Use the attached order cards to order your own or extra subscriptions to the **PRIVATE EDUCATION LAW REPORT**. . . the monthly newsletter service reporting the very latest private school law cases and late breaking legislation.

Order an extra subscription for your assistant, the school Personnel Officer, a board member or the faculty lounge. The attached order cards may be removed from the book for your order.

OUR GUARANTEE: If you are not satisfied with the **PRIVATE EDUCATION LAW REPORT**, for any reason, we will refund the unused portion of your subscription payment.

Yes, please send me _____ subscriptions to the **PRIVATE EDUCATION LAW REPORT** . . . the monthly newsletter service reporting the very latest private school law cases and late breaking legislation.

☐ Send two years at $167.00 (your best price)

☐ Send one year at $97.00

Name_____

Title _____

Address _____

City_____ State_____ Zip_____

Telephone Number _____

Purchase Order Number, if needed _____

Send order and check payable to: DATA RESEARCH, INC., P.O. Box 490, Rosemount, MN 55068

Yes, please send me _____ subscriptions to the **PRIVATE EDUCATION LAW REPORT** . . . the monthly newsletter service reporting the very latest private school law cases and late breaking legislation.

☐ Send two years at $167.00 (your best price)

☐ Send one year at $97.00

Name_____

Title_____

Address _____

City_____ State _____Zip_____

Telephone Number_____

Purchase Order Number, if needed _____

Send order and check payable to: DATA RESEARCH, INC., P.O. Box 490, Rosemount, MN 55068

PRIVATE SCHOOL LAW
IN AMERICA

"This publication is designed to provide accurate and authoritative information in regard to the subject matter covered. It is sold with the understanding that the publisher is not engaged in rendering legal, accounting or other professional service. If legal advice or other expert assistance is required, the service of a competent professional person should be sought."—*from a Declaration of Principles jointly adopted by a Committee of the American Bar Association and a Committee of Publishers and Associations.*

Published by
Data Research, Inc.
P.O. Box 490
Rosemount, Minnesota 55068

OTHER TITLES PUBLISHED
BY DATA RESEARCH, INC.:

Deskbook Encyclopedia of American School Law
Handicapped Students and Special Education

Library of Congress Cataloging-in-Publication Data

Private school law in America.

Includes index.
1. Private schools—Law and legislation—United States.
I. Data Research, Inc. (Rosemount, Minn.)
KF4220.P75 1987   344.73'072   87-5271
ISBN 0-939675-06-4   347.30472
ISBN 0-939675-05-6 (pbk.)

PREFACE

Private School Law in America is a completely updated encyclopedic compilation based on federal and state appellate court decisions in the field of private education. These decisions have been examined by the editorial staff of Data Research, Inc. for inclusion in the appropriate topic classifications. Federal statutory and regulatory requirements are included to the extent that they affect private education. This volume also contains an introduction offering a brief explanation of the American judicial system. The appendix includes a subject-matter table of private education cases decided by the U.S. Supreme Court.

To aid the reader in identifying any case, the case name and full legal citation, including the year of decision, have been supplied for all cases included in the text. Additionally, the case names have been alphabetized and placed in a Table of Cases following the Table of Contents. The text page numbers on which cases appear have been included for all listings in the Table of Cases.

The intent of *Private School Law in America* is to provide professional educators and lawyers with access to important case and statutory law in the field of private education.

EDITORIAL STAFF
DATA RESEARCH, INC.

INTRODUCTORY NOTE ON THE
JUDICIAL SYSTEM

In order to allow the reader to determine the relative importance of a judicial decision, the cases included in *Private School Law in America* identify the particular court from which a decision has been issued. For example, a case decided by a state supreme court generally will be of greater significance than a state circuit court case. Hence a basic knowledge of the structure of our judicial system is important to an understanding of private school law.

The most common system, used by nearly all states and also the federal judiciary, is as follows: a legal action is commenced in **district court** (sometimes called a trial court, county court, common pleas court or superior court) where a decision is initially reached. The case may then be appealed to the **court of appeals** (or appellate court), and in turn this decision may be appealed to the **supreme court**.

Several states, however, do not have a court of appeals; lower court decisions are appealed directly to the state's supreme court. Additionally, some states have labeled their courts in a nonstandard fashion.

In Maryland, the highest state court is called the Court of Appeals.

In the state of New York, the trial court is called the Supreme Court. Decisions of this court may be appealed to the Supreme Court, Appellate Division. The highest court in New York is the Court of Appeals.

Pennsylvania has perhaps the most complex court system. The lowest state court is the Court of Common Pleas. Depending on the circumstances of the case, appeals may be taken to either the Commonwealth Court or the Superior Court. In certain instances the Commonwealth Court functions as a trial court as well as an appellate court. The Superior Court, however, is strictly an intermediate appellate court. The highest court in Pennsylvania is the Supreme Court.

While supreme court decisions are generally regarded as the last word in legal matters, it is important to remember that trial court and appeals court decisions also create important legal precedents.

TABLE OF CONTENTS

_____ **Page**

PREFACE iii

INTRODUCTORY NOTE ON THE JUDICIAL SYSTEM v

TABLE OF CASES xiii

CHAPTER ONE
OPERATION OF PRIVATE SCHOOLS 1

   I. LICENSING 3

  II. ACCREDITATION 6

 III. ADMISSIONS 8
     A. Racial Discrimination 8
     B. Sexual Discrimination 10
     C. Age Discrimination 10
     D. Handicap Discrimination 11
     E. Exclusion from Premises 12

 IV. BREACH OF CONTRACT TO EDUCATE 12
     A. Generally 12
     B. Tuition Refunds 14
     C. Dismissals from School 15
     D. Educational Malpractice 16
     E. Parental Obligations 17
     F. Student Privacy Rights 17
        1. Buckley Amendment 17
        2. Implied Contractual Privacy Rights 18

  V. LEASING OF PRIVATE SCHOOL
     FACILITIES 19

 VI. COMPULSORY ATTENDANCE 20
     A. Attendance at Private Schools 20
     B. Amish Exception 21
     C. Teacher Certification and Other
        Minimum Standards 21
     D. Home Instruction 26

 VII. SCHOLARSHIPS, GRANTS AND
     FINANCIAL AID 27

TABLE OF CONTENTS

VIII. STUDENT ORGANIZATIONS 30

IX. ON-CAMPUS INTERVIEWING AND RECRUITING 31

X. NATIONAL HONOR SOCIETY 32

XI. ATHLETIC PROGRAMS 33
  A. Eligibility of Players 33
  B. Eligibility of Schools 35
  C. Coaches 36
    1. Equal Pay Act 36
    2. Duty of Care 36
  D. Discrimination 37

XII. FUNDRAISERS 37

CHAPTER TWO
EMPLOYMENT 39

  I. WRONGFUL TERMINATION AND BREACH OF
     CONTRACT 40
  A. Breach of Contract—Generally 40
  B. Tenure Denials 45
  C. Letters of Intent 48
  D. Investigations, Hearings and Procedural Disputes 49
  E. Retirement Plans 50

  II. DISCRIMINATION 51
  A. Race 51
  B. Sex 54
  C. Religion 57
  D. Age 58
  E. Handicap 58
  F. Retaliatory Discharge 59
  G. Investigation of Discrimination Charges 60

  III. DEFAMATION 62

  IV. EMPLOYMENT BENEFITS 63
  A. Discrimination 63
  B. Income Tax Laws 64

TABLE OF CONTENTS

Page

V. UNEMPLOYMENT TAXATION 65

VI. COLLECTIVE BARGAINING 69
  A. First Amendment Limitations 69
  B. Managerial Employees 72

VII. STATE ACTION 73

CHAPTER THREE
ACCIDENTS, INJURIES AND DEATHS 75

  I. CHARITABLE IMMUNITY 76

  II. DUTY OF CARE 77
  A. Negligence 77
  B. Dram Shop/Social Host Liability 81
  C. Wrongful Death 83

  III. ATHLETIC INJURIES 84
  A. Participants 84
  B. Spectators 86

  IV. INSURANCE...87

CHAPTER FOUR
STATE AID TO PRIVATE SCHOOLS 89

  I. FIRST AMENDMENT 90

  II. TEXTBOOK LOANS 90

  III. BUS TRANSPORTATION 92

  IV. COOPERATIVE EFFORTS BETWEEN
  PUBLIC AND PRIVATE SCHOOLS 95
  A. Release Time Programs 95
  B. Public School Personnel on Parochial School Grounds 98
  C. Instruction Offered on Public School Grounds 100
  D. Leasing of Public or Private School Facilities 102

TABLE OF CONTENTS

V. STATE FUNDING OF INSTRUCTIONAL
    AND OTHER SERVICES 103
    A. Instructional Services 104
    B. Classroom Equipment 106
    C. Diagnostic and Therapeutic Services 107

VI. STUDENT AID 107
    A. Tuition Assistance 107
    B. Tax Deductions and Credits 110
    C. Tax Refunds 111

VII. FEDERAL AID TO SCHOOLS 111

VIII. BUILDING CONSTRUCTION, MAINTENANCE
    AND DISPOSAL 112
    A. Construction and Maintenance Programs 112
    B. Zoning 113
    C. Disposal of Federal Property 114

IX. TAXATION OF PRIVATE SCHOOLS 114
    A. Federal Income Taxation 114
    B. Local Property Taxation 116

CHAPTER FIVE
HANDICAPPED CHILDREN 119

I. STATES' DUTY TO EDUCATE 120

II. TUITION REIMBURSEMENT 121

III. CHANGE IN PLACEMENT 127

IV. CIVIL RIGHTS LAWSUITS 127

V. PRIVATE SCHOOL ELIGIBILITY TO
    EDUCATE HANDICAPPED CHILDREN 128

VI. FACILITIES AND PROGRAMS 130

VII. CONTRACT DISPUTES 131

TABLE OF CONTENTS

_____ **Page**

CHAPTER SIX
FEDERAL STATUTORY REQUIREMENTS 135

I. OVERVIEW 136

II. CIVIL RIGHTS ACT OF 1964 136
    A. Title VI: Racial Discrimination 136
    B. Title VII: Employment Discrimination ....,.138

III. EQUAL PAY ACT 144

IV. TITLE IX 145

V. REHABILITATION ACT OF 1973 157

VI. AGE DISCRIMINATION 165
    A. Age Discrimination in Employment Act 165
    B. Age Discrimination Act 167

VII. BUCKLEY AMENDMENT 169

VIII. RECONSTRUCTION CIVIL RIGHTS STATUTES 189
    A. Section 1981 189
    B. Section 1983 189

APPENDIX A
United State Constitution: Provisions of Interest to Private
Educators 191

APPENDIX B
Subject Matter Table of Recent Law Review Articles 197

APPENDIX C
Subject Matter Table of United States Supreme Court Cases
Affecting Private Education 207

TABLE OF CONTENTS

APPENDIX D
Text of Selected United States Supreme Court Cases 211

Runyon v. McCrary 212
Bob Jones University v. United States 232
Grove City College v. Bell 257

INDEX 275

TABLE OF CASES

Abram v. City of Fayetteville, 5

Abrams v. Baylor College of Medicine, 52

Aguilar v. Felton, 98, 101

Al-Khazraji v. St. Francis College, 53

Alferoff v. Casagrande, 78

Allen v. Wright, 115

American & Foreign Ins. Co. v. Church Schools in the Diocese of Virginia, 87

Americans United for Separation of Church & State v. Porter, 103

Arna v. Northwestern University, 51

Attorney General v. School Comm. of Essex, 94

Avins v. White, 63

Baker v. Lafayette College, 62

Baltimore Lutheran High School Ass'n v. Employment Security Administration, 68

Bangor Baptist Church v. State of Maine, 25

Baum v. Reed College Student Body, Inc., 77

Belliveau v. Rerick, 63

Berman v. Nat'l Council of Beth Jacob Schools, Inc., 77

Berschback v. Grosse Pointe Public School District, 34

Binet-Montessori v. San Francisco Unified School Dist., 20

Bischoff v. Brothers of the Sacred Heart, 41

Black v. St. Bernadette Congregation of Appleton, 40

Blount v. Redmond, 21

Board of Education v. Allen, 90

Board of Education v. Ambach, 125

Board of Education v. Ambach, 126

Board of Trustees of Keene State College v. Sweeney, 139

Bob Jones University v. United States, 114, 211, 232

Bodard v. Culver-Stockton College, 77

Brigham Young University v. Lillywhite, 77

Brown v. Dade Christian Schools, Inc., 9

Buford v. Southeast Dubois County School Corp., 103

Burlington School Committee v. Dep't of Education of Massachusetts, 121

California Teachers Ass'n v. Riles, 91

Campbell v. Board of Trustees of Wabash College, 81

Casualty Ins. Co. v. Town & Country Preschool Nursery, 88

Catholic High School Ass'n v. Culvert, 71

Chabert v. Louisiana High School Athletic Ass'n, 35

Chi Realty Corp. v. Colby College, 30

Christ the King Regional High School v. Culvert, 70

TABLE OF CASES

Christian School Ass'n v.
Commonwealth Dep't of Labor &
Industry, 67

Christofides v. Hellenic Eastern
Orthodox Christian Church, 77

Circle Pines Cent. v. Orangeville
Township, 116

City of New York v. American School
Publications, Inc., 5

Clevenger v. Oak Ridge School Board,
130

Cochran v. Louisiana State Board of
Education, 90

Committee for Public Education &
Religious Liberty v. Nyquist, 110, 112

Committee for Public Education &
Religious Liberty v. Regan, 105

Commonwealth v. Downing, 12

Cooper v. Oregon School Activities
Ass'n, 35

Council of Private Schools for Children
with Special Needs, Inc. v.
Cooperman, 128

Country Hills Christian Church v.
Unified School Dist. No. 512, 103

Czigler v. Ohio Bureau of Employment,
68

Darlene L. v. Illinois State Board of
Education, 120

Decker v. O'Donnell, 106

Decker v. U.S. Dep't of Labor, 106

Dep't of Social Services v. Emmanuel
Baptist Preschool, 3

DeVico v. Roman Catholic Diocese of
Rockville, 44

Dima v. Macchiarola, 129

District of Columbia v. Trustees of
Amherst College, 116

Dothard v. Rawlinson, 139

Dr. Franklin Perkins School v. Freeman,
131

EEOC v. Franklin & Marshall College,
61

EEOC v. Fremont Christian School, 63

EEOC v. Southwestern Baptist
Theological Seminary, 61

EEOC v. University of Notre Dame, 61

Elmira Business Institute, Inc. v. New
York Dep't of Education, 27

Erickson v. Bd. of Educ., 36

Everson v. Board of Education, 92, 94

Exeter-West Greenwich Regional School
District v. Pontarelli, 108

Fannin v. Williams, 91

Fassett v. Delta Kappa Epsilon (New
York), 82

Fellowship Baptist Church v. Benton, 23

Feng v. Sandrik, 56

Fiedler v. Marumsco Christian School, 8

Flint v. St. Augustine High School, 16

Ford v. Manuel, 100

Franklin & Marshall College v. EEOC,
61

Gamble v. Lovett School, 47

Garnet Valley School Dist. v. Hanlon,
93

Gay Rights Coalition v. Georgetown
University, 31

Gillespie v. St. Joseph's University, 42

Gold v. Gallaudet College, 54

TABLE OF CASES

Grand Rapids School Dist. v. Ball, 98, 102

Grove City College v. Bell, 111, 148, 211, 257

Grove School v. Guardianship & Advocacy Comm'n, 4

Gubbe v. Catholic Diocese of Rockford, 77

Hahner v. Bd. of Educ., 93

Hanson v. Kynast, 86

Hanson v. Prudential Insurance Co. of America, 130

Havas v. Temple University, 50

Hornyak v. Pomfret School, 84

Horowitz v. Camp Cedarhurst and Town & Country Day School, Ltd., 79

Huff v. Notre Dame High School of West Haven, 16

Hunt v. McNair, 112, 113

In re Cert. of Question: Elbe v. Yankton Indep. School Dist. No. 63-3, 90

In re John K., 123

Jeffrey v. Whitworth College, 77

John Carroll University v. United States, 64

Johnson v. Charles City Comm. Schools Bd. of Educ., 24

Johnson v. Howard University, 59

Johnson v. Lincoln Christian College, 18

Johnson v. Transportation Agency, 140

Jones v. Grunewarld, 28

Jones v. Howe Military School, 16

Jones v. Jones, 17

Juneau Academy v. Chicago Board of Education, 133

Karnstein v. Pewaukee School Bd., 32

Kent S. v. California Interscholastic Federation, 33

Knipmeyer v. Diocese of Alexandria, 48

Koolau Baptist Church v. Dep't of Labor, 66

Krotkoff v. Groucher College, 43

Lanner v. Wimmer, 97

LaTorre v. First Baptist Church Ojus, 78

Leftwich v. Harris-Stowe College, 58

Lemon v. Kurtzman, 90, 101, 103, 104, 106

Levitt v. Committee for Public Education and Religious Liberty, 105

Lewis v. Loyola University of Chicago, 46

Linn v. Andover-Newton Theological School, 44

Luetkemeyer v. Kaufmann, 95

Maguire v. Marquette University, 57

Malloy v. Fong, 77

Marjorie Webster Junior College, Inc. v. Middle States Ass'n of Colleges & Secondary Schools, 7

Marquette University v. United States, 64

Matter of Adam D., 26

Mazanec v. North Judson-San Pierre School Corp., 26

McCollum v. Board of Education, 96

McConnell v. Howard University, 41

TABLE OF CASES

McDonough v. Alyward, 111

Meek v. Pittenger, 103, 106, 107

Members of Jamestown School
Committee v. Schmidt, 94

Merrill v. Southern Methodist
University, 55

Middlebury College v. Town of
Hancock, 116

Miller v. Catholic Diocese of Great
Falls, 40

Miller v. Macalester College, 77

Mlynarski v. St. Rita's Congregation, 77

Moore v. Vanderloo, 80

Moyse v. Runnels School, Inc., 14

Mozert v. Hawkins County Pub.
Schools, 109

Mueller v. Allen, 110

Nampa Christian Schools v. State, 66

NLRB v. Bishop Ford Cent. Catholic
High School, 69

NLRB v. Catholic Bishop of Chicago,
69, 70, 71

NLRB v. Cooper Union for the
Advancement of Science & Art, 73

NLRB v. St. Francis College, 72

NLRB v. Yeshiva University, 72, 73

Nordgren v. Haftner, 7

North Jersey Secretarial School v. Nat'l
Ass'n of Trade & Tech. Schools, 6

Norwood v. Harrison, 91

Nydeggar v. Don Bosco Prep. High
School, 36

O'Connell v. Virginia High School
League, 35

Ohio Civil Rights Comm'n v. Dayton
Christian Schools, 60

Opinion of the Justices, 105

Paladino v. Adelphi University, 16

Parents' Association of P.S. 16 v.
Quinones, 101

Perkaus v. Chicago Catholic High
School Athletic League, 85

Peterson v. Multnomah County School
Dist. No. 1, 84

Petock v. Thomas Jefferson University,
10

Petrowski v. Norwich Free Academy, 50

Phan v. Commonwealth of Virginia, 108

Phelps v. Washburn University of
Topeka, 9

Pierce v. Society of Sisters, 20, 26

Pizza Hut of America, Inc. v. Pastore,
113

Pollock v. Collipp, 83

President & Directors of Georgetown
College v. Hughes, 77

Price v. Young, 32

Pub. Funds for Pub. Schools of New
Jersey v. Byrne, 111

Pundt v. Millikin University, 42

Rackmyer v. Gates-Chili Cent. School
Dist., 93

Radosevic v. Virginia Intermont
College, 76

Record v. Mill Neck Manor Lutheran
School for the Deaf, 56

Regents of University of California v.
Bakke, 136

Reimer v. Tien, 14

TABLE OF CASES

Rendell-Baker v. Kohn, 74, 136

Riley v. Ambach, 129

Rivera v. Philadelphia Theological Seminary, 76

Roemer v. Board of Public Works, 113

Roman Catholic Church v. Keenan, 77

Runyon v. McCrary, 8, 189, 211, 212

Russell v. Salve Regina College, 18

St. Martin's Evangelical Lutheran Church v. South Dakota, 65

Save Immaculata-Dunblane, Inc. v. Immaculata Preparatory School, 13

Schimmel v. Spillane, 122

School Board of Nassau County v. Arline, 58

Seidman v. Fishburne-Hudgins Educ. Foundation, 83

Selective Service System v. Minnesota Public Interest Research Group, 29

Sheridan Road Baptist Church v. Department of Education, 22

Sherry v. New York State Department of Education, 127

Smith v. Archbishop of St. Louis, 79

Smith v. Smith, 96

Snyder v. Charlotte Public School District, 97

Sola v. Lafayette College, 45

Southeastern Community College v. Davis, 11

Spinelli v. Immanuel Evangelical Lutheran Congregation, 49

Sprunger v. East Noble School Corp., 86

Stark v. St. Cloud State University, 99

State Fire Marshall v. Lee, 5

State v. Alioto, 20

State v. Popanz, 24

State v. Shaver, 24

State v. Thompson, 97

State v. Whisner, 25

Steinberg v. Chicago Medical School, 12

Stone v. Belgrade School District No. 44, 139

Stuart v. Nappi, 127

Supervisor of Assessments of Baltimore City v. Friends School, 117

T.A.F. & E.M.F. v. Duval County, 26

Talley v. South Carolina Higher Education Tuition Grants Committee, 29

Taylor v. James F. Byrnes Academy, Inc., 37

T.G. v. Board of Education, 120

Thomas v. Schmidt, 19

Tidwell v. Emory University, 48

Till·v. Delta School of Commerce, Inc., 15

Tilton v. Richardson, 112

Transport Careers, Inc. v. National Home Study Council, 6

Trustee of St. Joseph's College, 70

U.S. v. City of Philadelphia, 31

United Steelworkers of America v. Weber, 140

Universidad Central de Bayamon v. NLRB, 71

Usery v. Columbia University, 145

TABLE OF CASES

Valencia v. Blue Hen Conference, 36

Valley Forge Christian College v. Americans United for Separation of Church & State, 114

Van Scoyk v. St. Mary's Assumption Parochial School, 58

Vander Malle v. Ambach, 129

VanLoock v. Curran, 12

Village Community School v. Adler, 132

Virginia Education Fund v. Commissioner of Internal Revenue, 115

Wall v. Tulane University, 43

Walsh v. Louisiana High School Athletic Ass'n, 35

Waring v. Fordham University, 46

Wayte v. United States, 30

Wexler v. Westfield Board of Education, 124

Wheeler v. Barrera, 99

Whipple v. Oregon School Activities Ass'n, 34

Whitlock v. Duke University, 80

Wiley House v. Scanlon, 128

Wisconsin v. Yoder, 21

Witters v. Washington Dep't of Servs. for the Blind, 107

Wolman v. Walter, 93, 103, 105, 106, 107

Woods Schools v. Commonwealth Department of Education, 127

Wright v. Columbia University, 37

Zorach v. Clauson, 96

CHAPTER ONE
OPERATION OF PRIVATE SCHOOLS

                                                              Page

    I. LICENSING 3

   II. ACCREDITATION 6

  III. ADMISSIONS 8
       A. Racial Discrimination 8
       B. Sexual Discrimination 10
       C. Age Discrimination 10
       D. Handicap Discrimination 11
       E. Exclusion from Premises 12

  IV. BREACH OF CONTRACT TO EDUCATE 12
       A. Generally 12
       B. Tuition Refunds 14
       C. Dismissals from School 15
       D. Educational Malpractice 16
       E. Parental Obligations 17
       F. Student Privacy Rights 17
           1. Buckley Amendment 17
           2. Implied Contractual Privacy Rights 18

    V. LEASING OF PRIVATE SCHOOL
       FACILITIES 19

  VI. COMPULSORY ATTENDANCE 20
       A. Attendance at Private Schools :......................20
       B. Amish Exception 21
       C. Teacher Certification and Other
          Minimum Standards 21
       D. Home Instruction 26

 VII. SCHOLARSHIPS, GRANTS AND
       FINANCIAL AID 27

VIII. STUDENT ORGANIZATIONS 30

  IX. ON-CAMPUS INTERVIEWING AND RECRUITING 31

    X. NATIONAL HONOR SOCIETY 32

  XI. ATHLETIC PROGRAMS 33
       A. Eligibility of Players 33

    B. Eligibility of Schools 35
    C. Coaches 36
        1. Equal Pay Act 36
        2. Duty of Care 36
    D. Discrimination 37

XII.   FUNDRAISERS 37

2

I. LICENSING

Under the "police powers" which are inherent in all state governments, states have extensive regulatory authority over private schools. This regulatory authority is generally manifested in two ways: 1) incorporation or chartering, and 2) licensing. While it is usually a simple matter for a private school to become incorporated or chartered, licensing requirements may be much more stringent. This fact is often vitiated by the practice in some states of exempting private schools from licensing requirements if the school is approved by a regional accrediting institution.

A recent case involved a challenge to state regulatory requirements based on the First Amendment's guarantee of religious freedom. Here the Emmanuel Baptist Bible Church, a fundamentalist church in Michigan, operated the Emmanuel Preschool. The church had a provisional preschool day care license. In 1979, the Department of Social Services (DSS) informed the church that its school was operating in violation of DSS licensing rules. Church officials informed the DSS that they would not comply with the agency's rules and no longer desired licensing because of religious beliefs. The church continued to operate the preschool without a license. The DSS sued in state circuit court to enforce the licensing requirements. The court ruled that the church must obtain licensing for the school, but held that DSS regulations on staff qualifications, programs and discipline would not be enforced. The church and the DSS both appealed to the Michigan Court of Appeals, which held that the licensing requirement did not infringe upon the church's freedom of religion under the First Amendment. In arguing against the DSS regulations the church contended that the rule requiring the head of a child care center to be a qualified college graduate burdened its constitutional right to free exercise of religion by requiring a graduate of an accredited college or university rather than a nonaccredited fundamentalist Christian college. The court, however, found that the qualification guidelines for child care professionals served a "compelling state interest" in assuring that young children are provided with quality preschool programs.

In addition, the court found that the DSS rule that the children be taught a positive self-image "was a rational means to serve the state's interest in protecting a child's emotional well-being," and that the church must be required to abide by it. The court also held that the DSS rule allowing only a light spanking with a flat hand should be adhered to by the school. The church advocated a literal interpretation of the principle, "spare the rod, spoil the child." The court found that the state's interest in preventing infliction of potentially abusive punishment upon children was "clear and compelling" and outweighed the church's religious belief to the contrary. Further, the licensing rules and the other DSS regulations created no "excessive entanglement" between church and state in violation of the First Amendment. The school's claim that the rules were unconstitutionally vague, subjective and ambiguous was also rejected. In sum, the court found no violation of the church's constitutional right to religious freedom through the licensing rules and the other DSS regulations, and it held that the school must be licensed in accordance with DSS rules in order to operate. *Dep't of Social Services v. Emmanuel Baptist Preschool*, 388 N.W.2d 326 (Mich.App.1986).

In an Illinois case, the scope of a state's authority to investigate private schools was examined. The Grove School, a private residential school for handicapped children, brought a civil rights lawsuit against the Illinois Guardianship and Advocacy Commission alleging that the commission had instituted a campaign to unlawfully harass the school. The commission had received complaints from several individuals who said that the Grove School's residents were inadequately supervised. The commission held a public hearing in which it publicized charges of unlicensed staff at the Grove School and abuse of residents, and commission members criticized the school for its nonconformist philosophy with regard to educating handicapped children. A U.S. district court dismissed the Grove School's claim that the commission's actions violated the school's due process rights under the Fourteenth Amendment. The commission was dismissed as a defendant in the case, and the only remaining claim by the school was that the individual commission members had violated the school's First Amendment right to freedom of speech. The Grove School argued that by investigating its practices and threatening to revoke its license, the commission had actually been seeking to silence the school's advocacy of alternative approaches to education. It contended that the commission's investigation had been a pretext for harassment and that the commission knew that the charges leveled against the Grove School were baseless, having been made by individuals who held grudges against the school. As evidence for the school's charge that the commission had sought to extinguish the school's First Amendment right to advocate nonconformist educational methods, the school cited the following comment made by a commission member at the public hearing:

> I think one of the most truly disturbing [things] that came through in our investigation was that the Executive Director, who is not a qualified professional in even a related field of education,... has demonstrated through his actions that he feels that he is more qualified than professionals to decide what is important and not important for handicapped students to learn. He has blatantly held himself up above the law and has acted in total disregard of the regulations. He is running Grove School by his own philosophy according to his own rules and regulations in complete disregard of the law and this is just absolutely appalling.

Despite this evidence the U.S. district court found it unnecessary to determine whether the commission had infringed upon the school's rights by investigating it. Because the commission members were state officials, they could be held liable under § 1983 of the Civil Rights Act only if they had violated "clearly established constitutional rights" possessed by the school. Thus, the question was not whether the First Amendment rights of the school had been violated, but whether the commission members had violated constitutional rights which, at the time of the alleged violation, were clearly established. The court held that the school had failed to prove this. It was likely that the commission had been seeking to deter *conduct*, not speech, which the commission perceived to be harmful to handicapped students. The reference by the commission member to the Grove School's allegedly questionable philosophy was insufficient to transform the school's conduct in educating handicapped children into advocacy of educational ideas. Thus, the court ruled that the commission members had not acted in violation of any clearly established constitutional right possessed by the school. The individual commission members were therefore immune from suit under the Civil Rights Act and the remainder of the lawsuit was dismissed. *Grove School v. Guardianship & Advocacy Comm'n*, 642 F.Supp. 1043 (N.D. Ill.1986).

The following two cases illustrate the general rule that private schools, regardless of whether they are religiously affiliated, must comply with reasonable fire code, zoning and land use regulations.

A Christian church purchased three modular classrooms from a Michigan school district. The classrooms were then converted for use as a church and as a church-related day school. While the classrooms had passed the state fire marshall's inspection when they were being used as public school classrooms, they were cited for several violations after they were put into use by the church school. The church appealed to the Michigan Court of Appeals. The court agreed that the sequence of the fire marshall's inspection and subsequent citation for code violations appeared to be a case of harassment against the church. The court noted that the classrooms may have been in violation of the code when used by the public school. But, since the safety of the children attending the church school was at issue, the school was required to correct the causes of the violations. *State Fire Marshall v. Lee*, 300 N.W.2d 748 (Mich.App.1980).

A Baptist church in Arkansas had received a building permit to erect a church but had not received approval for building or operating a school. It opened a school anyway. A state trial court enjoined operation of the parochial school unless a conditional use permit was obtained. The church appealed the order, alleging that the parochial school was an integral and inseparable part of the function of the church and that it was not within the province of a municipality to determine the substance of religious activity. The Arkansas Supreme Court affirmed the trial court's order. It held that the ordinance in question was a land use regulation and that the distinction between churches and schools was valid. A school operating from 8:30 a.m. to 3:15 p.m. each weekday is a more intensive use of land than a church, observed the court. *Abram v. City of Fayetteville*, 661 S.W.2d 371 (Ark.1983).

The final case in this section involved the lack of a valid licensing procedure, which resulted in a private school being allowed to distribute its literature on public sidewalks. In this New York case a private institution offering short, nonaccredited courses sought to distribute a magazine free of charge throughout New York City by the placement of newsracks on sidewalks. The city had no regulation authorizing the placement of newsracks. Instead, municipal officers determined which publications could use newsracks based upon their own assessment of the publication's content. When the city denied the school permission to disseminate its magazine through newsracks on the ground that the magazine was merely an advertisement for the school, the school began installing newsracks anyway. The city sought a court injunction preventing the school from installing any more newsracks. The New York Supreme Court, however, denied the city's request based upon freedom of speech under the First Amendment.

On appeal to the Supreme Court, Appellate Division, the city argued that the First Amendment's guarantee of freedom of speech did not entitle the school to install newsracks on the city's sidewalks and that municipal authorities have the right to maintain control over public areas. The court stated that the issue was not the city's right to bar newsracks from sidewalks, which it clearly has, but its right to deny the school the same privilege that it has granted others. Based on the U.S. Supreme Court's standards for evaluating "commercial" speech, the school's publication was clearly within the fully-protected noncommercial category, stated the court, because it contained a variety of material on various subjects in addition to advertisements. For this reason, the court ruled that in the absence of a regulation to administer the placement of newsracks on sidewalks, the city must either allow all applicants equal access to newsracks, or allow no access at all. The lower court's ruling against the city was affirmed. *City of New York v. American School Publications, Inc.*, 505 N.Y.S.2d 599 (A.D.1st Dept.1986).

II. ACCREDITATION

Regional and other accrediting institutions have been sued by private schools after accreditation was withdrawn. The general rules emerging from such cases are 1) actions of accrediting institutions are not "state action" triggering due process requirements, 2) a school may maintain a breach of contract lawsuit against an accrediting institution if the institution fails to follow its own rules and procedures, and 3) federal antitrust law applies to accrediting institutions.

A trade school brought suit against a national accrediting association after the association withdrew the school's accreditation on grounds of financial instability. Accreditation by the association was a prerequisite to the receipt of federal Department of Education financial assistance. The school alleged that the association's withdrawal of accreditation was a breach of contract, breach of fiduciary duty and an intentional interference with contractual relations. A U.S. district court held that since there was no evidence that the association had acted with malice or intent to injure, it could not be liable for intentional or improper interference with contractual relations. *North Jersey Secretarial School v. Nat'l Ass'n of Trade & Tech. Schools*, 597 F.Supp. 477 (D.D.C.1984).

Transport Careers, Inc. (TCI) is an Indiana-based corporation which trains students to operate semi-trucks and work on diesel engines. Its courses involve home correspondence study and residential training at one of its two training sites. The National Home Study Council (NHSC) is a not-for-profit association of public and private home study schools and is based in Washington, D.C. It is a nationally recognized accrediting body designated by the Secretary of Education to accredit home study courses in accordance with federal rules. TCI was accredited by the NHSC and was a member of NHSC from 1976 to 1986. In 1986 the NHSC terminated TCI's accreditation. TCI appealed the accreditation decision to a U.S. district court. The court observed that several of TCI's claims shared a common defect in that they erroneously relied on the U.S. Constitution. For example, TCI alleged that it had been denied accreditation in violation of the due process requirements of the Fifth Amendment. According to the court, it is fundamental that the U.S. Constitution does not extend protection to those who have been injured by private conduct. Since the NHSC's accreditation function did not constitute state action, the Constitution did not afford protection to TCI. Even though TCI's accreditation by the NHSC was a prerequisite to its eligibility for federal financial assistance, "[m]ere approval of or acquiescence in the initiatives of a private party" does not make the state responsible for those actions. TCI's constitutional claims were unfounded.

TCI also contended that the NHSC's standards were indefinite and unconstitutionally vague in setting accreditation standards. In denying this claim the court concluded that the guidelines of accreditation are not matters for lay people, but are for educational professionals, and that definiteness in one situation may prove to be arbitrary in another. The court also concluded that TCI's "due process" rights were not violated when NHSC considered a new TCI sales manual of which had not been submitted earlier. The court ruled that it would be preposterous for the court to hold that TCI was not given a fair hearing because the NHSC considered a document further illustrating TCI's noncompliance with the NHSC's advertising standards. Lastly, TCI contended that the NHSC is a "quasi public organization with a fiduciary duty to the public at large, the school, and the school's prospective students." The court observed that other courts have recognized that there is a common law fiduciary duty to follow fair procedures that are reasonably related to legitimate purposes. The court ruled that assuring compliance with the NHSC's business standards relating to advertising and other minimum standards for educational institutions were legitimate purposes. The decision by the NHSC to terminate TCI's accreditation was affirmed by the district court. *Transport Careers, Inc. v. National Home Study Council*, 646 F.Supp. 1474 (N.D. Ind.1986).

When a private junior college applied to the Middle States Association seeking accreditation, the association rejected the college because the college was operated on a for-profit basis. The college sued the association under federal antitrust laws. A U.S. district court ruled that the accrediting association's practice of excluding for-profit colleges was a restraint of trade and it ordered the association to abandon its for-profit, not-for-profit distinction. On appeal, the U.S. Court of Appeals reversed the district court's ruling. The appeals court held that while the Sherman Antitrust Act applied to accreditation decisions, such decisions would violate the Act only if made with an intent to affect a profession's commercial activities. A "commercial motive" was needed to find a violation of the Act. Since the appeals court found that the Middle States Association's ground for denying the junior college's application was an educational reason only peripherally related to commerce, the lower court's decision in favor of the junior college was reversed. *Marjorie Webster Junior College, Inc. v. Middle States Ass'n of Colleges & Secondary Schools*, 432 F.2d 650 (D.C.Cir.1970).

A female law school graduate was denied a Mississippi bar exam application because she had graduated from a California law school which was not accredited by the American Bar Association. She claimed that she should have been allowed to take the bar exam because she met the state's alternative requirement of a six-year course in legal study. The woman filed a civil rights lawsuit in federal district court challenging the constitutionality of Mississippi's bar admission rules, which allow a non-ABA accredited Mississippi law school graduate to take the bar exam, but do not allow a graduate of a non-ABA accredited out-of-state law school to take the exam. The district court granted the state's summary judgment motion and the woman's suit was dismissed. The woman appealed the decision to the U.S. Court of Appeals, Fifth Circuit. The court upheld the dismissal, reasoning that the state legislature could readily assess the educational quality of a nonaccredited law school in the state of Mississippi and determine whether their graduates should take the state bar exam. The court found it unreasonable to expect the state to make the same assessment of the educational quality of nonaccredited law schools in other states. *Nordgren v. Haftner*, 789 F.2d 334 (5th Cir.1986).

III. ADMISSIONS

Private schools which are open to the public may not maintain racially discriminatory admissions policies. Private undergraduate institutions may, however, maintain admissions policies which discriminate on the basis of sex. Private graduate schools may not exclude individuals on the basis of sex, but private professional schools which are affiliated with single-sex undergraduate institutions may exclude based upon sex. Further, Title IX provides that religiously-affiliated institutions may operate free of the prohibitions on sex discrimination in admissions.

A. Racial Discrimination

Section 1 of the Civil Rights Act of 1866 (42 U.S.C. § 1981) (see Chapter Six, Section VIII) prohibits racial discrimination in the making and enforcement of private contracts. Congress' authority for the enactment was the Thirteenth Amendment, and the Act's purpose was to remove one of the "badges and incidents of slavery" from blacks by reaffirming their civil right to enter into contracts. The courts have applied § 1981 to the private school setting.

In the landmark case of *Runyon v. McCrary*, the U.S. Supreme Court relied on § 1981 in declaring that blacks could not be excluded from all-white elementary schools. In this Virginia case, parents of black students sought to enter into contractual relationships with private nonreligious schools for educational services advertised and offered to members of the general public. The students were denied admission because of their race. The Supreme Court recognized that while parents have a First Amendment right to send their children to educational institutions which promote the belief that racial segregation is desirable, it does not follow that the practice of excluding racial minorities from such institutions is also protected by the same principle. The school's argument that section 1981 does not govern private acts of racial discrimination was rejected. However, the Court observed that its holding did not extend to religious schools that practiced racial exclusion on religious grounds. *Runyon v. McCrary*, 96 S.Ct. 2586 (1976).

A fundamentalist Christian church in Virginia operated a school open to the public without regard to race or religious beliefs. The pastor of the church also served as the school principal. Although the school was open to people of all races, the principal held very strong beliefs against interracial relationships and he expressly forbade interracial romantic relations between students. After warning a white fourteen-year-old girl against speaking to a specific black male student whom the principal believed to be romantically involved with the girl, the principal discovered the two of them speaking to one another in the school hallway. The girl was immediately expelled. In a subsequent lawsuit, the girl alleged that her civil right to contract free of racial discrimination had been violated. Notwithstanding the school's arguments that it was a religious school operating under certain religious beliefs free from governmental regulation, the U.S. Court of Appeals, Fourth Circuit, held that the Civil Rights Act prohibits a commercially- operated private sectarian school from discriminating on the basis of race. The court held that the school could not terminate its contractual relationship with a white student because of her association with a black student. *Fiedler v. Marumsco Christian School*, 631 F.2d 1144 (4th Cir.1980).

A black mother attempted to enroll her two children in a private religious school but was rebuffed after being handed a card which advised her that the school's policy was one of nonintegration. In a lawsuit which followed she contended that 42 U.S.C. § 1981 provides that all persons have an equal right to make contracts regardless of race and, therefore, she was entitled to contract with the school for the education of her children. The school contended that its members held sincere religious beliefs that socialization between the races would lead to intermarriage and that they had a right to hold such beliefs under the Free Exercise Clause of the First Amendment. The U.S. Court of Appeals, Fifth Circuit, observed that, based on the evidence presented, if the school's alleged belief in racial segregation was religious in nature, neither the officers of the school nor the congregation of the church were aware of it. It appeared that as social conditions changed and the racial issue arose, a policy was formulated by the school leaders. The court said that there was ample evidence to support the holding that the school's segregation policy was nothing more than a recent policy developed in response to the growing segregation-integration issue. *Brown v. Dade Christian Schools, Inc.*, 556 F.2d 310 (5th Cir.1977).

In a Kansas case two sisters and their brother, unsuccessful applicants to the Washburn University School of Law, filed suit against the school and individual members of the admissions committee alleging that they had been denied admission in retaliation for their family's association with civil rights causes through the family law firm. They argued that because their family's law firm often associated with minorities (a protected class), they were also a protected class under 42 U.S.C. § 1981. They also argued that they had a protected "property interest" in admission to the law school. A U.S. district court observed that there was no evidence of any bias against the family's law firm when their applications were reviewed by the admissions committee. Moreover, the court noted the strong civil rights interests of the individual members of the admissions committee, some of whom were minority group members.

Regarding their § 1981 claim, the court stated that merely because their family's law firm associated with blacks and civil rights causes, and because they, in turn, were associated with their father, did not place them in a protected class under § 1981. Furthermore, even if they were a protected class, they did not have a legitimate property interest in admission to the law school. Merely having an abstract need or desire for something, stated the court, does not confer a property interest. There must be a legitimate claim of entitlement. In conclusion, the court noted that the sisters and brother had filed a separate lawsuit in which they accused the same individuals of reverse discrimination, arguing that they had been denied admission to the law school because of the affirmative action treatment given to black applicants who were less qualified. Ruling that the evidence showed no hint of discriminatory conduct by the admissions committee, the court dismissed the case. *Phelps v. Washburn University of Topeka*, 634 F.Supp. 556 (D.Kan.1986).

Title VI of the Civil Rights Act of 1964 (42 U.S.C. § 2000d) prohibits discrimination on the basis of race, color or national origin in "programs or activities" (see Chapter Four, Section VII) receiving federal financial assistance. Since Title VI applies only to federally assisted public or private programs, its scope is not as broad as 42 U.S.C. § 1981 (see also Chapter Six).

B. Sexual Discrimination

Because the Civil Rights Act of 1866 (42 U.S.C. § 1981) applies only to racial discrimination, it is inapplicable to sexually discriminatory admissions policies. In the context of private higher educational institutions, Title IX is applicable to recipients of federal funding. Title IX, however, specifically allows private undergraduate institutions to discriminate on the basis of sex in admissions (20 U.S.C. § 1681(a)(1); see also Chapter Six, Section IV).

C. Age Discrimination

Having been denied readmission to Thomas Jefferson University Medical School, a student who was also a practicing attorney sued the school alleging age discrimination, breach of contract, fraud and duress. The student claimed that he was discriminated against by the school because he was older than his classmates. He based his claim on the Age Discrimination Act of 1975, which prohibits discrimination on the basis of age in programs or activities receiving federal financial assistance. To prove his claim, he attempted to show that the school improperly failed him in Family Medicine, gave him less than average evaluations in Pediatrics, denied his request for transfer of his Internal Medicine clerkship, and denied his application for readmission after he had withdrawn from the school. Claiming that he had been fraudulently induced to sign an agreement withdrawing from the school and that he signed it under duress, he contended that the attorney for the school induced him to sign the agreement by stating that he had received a failing grade in his Family Medicine written examination when, in fact, the exam had not yet been graded. The student, an experienced attorney, had drafted the agreement himself. It specified that if he were allowed to resign from the school in good standing, he would agree to withdraw an age discrimination complaint he had filed with the U.S. Department of Health and Human Services.

A federal district court rejected the age discrimination claim noting that the testimony and exhibits introduced at the trial showed that younger students had also failed courses under similar circumstances and had received evaluations based on the same criteria as were used to evaluate the plaintiff. In addition, merely because a school would not change its policies and make "extraordinary efforts" to enable the student to practice law and study medicine simultaneously was not indicative of age discrimination. Regarding the claims for fraud and duress, the court pointed out that according to the testimony of the student, the withdrawal and release agreement was completed before the alleged conversation with the school's attorney took place. For this reason, the student could not have relied on the school attorney's statements in decididng to withdraw, and his claim that he was fraudulently induced by the attorney's statements to sign the agreement could not overcome the weight of the evidence to the contrary. Furthermore, the court found no evidence which tended to show that the student was under duress so as to invalidate the agreement. The court also held that the student's claim for breach of contract was without substance. Although the student charged that he was graded and evaluated arbitrarily and capriciously in violation of his contractual rights as a student, the court determined from the testimony that academic evaluations of the student were based on standard criteria rationally based on the quality of his work. The court directed a verdict in favor of the school. *Petock v. Thomas Jefferson University*, 630 F.Supp. 187 (E.D.Pa.1986).

D. Handicap Discrimination

The U.S. Supreme Court's ruling in *Southeastern Community College v. Davis* set the standard for all institutions whose programs or activities receive federal financial assistance, including private schools, for evaluating claims of handicap discrimination. In this case a female nursing school applicant, who was severely hearing impaired, claimed that her denial of admission violated § 504 of the Rehabilitation Act. Section 504 states that an "otherwise qualified handicapped individual" may not be excluded from a federally funded program "solely by reason of his handicap" (see Chapter Six). In refusing to admit the applicant, the nursing school explained that the hearing disability made it unsafe for her to practice as a registered nurse. The school pointed out that even with a hearing aid the applicant had to rely on her lipreading skills. It argued that patient safety demanded that she be able to understand speech without reliance on lipreading. Agreeing with the school, the Supreme Court held that the term "otherwise qualified handicapped individual" meant an individual who is qualified in spite of his or her handicap. The applicant's contention that her handicap should be disregarded for purposes of determining whether she was otherwise qualified was rejected, as was her contention that § 504 imposed an obligation on the school to undertake affirmative action to modify its curriculum to accommodate her disability. While a school may be required to make minor curricular modifications to accommodate a handicap, here the applicant was physically able to take only academic courses (clinical study would be foreclosed due to patient safety concerns). The Court held that § 504 did not require a major curricular modification such as allowing the applicant to bypass clinical study.

The school's denial of admission was upheld. *Southeastern Community College v. Davis*, 442 U.S. 397 (1979).

E. Exclusion from Premises

A Pennsylvania case illustrates private schools' right to exclude individuals from their premises. Here a man was convicted of "defiant trespass" as a result of an incident at the Temple University law library. The man, who was not affiliated with the university, applied for and received a library card to obtain access to the library. Prior to law school exams, however, a notice was posted restricting the library to students, faculty and staff of the law school from December 4 through December 23. After meeting with the law school's legal counsel on two occasions, the man was unsuccessful in obtaining permission to use the library. He nevertheless went to the library and after several unsuccessful efforts by campus security to persuade him to leave, he was arrested and charged with defiant trespass. Although he was convicted in a common pleas court, the Pennsylvania Superior Court reversed his conviction on the ground that he had a legal right to use the library because it was open to members of the public. On appeal by the state, the Pennsylvania Supreme Court noted that although Temple University receives public funds, its character as a private educational institution has not been altered. Since Temple's property is essentially private property, persons not affiliated with the law shcool are permitted access to the library not as invitees but merely as guests. If and when the university determines that their presence interferes with its students' right to use the library, it may restrict access. The court further noted that the private nature of the library has not been altered by its designation as a Federal Depository Library. Nothing in the evidence suggested to the court that the man was denied free use of government publications. The superior court's ruling was reversed and the man's conviction was reinstated. *Commonwealth v. Downing*, 511 A.2d 792 (Pa.1986).

IV. BREACH OF CONTRACT TO EDUCATE

Like other legal entities, private schools may sue or be sued for breach of contract. Such lawsuits are governed by traditional contract principles (most of which are beyond the scope of this book). Courts generally will hold that a valid educational contract is created upon acceptance of a student for admission. The terms of such contracts are found in the tuition agreement, college catalogues or brochures and student handbooks.

A. Generally

In addition to the above principles, at least one court has held that upon acceptance of a prospective student's application fee, a private school is obliged to follow its admissions standards as set forth in its catalogue. If the school uses unstated criteria in making its decision whether to accept or reject the applicant, the school is liable for breach of contract and/or fraud. *Steinberg v. Chicago Medical School*, 354 N.E.2d 586 (Ill.App.1st Dist.1976).

The Alabama Supreme Court held that the parents of three boys enrolled at the Holy Family School, a Catholic school in Mobile, Alabama, could sue the school for breach of contract and fraud. The three boys, who had attended Holy Family all their lives, were enrolled in the first, fifth and sixth grades. All three boys were on the honor roll and each was promoted to the next grade at the end of the 1983-84 school year. One year later, in the spring of 1984, the parents filled out preregistration forms for the boys and paid preregistration fees for the next school year as provided by the Holy Family Parent-Student Handbook. The school accepted the preregistration fees, but on the last day of the 1983-84 school year the parents were informed that their children would not be allowed to return to Holy Family for the next year. The parents were refunded their preregistration fees but Holy Family did not provide an explanation why the boys would not be allowed to attend school. The parents initiated grievance proceedings as allowed by the school handbook. After a hearing, the grievance board voted three to two to reinstate the children in school. Holy Family's principal appealed to the superintendent of Mobile's Catholic schools, who overturned the board's decision and excluded the children from Holy Family for the next school year. The parents filed a lawsuit against the school in an Alabama circuit court, which promptly dismissed the suit.

The parents appealed to the Alabama Supreme Court, which reversed the circuit court and held that the parent's claim should not have been dismissed. A jury should have been allowed to decide whether the family and the school had entered into a contract once the preregistration fees had been paid. If a jury found that the school and family had formed a contract through payment and acceptance of the preregistration fees, then the school would be obligated to educate the children and failure to do so would breach the contract. The court also held that the family should have been allowed to have a jury decide their claim of fraud. It said that a fraud claim could be made if the parents proved that the school deliberately misled them into believing that currently enrolled children who paid preregistration fees and complied with school rules and regulations would not be denied enrollment and admission. The parents' claim for breach of contract and fraud was sent back to the circuit court to be heard by a jury. *VanLoock v. Curran*, 489 So.2d 525 (Ala.1986).

In 1965 the Sisters of Providence of St. Mary's of the Woods, Inc. (the "Order") formed a separate nonprofit corporation to administer its two Washington, D.C. area schools, Dunblane Academy for fifth through eighth graders and Immaculata Preparatory School for high schoolers. In March, 1982, the Order decided to dissolve the institutions because of financial difficulties and began negotiations to sell the properties to American University. The schools continued to operate and matriculate students. In October, 1984, the Order announced that the schools would close in 1986 with proceeds from the sale to be placed into the Order's retirement fund. The announcement stated that present juniors and seniors would graduate but younger students would have to find other schools. A group of concerned parents and alumnae (Save Immaculata-Dublane, Inc.) sued the Order in a superior court which ruled on the issue of breach of contract, among other things. When the superior court found in favor of the Order, Save Immaculata appealed to the District of Columbia Court of Appeals.

Four issues were presented in the case. First, Save Immaculata contended that the schools were trust-based nonprofit corporations and that a property held by a charitable corporation must be held and used only according to its corporate purpose and no other. The court of appeals ruled against Save Immaculata, and held that there was no evidence of an express trust nor was there authority to support the imposition of an implied trust. Second, Save Immaculata contended that the Order breached a contractual agreement when students were offered a place in the class called "Class of 1987 or 1988" but closed the high school before the students graduated. Although observing that there was a contractual relationship between the schools and the students, the court concluded that the contracts were for one-year terms only. Third, Save Immaculata argued that the Order fraudulently misrepresented the facts when it advertised a four-year education while planning to close the school. The court ruled that there was no fraud since the students paid only for education which they actually received. Fourth, Save Immaculata contended that the Order was liable for unlawful trade practices under the District of Columbia Consumer Protection Procedures Act. The court denied this claim, ruling that the Act did not apply since the schools were nonprofit educational institutions and not "merchants." The court dismissed the claims of Save Immaculata and the schools were allowed to close. *Save Immaculata-Dunblane, Inc. v. Immaculata Preparatory School*, 514 A.2d 1152 (D.C.App.1986).

B. Tuition Refunds

Courts will award tuition refunds only where a private school has breached its contractual obligations or where school handbooks or bulletins provide for such refunds.

At issue before the Louisiana Court of Appeal was whether the parents of a private school student were entitled to recover prepaid tuition after they withdrew their son from school prior to the beginning of the school term. The contract between the parents and the school provided that catastrophic illness, transfer out of the locale or disenrollment initiated by the school were the only three bases for a refund of prepaid tuition. The parents had admittedly withdrawn their son from the school after another, more preferred school accepted the child for enrollment. The court of appeal held that because the cancellation of the child's enrollment was not for one of the three accepted reasons enumerated in the contract, the parents were responsible for the full year's tuition and fees. *Moyse v. Runnels School, Inc.*, 457 So.2d 767 (La.App.1st Cir.1984).

In September, 1985, a medical student from Pennsylvania enrolled in the medical school at American University of the Caribbean (American). She stayed on campus for eleven days before she left school. After arriving home, she contacted American seeking a tuition refund. When the refund was not forthcoming she sued American in a Pennsylvania trial court. When the student was awarded only $3,500 on her breach of contract claim she appealed to the Pennsylvania Superior Court. At issue was whether American was liable for fraudulent misrepresentation and intentional infliction of emotional distress, among other things. The court ruled that a two-day delay in student orientation and a misrepresentation of some class sizes was not fraudulent misrepresentation. Concerning the intentional infliction of emotional distress claim, the court observed that there is liability for this tort only where "one who by extreme and outrageous conduct intentionally or recklessly causes severe emotional distress to another...." The court concluded that the evidence was not sufficient to constitute a valid claim of intentional infliction of emotional distress. It upheld the award of damages for breach of contract but dismissed the other contentions. *Reimer v. Tien*, 514 A.2d 566 (Pa.Super.1986).

In a second Louisiana case the Delta School of Commerce, Inc., a private business college, was ordered by the state court of appeal to refund to a student the full amount of her tuition including a PELL grant paid to the school on her behalf. The court found that the college was liable to the student because the school had misled her into believing that she could receive an associate degree in accounting that would transfer with full credit to a four-year college. The student had met with an admissions representative before applying to the school. At trial, she testified that he told her that her two years of credits at the business college could transfer to a four-year institution. Two other students also testified that they were led to believe that their credits would transfer. However, the admissions representative testified he never discussed the accounting program with the student. In February, the student spoke to the admissions representative and he told her that the transfer of her credits would be decided by whatever university she decided to attend. He told her that she would receive an associate degree in occupational studies, not accounting. She was told that if she dropped out at that time, she would receive a full refund. She decided to continue, but in April, she was dismissed from the college for excessive tardiness and attitude problems.

The student then filed a lawsuit in state court against the school for breach of contract in failing to provide a program with an associate degree in accounting that was transferable to a four-year college. At trial, the student was awarded the entire amount of her tuition. When the trial judge gave his oral reasons for the decision, he said that the student had been led to believe that she would receive a certain degree, when in fact she would not. The court of appeal upheld the trial court's decision. The court observed that an occupational studies degree was not listed in the student handbook, so it would not have been possible for the student to receive a degree in that area. Further, the college was not allowed to keep the PELL grant because it was awarded to the student, not the school. The court also assessed the cost of the trial court proceedings against the college. *Till v. Delta School of Commerce, Inc.*, 487 So.2d 180 (La.App.3d Cir.1986).

C. Dismissals from School

Courts will uphold the dismissal or expulsion of private school students for failure to comply with school rules, even where such compliance is not expressly required by the contractual agreement between school and student. Further, while private schools are not bound by the strict due process requirements imposed on public schools, there is a growing trend in the courts in favor of granting private school students the right to some minimal procedural safeguards upon dismissal.

In an Indiana case, the mother of a military school cadet sued the school on behalf of her son claiming that his bad-conduct dismissal from the seventh grade constituted a breach of the contract to educate her son. During the first semester the boy had accumulated more than twice the number of demerits allowed at the school for such conduct as "pushing, punching, teasing and shoving" other cadets. Two warning letters were sent to his mother and he was counseled twice about his behavior by the school's superintendent. The cadet persisted in his misconduct. In the last week of the first semester he brutally beat another cadet, rupturing the boy's eardrum in the process. A U.S. district court dismissed the breach of contract suit brought by the boy's mother, stating that "implicit in the student's contract with the school upon matriculation is the student's agreement to comply with the school's rules and regulations." The court held that the boy's continuing misconduct justified his dismissal from the school. *Jones v. Howe Military School*, 604 F.Supp. 122 (N.D.Ind.1984).

A fifteen-year-old Connecticut student was dismissed from a Catholic high school for disciplinary reasons. The youth contended that the school's receipt of governmental aid and the imposition of governmental regulations in accreditation converts a private school into a state agency for purposes of constitutional due process requirements. A U.S. district court held that state aid alone does not render a private school a state agency, nor does accreditation by a state agency result in the private school becoming an agency of the state. The student, said the court, was therefore was not entitled to due process. *Huff v. Notre Dame High School of West Haven*, 456 F.Supp. 1145 (D.Conn.1978).

In a similar case, students in a private high school in Louisiana were expelled following their second violation of the school's no-smoking rule. The rule was contained in the student handbook and provided for a $10 fine for the first violation and dismissal from school for the second violation. However, the penalty of dismissal had never before been enforced for a second offense although many students had repeatedly been caught violating the no-smoking rule. Based upon this lack of uniformity in enforcing the no-smoking rule, a lower court ordered that the students be reinstated. However, the Louisiana Court of Appeal reversed the lower court's decision and upheld the no-smoking rule and its enforcement. The court held that private institutions such as this have a near absolute right and power to control their own internal disciplinary procedures which includes the right and power to dismiss students. The court said that while due process safeguards cannot be completely ignored, in this case at least, such minimum safeguards were present. *Flint v. St. Augustine High School*, 323 So.2d 229 (La.App.4th Cir.1975).

D. Educational Malpractice

The courts have been extremely reluctant to recognize lawsuits based upon educational malpractice.

In a New York case, parents sued a private elementary school seeking to recover damages for breach of contract upon the alleged failure of the school to provide a quality education to an enrolled student. The New York Supreme Court, Appellate Division, citing prior decisions precluding educational malpractice as a ground for recovery against public schools, extended this doctrine to private schools. The judiciary's reluctance to attempt to determine the propriety of a course of instruction, which has repeatedly manifested itself in cases involving public schools, is no less appropriate when a private school is involved. The court stated that claims such as this require an analysis of the educational function itself, an analysis which is better left to professional educators. *Paladino v. Adelphi University*, 454 N.Y.S.2d 868 (A.D.2d Dept.1982).

E. Parental Obligations

An eighteen-year-old woman filed a lawsuit against her father seeking to force him to pay for her college education. Her parents had been divorced in 1980 and she had lived with each of them at different times. The total estimated cost for her to earn a degree in journalism from a four-year college was $25,000. At the time of the trial, she was working part-time and planned to continue to work during the school year, but she asserted that her salary would not be enough to cover the cost of a college education. Her mother, who totally supported the girl, could not afford the cost of a college education without her ex-husband's assistance. The daughter claimed that her father could give her the $3,600 a year she needed from his income of more than $60,000 a year without undue financial burden. The daughter brought her suit under California Civil Code § 206, which provides that "it is the duty of the father, the mother, and the children of any person in need who is unable to maintain himself by work, to maintain such person to the extent of their ability." The statute had been adopted in California in 1872. It put the financial burden on the parents to support a child of majority age unable to work and be self-sufficient. The state courts have since limited the statute to children with a mental or physical disability, or some other inability to find work because of factors outside of the child's control. The daughter claimed to be a "person in need" because she needed and expected the college education that she could not afford. The California Court of Appeal, however, did not find her "in need." The court held that the word "child" was used in the statute only to mean a minor or a disabled adult. According to the statute, the parent is only responsible for providing a nondisabled person with a high school education. *Jones v. Jones*, 225 Cal.Rptr. 95 (App.2d Dist.1986).

F. Student Privacy Rights

The contract to educate, as well as federal law, requires protection of students' privacy.

1. Buckley Amendment

The Family Educational Rights and Privacy Act of 1974 [20 U.S.C. § 1232(g)], also called the Buckley Amendment, applies to any educational institution receiving federal funds. The Amendment along with U.S. Department of Education regulations (found at 34 CFR Part 99) contain extremely detailed requirements regarding the maintaining and disclosing of student records. These requirements become applicable only upon a student's attendance at the school (see also Chapter Six, Section VII).

2. Implied Contractual Privacy Rights

The common law of most states recognizes a right of privacy inherent in the school-student relationship.

A five-foot, six-inch 315 lb. woman was enrolled in the nursing program at Salve Regina College in Rhode Island during the 1983-84 school year. In her junior year the student agreed to a contract with the college to make her further participation in the nursing curriculum contingent upon an average weight loss of two lbs. per week. When she failed to meet the terms of the agreement the college dismissed her from the nursing program in August, 1985. Subsequently, the student sued the college in a U.S. district court, and the college asked the court to dismiss the case. Among other things, the student contended that the college was liable for intentional infliction of emotional distress. The district court ruled that although Rhode Island did not recognize a lawsuit for negligent infliction of emotional distress, the state would recognize a lawsuit for harm resulting from intentional infliction of emotional distress. The court stated that although a private college must be afforded wide discretion in formulating scholastic standards and disciplining students, there is no justification for debasement, harassment, or humiliation.

The evidence showed that the student in this case had been used by faculty members to demonstrate hospital procedures regarding the care of obese patients and subjected to lectures and discussions about the necessity of weight loss. The court observed that as a result the student suffered nightmares, sleeplessness, nausea, vomiting and diarrhea after her dismissal. These results indicated that the college had recklessly disregarded the probability of causing emotional distress to the student. The college's conduct was justly described as extreme and outrageouus. The court held that in these circumstances, the student had a legitimate claim for intentional infliction of emotional distress.

The student also contended that her right to privacy had been violated when the college consistently intruded upon her physical solitude and seclusion regarding a personal matter such as obesity. These intrusions were illustrated by the college's continual inquiry into the progress of the student's diet and its exaggerated interest in "forbidden" food that the student ate. The court observed that these actions on the part of the college could lead a jury to find that her privacy rights had been violated. The court also reasoned that the student may have a viable breach of contract claim because she was dismissed for obesity while her academic accomplishments in the nursing program were sufficient to warrant her continuing in the program. The court therefore refused the college's motion to dismiss the claims of intentional infliction of emotional distress, violation of privacy and breach of contract. The student's lawsuit was allowed to proceed. *Russell v. Salve Regina College*, 649 F.Supp. 391 (D.R.I.1986).

A man was a student at Lincoln Christian College in Illinois from September, 1976, to March, 1981. During the man's last semester the dean of students was told by another student that the man might be a homosexual.

Consequently, the man was told that he would graduate only if he sought counseling from a college-designated counselor. In reliance upon the college's assurances that he would graduate if he sought counseling the man repeatedly traveled out of town to obtain counseling. Thinking that the information he divulged to the counselor would be held in confidence the man revealed many personal facts about his homosexuality that he had never told anyone else. When the counselor reported the man's tendencies to the dean of students, the dean informed the man that the college would hold a hearing in less than twenty-four hours where he would be required to defend himself against the rumor that he was a homosexual. Afraid that the accusation of homosexuality on his transcript would destroy his career prospects, the student withdrew from the college. The hearing was held anyway and subsequently the dean informed the student's mother that her son was being dismissed because he was a homosexual. In November, 1984, the student sued the college and the counselor in an Illinois circuit court. When the circuit court granted motions to dismiss the student's complaint he appealed to the Appellate Court of Illinois.

Among other things, the student alleged that the college breached its contract with him by arbitrarily and in bad faith denying him his diploma. The appellate court observed that the implied contract between a college and a student is legally enforceable. A student's application constitutes an offer to enroll at a college and the college accepts the student's offer when the student is admitted. The student pays tuition and attends classes in exchange for the college's provision of facilities and instruction. Upon the student's satisfactory completion of the college's academic requirements the college becomes obligated to issue the student a diploma. Because a college cannot act maliciously or refuse in bad faith to award a degree to a student who fulfills its degree requirements, the court concluded that the student's complaint stated a valid legal basis for breach of an implied contract. The court also ruled that the college violated the Illinois Confidentiality Act by disclosing information learned from the counselor to faculty members, students and members of the man's family. It also concluded that the lower court was wrong in dismissing the man's claim that the college tortiously interfered with the man's contract with the counselor and that the counselor's disclosure of confidential information tortiously interfered with the man's contract with LCC. These matters were remanded to the circuit court for further proceedings. *Johnson v. Lincoln Christian College*, 501 N.E.2d 1380 (Ill.App.4th Dist.1986).

V. LEASING OF PRIVATE SCHOOL FACILITIES

When a unit of government leases or otherwise puts to use classrooms or other facilities belonging to private or parochial schools, the government must take care to avoid a violation of the Establishment Clause of the First Amendment to the U.S. Constitution (see also Chapter Four).

Residents and taxpayers in Rhode Island sued their school district asking the court to prohibit the expenditure of public funds to lease classroom space for the school district from a Catholic institution. The claim was based on the contention that the lease agreement violated the First Amendment in that it provided state funds to a sectarian institution, involved excessive government entanglement with religion and constituted compulsory taxation for religious purposes. A U.S. district court rejected these claims and upheld the lease agreement. In so doing, the court noted that the leased premises were physically isolated from the religious atmosphere of the rest of the building and that public school authorities had taken other precautions to insulate the public school students from religious influence. *Thomas v. Schmidt*, 397 F.Supp. 203 (D.R.I.1975).

The California Court of Appeal rejected the San Francisco School District's attempt to keep a private school from bidding on a lease of a vacant school building by placing a proviso in the bid specifications which stated that the winning bid would be void if entered by a private school. The school district argued that the private and public school systems were competing for the same students and to allow the private school to bid on vacant public school property was self-defeating for the public schools. Further, the school district argued that a court-ordered school desegregation plan could be adversely affected by the enrollment composition of a private school. The court held that the two school systems provided healthy competition which ultimately benefited both systems. With respect to the desegregation plan, the court said that the bid specification could have contained a proviso that any private school enrollment must not cause the public school to fall short of the court-ordered guidelines for the district. However, the court held that the exclusion provision in the district's bid specification was unconstitutional. *Binet-Montessori v. San Francisco Unified School Dist.*, 160 Cal.Rptr. 38 (App.1st Dist.1979).

Wisconsin legislation which permitted the state to contract with private or parochial institutions for special education needs of handicapped children was held to be constitutional by that state's supreme court. The state had been forced to seek outside services for handicapped children because of a lack of public facilities. The objection to purchasing these services from religiously oriented facilities was that such purchases constituted aid to help advance religious causes. The court said that the mere contracting for goods and services with a private sectarian institution was appropriate. Since the primary effect of the legislation was to provide special education services to handicapped children and any possible religious advancement was incidental, the court held that the legislation was constitutional. *State v. Alioto*, 219 N.W.2d 585 (Wis.1974).

VI. COMPULSORY ATTENDANCE

Virtually every state requires children to attend school. The U.S. Constitution places limits, however, on compulsory school attendance laws.

A. Attendance at Private Schools

Under the U.S. Constitution, states must recognize that attendance at a qualified private school satisfies compulsory school attendance requirements.

In 1922, the voters of the state of Oregon enacted by initiative a law requiring that all school-age children attend public schools only. A Catholic parochial school and a military academy challenged the law in federal court. An injunction was granted to the private schools preventing enforcement of the law, and the state of Oregon appealed to the U.S. Supreme Court. Affirming the lower court's injunction, the Supreme Court held that while the state has a strong interest in educating its citizens, parents have a strong interest in directing the upbringing of their children. The Court resolved the conflict between these competing interests by declaring that "[t]he child is not the mere creature of the State." Although states may require children to attend school, requiring attendance at public schools only is an infringement of parents' constitutional rights. *Pierce v. Society of Sisters*, 268 U.S. 510 (1925).

B. Amish Exception

The general principle expounded by the Supreme Court in *Pierce v. Society of Sisters*, that the states could require some form of school attendance of all children, was tempered by the Court with its subsequent recognition of an "Amish exception" to compulsory school attendance. In this case, *Wisconsin v. Yoder*, Amish parents were convicted of failing to send their children to either a public or private school up to age sixteen, as required by state law. The parents had sent their children to public school only until they completed the eighth grade and were fourteen or fifteen years old. The Supreme Court held that the state of Wisconsin's interest in compelling Amish children to attend school after the eighth grade was minimal, and accordingly it upheld a lower court's reversal of the parents' criminal convictions. The Court cautioned that its holding was limited to children residing in traditionally discrete and isolated communities such as the Amish. *Wisconsin v. Yoder*, 406 U.S. 205 (1972).

C. Teacher Certification and Other Minimum Standards

Most states have enacted one or all of the following requirements: 1) that teachers in private schools be certified by the state, 2) that the instruction offered to nonpublic school children be "equivalent" to that offered in the public schools, and 3) that nonpublic education conform with certain curriculum standards. The cases in this section involve disputes arising under these requirements.

During the 1985-86 school year, a Maine couple enrolled their children in the satellite (correspondence type) school system of Christian Liberty Academy, headquartered in Prospect Heights, Illinois. The academy's satellite program required the couple's children to attend their home school at least 185 days a year and complete a course outlined by the academy. Prior to the 1985-86 school year the couple received a copy of the local school district's "Home Instruction Policy." The couple did not comply with this policy but submitted (in August, 1985) a letter alleging that they were in compliance with the school district's "Guidelines for Equivalent Instruction in Nonapproved Private Schools." The couple was informed by the State Department of Education in September, 1985, that the guidelines for nonapproved private schools did not apply to their home instruction program and, therefore, their request for nonapproved private school status would be denied. In

March, 1986, the couple was notified by the local school district that it would proceed with a truancy hearing according to Maine state law. In September, 1986, the school district referred the case to the district attorney for prosecution under state truancy law. The couple then sued the Commissioner of Education seeking a temporary restraining order against the truancy proceeding. When the request was denied the couple filed an amended complaint and a renewed motion for a temporary restraining order in a U.S. district court. The district court treated the couple's request as a request for a preliminary injunction and stated that the criteria for such an injunction were well settled:

> The court must find: (1) that plaintiff will suffer irreparable injury if the injunction is not granted; (2) that such injury outweighs any harm which granting injunctive relief would inflict on the defendant; (3) that plaintiff has exhibited a likelihood of success on the merits; and (4) that the public interest will not be adversely affected by the granting of the injunction.

Concluding that the couple failed to demonstrate a likelihood of success, the district court applied the *Younger* abstention doctrine. In *Younger* the U.S. Supreme Court ruled that a federal court could abstain from ruling on state criminal proceedings which the federal court plaintiffs claimed had been brought under an unconstitutional state law. The district court reasoned that the state's interest in educating its citizens justified the imposition of reasonable regulations for the control and duration of basic education. This state interest justified the enforcement of the truancy laws. The coupled argued that the *Younger* abstention doctrine should not apply because no state court lawsuit was pending at the time they filed their federal lawsuit. The court rejected this argument, ruling that state criminal proceedings do not have to be pending in order for *Younger* to apply.

The couple also claimed that the enforcement of the requirement that their home education program be state-approved burdened their parental rights and religious liberties. Specifically, they contended that the truancy policy placed substantial pressure on them to modify their behavior, thereby violating their sincerely-held religious beliefs. They further argued that the pending truancy proceeding hindered the exercise of their constitutional rights under the First Amendment. In denying the irreparable harm claim, the court stated that the couple could not argue that the state policy requiring prior approval of home education programs deprived them of the constitutional right to educate their children since they had made a choice to go forward with their unapproved home education program. The court also observed that the cost and inconvenience of having to defend against a truancy prosecution could not, by itself, be considered "irreparable" in the special legal sense of the term. It noted that the issue of irreparable injury was narrow in this case. The argument of the couple amounted to a claim that they would be irreparably injured if they were forced to argue their constitutional claims in a state court rather then a federal court. The couple's motion for preliminary injunctive relief was denied and the truancy charges were allowed to proceed. *Blount v. Redmond*, 649 F.Supp. 319 (D.Me.1986).

A 1921 Michigan law provides that the superintendent of public instruction is to supervise "all the private, denominational and parochial schools" in the state. This provision includes the examination of curriculum and ensuring that all private and parochial teachers "hold a certificate such as would qualify him or her to teach in like grades of the public schools of the state." In 1979, the State Department of Education sought to obtain information about teacher qualifications from two private church-run K-12 schools. The schools had no separate corporate existence from the churches. The church schools refused to provide the requested information and sued the department in a circuit court. The church schools contended that the 1921 state law was unconstitutional on the basis of the First Amendment to the U.S. Constitution and certain articles of the state constitution. The circuit court ruled in favor of the church schools, noting that the requirement of teacher certification was unconstitutional because it violated the church schools' free exercise rights and created excessive government entanglement with religion. The department appealed to the state court of appeals, which reversed the trial court decision. The church schools appealed to the Michigan Supreme Court. The supreme court voted three to three, which under Michigan law affirmed the appeals court decision in favor of the department. The prevailing opinion listed four rules used to decide the case: 1) the church schools' "claims must be rooted in religious belief;" 2) if the state law does not infringe on the church schools' free exercise of religion, the law will be upheld; 3) incidental burdens on the free exercise of religion may be justified by a compelling state interest, and 4) if no less obtrusive form of regulation is avilable to the state, the law will be upheld.

The prevailing opinion denied the church schools' reasoning on the last three rules. The schools claimed their religious interests would be burdened because "no one may carry out a teaching ministry in a church-school without a government permit to do so." They also contended that enforcement of the law gave the state excessive discretion in determining whether a teacher receives a provisional certificate. The court agreed that licensing the schools' teachers did affect their free exercise rights but observed that the burden on the schools was outweighed by the compelling state interest in educating its youth. The prevailing opinion reasoned that the infringement on the schools' free exercise rights was minimal since the teachers can secure all the certification requirements at either a religious or nonreligious institution. The schools argued that student achievement testing was an adequate method of state monitoring. However, the prevailing opinion reasoned that standardized student achievement tests would not be an adequate, less intrusive means of state monitoring since deficient teaching would come to light only after the damage is done. *Sheridan Road Baptist Church v. Department of Education*, 396 N.W.2d 373 (Mich.1986).

Operators of Baptist schools in Iowa filed suit in federal court arguing that their religious freedoms were being infringed by the state. In particular they objected to a statutory requirement that teachers in any nonpublic school be certified. One prerequisite to teacher certification was a human relations component which enabled teachers to "[r]ecognize and deal with such dehumanizing biases as sexism, racism, prejudice, and discrimination, and become aware of the impact that such biases have on interpersonal relations" [Iowa Admin. Rules, Pub. Ins. Dept. 670-13.21(257)]. The reference to "sexism" as a "dehumanizing bias" was alleged to be an unconstitutional interference by the state with the Baptist schools' sincere religious belief that

God intended men and women to assume different familial roles. The district court rejected this contention, holding that although Baptist teachers were required to satisfy the human relations component, nothing required them to agree with its viewpoints. The teachers could still hold their traditional biblical beliefs concerning the roles of the sexes. The court dismissed the remainder of the plaintiffs' arguments and upheld the constitutionality of Iowa's teacher certification laws. *Fellowship Baptist Church v. Benton*, 620 F.Supp. 308 (D.C.Iowa 1985).

In a second Iowa case, a pastor and certain members of a fundamentalist Baptist church decided to form a parochial school where the children of church members could be educated. They sought a ruling from state education officials that the school would be exempt, under the Amish exception, from complying with certain aspects of Iowa's compulsory school attendance laws. The Amish exception under Iowa law allows children to be instructed by individuals who do not possess state teacher certification. While acknowledging the validity of the statute requiring that all children attend a private or public school, the parents contended that their church school could not be required to hire only certified teachers. Education officials refused to apply the Amish exception to the school and the parents filed suit. A state trial court upheld the administrative decision and the parents appealed. The Iowa Supreme Court held that the church school must comply with the certification requirements of Iowa law. The Amish exception from teacher certification is available only to children who will live in isolated communities and hence will not require a great deal of learning. In this case, the organizers of the church school had no compelling justification for avoiding the certification requirement. The supreme court therefore ordered that the church school comply with all state requirements. *Johnson v. Charles City Comm. Schools Bd. of Educ.*, 368 N.W.2d 74 (Iowa 1985).

Parents of two North Dakota school children were convicted of failure to comply with the state's compulsory school attendance laws. The parents, members of the Bible Baptist Church, sent their children to a church-sponsored school rather than a public school or an accredited private school. The church-sponsored school was not accredited, employed no certified teachers, and followed a curriculum entitled Accelerated Christian Education which incorporated scripture passages within the teaching materials. Uncontroverted evidence showed that the parents were sincere in their belief that it was a religious mandate to educate their children in Christian schools. Evidence also showed that even though the school was not accredited, many of the children were, when tested by the California Achievement Tests, scoring higher than their public school counterparts. However, the North Dakota Supreme Court upheld the parents' lower court convictions, ruling that the state's compelling interest in educating its citizens and regulation of that education through minimum standards did not violate the religious tenets of the Bible Baptist Church. Because the church school failed to meet the minimum accreditation requirements, the school was not acceptable for purposes of fulfilling the compulsory school attendance laws. *State v. Shaver*, 294 N.W.2d 883 (N.D.1980).

A Wisconsin father of three children was convicted of violating that state's compulsory school attendance laws when he sought to have his child attend a private church-affiliated school called the Free Thinker School. He notified school authorities of the facts and asked that his daughter's school records be forwarded to the new school. A district school administrator, however, determined that before he would recognize the school as a private school for purposes of the compulsory school attendance law, it would have to be listed in the Wisconsin Nonpublic School Directory issued by the Department of Public Instruction. The directory is compiled from information received from local school administrators who advise of the existence of private schools in their districts. There is no statutory or regulatory definition of private schools. Since the Free Thinker School was not listed in the directory, the father was arrested and convicted of violating the compulsory school attendance law. The Supreme Court of Wisconsin, reversing the conviction, held that the definition of what constituted a private school was vague and therefore unconstitutional as a violation of the Due Process Clause of the U.S. Constitution's Fourteenth Amendment and also the Wisconsin Constitution. The court noted that the statute, lacking such a definition, left it to the school administrators and courts to define "private school." This could lead to arbitrary application of the law bases on subjective standards. The court noted that such discriminatory enforcement is contrary to the basic values underlying the principles of due process. *State v. Popanz*, 332 N.W.2d 750 (Wis.1983).

The Supreme Court of Ohio, reversing two lower courts, permitted the continuance of a religious school. The school was established by the Tabernacle Christian sect in order to provide children of that sect with an education based upon certain religious beliefs and untainted by what the members of the sect felt were unhealthy outside influences. The school was not completely inconsistent with Ohio educational standards but did have Biblical references interjected into almost all areas of the curriculum. Because of this, the state department of education refused to grant a charter to the school. This resulted in the parents being indicted for failure to send their children to a properly approved school. The supreme court held that the state minimum standards overstepped the boundary of reasonable regulation of nonpublic religious schools. *State v. Whisner*, 351 N.E.2d 750 (Ohio 1976).

A group of private religious schools brought suit against the Maine State Board of Education seeking an injunction preventing the board from bringing actions against the schools on the ground that they induced truancy. The board filed a countersuit for an injunction prohibiting the schools from operating based upon their failure to obtain statutory approval to operate as private institutions. The schools, concerned about increasing governmental involvement in sectarian education, had declined to submit a five-year educational plan. The board argued that since the schools were unapproved, the students were not receiving an education equivalent to that provided in public schools and, therefore, were violating compulsory attendance laws. A U.S. district court held that the Maine compulsory attendance law does not prohibit the schools from operating merely because they are unapproved. Thus, the state was not entitled to injunctive relief against the schools. The private schools' request for an injunction was granted. The court perceived the board's attempt to close the schools by judicial means as a way of circumventing procedural safeguards required by law. Any action against the schools for inducing truancy by preaching that the Bible commands a fundamentalist Christian education for children would inhibit the schools' right to free speech. *Bangor Baptist Church v. State of Maine*, 576 F.Supp. 1299 (D.Me.1983).

D. Home Instruction

While the decision in *Pierce v. Society of Sisters* establishes a right to attend a private rather than a public school, *Pierce* does not establish a right to home education. States may choose, however, to permit home education. Parents providing home education must comply with applicable state regulations.

A Florida court held that a "school" set up in a home did not qualify as a denominational or parochial school. The parents refused to send their children to a public school because they believed that race mixing in public schools was sinful. Instead, the children stayed at home where the mother, not trained as a teacher, taught them. The court said that under these circumstances the children were truants and they were therefore placed under the supervision of a juvenile counselor of the court. *T.A.F. & E.M.F. v. Duval County*, 273 So.2d 15 (Fla.App.1st Dist.1973).

When a nine-year-old home schooled boy was thought to be academically deficient a New York family court ordered achievement testing in August, 1985. The boy was found to be unable to read and the court instructed the parents to make competent efforts to educate him. Further testing took place in April, 1986, indicating that he had made strong progress in several subjects but was still lacking in others. Consequently, the local school district petitioned the family court for an order that the boy be required to attend the local public school or an approved private school, or that the school district be allowed to extensively monitor the boy's home education. The court observed that home schooling was allowed by New York law when the education given and received was substantially equivalent to the education given and received in the local public schools. The court pointed out that the local public school board of education was responsible for determining whether the child received instruction that was substantially equivalent in time and in quality to that given in the public school. The court concluded that the parents must send their boy to a full-time instruction program at a public or private school or agree to have the boy's progress monitored by the local school board. The court observed that monitoring included curriculum evaluation, teacher competency, inspections, achievement testing, and the regular keeping of attendance records. Reiterating that the issue was not whether home schooling was right, but whether the child was receiving an adequate education, the court ruled that the parents must acquiesce in the local school system's efforts to determine whether the boy's education was adequate. *Matter of Adam D.*, 505 N.Y.S.2d 809 (Fam.Ct.1986).

Convinced that the environment and education provided by Indiana public schools were incompatible with their family's religion, an ordained minister of the Jehovah's Witnesses decided to start her own home school, the Greenhouse Academy. The superintendent and attendance officer of the local school district swore out a complaint with a prosecuting attorney after the woman and her husband refused to cooperate with him in verifying the educational program of the Greenhouse Academy. The charges against the couple were dropped, however, after they made efforts to bring her school into compliance with the Indiana compulsory attendance law. The couple then brought suit against the superintendent and the school district alleging that the state compulsory attendance law and the superintendent's attempts to enforce it violated their civil rights. They asked for damages and an injunction preventing local school officials from interfering in their decision to educate their children at home. A U.S. district court ruled in favor of the superintendent and the couple appealed. The U.S. Court of Appeals, Seventh Circuit, stated that the prosecution under the state compulsory attendance statute was a result of the couple's failure to cooperate with the superintendent in monitoring compliance rather than a result of the application of the statute itself. Once the couple made attempts to comply with the law, the charges were dropped. Thus, a federal court injunction against the school officials was not warranted. The court also ruled that the superintendent's acts did not arise out of any hostility to home schooling or to the Jehovah's Witnesses but were merely attempts to enforce the law. The decision of the district court was affirmed. *Mazanec v. North Judson-San Pierre School Corp.*, 798 F.2d 230 (7th Cir.1986).

VII. SCHOLARSHIPS, GRANTS AND FINANCIAL AID

Disputes involving various types of financial aid offered by private schools are governed by contract law principles. Receipt of federal funding may impose additional obligations on institutions. As the second case in this section illustrates, students have attempted (usually unsuccessfully) to hold private schools to the heightened due process standards applicable to public institutions on the basis of state funding. The final two cases address the constitutional challenges which have been brought against the draft registration requirement for the receipt by male students of federal financial aid.

The New York Supreme Court, Appellate Division, affirmed the state Department of Education's adoption of an audit report compiled by the state comptroller which found that Elmira Business Institute, a private business school, had not offered programs for the 1975 through 1985 academic years in accordance with regulations pertaining to New York's Tuition Assistance Program (TAP). TAP awards grants to schools on behalf of students and the grants go toward paying students' tuition. Under TAP regulations, each institution is required to provide each student with at least 1,440 hours of instruction in each area of study. The school had first been approved to receive TAP grants in 1975, and in 1977 the New York comptroller began auditing the school. A report was issued in 1982 which concluded that the school had been overpaid $264,263. The report found that the school had not complied with the program and students were receiving less hours of classroom instruction that the school had originally proposed. The school was also including unapproved and unstructured classes into the tabulation of credit hours for TAP. A lower court held that the government could not collect the money that the school owed because 1) the audit had taken too long, 2) the school had the right to decide to change its curriculum, and 3) the government could not demand repayment once it had approved the program. On appeal, the appellate court disagreed with these determinations and reversed the decision. The court found no evidence of prejudice to the school caused by the length of time it took to complete the audit. The court agreed that the school could change its original course offerings but held that the changes needed to be approved by the state. According to the court, the school had an obligation to comply with the dictates of an authorized program and its failure to do so made the school responsible for repaying $264,263 in TAP funds. *Elmira Business Institute, Inc. v. New York Dep't of Education*, 500 N.Y.S.2d 833 (A.D.3d Dept.1986).

An inmate at a state prison facility in Ossining, New York, was admitted to the educational program operated by Mercy College at the prison. The inmate completed the 1984 spring semester with honors and then asked a college administrator about the availability of an academic scholarship so he could continue in the program. When the administrator informed him that scholarships were not available to inmates, the inmate wrote a letter to the president of Mercy College. After the inmate failed to receive satisfaction he sued Mercy College in U.S. district court under the Civil Rights Act contending that Mercy's failure to grant him the scholarship to further his college education violated New York corrections law and deprived him of his constitutional rights. In denying the inmate's claim the district court reasoned that the inmate must allege 1) that Mercy had deprived him of a right secured by federal law and 2) that in doing so Mercy acted under the color of state law. The court further observed that the inmate would not prevail unless the actions upon which his claims were based were "fairly attributable to the state." The issue was whether the actions of the Mercy College employees had been taken under the color of state law. The court inferred that the inmate attempted to link Mercy and the state of New York because Mercy received state funding, but concluded that the fact that Mercy was partially supported by state funds failed to satisfy the requirement of state action. The court noted that the U.S. Supreme Court has ruled that the "mere receipt of public funds by an entity 'does not make [that entity's] discharge decisions acts of the state'." The district court stated that even the presence of large amounts of public funds is insufficient to change the action of a private institution into a state action. The inmate did not demonstrate any other "state entanglement" with Mercy.

The inmate also contended that his constitutional rights had been violated because he had not been afforded the same educational opportunities that are given to wealthier, nonincarcerated applicants. Specifically, he alleged that Mercy violated his equal protection and due process rights by failing to provide him with a scholarship simply because he was a prisoner. The court rejected this argument, observing that New York corrections law "does not confer a right to both a full-time education and a full-time job." The court noted that correctional law provided for education designed to return the inmate to society as a "wholesome citizen" but did not confer either a property or liberty interest in a full-time education, which is necessary for a successful due process claim. His equal protection claim was dismissed when the court reasoned that a state-funded college education is not a fundamental right for anyone, prisoner or not. All of the inmate's claims were dismissed. *Jones v. Grunewarld*, 644 F.Supp. 256 (S.D.N.Y.1986).

A student at a "for profit" college was denied a state educational grant and sued the South Carolina Higher Education Tuition Grants Committee in state court seeking to have a provision of the state General Appropriations Act (GAA) limiting state grants to students at nonprofit institutions declared unconstitutional. The court ruled that the provision was unconstitutional but it declined to order the Tuition Grants Committee to consider the student's application for an educational loan. Both parties appealed to the Supreme Court of South Carolina. Section 18 of the GAA stated that loans shall only be made to students attending "independent, nonprofit, post-secondary institutions." The supreme court reversed the lower court decision and agreed with the Tuition Grants Committee that the nonprofit/for profit distinction in the GAA was not a violation of the Equal Protection Clause of the U.S. Constitution. The court referred to a Virginia case which stated "it is certainly rational, and therefore compatible with the Equal Protection Clause, for government to pursue a policy which does not funnel state loans into the hands of students who, attending institutions conducted for profit, necessarily are paying tuition fees at a level which makes possible that profit." Under this rationale, the court concluded that the distinction between nonprofit and for profit schools did not violate the student's equal protection rights. *Talley v. South Carolina Higher Education Tuition Grants Committee*, 347 S.E.2d 99 (S.C.1986).

The U.S. Supreme Court held that a federal law denying Guaranteed Student Loans, as well as other federal financial aid, to male students who fail to register for the draft was constitutionally valid. The law was challenged by a group of students in Minnesota who brought suit against the Selective Service System. The students claimed that the law imposed an automatic "punishment" upon nonregistering male students without the benefit of a judicial trial. They also argued that requiring students to disclose whether they had registered for the draft violated the Fifth Amendment privilege against self-incrimination. The Supreme Court upheld the law and rejected the students' claims that the law was a "bill of attainder," i.e., a law which imposes a penalty without a trial. The law clearly gave nonregistrants thirty days after receiving notice that they were ineligible for federal financial aid to register for the draft and thereby qualify for aid. Further, the proscription in the U.S. Constitution against bills of attainder applies only to statutes that inflict punishments on specified individuals or groups, for example, "all members of the Communist Party." The Court did not believe that the statute had singled out a specific group for punishment. The Court also held that merely because Congress had established certain requirements in order for students to qualify for federal financial aid did not necessarily mean that the nonregistering students had been "punished." In this regard, the Court quoted a U.S. Senator who had supported the legislation: "If students wish to further their education at the expense of their country, they cannot expect these benefits to be provided without accepting their fair share of the responsibilities to that Government." Finally, the law did not violate the Fifth Amendment privilege against compelled self-incrimination because there was nothing forcing the students to apply for federal financial aid. *Selective Service System v. Minnesota Public Interest Research Group*, 104 S.Ct. 3348 (1984).

In 1985, the U.S. Supreme Court issued another ruling on the issue of draft registration. In this case the Court held that the U.S. Department of Justice could legitimately prosecute only those individuals who were known to have failed to register with the Selective Service System. Thus the indictment of a California man who had written letters to the government announcing his refusal to register for the draft was upheld against a First Amendment challenge. The man claimed that he had been singled out for prosecution solely because he was a vocal opponent of draft registration, and he argued that this was an infringement of his right of free speech. The Court rejected this claim and upheld the right of the Justice Department to prosecute only those individuals whose nonregistration had in some way been brought to the attention of the Department. *Wayte v. United States*, 105 S.Ct. 1524 (1985).

VIII. STUDENT ORGANIZATIONS

Private educational institutions, unlike their counterparts in the public sector, have wide discretion in deciding whether to recognize or charter student clubs and organizations. This is due to the fact that generally the U.S. Constitution is inapplicable in the private school setting. Some states, however, have enacted laws protecting students' speech and association rights in both the public and private school context. In such states, conflicts may arise between institutional religious or academic freedom and student free speech rights.

In 1984 the trustees of Colby College decided to withdraw recognition from all fraternities on the campus. A realty company, on behalf of a fraternity, sued the college for breach of contract in a state superior court. The court ruled in favor of the college and the realty company appealed to the Supreme Judicial Court of Maine. The dispute arose over a Memorandum of Agreement executed in 1951 between the realty company and the college. Section III(e) of that agreement stated that the college could cancel the agreement only in the following circumstances:

> In the event the ZETA PSI Fraternity ceases to have a chapter at Colby College, or in the event the Chapter is suspended or expelled for reason either by the College or the National Fraternity....

The realty company contended that the action of the college did not fall within the "expelled for reason" provision. It further claimed that the term "expelled for reason" must be construed as including only reasons amounting to a breach of the contract. Hence, the fraternity could only be expelled if it failed to maintain the social and academic standards prescribed by the college. The realtor concluded that the fraternity was at least entitled to a trial to determine whether it had failed to maintain the required standards. The college maintained, however, that the "expelled for reason" phrase should be construed according to its common meaning, i.e., a "rational justification," a definition which would preclude only arbitrary or capricious actions by the college. The college rationally justified its decision to oust all fraternities from the campus as a move to more fully "integrate the housing units into the academic program of the college." The court observed that the president and trustees of the college had the right and responsibility to periodically evaluate and change policies for the purpose of achieving certain educational goals. The court ruled that the 1984 decision by the college president and trustees to eliminate fraternity chapters at the college was a legitimate exercise of the college's supervisory authority. The college, therefore, properly ended its relationship with the realtor and fraternity under the 1951 lease agreement. The decision of the superior court in favor of the college was affirmed. *Chi Realty Corp. v. Colby College*, 513 A.2d 866 (Me.1986).

A three-judge panel of the District of Columbia Court of Appeals ordered Georgetown University to offically recognize two gay rights groups as approved student organizations. The university, a Catholic institution historically owned and controlled by the Jesuits, had been sued in superior court by the gay rights groups when it refused to extend full university recognition as student organizations. The superior court held that the Free Exercise Clause of the U.S. Constitution required that the university be allowed to deny recognition to groups which espoused goals inimical to the religious beliefs of the university. The panel reversed this decision, stating that the District of Columbia Human Rights Act prohibited the university from discriminating against gays. The evidence indicated that although official recognition had been denied to the gay student groups, the university had allowed the groups to conduct meetings on campus and invite speakers. The panel held that since for all practical purposes the groups had been allowed to operate as recognized student clubs, to require official university recognition would only minimally burden the university's religious freedom. "Recognition" would not equal "approval." The university was thus ordered by the panel to extend recognition to the gay student groups. *Gay Rights Coalition v. Georgetown University*, 496 A.2d 567 (D.C.App.1985). This decision, however, was vacated by the full court sitting *en banc* on the same day the panel issued its decision. The *en banc* court's unusual action demonstrates the judicial uncertainty in questions of this nature. The *en banc* court ordered that the case be reargued before all the judges of the court of appeals for a new decision. *See* 496 A.2d 587.

IX. ON-CAMPUS INTERVIEWING AND RECRUITING

Generally, private educational institutions may allow any groups they desire to enter their campuses for employment recruiting purposes. In denying access to certain groups, however, programs which receive federal funding must comply with civil rights laws (see Chapter Six). In addition, the following case shows that in certain instances private schools *must* allow on-campus interviewing.

The Temple University School of Law operated a placement service that arranged interviews between employers and students. One of the potential employers was the Judge Advocate General (JAG) Corps of the U.S. Army, Navy and Marines. These branches do not employ homosexuals. After being notified of the practice, the Pennsylvania Commission on Human Relations issued a complaint against the law school, alleging that it had violated the Philadelphia Fair Practices Ordinance in permitting the JAG Corps to interview at the law school. The commission claimed that the law school had violated the ordinance when referring persons to the JAG Corps knowing that it was discriminatory in its hiring practices. A U.S. district court ruled in favor of the law school and the commission appealed. The U.S. Court of Appeals, Third Circuit, observed that all parties were in agreement that the commission could not directly keep the military from recruiting persons on whatever terms it deemed appropriate. However, the parties sharply disagreed as to whether the commission could prevent the school from making its placement service available to the JAG Corps for recruitment when it discriminated on the basis of sexual orientation. In ruling in favor of the JAG Corps and the law school, the court of appeals referred to the federal Department of Defense Authorization Act of 1973, in which Congress declared that access to college and university employment facilities was of paramount importance. The court observed that in the above-mentioned act (and others similar to it) the government had shown that recruitment on a variety of campuses is essential to having a broad scope of skilled personnel in the U.S. military. The court ruled that to uphold the commission's complaint would potentially frustrate effective military recruiting in the area. The Philadelphia Fair Practices Ordinance was in direct conflict with federal legislative policy, and the court ruled that federal law took precedence. The local ordinance therefore could not be enforced against the law school. *U.S. v. City of Philadelphia*, 798 F.2d 81 (3d Cir.1986).

X. NATIONAL HONOR SOCIETY

The following public school cases establish that membership in the National Honor Society is not a right protected by the U.S. Constitution.

The father of a public school student in Arkansas brought suit against a local school board on behalf of his son alleging that his son's civil rights and the Family Educational Rights and Privacy Act of 1974 (FERPA) were violated because of the school's rejection of his son from the National Honor Society. Apparently the boy was academically eligible for membership in the society but anonymous evaluations of him submitted by his teachers prevented his inclusion. A U.S. district court held that membership in the society did not give rise to a property interest which would entitle the student to due process of law. There was also no violation of equal protection as all candidates for admission were fully apprised of the rules for admission and were treated equally. Finally, the FERPA does not provide a private right of action to challenge rejection from a school society. *Price v. Young*, 580 F.Supp. 1 (E.D.Ark.1983).

A similar Wisconsin case involved a student who also was not chosen for membership in the NHS. He and his father sought to have that decision reversed, ultimately filing a lawsuit claiming a violation of due process rights. In rejecting that claim, the court said that due process merely requires fair treatment under the circumstances, and here the procedures were fair. "Most honors are alike in that some individual or committee must review what someone has accomplished and make a subjective judgment of whether that conduct is deserving of reward or recognition. Inherent in such a system is the possibility of error.... Courts would indeed be entering into a prickly briarpatch were they to get involved in reviewing these kinds of subjective judgments." *Karnstein v. Pewaukee School Bd.*, 557 F.Supp. 565 (E.D. Wis.1983).

XI. ATHLETIC PROGRAMS

Private school athletic programs give rise to many of the same legal questions as are found in the public sphere. Player and school eligibility rules, coaching contracts, and Title IX rules (see Chapter Six) are frequent bases for lawsuits.

A. Eligibility of Players

Along with the majority of other courts, the Court of Appeal of California decided that the right of a student to participate in interscholastic athletics is not a "fundamental right" on a par with the right, under the California Constitution, to a free public education. In this case the court examined a regulation limiting interscholastic athletics and allowed it to stand. The defendant in this case, the California Interscholastic Federation (CIF), is a statewide organization established to enact and enforce regulations governing secondary school interscholastic athletics in California. At issue in this case was CIF Rule 214, which provides:

> A student who transfers from a school located in the United States, a U.S. territory or U.S. military base (to be referred to as school A) to school B without a change of residence on the part of the parents or legal guardian from school attendance area A to attendance area B shall be residentially eligible for all athletic competition, except varsity level competition in sports in which the student has competed in any level of interscholastic competition during the twelve calendar months preceding the date of such transfer, provided the athletic eligibility is approved by both principals of the schools involved. The student shall be ineligible for all sports for one calendar year in the event that either or both principals decline to approve athletic eligibility....

The plaintiff, a high school student, challenged this rule and requested an order from the court to prevent the schools involved from enforcing it. In his sophomore year in 1983-84, the plaintiff attended Brentwood School, a private school in Los Angeles County, and participated in varsity sports. At the end of his sophomore year, his parents decided to transfer him to Palisades High School (Pali High), a public school in the same general area. The plaintiff had not been recruited nor encouraged to change schools for athletic purposes by any of the personnel at Pali High. The principal of Brentwood refused to approve a waiver from athletic ineligibility after the transfer and the plaintiff was barred from athletic participation by Rule 214. The student sued in state court alleging that Rule 214 impermissibly deprived him of his "fundamental right to participate in extracurricular activities."

In its opinion, the appeals court reasoned that although public education is not a fundamental right under the federal constitution, it is under the California Constitution. Nevertheless, this did not compel the finding that the right to participate in interscholastic athletics is also a fundamental right.

Since there was no fundamental right to participate in interscholastic athletics, Rule 214 would be upheld if there were any rational basis for the rule. The court then described Rule 214 as being "rationally related to the State's valid and legitimate interest in eliminating or minimizing athletic recruitment problems in secondary schools." In ruling in favor of the CIF, the court stated: "The rules, regulations and procedures discussed herein, as they relate to the interscholastic athletic transfer rule, are prophylactic in nature, reasonable in scope and rationally based. As such, they neither trammel upon fundamental rights nor occasion unnecessary burdens. Curtailment or reduction of the abuses and transgressions which threaten to undermine student athletics are salutory goals which preserve equity between schools and protect the integrity of extracurricular programs." The student's request to suspend enforcement of the rule was thus denied. *Kent S. v. California Interscholastic Federation*, 222 Cal.Rptr. 355 (App.2d Dist.1986).

The Michigan High School Athletic Association's transfer eligibility rule states that "[a] student who transfers from one high school...to another...is ineligible to participate in an interscholastic athletic contest for one full semester in the school to which the student transfers...." In September, 1985, two students transferred from parochial high schools to public high schools for primarily academic reasons. Since both students desired to play interscholastic athletics in the fall of 1985 they requested a waiver of the transfer eligibility rule. When both requests were denied the students sued the individual school districts and the MHSAA in a Michigan circuit court. When the circuit court ruled against the students they consolidated their cases and appealed to the state court of appeals. Both students contended that the transfer eligibility rule denied them equal protection of the law in violation of the Fourteenth Amendment. The court noted that all of the parties in the case correctly assumed that the MHSAA did involve "state action" for purposes of the Fourteenth Amendment, even though it was technically a private entity, since the MHSAA was comprised primarily of public school members and was statutorily described as the "official association of the state." The students argued that because the primary reason for the transfer eligibility rule was to prevent interscholastic athletic recruiting, its application in their situations was overbroad. The court observed that because athletic participation is not a fundamental constitutional right, the rule would be upheld against an equal protection challenge if it was rationally related to a legitimate governmental interest. Since the rule related to the legitimate regulatory purpose of discouraging the recruitment of high school athletes, it did not constitute a denial of equal protection to the students. The students also argued that the procedures used by the MHSAA and the public high schools in evaluating and then denying their applications for waiver of the rule violated their right to due process. The court concluded that although the Fourteenth Amendment forbids a state to deprive any person of life, liberty or property without due process of law, the right of a student to participate in interscholastic sports was not a "property interest" protected by the Amendment. The decision of the lower court in favor of the transfer eligibility rule was upheld. *Berschback v. Grosse Pointe Public School District*, 397 N.W.2d 234 (Mich.App.1986).

The Court of Appeals of Oregon, in two separate opinions, upheld the rules of the Oregon School Activities Association regarding eligibility of transfer students. Both cases addressed the question of whether the OSAA transfer rule violates any of the plaintiffs' state or federal constitutional rights. Both decisions held the rule to be constitutional. The first case involved a girl who had transferred out of a district to a second district and then returned to the first district. She was not allowed to participate in interscholastic athletics upon her return even though her school board had filed for a hardship exemption and it was agreed that there was no recruitment or proselytizing involved. The transfer had been made solely for academic reasons. The court agreed that the rule here swept broadly and was perhaps unfair to the individual, but it noted that rules such as this do not have to apply to all parties with computer-like precision. It was also noted that no procedural or substantive due process rights were violated. *Whipple v. Oregon School Activities Ass'n*, 629 P.2d 384 (Or.App.1981).

The second case involved the transfer of students from parochial to public high schools. This case had the added element of a contention that the rule was a violation of the free exercise of religion. The court of appeals, in upholding a lower court, held that nothing in the rule impinged upon the plaintiffs' right to attend a parochial school. Nor was there a violation of any other constitutional privilege. Therefore, in both cases, the rule regarding transfers was upheld. *Cooper v. Oregon School Activities Ass'n*, 629 P.2d 386 (Or.App.1981).

Two Louisiana cases included challenges to that state's eligibility rules prohibiting students from athletic participation for one year where they attended religious schools located outside of their public school attendance zone. Both cases involved religious schools which served the entire parish irrespective of traditional public school boundaries. In each case, the students had attended Catholic or Lutheran grade schools and entered a parish-wide Catholic or Lutheran high school. But because the schools were outside their public school attendance zones, the students were required to sit out one year of athletic eligibility. The first case was brought before the Louisiana Supreme Court. The court held that the student's right to religious freedom had not been compromised and that the legitimate state interest in preventing illegal recruiting of high school athletes compelled the courts to permit the rule to stand. *Chabert v. Louisiana High School Athletic Ass'n*, 323 So.2d 774 (La.1975). The second case came before a U.S. district court, which also upheld the Louisiana transfer rule. *Walsh v. Louisiana High School Athletic Ass'n*, 428 F.Supp. 1261 (E.D.La.1977).

B. Eligibility of Schools

The U.S. Court of Appeals, Fourth Circuit upheld a Virginia public school league's decision to deny entry of several private schools in the public schools' athletic league. The private schools argued that to deny their students the opportunity to compete was an unreasonable and arbitrary action which denied the private school students equal protection. The court ruled in favor of the public school league's decision. The league argued successfully that the parochial schools do not abide by the same attendance rules as the public schools, thus opening up the possibility of recruiting of athletes by private schools. Further, the public schools contended, the transfer policies would be greatly disrupted if a parochial student was allowed to transfer from public to private schools during subsequent athletic seasons. The court of appeals agreed with the public school league that its interests in preventing actual or potential abuses by student athletes was sufficient to deny parochial schools admission to the state public school league. *O'Connell v. Virginia High School League*, 581 F.2d 81 (4th Cir.1978). See also *Valencia v. Blue Hen Conference*, 476 F.Supp. 809 (D.Del.1979).

C. Coaches

1. Equal Pay Act

In an Illinois case, female high school athletic coaches in Illinois brought suit against a local board of education alleging a violation of the Equal Pay Act and also a violation of an Illinois constitutional article prohibiting discrimination on the basis of sex. The coaches claimed that they were being paid less than male coaches for jobs of the same skill, effort and responsibility. The Appellate Court of Illinois upheld a trial court ruling in the board's favor, saying that any reference to "men" and "women" in a collective bargaining agreement setting out coaches' salaries referred to the sex of student participants in athletics who received coaching. The coaching was such that in some instances male coaches assisted girls in their sports and in one situation a woman had served as a gymnastic coach for boys. Coaches who served in this capacity received a higher salary in accordance with the collective bargaining agreement setting out coaches' salaries. Therefore, the compensation given to coaches did not vary on the basis of sex of the coach but rather the sex of the pupils who received the coaching. Since one of the exceptions to the Equal Pay Act is "a differential based on any other factor other than sex," which the court found to refer only to the sex of the employee, the court ruled in favor of the board of education. *Erickson v. Bd. of Educ.*, 458 N.E.2d 84 (Ill.App.1st Dist.1983) (see also Chapter Six).

2. Duty of Care

In a New Jersey case, a member of a varsity soccer team sustained a serious injury caused by an opposing player during the course of a game. Both teams were private school teams, but they participated in the public/private interscholastic athletic league. The injured student brought suit against the opposing coach who admitted to instructing his players to compete in an intense and aggressive manner; victory was all-important. The Superior Court of New Jersey dismissed the case and held that a participant in high school athletics may not sue an opposing coach for injuries absent evidence that the coach instructed his players to commit wrongful acts. The court noted that "[i]mposing liability upon schools and coaches based on negligent or wrongful acts of players, committed during the course of play, would have the practical effect of eventually eliminating interscholastic athletics.... [A] coach cannot insure or guarantee that each and every member of his team will not commit a foul...or do an act beyond that which is acceptable." Because no evidence existed that the coach had encouraged any wrongful behavior on the part of his players, the injured player's suit was dismissed. *Nydeggar v. Don Bosco Prep. High School*, 495 A.2d 485 (N.J.Super.1985).

D. Discrimination

Title IX (20 U.S.C. § 1681 *et seq.*; see also Chapter Six) addresses sex discrimination in school athletics. It currently applies only to athletics programs which receive federal financial assistance. The most important of the federal regulations implementing Title IX provides as follows:

> [An institution] may operate or sponsor separate teams for members of each sex where selection for such teams is based upon competitive skill or the activity involved is a contact sport. However, where a recipient operates or sponsors a team in a particular sport for members of one sex but operates no such team for members of the other sex, and athletic opportunities for members of that sex have previously been limited, members of the excluded sex must be allowed to try out for the team offered unless the sport involved is a contact sport. For the purposes of this part, contact sports include boxing, wrestling, rugby, ice hockey, football, basketball, and other sports the purpose or major activity of which involves bodily contact [34 CFR § 106.41(b)].

The Rehabilitation Act of 1973 (see Section III above; see also Chapter Six) and its accompanying regulations similarly forbid discrimination against the handicapped in school athletics:

> (1)In providing physical education courses and athletics and similar programs and activities to any of its students, a recipient that offers physical education courses or that operates or sponsors intercollegiate, club, or intramural athletics shall provide to qualified handicapped students an equal opportunity for participation in these activities.
> (2)A recipient may offer to handicapped students physical education and athletic activities that are separate or different only if separation or differentiation is consistent with the requirements [that the program be operated in "the most integrated setting appropriate"] and only if no qualified handicapped student is denied the opportunity to compete for teams or to participate in courses that are not separate or different [34 CFR § 104.47(a)].

A New York case upheld the right of a student, blind in one eye, to play intercollegiate football. *Wright v. Columbia University*, 520 F.Supp. 789 (S.D.N.Y.1981).

XII. FUNDRAISERS

Occasionally, fundraising efforts such as bingo games, raffles or other contests have given rise to legal disputes. Such disputes are generally resolved through reference to contract law or state statutes which address this area.

The following case involved an attempt to characterize a school's alleged refusal to turn over bingo prize money as a "conversion" rather than a breach of contract. Because conversion (unlawful interference with another's property) is a tort, such a characterization would entitle a plaintiff to compensatory and/or punitive damages. Such damages are unavailable in breach of contract lawsuits, where a plaintiff is entitled only to the "benefit of the bargain."

The James F. Byrnes Academy is a private school for grades K-12 in South Carolina which periodically raises money for the school through bingo games. The rules of bingo, set forth in South Carolina law, require that the prize be awarded without delay to the first person who reaches the winning combination of squares. When there are multiple winners, the rules direct that the prize be equally divided among the multiple winners. In October, 1983, the academy conducted a bingo game with 5,000 players in attendance. During the evening a woman received a winning number and began shouting "bingo," but there was no usher who heard her call the word. The woman proceeded as quickly as she could to the caller and while she was proceeding, an usher came up to her and asked her to sign the back of her card. The woman asked the usher to stop the next call but the number was called and three other persons claimed bingo on that call. The woman claimed that she was entitled to the entire $3,000 prize since she was the first to achieve bingo but the school offered her $1,500 or nothing. The woman accepted the proposal and was required to sign a W-2G tax form. When the woman again approached the school for the total $3,000 prize and was refused, she sued the school for conversion in a court of common pleas. The court ruled for the woman and the school appealed to the Court of Appeals of South Carolina.

The court had to decide whether the refusal to award the total prize money at the bingo game could be the basis for a conversion action against the school. The school argued that if it had done anything wrong, it was at most liable for breach of contract (the "contract" being the bingo rules). The woman contended that the school's failure to award her the total prize money was a breach of a duty set forth in a contract which led to a conversion. In ruling that the school and the woman had entered into a contract, the court quoted from a case reporter:

> The general rule of the law of contracts that where an offer or promise for an act is made, the only acceptance of the offer that is necessary is the performance of the act, applies to prizewinning contests. The promoter of such a contest, by making public the conditions and rules of the contest, makes an offer, and if before the offer is withdrawn another person acts upon it, the promoter is bound to perform his promise.

In conducting the bingo game the school acted as an offeror and was bound to award the prize money to anyone and everyone who accepted the offer by achieving the right combination of numbers in the bingo game. The school fulfilled its contractual obligations to the woman when it awarded her $1,500 according to the state law regarding multiple winners. The woman's claim did not give rise to conversion, and thus the lower court decision was reversed. *Taylor v. James F. Byrnes Academy, Inc.*, 349 S.E.2d 888 (S.C. App.1986).

CHAPTER TWO
EMPLOYMENT

Page

I. WRONGFUL TERMINATION AND BREACH OF
   CONTRACT 40
   A. Breach of Contract—Generally 40
   B. Tenure Denials 45
   C. Letters of Intent 48
   D. Investigations, Hearings and Procedural Disputes 49
   E. Retirement Plans 50

II. DISCRIMINATION 51
    A. Race 51
    B. Sex 54
    C. Religion 57
    D. Age 58
    E. Handicap 58
    F. Retaliatory Discharge 59
    G. Investigation of Discrimination Charges 60

III. DEFAMATION 62

IV. EMPLOYMENT BENEFITS 63
    A. Discrimination 63
    B. Income Tax Laws 64

V. UNEMPLOYMENT TAXATION 65

VI. COLLECTIVE BARGAINING 69
    A. First Amendment Limitations 69
    B. Managerial Employees 72

VII. STATE ACTION 73

I. WRONGFUL TERMINATION AND BREACH OF CONTRACT

A good deal of the case law involving private education arises in the context of employment. Sources generally relied upon for resolution of employment disputes include state and federal civil rights laws, academic custom and usage, American Association of University Professors (AAUP) guidelines, and the employment contract itself.

A. Breach of Contract—Generally

A Wisconsin case restated the general rule that where a religious school's employment decision is grounded on religious considerations, the courts will refuse to pass on the merits of the decision. Here a former parochial school principal brought suit against a local church congregation, church diocese and bishop after he was dismissed. A schism had developed within the congregation when some church leaders opposed the principal's appointment and the parish priest supported him. Attempting to end the dispute, the bishop terminated the principal's employment. The Court of Appeals of Wisconsin found that the bishop's reason for terminating the principal's employment was ecclesiastical in nature, thereby precluding judicial review of the merits of the termination. Matters of internal church government, found the court, are at the core of ecclesiastical affairs and are thus beyond the province of judicial review. *Black v. St. Bernadette Congregation of Appleton*, 360 N.W.2d 550 (Wis.App.1984).

A recent decision of the Montana Supreme Court extended the above principle to any lawsuit based on the implied contractual duty of good faith and fair dealing, at least in the parochial school context. In this case, during the early fall of the 1984-85 school year a teacher in a Montana parochial school was told on several occasions by a supervisor that the teacher's classroom methods were unsatisfactory. The supervisor claimed there was a lack of discipline in the classroom. In November, 1984, the teacher was fired by a school administrator because of the alleged lack of discipline. The teacher sued the school in a state district court. When the district court ruled for the school, the teacher appealed to the Montana Supreme Court. The teacher contended that there had been a breach of the covenant of good faith and fair dealing in employment on the part of the school. The school argued that the Free Exercise of Religion clauses of both the U.S. and Montana constitutions barred consideration of the tort of breach of the covenant of good faith and fair dealing in the firing of the teacher for her failure to maintain discipline in the classroom. The school also argued that all aspects of parochial school education, including discipline, are permeated with the religious mission of the school and that the school was an integral part of the religious mission of the Catholic Church.

The teacher argued that the court could consider her methods of discipline without involving itself in the religion issue, but the court disagreed. The court observed that the discharged teacher's lack of classroom discipline made it impossible for the school's religion teacher to teach religion effectively in the discharged teacher's classroom. It concluded that "discipline in the classroom is so intertwined with teaching which in turn is so intertwined with religious principles that a court cannot properly make the determination requested here without interfering with a legitimate claim to the free exercise of religion." The court held that the teacher's breach of good faith lawsuit was barred by both the U.S. and Montana constitutions.

The teacher also argued that to rule in favor of the school would result in excessive government entanglement with religion in violation of the Establishment Clause of the U.S. Constitution. The court observed that a three-factor balancing test has been developed for evaluating Establishment Clause claims. "The factors are: (1) the character and purpose of the institution involved; (2) the nature of the law's intrusion into church affairs; and (3) the resulting relationship between the government and the religious authority." The court concluded that denying application of the tort of bad faith in this case did not result in an intrusion into church affairs. The court also noted that because its holding only applied to this particular situation, the resulting relationship between the government and the church was negligible at best. After examining all three of the above factors, the court ruled that prohibiting the teacher's lawsuit did not violate the Establishment Clause. The teacher's breach of good faith and fair dealing in employment claims were rejected. *Miller v. Catholic Diocese of Great Falls*, 728 P.2d 794 (Mont.1986).

When a court *does* reach the merits of an employment dispute, traditional contract law rules will govern the case.

A would-be teacher of religion at a Catholic high school in New Orleans sued for breach of contract after a signed contract was withdrawn by the school prior to the beginning of the school term. The withdrawal came following discovery by the school that the teacher had been divorced and re-married, a situation contrary to the teachings of the Catholic Church and a fact not revealed prior to the signing of the contract. The teacher sued for lost wages, mental anguish, damages to his career and attorney's fees. The Louisiana Court of Appeal held that the teacher had misled the school because, due to his expertise in Catholic doctrine, he should have known that his marital status would have been crucial to the making of the contract. The court concluded that the teacher's bad faith caused error and the contract was void from its inception. *Bischoff v. Brothers of the Sacred Heart*, 416 So.2d 348 (La.App.4th Cir.1982).

A white math professor at Howard University began the fall semester of the 1983-84 academic year by advising his Elementary Functions students, who all were black, that they should reduce their credit loads. This advice rested on his perception that Howard students traditionally performed poorly in math. At a later class session he renewed his suggestion and illustrated it with a story about a monkey that caught its hand in a food jar and lacked the good sense to drop the food in order to escape. One student reacted by calling the professor a "condescending patronizing racist." After this incident, the professor refused to continue teaching the class unless the student either apologized or dropped the class. The university refused to remove the student from the class, and the professor was repeatedly asked to resume his teaching duties. When he failed to do so he was dismissed for "neglect of professional responsibilities." He sued the university in federal court, claiming that neglect of professional responsibilities was an ambiguous contractual term which could not be used to support his dismissal. The district court stated: "There are obviously two (or more) sides to the controversy between the plaintiff, the student, and the University. There is nothing ambiguous, however, about the obligation of a professor to teach assigned classes and plaintiff's failure to teach his class is undisputed." The professor's dismissal was therefore held to be justified. The court also ruled against the professor on his defamation of character claim, as it is well-settled that evaluative opinions (absent any false statements of fact) may not be used to establish defamation. *McConnell v. Howard University*, 621 F.Supp. 327 (D.D.C.1985).

A groundskeeper at a private university in Pennsylvania was discharged from employment after being accused of a crime involving dishonesty. Two years later he sued the university claiming that he had been wrongfully discharged. A state trial court ruled in favor of the university and the man appealed to the Superior Court of Pennsylvania. On appeal, the man urged the court to apply a balancing test to determine whether a legitimate claim for wrongful dismissal exists when an employee has been falsely accused of a crime and dismissed as a result of the accusation. The court responded that an employee can maintain a lawsuit for wrongful discharge against an employer if the discharge was motivated by a particular intent to harm the employee or if the discharge "violates a clear mandate of public policy." The court stated that the man failed to allege in his complaint that the university had a specific intent to harm him. The court also found that the man's discharge was not a great enough violation of public policy to maintain an action for wrongful discharge. Accordingly, the claim for compensatory and punitive damages was denied. The decision of the lower court in favor of the university was affirmed. *Gillespie v. St. Joseph's University*, 513 A.2d 471 (Pa.Super.1986).

The following two cases illustrate the rule that written material not specifically included in an employment contract (handbooks, AAUP guidelines, etc.) may nevertheless be deemed to be incorporated into the contract by virtue of the common law doctrine of estoppel. In the first case, the court held that employee handbook provisions regarding dismissal were incorporated into an employee's contract. In the second case, however, the court refused to foreclose the school's right to unilaterally change a handbook provision regarding fringe benefits.

When a security guard at an Illinois not-for-profit corporation (Millikin University) was terminated, he sued the university for breach of contract. When a circuit court dismissed the claim, he appealed to the Appellate Court of Illinois. The dispute concerned whether the university's staff handbook was an employment contract between the security guard and the university. The security guard alleged that the staff handbook was presented to him as an employment contract which provided that "the university will, to the best of its ability ... provide security of employment to those who are constantly industrious, loyal, cooperative and honest." It further provided that full-time employees "may be discharged for cause only." The security guard alleged that he was fired without just cause as outlined in the handbook, that he had fully complied with the grievance procedures, and had been denied reinstatement or reemployment with the university. In ruling that the handbook was a part of the security guard's contract, the court observed that when the university prepared the handbook, the security guard had a right and expectation that the handbook policies would be followed by the school. The court further observed that "where an employer ... provides a handbook, states its purpose, indicates that the permanent employee will be discharged for good cause only, and provides what those good cause reasons are, it cannot say it does not follow the handbook and is not bound thereby." Because there was no other written contract and because the handbook was deemed by the court to be at least part of the security guard's employment agreement with the university, the university was liable for a breach of contract claim when it failed to abide by the handbook policies. *Pundt v. Millikin University*, 496 N.E.2d 291 (Ill.App.4th Dist.1986).

A former employee of Tulane University sued the university in a Louisiana district court. He alleged that he was damaged by Tulane's action in changing its employee tuition waiver policy so that fewer courses could be taken by employees tuition-free. The man claimed that in reliance on Tulane's original policy, which allowed employees to take an unlimited number of tuition-free courses, he had foregone more lucrative employment in order to complete his education at Tulane. The district court ruled for Tulane and the Louisiana Court of Appeal affirmed. It observed that documents submitted by Tulane established that the man had been hired for an indefinite term. These documents also indicated that the man was not promised an indefinite continuation of the original tuition waiver program. The court further held that the Tulane staff handbook, which described the benefits and conditions of employment with Tulane, was not a part of the man's employment agreement. The handbook was primarily informational in nature and did not constitute a binding promise by Tulane to continue indefinitely the unlimited tuition waiver program. Because the man was hired for an indefinite period of time and because no promise was made to him concerning the duration of the tuition waiver program, the man's claim was properly dismissed by the lower court. *Wall v. Tulane University*, 499 So.2d 375 (La.App.4th Cir.1986).

The following case illustrates that financial exigencies will justify termination of teaching contracts, as long as the exigencies are *bona fide*.

A small private college facing severe financial problems did not renew a tenured professor's contract. She sued, claiming the termination was in violation of the provisions of her contract. Both a U.S. district court and the U.S. Court of Appeals, Fourth Circuit, found in favor of the college. The issue was whether the professor's contract permitted her termination by discontinuing her teaching position because of financial exigencies. In answering affirmatively, the court noted that AAUP guidelines incorporate the notion that a college may refuse to renew a tenured teacher's contract because of a financial exigency, as long as its action is demonstrably *bona fide*. Here, a thorough study had been made of possible alternatives and everything that could be done had been done for the professor. Hence the nonrenewal was upheld. *Krotkoff v. Groucher College*, 585 F.2d 675 (4th Cir.1978).

A Massachusetts case involved contractual due process rights. Here the executive committee of a seminary's board of trustees ordered the president of the seminary to reduce the budget by at least $50,000. As a result a sixty-two-year-old tenured faculty member, who had taught there for thirty-one years, was fired. The faculty member later sued in U.S. district court alleging that the termination breached his employment contract with the seminary. The court observed that in order for the faculty member to prevail, he must "establish that (1) a contract was in force between the parties, (2) the contract established the procedures to be followed in the event of plaintiff's discharge, and (3) these procedures were not followed by the defendant in discharging the plaintiff." The court noted that both parties agreed that a contract existed and that it established procedures to be followed in the event of a dismissal. The seminary further agreed that the contract was subject to the American Association of University Professors Recommended Institutional Regulations on Academic Freedom and Tenure. This document, along with the faculty promotion and tenure policy of the seminary, contained provisions governing the firing of a tenured faculty member. The seminary claimed that the document did not require it to allow the fired teacher to participate in "any way at any stage" of the proceedings. The court observed, however, that the regulations required any faculty member facing termination to be allowed to participate in the dismissal proceedings before a faculty group and the governing board. It noted that without an opportunity to be heard, the faculty member had no opportunity to have pertinent issues reviewed and discussed in a meaningful way. The court therefore ruled that the seminary failed to follow its own regulations since the language of the document clearly expressed that an aggrieved faculty member had a "contractual right to request a review of his termination." In this case the discharged faculty member was denied that opportunity, which meant that the seminary had breached the faculty member's employment contract. *Linn v. Andover-Newton Theological School*, 638 F.Supp. 1114 (D.Mass.1986).

A recent New York case reaffirmed the principle that nontenured employees are generally subject to dismissal at any time. In this case a teacher was employed by the Roman Catholic Diocese of Rockville Centre. When the teacher was terminated he sued the diocese in a New York trial court alleging "abusive discharge" from employment and breach of employment contract. When the court ruled for the diocese the teacher appealed to the New York Supreme Court, Appellate Division. The appellate court affirmed the lower court's decision. The teacher's abusive discharge from employment claim was properly dismissed by the lower court because no such cause of action is recognized in the state of New York. The appellate court also ruled that the teacher's breach of an employment contract claim failed because he failed to establish the existence of a contract between himself and the diocese. It reasoned that the teacher's hiring was for an indefinite term (or employment "at will") and could be terminated by either party at any time for any reason, or even for no reason at all. The teacher also claimed that he had attained tenure by acquiescence, which is provided for in the teachers' handbook published by the diocese. This claim failed since the teacher possessed no bachelor's degree or provisional state certification, both of which are necessary to establish tenure by acquiescence. The teacher's claims were rejected and the lower court decision was upheld. *DeVico v. Roman Catholic Diocese of Rockville*, 508 N.Y.S.2d 886 (A.D.2d Dept.1986).

B. Tenure Denials

Absent a state statute specifically governing tenure at private educational institutions, and absent a claim of discrimination, tenure disputes at private schools are purely a matter of contract law. (See also the discussion of age discrimination in Chapter Six, Section VI.)

In 1976, a woman became an assistant professor at Lafayette College. In 1982, she applied for tenure at the college in the psychology department. Tenure decisions at the college are governed by the faculty handbook and college guidelines. The guidelines provide for tenure determinations to be made by the Appointments, Promotions and Dismissals Committee, which makes recommendations to the college president. The president then makes final recommendations to the board of trustees. If the committee's decision is unfavorable, the candidate may appeal to the college president or ask the committee to reconsider. An important factor in the committee's determination is the department chairperson's recommendation. This recommendation includes a judgment as to the probable effect of the award of tenure on other members of the department. Tenure guidelines at the college require that no more than two-thirds of a department may be tenured faculty unless the person seeking tenure is an exceptional, "guideline breaking" candidate. The department chairperson gave the woman a qualified recommendation, noting that a male professor, whom he viewed as a stronger candidate, would come up for tenure in three years. The chairperson informed the committee that the male professor's tenure appointment would be jeopardized if the woman was granted tenure since the two-thirds limit would be exceeded if both were appointed. When the committee did not recommend the woman, she appealed to the college president. The president affirmed the committee's decision and the woman sued the college in U.S. district court. The court ruled for the college and the woman appealed to the U.S. Court of Appeals, Third Circuit.

The woman claimed that the college was liable for wrongful discharge because it had denied her request for tenure. She claimed that the tenure quota adopted by the college violated public policy by threatening the principles of academic freedom, and that the tenure decision came within the public policy tort of wrongful discharge. The court of appeals, however, was not persuaded that her claim of a potential threat to the tenure system rose to the level of the public policy concerns that had been previously recognized in wrongful discharge cases. In fact, the court observed that significant policy concerns counseled against recognizing her claims, since evaluation of and changes in the college's tenure quota system by the courts would threaten the college's academic freedom more than did the quota system itself. The denial of the wrongful discharge claim was therefore affirmed. The woman also claimed that the district court was wrong in not finding that the college had violated state law by failing to consider her gender in a positive light in the tenure decision. The court of appeals reasoned that this affirmative action claim should have been considered by the district court and it remanded the issue for further proceedings. *Sola v. Lafayette College*, 804 F.2d 40 (3d Cir.1986).

When a professor at a private university was denied tenure, she sued the university in U.S. district court. The professor alleged that her denial of tenure was in violation of established university policies and was therefore a breach of her contract. Additionally, she claimed that the university discriminated against her because she suffered from tinnitus, or ringing in the ears. Although the professor alleged that the university used a quota system in granting tenure, the court observed that the university had in fact limited tenured positions to sixty percent of the faculty in the various schools of the university in accordance with the "1940 Statement of Principles" of the American Association of University Professors, which the university had adopted. A 1973 statement by the AAUP opposing quotas was deemed by the court to be irrelevant to the issue involving the professor's contractual rights. The professor further claimed that because she was considered along with three other professors by the University Tenure Review Committee, she was wrongly denied a tenured position on the university faculty. She claimed that had she been considered alone, her appointment would not have been subject to the sixty percent policy that the university had established. The court concluded, however, that the university's sixty percent policy would be completely undermined if each applicant involved in a multiple tenure decision had the right to be considered in isolation with respect to the tenure limit.

The professor also contended that since one of the three professors who had been denied tenure with her failed to appeal the decision, she should have been automatically granted a tenured position. The court rejected this contention and stated that neither the circumstances nor the university regulations allowed for automatic tenure in this case, because evaluations by both the university vice president and president were necessary in order for formal reconsideration to take place. Concerning the professor's claim that the reconsideration of her application for tenure violated university regulations, the court observed that this claim was the "most baffling" of all because the professor stood only to benefit from a second review, having received the fewest number of votes. The court also found no evidence of discrimination by the university against the professor on the basis of her tinnitus affliction. The only thing the professor had shown, stated the court, was that she had tinnitus and was denied tenure. Since the professor failed to state a claim upon which legal relief could be granted, the court granted the university's request that the case be dismissed. *Waring v. Fordham University*, 640 F.Supp. 42 (S.D.N.Y.1986).

In June, 1979, Chicago's Loyola University approached a man concerning the chairmanship of a department in its medical school. After lengthy negotiations and two letters from the dean of the medical school in which the professor was promised an early tenure beginning in September, 1981, he agreed to accept the chairmanship position in June, 1980. The professor accepted letters of appointment for the next two academic years and in April, 1982, the professor was sent a letter of appointment for the period July 1, 1982, through June 30, 1983. On May 19, 1982, he received a letter relieving him of his duties as department chairman effective immediately; one week later he was advised that his 1982-83 faculty contract would not be renewed beyond June 30, 1983. The professor sued the university for breach of contract alleging deprivation of tenure. When an Illinois circuit court ruled in favor of the professor the university appealed to the Appellate Court of Illinois.

The university argued that the trial court was wrong in admitting into evidence two letters to the professor from the dean in which the professor was told that the dean would propose an early approval of tenure in September, 1981. The university stated that the terms of the May 14, 1980, letter of appointment were clear and unambiguous and that the two letters from the dean promising tenure were unnecessary as evidence at the trial court level. The appellate court disagreed, noting that although it is well settled that where contract terms are clear and unambiguous, they must be given their ordinary meaning, it is also well established in contract law that preliminary negotiations to contract are "merged" into the final written agreement and that the final agreement includes all material terms. The court ruled that the conversations, meetings and correspondence over the negotiation period of the year should all be considered as part of the contract terms.

The university also argued that even if the letters from the dean to the professor were part of the contract, those promises did not constitute a guarantee of tenure. The court ruled for the professor, reasoning that objective criteria considered at the trial court level indicated that the only reason the professor was not granted tenure in 1981 was that the dean failed to bring up the tenure matter at the administrative meeting. A university administrative authority had testified in the trial court that occasionally a dean's recommendation is denied but that such an occurrence is uncommon. The trial court's decision in favor of the professor was upheld. *Lewis v. Loyola University of Chicago*, 500 N.E.2d 47 (Ill.App.1st Dist.1986).

A teacher in Georgia was employed by a private, K-12 grade school in 1959. He taught for the school until 1981. He allegedly obtained tenure, which was granted to those who worked at least three years beginning in September, 1966. When the teacher's employment with the school was not renewed for the 1981-82 school year he claimed that his right to tenured employment was breached. The teacher claimed that he was terminated without cause and that the board of trustees did not consider his renewal or offer him a hearing. He alleged that the breach of contract occurred in 1981 and sought recovery for lost wages and nominal damages in a Georgia superior court. After the court ruled for the school the teacher appealed to the Georgia Court of Appeals. The appellate court observed that the school's board of trustees approved a provision regarding teacher tenure in 1970 and that during the period of 1966-1972, the teacher's employment contracts contained wording that required the school to responsibly consider the tenure of teachers in employment decisions. However, in 1972 the school employed a new headmaster who was opposed to tenure. He omitted tenure from the teachers' handbooks and any reference to tenure was stricken from employment agreements. The school argued that the teacher had no right to tenure, but if he did have a right to tenure, the breach of tenure occurred in 1972 when the new headmaster took over and not in 1984 when the teacher sued the school for breach. The appellate court agreed with the school, noting that the teacher lost his "security in employment" in 1972 and that it was then that the breach of contract, if any, occurred. The court reasoned that in contract lawsuits the time of the breach controls, not the time that the actual damages result or are discovered. The teacher understood in 1972 that tenured job security was no longer a part of his faculty benefits and should have sued the school for breach of contract at that time. It was too late for the teacher to file a breach of contract claim when the actual damage occurred. The lower court's decision was upheld. *Gamble v. Lovett School*, 350 S.E.2d 311 (Ga.App.1986).

C. Letters of Intent

A letter (or statement) of intent regarding future employment is generally not enforceable against an employer unless the letter evinces a bilateral understanding that employment will be forthcoming. A unilateral, subjective expectation on the part of an employee (or future employee) is insufficient to subject an employer to liability.

In the fall of 1979 a former principal of a Louisiana Catholic school returned to the school as principal. In April, 1983, she received a one-page "letter of intent" survey from the school board on which she was to express whether she wanted to return as principal for the 1983-84 school year. The form contained her proposed salary and a place for her to sign. She returned the form, expressing that she would be willing to serve as principal at the stated salary. After the school board met in May, 1983, it informed her that she would not be offered a contract for the coming year. The principal sued the school board in a state district court for breach of contract. The court awarded her salary for the 1983-84 school year. The board appealed to the Louisiana Court of Appeal. At issue was 1) whether the board had given the principal reasonable notice of the nonrenewal of her contract, and 2) whether the letter of intent was indeed a contract.

The court concluded that the principal was well aware that a contract could not be offered to her until after the May, 1983, school board meeting. It noted that the principal herself, as an administrator, had attended board meetings where the board had voted to extend her contract for another year. The court also noted that the principal was notified within the school year which was within the notice guidelines of the previous contract. With regard to the principal's claims that the "letter of intent" was a contract and that the board should be bound to pay her for the 1983-84 school year, the court ruled that the letter of intent was not a contract in light of a state law which says that "when in the absence of a legal requirement the parties have contemplated a certain form it is presumed that they do not intend to be bound until the contract is executed in *that form*." The principal was reasonably notified of the nonrenewal of her contract and the school board did not have to pay her 1983-84 salary. *Knipmeyer v. Diocese of Alexandria*, 492 So.2d 550 (La.App.3d Cir.1986).

In a Georgia case, a man applied for and was offered employment by a private university in the capacity of an "at will" research technician. The professor he was working with informed him that "if things worked out" the university might keep him on in a nontenured faculty position. The research technician assisted the professor in preparing an application for a two-year research grant which was to be submitted by the university to the American Cancer Society. The application listed the research technician as a "co-investigator" at a stated salary in each of the two years of the grant. The application was accepted but the research technician was informed by the university that he would not be permitted to participate in the cancer research project and that he could only continue as a research technician if he made an effort to get along with the other employees. The research technician was fired several months later. He sued the university in a Georgia superior court claiming breach of contract. The court ruled for the university and the research technician appealed.

In affirming the superior court decision, the Georgia Court of Appeals observed that the research technician had secured no contractual rights of employment as a result of the research grant from the Cancer Society. The research technician argued that although the application for the Cancer Society grant was not a contract, it should render his oral contract of employment on the research project enforceable because the application showed that he was to be employed for a definite period of two years at a specific salary. The court of appeals stated that although a promise is usually enforceable as a contract against the party making it, "the promise...must be of such a character as to be capable of enforcement against the party making it...." Here, the court of appeals ruled that the research technician's subjective opinions regarding the university's *intent* were not the equivalent of a definite promise of employment that would be enforceable against the university. Because there was no underlying oral promise of employment by the university, the research technician's claim was denied. *Tidwell v. Emory University*, 349 S.E.2d 245 (Ga.App.1986).

D. Investigations, Hearings and Procedural Disputes

In an Illinois case, an employment records disclosure statute was held to be unconstitutionally vague and ambiguous. Here a private school, Immanuel Evangelical Lutheran Congregation, employed a teacher from August, 1980, to June, 1984, under a series of one-year contracts. When the teacher's last employment contract expired, however, the school decided not to renew it for the following year. The teacher then requested to see her personnel file pursuant to the Illinois personnel disclosure law. The school permitted the teacher to inspect her records with the exception of three letters written by unnamed individuals who made various comments about the teacher. After the school refused to turn over the letters for inspection, the teacher sued. A trial court ruled in favor of the teacher. On appeal before the Illinois Appellate Court, the school argued that the letters were not subject to disclosure because of two exceptions under the statute dealing with "letters of reference" and "management planning." The court explained that since the school did not argue in the trial court that the letters were letters of reference, the school could not raise that argument on appeal.

Turning to the statute, the court noted that the term "management planning" created problems of interpretation. The teacher argued that the term referred only to "management employees" while the school contended that it meant the "formulation of a program of employment." To resolve the ambiguity, the court examined the legislative history of the statute and found that the act was so vague and uncertain that it violated the due process rights of employers. In light of its ambiguous and inconsistent provisions, the court ruled the statute unconstitutional. It concluded that "an employer of ordinary intelligence, by reading the statute, has no way of knowing with reasonable certainty what rights it confers and what obligations it imposes." The decision of the trial court ordering disclosure of the letters was reversed. *Spinelli v. Immanuel Evangelical Lutheran Congregation*, 494 N.E.2d 196 (Ill.App.2d Dist.1986).

When a tenured teacher at a Connecticut private secondary school received notice that the termination of her contract was being considered, she requested a hearing before the school's board of trustees. Under state law [C.G.S.A. § 10-151(b)] the teacher had a choice of having her case adjudicated by the board of trustees of the school or by a three-person "impartial hearing panel." During the hearing before the board of trustees, the teacher sought to have two members of the board disqualify themselves on the basis of their membership in a law firm which represented the school in other matters unrelated to the proceeding at hand. The two members refused and continued to participate in the hearing. The board voted unanimously to terminate the teacher's employment contract.

The teacher appealed the decision to a superior court, contending that the participation of the two attorneys unfairly biased the decision of the board against her. The court disagreed and dismissed the teacher's appeal. She appealed further to the Appellate Court of Connecticut, which reversed the decision of the superior court and held that the presence of the two attorneys on the board of trustees was a *per se* violation of the teacher's due process rights because it "created an appearance of impropriety." The school then appealed to the Supreme Court of Connecticut, which rejected the contention that the hearing lacked due process. The court pointed out that the teacher had chosen to have her case adjudicated by the board of trustees rather than by a three-person "impartial hearing panel" as allowed by statute. It ordered reinstatement of the Superior Court decision which found that neither of the two attorneys on the board were prejudiced against the teacher. The termination of the teacher was upheld. *Petrowski v. Norwich Free Academy*, 506 A.2d 139 (Conn.1986).

E. Retirement Plans

(See also Chapter Six, Section VI.)

On April 3, 1980, Temple University announced that it and the American Association of University Professors, a collective bargaining agent for the faculty, had agreed on a new voluntary early retirement plan. A tenured professor at the university filed an application with the school on June 25, 1980, requesting an early retirement according to the terms of the plan. Assuming that he would obtain early retirement status, the professor had taken the liberty of arranging for several off campus teaching responsibilities in the spring of 1981. He asked that the early retirement be effective January 1, 1981. On November 20, 1980, the request was denied and the professor's early retirement did not take effect until July 1, 1981. In order to keep the professional commitments he had made for the winter and spring of 1981, and in contemplation of the early retirement approval, the professor took a leave of absence without pay from January 1, 1981, to June 30, 1981. The professor sued the university for lost wages in April, 1982, and a trial court ruled for the university. The professor appealed to the Superior Court of Pennsylvania which remanded the case to the trial court. When the trial court ruled for the professor on the principle of estoppel (a contract law doctrine protecting persons who act in reliance on another's assurances), the university appealed, bringing the case before the superior court for the second time.

The question was whether the university could be prevented from denying the early retirement request when there was neither agreement nor a promise by the university to approve the professor's request. The superior court observed that "[a]n estoppel requires the presence of two essential elements. The first is an inducement to act. The second is a justifiable reliance upon that inducement." In reversing the trial court decision in favor of the university, the court observed that neither element was present. The plan expressly stated that "[a]n application for voluntary early retirement must be recommended, and...justified, by the department chairperson and dean, and must be accompanied by a written statement from the dean. An application requires the approval of the Vice President and Dean of Faculties before submission to the President for final approval or disapproval." The court reasoned that it would be unfair to allow the professor "to raise an estoppel by his own carelessness in failing to read and become aware of the terms and the conditions for acceptance into" the plan and that there was no suggestion in the plan that acceptance would be automatic. The court observed that the professor recognized that approval was not automatic since he repeatedly called the university vice president between June 25, 1980, and November 20, 1980, to determine whether his application would be approved. The professor was denied recovery for lost wages because he had acted without complying with the terms of the voluntary retirement agreement. *Havas v. Temple University*, 516 A.2d 17 (Pa.Super.1986).

II. DISCRIMINATION

Title VII of the Civil Rights Act of 1964 prohibits discrimination in employment based upon race, color, sex, religion or national origin. Members of the Communist Party are excepted from Title VII's protection. Discrimination based upon age, handicap and alienage is covered by other federal statutes. (See also Chapter Six.)

A. Race

The prohibition against racial discrimination in employment extends to all "terms or conditions of employment," including hiring and firing decisions, promotions, salary, seniority, benefits, and work assignments. Reverse discrimination claims are also recognized under Title VII.

The following case involves Title VII's 180-day limitation period for filing a discrimination claim with the Equal Employment Opportunity Commission (EEOC).

A black former custodian for Northwestern University filed suit under Title VII alleging that he was subjected to "adverse and prejudicial treatment" because of his race. The custodian had been hired by Northwestern in 1981. He was later transferred to the landscaping department following a general layoff in the custodial department. Although his work record as a custodian was good, he experienced numerous problems with his supervisor while in landscaping. He alleged that he was singled out by his supervisor, treated unfairly, and that he was assigned the most difficult jobs without assistance from others; he also alleged that at the same time, whites were allowed to do no work at all and often engaged in personal activities while on the job. After receiving warnings and being suspended because of alleged poor work habits and a bad attitude, he was allowed to transfer back to the custodial department on "final warning status." Although he admitted that he was not discriminated against in the custodial department where his immediate supervisors were black, he was nonetheless terminated in September, 1983, allegedly for insubordination and a poor attitude on the job. He filed a charge of employment discrimination with the EEOC in March, 1984, and sued Northwestern in federal district court in May, 1984.

Although the man alleged that the racial discrimination was a continuing violation which began in the landscaping department and ended with his wrongful discharge, the court disagreed. According to Title VII, a charge of an unlawful employment practice must be made within 180 days after the violation occurred or when the victim knew or should have known that a violation occurred. Since he should have become aware of Northwestern's alleged discrimination against him when he worked in landscaping, the court ruled that his claim was barred by the 180-day statute of limitations for lawsuits under Title VII. The man further alleged that he was intentionally fired because of his race and that the charge was not time-barred by the statute of limitations. The court acknowledged that a Title VII action based on his termination would not be time-barred, but stated that the evidence did not support the charge. The court held that the man's termination while a custodian was based on a legitimate, nondiscriminatory reason—poor work performance. Since the man had no valid claim of discrimination that was not time-barred, the court dismissed the suit and ruled in favor of Northwestern. *Arna v. Northwestern University*, 640 F.Supp. 923 (N.D.Ill.1986).

In 1977, Baylor College of Medicine agreed to provide special cardiovascular services to King Faisal Hospital in Saudi Arabia. This presented physicians from the college with a greater opportunity for clinical experience in the treatment of childhood heart disease. The agreement provided that the college would send surgeons, anesthesiologists and other medical personnel to the hospital for a three-month rotation. The college would be reimbursed by the Saudis for most of the costs, including salaries, travel and fringe benefits to the medical personnel participating in the rotating program. Baylor purposely set the salaries of such personnel at almost twice that paid to stateside instructors so that the positions in Saudi Arabia would be adequately staffed. Those from the college who desired to participate in the program were simply required to express verbal interest to the college administrators in charge of the program. Shortly thereafter, the interested physician would be placed on a constantly changing scheduling sheet.

Two Jewish physicians on the college faculty verbally applied for the rotating positions but were told by the administrators that Jews were unable to secure visas to enter Saudi Arabia. This difficulty made it impossible for Jews to participate in the program. The Jewish physicians filed charges with the EEOC, which transferred the case to a U.S. district court. It found that the college had intentionally discriminated against the physicians on the basis of their Jewish religion. The court also awarded attorney's fees to the physicians. The college appealed the decision to the U.S. Court of Appeals, Fifth Circuit.

The court of appeals observed that Title VII of the Civil Rights Act of 1964 prohibits employment discrimination based on race, color, religion, sex or national origin. It further provides that employees must file their charges of discrimination within 180 days after the unlawful employment practice occurs. Although the complaint was filed substantially more than 180 days after the physicians first became aware of the "visa problems," the court observed that it had recognized "equitable considerations" in allowing claims to be heard after the 180-day limitation period. One such consideration involves continuing violations of a Title VII provision. The court held that where the unlawful employment practice manifested itself over a period of time the violation may be found to be a continuing one that would relieve the physicians from the burden of proving that the entire violation occurred within the 180-day period. College administrators testified in the district court that the makeup of the college's personnel rosters varied right up until the time of departure and that these departures of non-Jewish medical personnel had occurred within 180 days of the physicians' complaint. The complaint of the physicians therefore had been filed within the 180-day statutory period.

Addressing the substance of the physicians' claims, the court stated that the college could have legally asserted that "non-Jewishness" was a bona fide occupational qualification (BFOQ) for the Faisal Hospital rotation program if the college could have proven that this was the official position of the Saudi Arabian government. However, the college never presented any evidence to the district court to demonstrate that "non-Jewishness" was a BFOQ by showing that this was Saudi policy. The court of appeals affirmed the district court's decision in favor of the physicians, holding that exclusion of Jewish individuals from the program was a continuing violation of Title VII by the college. The question of the award of attorney's fees was remanded for redetermination. *Abrams v. Baylor College of Medicine*, 805 F.2d 528 (5th Cir.1986).

As noted in Chapter One, § 1981 of the Civil Rights Act makes it unlawful for any person or entity to discriminate on the basis of race in the making and enforcement of contracts. Section 1981 therefore provides an alternative basis for racial discrimination in employment claims.

The U.S. Court of Appeals, Third Circuit, ruled that a professor who was denied tenure can maintain a racial discrimination claim under § 1981 alleging that he was discriminated against because of his Arab descent. The professor, who was born in Iraq, was a U.S. citizen and member of the Muslim faith. A U.S. district court rejected the professor's claim and held that ethnic Arabs are taxonomically caucasians and are therefore not protected persons under § 1981. In reversing the district court, the court of appeals explained that the term "race" in the statute was not intended by Congress to refer to any particular scientific definition of the term. In the opinion of the court, "Congress's purpose was to insure that all persons be treated equally, without regard to color or race, which we understand to embrace, at the least, membership in a group that is ethnically and physiognomically distinctive." The court ruled that the professor could proceed with his discrimination claim in the district court. The college successfully petitioned the U.S. Supreme Court to review the case, and a decision will probably be handed down before the Court's July, 1987, recess. Educators should check with legal counsel regarding the continuing vitality of the court of appeals' ruling. *Al-Khazraji v. St. Francis College*, 784 F.2d 505 (3d Cir.1986).

B. Sex

Gallaudet College, a liberal arts college for deaf students, hired a female teacher in 1971. Between 1973 and 1979, she worked with a female supervisor and received an "outstanding" rating. This rating dropped to "above average" in the 1978-79 academic year. The supervisor commented that the teacher had seemed to "peak out." In 1980, the teacher came under the supervision of a man. This new supervisor lowered her rating on the ground that the teacher's female supervisor had practiced grade inflation. The teacher's lower grade reflected her new supervisor's disappointment in the teacher's drawing and illustration skills and in her artistic ability generally. A second male supervisor later wrote a memo to the teacher expressing his dissatisfaction with her work habits. At her request, the teacher was transferred to the college's Learning Center where she filed a grievance complaining of sexual harassment by one of the photographers who worked at the center. She testified that the supervisor investigated her complaint and put an immediate stop to the photographer's behavior. Nevertheless, she said the episode was an act of sexual discrimination because the supervisor knew of the harassment but allegedly let it continue until she made a formal complaint. Her supervisor was promoted and his position was filled by another male faculty member. The teacher then called a meeting to discuss her objections to not receiving the promotion to supervisor, and a proposal was made to relocate her office. The teacher informed her supervisor and the other faculty members present at the meeting that the replacement for the supervisor had made a slur about her being Jewish. The replacement supervisor was reprimanded and a note about the incident was placed in his permanent file. After her office was relocated, the teacher wrote a memo complaining of eye strain due to the office's poor lighting. [She later testified that the eye strain was caused by a foreign object in her eye and was unrelated to the absence of adequate light in her new office.] When the new supervisor did not respond to her memo, she confronted him about the inadequacies of her new office. She began shouting at him, allegedly because he told her she would not have been reassigned if she had kept her mouth shut. He denied making such a statement. After the incident, she contacted an attorney and filed a federal lawsuit against the college alleging sexual and religious discrimination.

The federal court noted that the U.S. Supreme Court has set out four requirements that must be met in a Title VII discrimination lawsuit. The teacher must show 1) that she belonged to a protected class, 2) that she applied for and was qualified for the position, 3) that she was rejected for the position, and 4) that after her rejection the position remained open for other applicants. The court held that despite the low evaluations the teacher may have received in the past, she did satisfy the minimal burden of showing that she was qualified for the supervisor's position. However, although the teacher had met the requirements for a sexual or religious discrimination suit, she did not convince the district court that her claims were valid. The teacher also made a retaliatory discharge claim, alleging that her supervisor had relocated her in retaliation for her criticism of the school's alleged discriminatory actions. However, the teacher impressed the court as an "overly sensitive person who took offense at the slightest criticism and viewed even the most routine supervisory decision as an act of discrimination. . . ." Therefore, the district court held that the school was justified in relocating the teacher. *Gold v. Gallaudet College*, 630 F.Supp. 1176 (D.D.C.1986).

In 1985, a female education professor applied for an assistant professorship position at Southern Methodist University. She was denied the position but was later hired to teach on a part-time basis at the university during the spring of 1976. She subsequently was hired to teach for three years with a promise that her tenure eligibility would be considered no later than the last year of her contract. At that time she was denied tenure. She requested the right to personally appeal to the education faculty. The faculty reaffirmed its previous unfavorable decision. After two more hearings were held at the university the woman filed a suit in a U.S. district court. The district court affirmed the university's decision and the woman appealed to the U.S. Court of Appeals, Fifth Circuit. The woman claimed that she was a victim of intentional sexual discrimination in the tenure decision and other areas. She argued that the terms of her earlier three-year teaching contract sexually discriminated against her in rank, salary and untenured status. The appeals court agreed with the district court that these claims were barred because they were filed too late. Title VII requires that a complaint be filed with the EEOC within 180 days of the occurrence. This limitations period starts running on the date the alleged discriminatory act occurs and not when a plaintiff first perceives that discrimination has taken place. The court of appeals observed that the Title VII limitations period is partially designed to protect employers from the burden of defending claims arising from employment decisions that are long past. The professor also contended that when the university evaluated her past publications record, her service to the university and the real needs of the department, it failed to correctly evaluate the criteria. The court ruled that the university had every right to consider its own teaching needs in deciding whether to grant tenure to the professor. It observed that the fact that the university's education department was eliminated subsequent to her tenure request indicated that the denial of tenure was legitimate. The court also observed that publication scholarship is not measured by volume alone but by comprehensiveness and direction of the research. It noted that the professor's publications were lacking in these areas. Finally, regarding the pay discrimination claim, the appellate court concluded that there is more to evaluating pay structure than the amount of hours a professor teaches in the classroom. Other things to consider are prior teaching experience, location of that experience, administrative responsibilities and professional achievements. The district court's denial of the discrimination claim was upheld by the court of appeals. *Merrill v. Southern Methodist University*, 806 F.2d 600 (5th Cir.1986).

A former assistant professor at Loyola University of Chicago and her spouse brought a sex discrimination suit against Loyola, the individual members of both the Board of Trustees and the Lay Board of Trustees and several university employees. The woman was a full-time assistant professor at the Loyola School of Dentistry for the 1970-79 academic years and received tenure in 1975. In September, 1979, she contacted Loyola's general counsel alleging that Loyola had engaged in a pattern of wage discrimination against female assistant professors since 1976. The woman was later informed that her salary would be reduced and her pending promotion was allegedly denied. In August, 1980, her contract of employment was not renewed. Several months later, she filed a sex discrimination charge with the Equal Employment Opportunity Commission. After the EEOC conducted an investigation and found no reasonable cause to believe that her allegations were true, it issued her a "right to sue" letter and this lawsuit followed.

In their complaint, based on Title VII of the Civil Rights Act of 1964, the Equal Pay Act, and § 1985 of the Civil Rights Act of 1871, the woman and her spouse sought compensatory and punitive damages. A U.S. district court ruled that the woman's spouse had no right to join in the suit because he had never been employed at Loyola and was therefore not a victim of the allegedly discriminatory employment practices. Regarding the Title VII claim, the court stated that since the woman had named only the university in her initial complaint to the EEOC, she could not now add the names of various other individuals to the complaint. The Title VII claim against Loyola, however, could still be maintained. Having ruled that the claim based on the Equal Pay Act was time-barred by the statute of limitations, the court further stated that the facts alleged in her complaint were not specific enough to suggest the existence of a "conspiracy" to discriminate against her pursuant to her § 1985 claim. The court noted, however, that she could still maintain the Title VII claim against Loyola and a claim under Illinois law for breach of an employment contract. *Feng v. Sandrik*, 636 F.Supp. 77 (N.D.Ill.1986).

As the following case indicates, discrimination based upon pregnancy constitutes discrimination based upon sex.

A Lutheran school for the deaf in New York hired a female art teacher in March, 1979. She possessed permanent certification as an art teacher but was not certified as a teacher for the deaf as required by state law. At the time she was hired, she was told that in order for the school to waive the certification requirement she would have to pursue courses toward deaf education certification. At the close of the 1980-81 academic year, however, the teacher had taken only two courses toward certification. In November, 1981, she left to have a baby and began her child-rearing leave in January, 1982. In March, 1982, school officials wrote to the woman and again informed her that in order to waive certification she must pursue at least six semester hours of study per year. She then met with the school superintendent, assuring him that she would continue to work toward certification. She was also granted an additional year of child-rearing leave. In March, 1983, the superintendent asked the woman if she intended to return to her position in the fall. He refused to extend her child-rearing leave, but told her that if she became pregnant again she would have "no trouble" in receiving additional pregnancy leave. At this time the woman told the superintendent that she had taken only three semester hours of courses toward certification in the past year. One month later she told the principal that she was pregnant. This prompted him to offer her a woodworking teacher position instead of art because when she would be forced to leave again in the fall, a woodworking teacher's sudden absence would be less disruptive to the learning process. The woman refused this offer and one month later she was dismissed. She sued in U.S. district court alleging unlawful discrimination due to pregnancy. The court disagreed with her claims, holding that the school had proven that the decision to terminate her employment was based upon her lack of deaf education certification. It was entirely proper for school officials to show concern for the continuity and quality of instruction at the school in the face of the woman's lack of certification and lengthy child-rearing leaves. The court noted that while pregnancy leaves are protected by Title VII, child-rearing leaves are not. Because no unlawful discrimination was proven, the court dimissed the woman's complaint. *Record v. Mill Neck Manor Lutheran School for the Deaf*, 611 F.Supp. 905 (E.D.N.Y.1985).

C. Religion

A Wisconsin case involved allegations of both sexual and religious discrimination. Here a woman applied to the theology department of Marquette University, a Catholic institution run by Jesuits, seeking an associate professorship. After her application was denied, she sued the university in U.S. district court under Title VII contending that she had been the victim of sexual discrimination: She also contended that her liberal views concerning abortion had been a factor in the refusal of Marquette to hire her. She demanded back pay and a court order entitling her to be hired as an associate professor of theology. The district court ruled against the woman, holding that the First Amendment to the U.S. Constitution prohibited any court from even considering her claim. "If the Court were to grant plaintiff the relief she requests, a place on Marquette's theology faculty, the government would, in effect, be forcing its interpretation of what Catholicism demands on the University and its students." The university's interest in the integrity of its theology department, as opposed to a geology or psychology department post, was held to be overriding. The court further noted that First Amendment considerations aside, § 702 of Title VII provides an exception for religiously oriented institutions. Under § 702, Marquette could legitimately discriminate against the applicant on the basis of her religious (abortion) views since she was a Catholic but not a Jesuit. Her religion, in effect, was different from that of her prospective employer. Under these circumstances, § 702 exempted Marquette University from Title VII's requirements. After dismissing the woman's academic freedom arguments on the ground that Marquette's theology department was entitled to enforce its views on abortion, the district court entered judgment for the university. *Maguire v. Marquette University*, 627 F.Supp. 1499 (E.D.Wis.1986).

A similar result was reached in a Kansas case in which two teachers sued the parochial school in which they taught. They charged the school with religious discrimination when the school did not renew their teaching contracts. The teachers were Protestant and the school in which they taught was Roman Catholic. The teachers filed a complaint with the Kansas Civil Rights Commission claiming they had been discriminated against on the basis of religion contrary to Kansas law. The Supreme Court of Kansas held that state laws prohibiting religious discrimination did not apply to sectarian employers. *Van Scoyk v. St. Mary's Assumption Parochial School*, 580 P.2d 1315 (Kan.1978).

D. Age

The Age Discrimination in Employment Act (ADEA) prohibits age discrimination against individuals who are over forty years of age. However, institutions of higher education may impose mandatory retirement upon individuals who reach the age of seventy. (See Chapter Six, Section VI.)

A case arising at Harris-Stowe College, a public institution, illustrates the general application of the ADEA and the "business necessity" defense found in the ADEA's § 623(f)(1). Here the college was reorganized by the legislature and currently employed faculty were allowed to reapply for employment at the new, reorganized college. A tenured biology professor was not reemployed due to the new administration's desire to hold down costs by establishing a preference for nontenured (and lesser paid) professors. The college also claimed that a preference in favor of younger nontenured professors would promote academic innovation and quality. A U.S. district court held that the college was guilty of age discrimination and the U.S. Court of Appeals, Eighth Circuit, affirmed. The college's claim that reemploying nontenured professors constituted a business necessity was rejected because cost savings was viewed as a prohibited reason in light of the fact that older professors earned higher salaries. *Leftwich v. Harris-Stowe College*, 702 F.2d 686 (8th Cir.1983).

E. Handicap

Unlike racial, sexual and religious discrimination in employment (forbidden by Title VII), discrimination against the handicapped is forbidden by federal law only in "programs or activities" receiving federal financial assistance. Section 504 of the Rehabilitation Act (29 U.S.C. § 794; see Chapter Six, Section V) states: "No otherwise qualified handicapped individual ... shall, solely by reason of his handicap, be excluded from the participation in, be denied the benefits of, or be subjected to discrimination under any program or activity receiving Federal financial assistance...."

In a decision affecting any private or public school program receiving federal financial assistance, the U.S. Supreme Court ruled that tuberculosis is a handicap under § 504 of the Rehabilitation Act. Federal law defines a handicapped individual as "any person who (i) has a physical or mental impairment which substantially limits one or more of such person's major life activities, (ii) has a record of such impairment or (iii) is regarded as having such an impairment." It defines "physical impairment" as disorders affecting, among other things, the respiratory system and defines "major life activities" as "functions such as caring for one's self...and working." The case involved a Florida elementary school teacher who was discharged because of the continued recurrence of tuberculosis. The teacher sued the school board under § 504 but a U.S. district court dismissed her claims. However, the U.S. Court of Appeals, Eleventh Circuit, reversed the district court's decision and held that persons with contagious diseases fall within § 504's coverage. The school board appealed to the U.S. Supreme Court.

The Supreme Court ruled that tuberculosis was a handicap under § 504 because it affected the respiratory system and affected her ability to work (a major life activity). The school board contended that in defining a handicapped individual under § 504, the contagious effects of a disease should be distinguished from the disease's physical effects. However, the Court reasoned that the teacher's contagion and her physical impairment both resulted from the same condition: tuberculosis. It would be unfair to allow an employer to distinguish between a disease's potential effect on others and its effect on the afflicted employee in order to justify discriminatory treatment. Allowing discrimination based on the contagious effects of a physical impairment would be inconsistent with the underlying purpose of § 504. According to the Court, that purpose is to ensure that handicapped persons are not denied jobs because of prejudice or ignorance. It noted that society's myths and fears about disability and disease are as handicapping as the physical limitations that result from physical impairment, and concluded that contagion cannot remove a person from § 504's coverage. The Supreme Court remanded the case to the district court to determine whether the teacher was "otherwise qualified" for her job and whether the school board could reasonably accommodate her as an employee. *School Board of Nassau County v. Arline*, 107 S.Ct. 1123 (1987).

F. Retaliatory Discharge

Title VII prohibits an employer from taking action against an employee because the employee has filed, or has participated in the investigation of, a discrimination complaint.

A male former employee of Howard University sued the university in U.S. district court, claiming that his firing was based on sex discrimination and was in retaliation for his December, 1982, filing of a sex discrimination complaint with the Equal Employment Opportunity Commission (EEOC). The court concluded that there was no basis for a charge of sex discrimination. Concerning the retaliatory discharge complaint, the court observed that

[i]n order to establish such a claim the plaintiff must show: first, protected participation or opposition under Title VII known by the alleged retaliator; second, an employment action or actions disadvantaging persons engaged in protected activities; and third, a causal connection between the first two elements, that is, a retaliatory motive playing a part

in the adverse employment action.... The plaintiff must first establish a prima facia case; the burden then shifts to the employer to articulate some legitimate, nondiscriminatory reason for the alleged acts of reprisal; and lastly, the burden returns to the plaintiff, who is given an opportunity to demonstrate that the employer's reasons are a mere pretext for discrimination taken in retaliation for participation in protected activities.

The court ruled that the male employee failed to demonstrate the required causal connection between his firing and the filing of the EEOC complaint. The court observed that his university supervisor had been dissatisfied with his "discourteousness, insubordination and failure to comply with rules and requirements and conditions of employment" for two years prior to his filing of the complaint and that he was afforded every opportunity to improve his performance. The sex discrimination and retaliatory discharge claims of the man were dismissed. *Johnson v. Howard University*, 641 F.Supp. 219 (D.D.C.1986).

G. Investigation of Discrimination Charges

When administrative agencies attempt to investigate discrimination charges, they frequently issue subpoenas for school employment records and may seek testimony from school officials regarding employment decisions. Schools are often reluctant to provide such information because of two factors: 1) the First Amendment's assurance that the government will not entangle itself in religious affairs (applicable only to religious schools), and 2) the perceived need to protect the integrity of the peer review process (applicable regardless of religious affiliation). While the lower courts are split on whether to allow broad inquiries by *federal* authorities into private school employment records, the U.S. Supreme Court has ruled that investigations by *state* agencies should be allowed to proceed unhampered by the federal courts.

In the case mentioned above, the Supreme Court ruled that the Ohio Civil Rights Commission (OCRC) could investigate an employment dispute at the Dayton Christian Schools, Inc. The Ohio private school had refused to renew the contract of a teacher after it discovered that she was pregnant, due to its belief that a mother should stay home with her young children. The teacher contacted an attorney and threatened the school with a lawsuit. The school rescinded its nonrenewal decision, but then terminated her because she had circumvented the school's internal grievance procedures, thus violating the "biblical chain of command." After the termination, she filed a sex discrimination complaint with the OCRC. When the OCRC began its investigation of the complaint, which included issuing subpoenas for large volumes of personnel records, the school sued in federal district court to prevent any action by the OCRC. The school based its arguments on the First Amendment's guarantee of freedom of religion. The district court dismissed the complaint, but the U.S. Court of Appeals, Sixth Circuit, reversed the decision. The court of appeals agreed that the OCRC investigation would impermissibly interfere with the practice of the school's religious beliefs. On appeal to the U.S. Supreme Court, the district court's ruling was reinstated.

The federal courts should be reluctant to interfere with a pending state administrative or judicial proceeding until the proceeding is completed. Further, the Supreme Court was unwilling to find that merely because a state administrative body had jurisdiction over a religious school the school's First Amendment rights would be violated. The school, noted the Court, would have an opportunity to raise its First Amendment arguments with the OCRC and with the state courts. Resort to the federal courts at this early stage was improper. The OCRC was allowed to go forward with its investigation. *Ohio Civil Rights Comm'n v. Dayton Christian Schools*, 106 S.Ct. 2718 (1986).

The U.S. Supreme Court also refused to intervene in *EEOC v. Franklin & Marshall College*, 775 F.2d 110 (3d Cir.1985). The high court's refusal to intervene allowed the U.S. Court of Appeals' decision in the case to stand. The case arose when a professor, who had been employed at Franklin and Marshall College (a private school in Pennsylvania) for three years, was denied tenure after he was reviewed by the school's Professional Standards Committee. The committee, composed of the dean and five faculty members, recommended that tenure not be granted to the professor. The committee's recommendation was also reaffirmed by the college's grievance committee. The professor then filed a complaint with the EEOC alleging discrimination based on his French national origin. The EEOC issued a subpoena for the committee's records. Although the EEOC offered to accept the records with names deleted, the school refused to disclose them. The EEOC then filed suit in federal district court to compel the college to comply with the subpoena. The district court ordered disclosure of the records and the college appealed. Before the court of appeals, the college argued that "the quality of a college and ... academic freedom, which has a constitutional dimension, is inextricably intertwined with a confidential peer review process." The court of appeals held that although the disclosure might burden the tenure process or invade the privacy of other professors, the records had to be disclosed because they were "relevant" to the EEOC's case. The records were ordered disclosed to the EEOC. The college appealed to the U.S. Supreme Court, but its petition for review was denied. *Franklin & Marshall College v. EEOC*, 106 S.Ct. 2288 (1986).

A black college professor filed a claim with the EEOC alleging racial discrimination after he was denied tenure by the University of Notre Dame. Pursuant to its investigation of the claim, the EEOC requested access to all the files of faculty members who were eligible for tenure at the time the claimant was eligible. The university refused to furnish the files unless it could first delete any identifying information of professors who had participated in the university's peer review process. The EEOC refused to sign a nondisclosure agreement as a condition to the release of any files. The U.S. Court of Appeals, Seventh Circuit, held that the need to preserve the integrity of the peer review process necessitated the removal of information identifying professors who had made evaluations of their colleagues. *EEOC v. University of Notre Dame*, 715 F.2d 331 (7th Cir.1983).

The Southwestern Baptist Theological Seminary of Fort Worth was sued by the EEOC, which attempted to establish jurisdiction over the seminary's employment practices. The seminary had sought and was given approval of its course of study by the Veterans Administration. This action, the EEOC argued, placed the seminary under the academic surveillance of the federal government. The seminary argued, and a U.S. district court agreed, that to place the institution's employment practices under government supervision would be an infringement of its First Amendment right to free exercise of religion. To require these types of employment relationships to be placed under government supervision would ultimately lead to excessive entanglement in the process of dissecting employment functions into religious and secular components. *EEOC v. Southwestern Baptist Theological Seminary*, 485 F.Supp. 255 (N.D.Tex.1980).

III. DEFAMATION

Defamation consists of an oral (slander) or written (libel) communication which injures a person's reputation. The defamatory material must have been disclosed to third parties who understand the material to refer to the plaintiff. Also, the plaintiff's reputation must have suffered in the minds of the third parties.

Several absolute defenses exist to a defamation lawsuit, the most important of which are truth, consent and opinion. Fair comment is an important conditional defense.

A Pennsylvania case involved the defense of consent. Here, an assistant professor of art at Lafayette College filed a lawsuit claiming that the school made defamatory statements about him when it declined to renew his contract. The professor's lawsuit was based on four documents containing statements relating to his performance as a faculty member at the school. Two of these documents were letters from the head of the art department which were highly critical of the professor's teaching ability, his grading standards, his willingness to contribute to the betterment of the department, and his relationships with other faculty members. One was a memorandum from a provost commenting unfavorably on the presence of the professor's wife in the classes. The other was a letter from the dean of Tyler School of Art to the same provost commenting on the professor's methods. The Superior Court of Pennsyvania stated the applicable rule of law in this case: "a publication is defamatory if it tends to harm the reputation of another so as to lower him in the estimation of the community or deter third persons from associating and dealing with him." The court, however, noted that "the consent of another to the publication of defamatory matter concerning him is a complete defense to his action for defamation." The court added that where an employment contract requires written statements of evaluation of an employee's record to be forwarded to interested persons for purposes of promotion, retention, discipline, or discharge, the employee has consented to the publication of these statements by being a party to the contract. By signing his employment contract, the professor agreed to the evaluation procedures as set forth in the faculty handbook and, according to the court, such publications by the college were "privileged communications." The court ruled that although the two documents written by the head of the art department were defamatory, they were privileged. On the other hand, the other two documents were not privileged communications, but neither were they defamatory. Thus, no actionable defamation took place and the professor's lawsuit was dismissed. *Baker v. Lafayette College*, 504 A.2d 247 (Pa.Super.1986).

A case involving similar circumstances occurred in Rhode Island. An assistant professor of chemistry applied for promotion to associate professor. The chairman of the department wrote a memorandum to the vice president of academic administration expressing serious reservations about the professor's promotion. In the chairman's opinion, the professor's record of publishing research was deficient. The chairman based his opinion on a publication summary list that the professor himself had provided. The Supreme Court of Rhode Island explained that a statement of opinion about matters which are publicly known is not defamatory as long as the opinion does not imply the existence of undisclosed defamatory facts. In this case, reasoned the court, not only were the facts upon which the opinion was based publicly known, but they had been supplied by the professor himself. The court therefore ruled that the memorandum written by the chairman was not defamatory. *Belliveau v. Rerick*, 504 A.2d 1360 (R.I.1986).

A person deemed to be a "public figure" may not succeed in a defamation lawsuit unless he or she proves that the defendant published the defamatory statements 1) knowing the statements were false or 2) in reckless disregard for the truth. Accordingly, a defamation lawsuit brought by the dean of the Delaware Law School was unsuccessful due to the U.S. Court of Appeals' conclusion that he was a public figure. The court observed that he was the "creator" and "chief architect" of the law school and had been actively involved in gaining its accreditation. *Avins v. White*, 627 F.2d 637 (3d Cir.1980).

IV. EMPLOYMENT BENEFITS

Like their counterparts in the public sector, many private schools offer a broad range of employment benefits to employees. These benefit programs are subject to federal civil rights and income tax laws. Employer-employee disputes concerning benefits will generally be resolved according to contract law rules (see Section I).

A. Discrimination

The prohibitions of Title VII and the Equal Pay Act apply to the provision of employee benefits.

A church-owned and -operated private school providing instruction from the preschool years through twelfth grade was recently held to be in violation of both Title VII and the Equal Pay Act. At issue was the school's practice of offering a health insurance plan only to "head of household" employees, which the school interpreted to be single persons and married men. The U.S. Court of Appeals based its decision on § 2000e-1 of Title VII which allows religious institutions to base relevant hiring decisions on religious preferences but forbids discrimination based on sex. The school's actions, in effect, discriminated against women by paying them less. The court rejected the school's argument that the Free Exercise and Establishment clauses of the First

Amendment prohibit the federal government from interfering with this re-
ligiously-motivated practice of granting health insurance to married men but
not to married women. Holding that the burden on the school's beliefs and
operations would be minimal, the court ordered the school to comply with
Title VII and the Equal Pay Act by abandoning its discriminatory "head of
household" distinction. *EEOC v. Fremont Christian School*, 781 F.2d 1362
(9th Cir.1986).

B. Income Tax Laws

As a nonstock, not-for-profit corporation, Marquette University has been
considered by the Internal Revenue Service as a tax-exempt educational
institution. From 1973 to 1978, the university provided certain fringe benefits
to its employees with commensurate salary reductions but did not withhold
federal income tax on the amounts by which the salaries of participating
employees were reduced. The university paid taxes on those amounts after
they were assessed by the IRS and then sued the government in U.S. district
court seeking a refund. The Internal Revenue Code defines gross income as
"all income from whatever source...including...compensation for services...." The district court observed that this included income obtained in
any form, whether services or property, and that the university would be
obligated to locate a specific statutory section which allowed it to exclude
the questionable amounts from "gross income." The three benefits at issue
were parking spaces, recreation center memberships and tuition payments
by the university for certain employees' children at area high schools.

The university claimed that the tuition payments remitted to the area high
schools were scholarships and therefore were exempt from taxation. The
district court ruled, however, that the tuition payments were not scholarships
since the payments were not remitted by the high schools to the university
or the employees. The tuition payments had been deducted from the salaries
of the employees and remitted to the high schools by the university and were
therefore to be considered part of the employee's taxable gross income. The
university also contended that waived parking fees and recreation center
memberships were not taxable income. The district court observed that "en-
tertainment, medical services, or so called 'courtesy' discounts furnished by
an employer to his employee generally are not considered as wages subject
to withholding if such facilities or privileges are of relatively small value and
are offered by the employer merely as a means of promoting the health,
goodwill, contentment, or efficiency of its employees." However, the court
concluded that the benefits here did not meet the criteria since they were
considered significant enough to be deducted from the employee's wages and
were only available to employees who agreed to the salary reduction in return
for the benefits. The university's attempt to recover the taxes paid was rejected by the court. *Marquette University v. United States*, 645 F.Supp. 1007
(E.D.Wis.1986).

John Carroll University is a not-for-profit institution exempt from federal
income taxes under §§ 501(a) and 503(c)(3) of the Internal Revenue Code.
The university established a retirement annuity plan for employees in which
participating employees agreed to take salary cuts in exchange for contributions by the university on their behalf toward the purchase of annuity

contracts. The university's contributions were excludable from the employees' gross income for federal income tax purposes. In April, 1983, and March, 1985, the university filed claims for refunds of FICA taxes paid for the years 1979 and 1981-83. After the IRS denied the university's claim for 1979 and failed to rule on the 1981-83 claim, the university sued the IRS in U.S. district court seeking a refund of FICA taxes for the years in question totaling $79,147 plus interest.

At issue was whether taxpayers acting pursuant to salary reduction agreements are exempt from FICA taxes paid on amounts contributed prior to January 1, 1984, toward the purchase of retirement annuities. The court observed that in 1965, the IRS decided that amounts withheld because of a salary cut agreement are to be included in the employee's taxable wage base for FICA tax purposes, even though the amounts withheld are excluded from gross income for federal income tax purposes. The court reasoned that if retirement annuity contributions were not included in the FICA wage base, individuals could control which part of their wage was to be included in the FICA wage base. In denying the university's claim, the court also referred to a 1981 U.S. Supreme Court decision in which the court held that "the term 'wages' must be interpreted consistently for purposes of both income tax withholding and FICA." The district court also concluded that a 1984 Act of Congress, which applied FICA taxation to remuneration paid on or before March 4, 1983, made retroactive taxation possible. The contributions of the university to the annuity plans were therefore subject to FICA taxes. The university's claim was dismissed. *John Carroll University v. United States*, 643 F.Supp. 675 (N.D.Ohio 1986).

V. UNEMPLOYMENT TAXATION

The Federal Unemployment Tax Act (FUTA) (26 U.S.C. § 3301 et seq.) establishes a federal program compensating persons who are temporarily unemployed. Although the federal Department of Labor oversees the program, the responsibility of administering the program is given to the states (when certain criteria are met). A major exemption from coverage is found in § 3309(b)(1) of the Act, which states: "This section shall not apply to service performed...in the employ of (A) a church or convention or association of churches, or (B) an organization which is operated primarily for religious purposes and which is operated, supervised, controlled, or principally supported by a church or convention or association of churches."

The U.S. Supreme Court held that a parochial school which has no separate legal existence from a church or an association of churches comes within the meaning of the word "church" as used in the Federal Unemployment Tax Act. Thus a parochial, church-supported school is exempt from payment of unemployment compensation taxes. The case arose when a South Dakota elementary Christian day school, financed and controlled by a church within the Wisconsin Evangelical Lutheran Synod, appealed a decision by the Department of Labor that it had to pay unemployment compensation insurance. The Supreme Court concluded that as long as a school is part "of a church or convention or association of churches" and is not separately incorporated, the school is exempt from the Act by its own terms. *St. Martin's Evangelical Lutheran Church v. South Dakota*, 101 S.Ct. 2142 (1981).

The Koolau Baptist Church operated the Koolau Baptist Academy, a private school in Hawaii for grades one through twelve. The school was sent a Notice of Contribution Assessment for delinquent contributions to the state unemployment compensation fund. The contributions were to be based on wages paid to the school's lay teachers and staff. Every employer was obligated to contribute to the fund unless it was granted a special exemption under the law, but the school refused to pay the amount assessed and appealed the case to the Referee for Unemployment Compensation Appeals. The school claimed that the payment of unemployment insurance deprived the school of funds "to further its religious mission" and resulted in the entanglement of church and state. The school also claimed that it was exempt under the Federal Unemployment Tax Act (FUTA) which, in turn, made them exempt under the state unemployment tax as well. The referee found that the school was not exempt, but he ignored the issues raised about church-state entanglement under the First Amendment to the U.S. Constitution. On appeal by the school, a state circuit court held that the exemptions and exclusions passed by Congress under FUTA preempted state law in order to be applied uniformly in all states. Since the school was exempt under FUTA, stated the court, the school must be exempt under state law. The state appealed.

Before the Hawaii Supreme Court the school argued that the teachers and staff were active in a *"per se* religious function" and should be free from financial burdens. The court noted, however, that the U.S. Supreme Court has held that not all burdens on religious activities are unconstitutional. To determine if a law infringes on religious freedom guaranteed by the First Amendment, it must be determined whether the law "has a secular legislative purpose; whether its primary effect is one that neither advances nor inhibits religion; and whether it fosters excessive government entanglement with religion." The school agreed that the unemployment insurance law had the secular purpose of providing a safety net for temporarily unemployed state residents; it also agreed that the law did not promote or inhibit religion. However, the school argued that the state unemployment law did not meet the third requirement of the test because it was too intrusive and too entangled with church affairs. As an example of this entanglement, the school argued that it could fire a lay employee over a religious doctrine dispute which would prompt a state inquiry into whether the termination was for "good cause."

The court, disagreeing, stated that a good cause termination investigation was rare and did not constitute "excessive" entanglement. In addition, even state inspection of the school's financial records would not entangle the state with church affairs. The court also observed that Congress had not intended that FUTA preempt state unemployment laws by creating a nationally administered unemployment compensation system. In addition, the Hawaii Employment Security Law makes no mention of strict conformity with federal law in the area of coverage requirements. For these reasons, the state supreme court ruled that the school was subject to the requirements of the state unemployment compensation system. The case was remanded to the trial court for a judgment consistent with this decision. *Koolau Baptist Church v. Dep't of Labor*, 718 P.2d 267 (Hawaii 1986).

A group of parents in Idaho interested in providing a private Christian education for high school students organized a nondenominational school, the Nampa Christian Schools, Inc. The school adopted a "Statement of Faith" which teachers were expected to integrate into every school course. Students signed the Statement of Faith and attended weekly chapel and Bible study meetings. Although eighty-five percent of the school's financial support came from tuition paid by the students, the Idaho Industrial Commission noted that the institution could not exist as a private school without the moral support of several local churches. This case arose when an office employee of Nampa Christian was dismissed and filed for unemployment insurance. The employee was denied benefits because the school did not pay unemployment taxes. She appealed to the Idaho Industrial Commission, which determined 1) that the school was for all practical purposes a church and 2) that the section of the Idaho Employment Security law dealing with exemptions from coverage violated the Establishment Clause of the U.S. Constitution. On appeal, the Idaho Supreme Court ruled that the school was not a "church." According to the court, the school could not maintain a separate legal identity from a church and still be a recognized as a church. The court examined various factors in making this determination including whether the school had:

> (1) a distinct legal existence; (2) a recognized creed and form of worship; (3) a definite and distinct ecclesiastical government; (4) a formal code of doctrine and discipline; (5) a distinct religious history; (6) a membership not associated with any church or denomination; (7) an organization of ordained ministers; (8) ordained ministers selected after completing prescribed studies; (9) literature of its own; (10) established places of worship; (11) a regular congregation; (12) regular religious services; (13) Sunday schools for religious instruction of the young; [and] (14) schools for preparations of its ministers.

The court noted that not all of the factors or even a majority of them would have to be present in order to recognize the church and school as one entity. However, since the court found that the school had met only the single factor of regular worship, it held that the school was not, constitutionally speaking, a church protected from taxation. On the other hand, under Idaho law a religious "association" is exempted from unemployment taxes. The evidence showed that the school was primarily for religious purposes and was operated, supervised and controlled by various churches which have members attending the school. Although the school could constitutionally be taxed because it was not recognized as a church, the school could not be taxed under Idaho law because it was part of a religious association. The court found no Establishment Clause violation and held that the school was exempt from unemployment taxes. *Nampa Christian Schools v. State*, 719 P.2d 1178 (Idaho 1986).

In Pennsylvania five private religious schools brought appeals from decisions of the Pennsylvania Department of Labor and Industry which determined that each school was subject to the provisions of the Unemployment Compensation Law and that each school should therefore be assessed unemployment contributions pursuant to state statutes. The schools sought refuge under FUTA's exemption for organizations operated primarily for religious purposes and operated, supervised and controlled by a church or a group of churches. The court held that the imposition of the assessment presented substantial risk of infringement upon the schools' First Amendment rights. Therefore, the schools were held to be exempt from the assessment. *Christian School Ass'n v. Commonwealth Dep't of Labor & Industry*, 423 A.2d 1340 (Pa.Cmwlth.1980).

A Lutheran high school in Maryland, because of its status as a religiously oriented institution, sought a ruling that its employees should be declared exempt from paying state unemployment insurance taxes. The Maryland Court of Appeals held that although the school had a Lutheran methodology of instruction, used the Bible in class and had mandatory chapel services, the primary purpose of the school was to provide its students with a secondary-level education. Analyzing the case under U.S. Supreme Court guidelines, the court of appeals found that the imposition of unemployment insurance taxes on the Lutheran school's employees would not unreasonably burden the school's operation nor conflict with its religious beliefs. The state's interest in maintaining an unemployment insurance system was found to outweigh the private school's interest in exempting its employes from the unemployment tax. *Baltimore Lutheran High School Ass'n v. Employment Security Administration*, 490 A.2d 701 (Md.1985).

A recent Ohio case involved the question whether employees of a religious school were excepted under state law from receiving unemployment benefits. Here a man was a teacher of Jewish religion courses at the Hillel Academy in Ohio from 1963 until 1983. When his employment contract was terminated he applied for unemployment benefits which were denied by the Bureau of Employment Services. The man appealed the bureau's decision to an Ohio common pleas court which reversed the bureau's decision and held in favor of the teacher. The bureau appealed that decision to the Court of Appeals of Ohio. The question before the court was whether Ohio unemployment compensation law applied in this situation. Ohio law provides as follows:

> "Employment" does not include...[s]ervice performed...in an organization which is operated primarily for religious purposes and which is operated, supervised, controlled or principally supported by a church...or association of churches.

The bureau contended that the exemption is determined by the purpose of the existence and operation of the school, which in this case was primarily religious. It argued that the school was primarily religious because traditional Jewish holidays were recognized and because the study of Hebrew and Jewish religion was mandatory. The teacher argued that the school was not primarily religious since the majority of the subjects were secular in nature. The court of appeals agreed with the bureau and reasoned that whether certain subjects constitute a majority of hours in the curriculum is irrelevant. The above-stated exemption simply requires that the purpose of the organization and its operation or support be primarily religiously-oriented in the conduct of its activity. Hillel Academy met this requirement. The exemption did not require or suggest the weighing of hours of secular and religious instruction in order to determine a school's purpose. Also, for the court to impose the responsibility of paying unemployment compensation upon the religious school would excessively entangle the state in its affairs. This is exactly what the unemployment compensation law was designed to avoid. The award of unemployment compensation by the common pleas court was reversed by the court of appeals. The academy was not required to pay unemployment compensation to the terminated teacher. *Czigler v. Ohio Bureau of Employment*, 501 N.E.2d 56 (Ohio App.1985).

VI. COLLECTIVE BARGAINING

The National Labor Relations Act (NLRA) (29 U.S.C. § 141 *et seq.*) governs unionization and collective bargaining matters in all aspects of the private sector, including private education.

A. First Amendment Limitations

The courts have ruled that "pervasively religious" schools may be able to avoid any obligation under the NLRA to bargain with employees. This exception to the NLRA's coverage is based upon First Amendment religious freedom considerations.

The right of employees of a Catholic school system to join together and be recognized as a bargaining unit was successfully challenged in a case decided by the U.S. Supreme Court. In this case, the unions were certified by the NLRB as bargaining units but the diocese refused to bargain. The court said that the religion clauses of the U.S. Constitution, which require religious organizations to finance their educational systems without governmental aid, also free the religious organizations of the obviously inhibiting effect and impact of unionization of their teachers. The court agreed with the employers' contention that the very threshold act of certification of the union by the NLRB would necessarily alter and infringe upon the religious character of parochial schools, since this would mean that the bishop would no longer be the sole repository of authority as required by church law. Instead he would have to share some decisionmaking with the union. This, said the court, violated the religion clauses of the U.S. Constitution. *NLRB v. Catholic Bishop of Chicago*, 440 U.S. 490 (1979).

In a similar case, the Catholic Diocese of New York transferred control and operation of a school to a lay board. The transfer was conditioned upon the continued operation of the school as a Roman Catholic institution. When the now-transferred school refused to recognize the Lay Faculty Association as the representative of the lay faculty, the NLRB applied to the courts for enforcement of its prior order that the association be recognized. The U.S. Court of Appeals, Second Circuit, held that the mere severance of daily control from the church did not alter the school's status as a church-operated school so as to warrant the placing of the school under the jurisdiction of the NLRB. To place the school under the NLRB's jurisdiction would bring about the very kind of excessive church-state entanglement the First Amendment seeks to avoid. *NLRB v. Bishop Ford Cent. Catholic High School*, 623 F.2d 818 (2d Cir.1980).

The National Labor Relations Board recently modified its jurisdictional stance regarding church-operated institutions of higher learning. The case involved a group of full-time lay teachers at St. Joseph's College who sought unionization for collective bargaining purposes. The college contended that the NLRB lacked jurisdiction over the matter since the college is operated by and financially dependent on a Catholic order, bringing it within the description of "church-operated" schools set forth in *NLRB v. Catholic Bishop of Chicago*. The St. Joseph's teachers argued that *Catholic Bishop* did not preclude the NLRB's assertion of jurisdiction because in that case the U.S. Supreme Court found only that religiously affiliated secondary schools were excluded from coverage under the National Labor Relations Act. The teachers further argued that even if *Catholic Bishop* applied to institutions of higher learning, St. Joseph's College was not "pervasively religious" so as to warrant exclusion from the NLRA's jurisdiction. In *Catholic Bishop* the NLRB attempted to assert jurisdiction on the ground that the schools involved were not completely religious but only "religiously associated." However, the Supreme Court found the schools to be church-operated and concluded that under the First Amendment the NLRB could not take jurisdiction over teachers at such schools.

In the St. Joseph's case, the NLRB ruled that whether it has jurisdiction must be determined on a case-by-case basis rather than a level-of-learning basis. The NLRB ruled that the decision in *Catholic Bishop* applies to all schools regardless of the level of education provided, and it stated that it would no longer generalize by saying that its involvement in labor matters in institutions of higher learning never presents a threat to First Amendment religious freedom concerns. The NLRB held that it would not assert jurisdiction in the St. Joseph's College dispute since the college was "pervasively religious." *Trustee of St. Joseph's College*, 282 NLRB No. 9 (Nov. 5th, 1986).

In February, 1982, seventy-three lay teachers employed by a New York City Catholic parochial school filed individual unfair labor practice charges against the school with the State Labor Relations Board (SLRB). The teachers alleged that the school had unlawfully refused to bargain with its bargaining agent, the Lay Faculty Association (an affiliate of the American Federation of Teachers). The teachers also claimed that the school had unlawfully discharged members of its faculty in violation of the State Labor Relations Act (SLRA). In December, 1982, the school asked the SLRB for an order dismissing the teachers' complaint because the National Labor Relations Board had exclusive jurisdiction over the church-operated school. Also in December, 1982, the school sued both the SLRB and the faculty association in U.S. district court. The school contended that the SLRB's assertion of jurisdiction over the school violated the Free Exercise and Establishment clauses of the First Amendment and that the National Labor Relations Act preempted the SLRB's attempt to assert jurisdiction. The school cited the three-point analysis used by the U.S. Supreme Court in resolving Free Exercise Clause questions. It argued:

(1) that the nature and extent to which the SLRB's assertion of jurisdiction burdens the free exercise of the [school's] religious beliefs is clear; (2) that the state cannot justify the burden which the assertion of jurisdiction by the SLRB will place on the religious liberty of [the school]; and (3) that accommodation by the state to [the school's] Free Exercise

concerns would not unduly interfere with the governmental interest of maintaining labor peace through the furtherance of collective bargaining.

The SLRB and the association claimed that the SLRA was concerned only with the secular issue of anti-union conduct, and that neither the SLRA's requirement nor the practices of the SLRB resulted in excessive entanglement between church and state or violated the Free Exercise Clause. In ruling for the association and the SLRB, the district court applied the principles of *Catholic High School Association of the Archdiocese of New York v. Culvert*, 753 F.2d 1161 (2d Cir.1985) (below), where the U.S. Court of Appeals ruled that the duty of church-operated schools to bargain with labor unions did not produce excessive administrative entanglement between church and state, since important religious issues were generally not involved. In *Culvert* the court also ruled that the NLRA did not preempt the SLRB from intervening in church school labor relations disputes. The district court therefore ruled that the Catholic parochial school was subject to SLRB jurisdiction. *Christ the King Regional High School v. Culvert*, 644 F.Supp. 1490 (S.D.N.Y.1986).

The U.S. Court of Appeals, First Circuit, was asked to decide whether the National Labor Relations Board could assert jurisdiction over an employment dispute at a religious university, the Universidad Central de Bayamon, and whether the NLRB could order the university to recognize and bargain with a union established through a vote of its full-time teachers. The court ruled that the union was entitled to recognition by the university. In its decision the court distinguished the case from *NLRB v. Catholic Bishop of Chicago*, in which the U.S. Supreme Court held that the unionization of lay teachers at a parochial secondary school was outside the scope of NLRB jurisdiction. The Supreme Court based its decision on First Amendment religious freedom concerns. The court of appeals held that the *Catholic Bishop* case was inapplicable because the Universidad Central de Bayamon's stated educational objective was to provide "humanistic education at an academic level," a seemingly secular purpose. Also, this case involved a university rather than a parochial secondary school. Finding that religious indoctrination was not a primary function of the Universidad Central de Bayamon, the court of appeals held that it was required to recognize the teachers' union. *Universidad Central de Bayamon v. NLRB*, 778 F.2d 906 (1st Cir.1985).

At issue before the U.S. Court of Appeals, Second Circuit, was whether the Establishment Clause of the First Amendment prohibited the New York State Labor Relations Board (SLRB) from exercising jurisdiction over labor relations between parochial schools and their already unionized lay teachers. The lay teachers' union had filed charges with the SLRB alleging that the Catholic High School Association had engaged in unfair labor practices by suspending 226 teachers who had protested the implementation of a policy that required teachers to teach the classes of absent teachers in addition to their own classes. The teachers also alleged that the Association wrote letters to individual teachers urging them to pressure the union into accepting the Association's offers, discouraged support for the union by referring to the futility of its efforts and announced other changes in working conditions that the Association would make unilaterally. The Association countered that the First Amendment prohibited the SLRB from exercising jurisdiction over labor relations between parochial schools and lay teachers. The court of appeals did not agree, finding that the duty of church-operated schools to bargain with labor unions does not involve excessive administrative entanglement between church and state. Even if the exercise of the SLRB's jurisdiction over the dispute between the school and the lay teachers' association had an indirect and incidental effect on employment decisions in parochial schools involving religious issues, minimal intrusion was justified by the state's compelling interest in collective bargaining. *Catholic High School Ass'n v. Culvert*, 753 F.2d 1161 (2d Cir.1985).

B. Managerial Employees

Managerial employees are not protected by the National Labor Relations Act.

In *NLRB v. Yeshiva University* the U.S. Supreme Court held that in certain circumstances, faculty members at private educational institutions could be considered managerial employees. Yeshiva's faculty association had petitioned the NLRB seeking certification as bargaining agent for all faculty members. The NLRB granted certification but the university refused to bargain. After the U.S. Court of Appeals declined to enforce the NLRB's order that the university bargain with union, the NLRB appealed to the U.S. Supreme Court, which upheld the appeals court. The Supreme Court's ruling was based on its conclusion that Yeshiva's faculty were managerial employees. It stated:

> The controlling consideration in this case is that the faculty of Yeshiva University exercise authority which in any other context unquestionably would be managerial. Their authority in academic matters is absolute. They decide what courses will be offered, when they will be scheduled, and to whom they will be taught. They debate and determine teaching methods, grading policies, and matriculation standards. They effectively decide which students will be admitted, retained, and graduated. On occasion their views have determined the size of the student body, the tuition to be charged, and the location of a school. When one considers the function of a university, it is difficult to imagine decisions more managerial than these. To the extent the industrial analogy applies, the faculty determines within each school the product to be produced, the terms upon which it will be offered, and the customers who will be served.

The Court noted that its decision applied only to schools that were "like Yeshiva" and not to schools where the faculty exercised less control. Schools where faculty do not exercise binding managerial discretion do not fall within the scope of the managerial employee exclusion. *NLRB v. Yeshiva University*, 100 S.Ct. 856 (1980).

However, in a case where the lay faculty of a Catholic Franciscan college were already represented by a union, the members of the Franciscan Order who also taught at the college were permitted to be represented by the same union. The U.S. Court of Appeals, Third Circuit, rejected the union's contention that there was no "community of interest" between the lay faculty and the Franciscan faculty members. The fact that the Franciscans donated a good portion of their salary to the college did not preclude them from being able to bargain for the same salaries paid to their lay counterparts inasmuch as salary is relevant to their status on the faculty. *NLRB v. St. Francis College*, 562 F.2d 246 (3d Cir.1977).

The Cooper Union for the Advancement of Science and Art, a private institution of higher education located in Manhattan, had an enrollment of 900 to 1,000 students and employed 55 to 60 full-time faculty members. In 1974, the Cooper Union Federation of College Teachers was certified to represent a bargaining unit of full-time faculty members and librarians. In 1980, however, after the U.S. Supreme Court's decision in *NLRB v. Yeshiva University*, the school withdrew its recognition of the bargaining unit and refused to bargain with it. In cases before *Yeshiva*, the Supreme Court had held that although the National Labor Relations Act does not expressly exclude managerial employees as it does supervisors, such an exclusion would be implied. According to the court, the rationale behind this exclusion was that "an employer is entitled to the undivided loyalty of its representatives." In *Yeshiva*, the Court ruled that a college faculty need only exercise "effective recommendation or control, rather than final authority," to be considered managerial. Recommendation or control as defined in *Yeshiva* refers to the faculty's authority to make policy decisions in both curricular and noncurricular matters. The Yeshiva faculty were deemed to be managerial employees outside the protection of the NLRA. Nevertheless, the Supreme Court noted that some faculties at other colleges may be nonmanagerial, depending on the circumstances.

The U.S. Court of Appeals, Second Circuit, noted several distinctions between Cooper Union and Yeshiva. Cooper Union's faculty had no "effective recommendation or control" of management decisions, and lacked the authority possessed by the Yeshiva faculty. Also, the Cooper Union faculty had little or no authority over financial concerns and other nonacademic matters and merely had restricted access to ordinary office supplies. In addition, the authority of Cooper Union's faculty over academic matters was relatively weak. In light of these differences, the court ruled that the holding of the *Yeshiva* case could not be applied to Cooper Union. Therefore the Cooper Union faculty was held to be nonmanagerial and was entitled to the protection of the NLRA. The court affirmed the decision of the National Labor Relations Board and ordered Cooper Union to bargain with the faculty bargaining unit. *NLRB v. Cooper Union for the Advancement of Science & Art*, 783 F.2d 29 (2d Cir.1986).

VII. STATE ACTION

Section 1983 of the Civil Rights Act (see Chapter Six, Section VIII) forbids action taken under the color of state law which deprives any person of federal constitutional or statutory rights. Recently, the Supreme Court sharply limited the circumstances in which an ostensibly private institution can be found to be acting "under the color of state law."

The Fourteenth Amendment prohibits any state action which deprives any person within that state's jurisdiction from any rights, privileges or immunities secured by the U.S. Constitution. When a privately operated school in Massachusetts fired a teacher for speaking out against school policy, she sued under the Civil Rights Act of 1871 (42 U.S.C. § 1983) on the grounds that the state, acting through a private school it allegedly controlled, had abridged her First Amendment right to free speech. As evidence of the control the state had over the private school she cited the fact that 1) the school issued diplomas approved by the local school districts whose special students this private school contracted to teach, 2) the private school received ninety-nine percent of its funding from state sources, and 3) this teacher's position on the private school staff had been created and funded by a state agency. The U.S. Supreme Court ruled that even though all of her examples of state control and funding were true, these factors in themselves were not sufficient to show that the state had created an agency or so controlled this private school as to make the school's actions its own. Absent a showing of actual control by the state, any deprivations of consitutional rights claimed by this teacher were matters between the teacher and another private party. Such complaints between private parties are not within the scope of the 1871 Civil Rights Act. Her dismissal was allowed to stand. *Rendell-Baker v. Kohn*, 102 S.Ct. 2764 (1982).

CHAPTER THREE
ACCIDENTS, INJURIES AND DEATHS

Page

I. CHARITABLE IMMUNITY 76

II. DUTY OF CARE 77
  A. Negligence 77
  B. Dram Shop/Social Host Liability 81
  C. Wrongful Death 83

III. ATHLETIC INJURIES 84
  A. Participants 84
  B. Spectators 86

IV. INSURANCE 87

I. CHARITABLE IMMUNITY

Under the common law, charitable and nonprofit institutions enjoyed immunity from personal injury lawsuits and other tort claims. Private schools operated by or affiliated with churches, as well as nonprofit but secular private schools, benefited greatly from the charitable immunity doctrine in the past. However, in recent years charitable immunity (like sovereign immunity) has been subjected to a high degree of judicial scrutiny. Many states have eliminated or restricted the doctrine as it applies to private schools, and it is generally recognized that the law of charitable immunity is in a state of flux.

A student at Virginia Intermont College, a private school, was injured when a roof access hatch cover blew off during a storm. She filed a claim against the college in federal district court. The college contended that it was immune from personal injury claims under Virginia law because the state had recognized the doctrine of charitable immunity in which beneficiaries of charitable institutions cannot bring negligence suits against them unless the negligent hiring of a charitable institution's employee is at issue. The issue before the court was whether Virginia Intermont College was a charitable institution within the scope of the doctrine. The court determined that two elements must be present for a private college to be considered a charitable institution. First, the school charter must restrict operations to charitable purposes; and second, the charity must not be operated for profit. According to its charter, Intermont was established as a private educational institution governed by a board of trustees affiliated with the Baptist Church. However, nothing in the charter limited the school to conducting its affairs as a religious, benevolent or charitable institution. The school was funded by charitable contributions, but students were required to pay for their own educations. Furthermore, for the nine years preceding this lawsuit, the college had shown a profit. The court observed that public policy in Virginia favored a more restrictive approach in determining whether an institution is immune under the charitable immunity doctrine. This was evidenced by the legislature's decision to abolish charitable immunity for hospitals and by the Virginia Supreme Court's refusal to automatically apply the charitable immunity label to various institutions. In light of the above observations, and the fact that the college carried liability insurance and was protected in the event that such an accident arose, the court ruled that the doctrine of charitable immunity did not apply to Intermont and that the student's case would be heard. *Radosevic v. Virginia Intermont College*, 633 F.Supp. 1084 (W.D. Va.1986).

A twelve-year-old Pennsylvania boy drowned in the Philadelphia Theological Seminary's indoor pool while attending a swimming party organized for altar boys of a nearby Catholic church. While the boys were in the pool, the priest who brought them went into the locker room to look up the number of a pizza shop where he planned to take the boys after the swim. No other adult was supervising the boys. Once he was informed of the emergency, the priest, who was an excellent swimmer and trained in water rescue, dove into the pool and retrieved the boy. His attempts to revive him were unsuccessful.

The priest had not obtained permission or warned any of the seminary personnel that he was bringing a group of altar boys from his parish to the pool. Having brought the boys in through a fire door, no seminary personnel knew the group was there. The priest, who was a graduate of the seminary, had brought 75 to 100 groups to the pool during his two and one-half year tenure at a nearby church. He testified that he had thought the pool was open to priests and their guests. The mother of the boy brought suit against the church, the seminary and the priest. The jury returned a verdict in favor of the mother finding the church 65% negligent and the seminary 30% negligent. The jury also found the deceased boy 5% contributorily negligent. While the trial court held that the priest should not be included in the lawsuit, the church and seminary moved for a new trial. The Superior Court of Pennsylvania granted the motion and the deceased boy's mother appealed. The Supreme Court of Pennsylvania reinstated the judgment against the church but granted the seminary a new trial only to determine the extent of its liability, having found that the instructions given to the jury on the seminary's liability were confusing. The seminary argued that it should have been immune from the suit under the state's Recreational Use Law. The law was developed to encourage the opening up of large private landholdings for outdoor recreational use by the general public by limiting the liability of the landowner. The court was unwilling to hold that the seminary's indoor pool was covered by the recreational use law. The case was sent back to the trial court for a determination of the extent of the seminary's liability based on clear jury instructions. *Rivera v. Philadelphia Theological Seminary*, 507 A.2d 1 (Pa.1986).

Cases abolishing the charitable immunity doctrine in the private school context include: *Roman Catholic Church v. Keenan*, 243 P.2d 455 (Ariz.1952); *Malloy v. Fong*, 232 P.2d 241 (Cal.1951); *President & Directors of Georgetown College v. Hughes*, 130 F.2d 810 (D.C.App.1942); *Gubbe v. Catholic Diocese of Rockford*, 257 N.E.2d 239 (Ill.App.1970); *Miller v. Macalester College*, 115 N.W.2d 666 (Minn.1962); *Bodard v. Culver-Stockton College*, 471 S.W.2d 253 (Mo.1969); *Christofides v. Hellenic Eastern Orthodox Christian Church*, 227 N.Y.S.2d 946 (1962); *Baum v. Reed College Student Body, Inc.*, 401 P.2d 294 (Or.1965); *Brigham Young University v. Lillywhite*, 118 F.2d 836 (10th Cir.1941) (applying Utah law), *cert. denied* 314 U.S. 638; *Jeffrey v. Whitworth College*, 128 F.Supp. 219 (D.C.Wash.1955); and *Mlynarski v. St. Rita's Congregation*, 142 N.W.2d 207 (Wis.1966).

II. DUTY OF CARE

The types of tort lawsuits brought against private educational institutions are usually closely related to the tort of negligence, which has three general components: 1) a duty on the part of the school or school officials to protect others from unreasonable risk of harm, 2) the school's failure to exercise the duty of care appropriate to the risk involved, and 3) an injury or loss caused by such failure.

A. Negligence

A fourteen-year-old deaf girl contracted rheumatic fever while attending a summer camp operated by the National Council of Beth Jacob Schools,

Inc. Due to the camp's negligence, the girl's disease was neither detected nor treated until she returned home at the end of the summer. As a result of the disease she developed polyarthritis, an enlarged heart, a heart murmur and a leakage of her aortic valve. The girl was forced to miss two and one-half months of school. At the time the case went to trial (three years after she caught the disease) the girl tired easily and had a susceptibility to heart problems. Her medical expenses totalled $2,900. A New York trial court, sitting without a jury, awarded the girl $30,000 in damages and her mother $2,000. The girl's mother appealed, contending that the trial court's award of damages was insufficient. The New York Supreme Court, Appellate Division, noted that under state law, nonjury damage awards are freely reviewable by an appellate court. It agreed with the mother's contentions and modified the award to $50,000 for the child and $5,000 for the mother. The appellate court reasoned that the trial court's award was inadequate because the child, who already had been afflicted with one handicap, was now required to deal with a heart condition that showed no signs of improving. *Berman v. Nat'l Council of Beth Jacob Schools, Inc.*, 501 N.Y.S.2d 413 (A.D.2d Dept.1986).

At the Holy Name of Jesus School in New York, a student suffered permanent loss of vision in her left eye and subsequent psychological trauma when she was struck by an eraser thrown by another student. At the time of the incident, the teacher had temporarily stepped out of the classroom. The injured student later brought a personal injury lawsuit against the school and the Roman Catholic Diocese of Brooklyn alleging that the teacher failed to provide adequate supervision. A jury verdict found the school and the diocese eighty-five percent at fault and awarded the student $650,000, but the trial judge later reduced the award to $350,000. The school and diocese appealed the jury's determination of negligence; the student appealed the reduction of the damage award. The Supreme Court, Appellate Division, stated that the trial court had correctly imposed liability upon the school for the consequences of a foreseeable act by a student. The failure of the teacher to adequately supervise a class constituted negligence. That negligence, reasoned the court, was the "proximate cause" of the student's injuries because the teacher was aware that the students regularly behaved in a rowdy and disruptive fashion in the teacher's absence. The court also ruled that the trial court did not err in reducing the student's award of damages. The jury verdict that the school and the diocese were eighty-five percent at fault and the trial court's award of $350,000 to the injured student were upheld. *Alferoff v. Casagrande*, 504 N.Y.S.2d 719 (A.D.2d Dept.1986).

A child care center for preschool children was operated by a church in Florida. After a one and one-half year old boy was bitten by ants in the outside play area of the center, his parents sued the church in a state circuit court. They alleged that the church was negligent and that its negligence resulted in the boy's having assorted physical, mental and emotional problems. The jury returned a verdict in favor of the church and the parents appealed to the Florida District Court of Appeal. The parents raised two issues on appeal. First, they contended that the circuit court was wrong in refusing to instruct the jury as to the violation of certain health department regulations governing the child care center. The court had refused to instruct the jury regarding a regulation which required that "[t]here shall be a minimum of forty-five (45) square feet of usable, safe and sanitary outdoor play area per child." The district court of appeal ruled that a finding of negligence was mandatory since the presence of ants in the play area was a clear violation of the "sanitary" provision. The parents also contended that they should have been allowed to introduce into evidence the deposition of the maintenance director of the child care center during the jury trial. The circuit court judge had disallowed the deposition because the maintenance director testified as a live witness. The district court of appeal also reversed the circuit court on this matter. It quoted from a Florida law which stated that "[t]he deposition of a party or of anyone who at the time of taking of the deposition was an officer, director or managing agent...may be used by an adverse party for any purpose." The director had stated in the deposition that whenever ants appeared in the play area, he or another committee member would pour some chemical on them to eliminate them. The director failed to corroborate that statement in his trial testimony. The circuit court was wrong in disallowing the use of the deposition during the jury trial. The district court of appeal reversed the decision of the lower court and remanded the case for a new trial. *LaTorre v. First Baptist Church Ojus*, 498 So.2d 455 (Fla.App.3d Dist.1986).

Suit was brought against the archdiocese of St. Louis for damages suffered by an eight-year-old second grade student who was burned when her costume for a school play caught fire from a lighted candle on her teacher's desk. The candle had been lit each school day during the month of May because May was dedicated to the Mother of Jesus. The costume the student was wearing at the time of the accident was a bluebird costume which included crepe paper and tissue to simulate feathers. While the students were changing into their costumes for the school play and the teacher was in the rear of the classroom assisting with another student's costume, the bluebird costume caught fire. The teacher doused the flames with water from a flower vase, but the child sustained burns over twenty-two percent of her body. A lower court jury awarded the child $1,250,000 in damages, and this verdict was affirmed by the Missouri Court of Appeals. The court rejected the archdiocese's contention that there was no evidence that the teacher was negligent, observing that the lighted candle posed a danger which was known to the teacher. The court further held that while the verdict was substantial, it was not excessive when viewed against the severe physical and emotional scars the child would carry. *Smith v. Archbishop of St. Louis*, 632 S.W.2d 516 (Mo.App.1982).

A three-year-old boy was attacked by another three-year-old boy at Camp Cedarhurst, which was owned and operated by Town and Country Day School, Ltd. The father of the boy sued the camp for failing to provide safe surroundings for the boy. The father claimed the camp was aware of the other boy's violent propensities, because he was involved in previous violent episodes. The camp responded to the lawsuit by claiming not to have had any knowledge of the boy's past violent episodes. The camp was ordered by the court to turn over the boy's records, so the court could verify that the camp had no knowledge of the boy's violent behavior. The camp refused to turn over the records for over fifteen months. The camp's continuous failure to turn over the records compelled the court to strike the camp's explanation that it did now know of the boy's violent tendencies from the camp's answer to the father's lawsuit. The camp thus could not defend itself during the trial by claiming it did not know of the boy's violent tendencies. *Horowitz v. Camp Cedarhurst and Town & Country Day School, Ltd.*, 500 N.Y.S.2d 726 (A.D.2 Dept.1986).

A case involving a research program conducted by Duke University of North Carolina resulted in a finding of no liability. The program consisted of a series of experimental simulated deep dives to study high pressure nervous syndrome in humans. One of the participants in the experiments was a graduate of the Florida Institute of Technology and an experienced diver who wished to take part in the program to further his career. Prior to his participation, he signed an "informed consent" form advising him of the known risks associated with the activity. After setting a world record for a simulated depth of 2,250 feet, the participant sued the university alleging that the experiment had caused him organic brain damage and that Duke had fraudulently and negligently failed to warn of this risk. A U.S. district court observed that although North Carolina law defines the degree of disclosure required for informed consent in therapeutic research, the statute does not apply to human experimentation outside the scope of health care as was the case here. For guidance, the court looked to the Nuremburg Code as adopted by the United States Military Tribunal at Nuremburg and a regulation of the Department of Health and Human Services, 45 CFR 46.116(a)(2), which was similar. The court concluded that the higher degree of disclosure of risks mandated by the latter two sources was the proper standard for a researcher obtaining informed consent from a subject of nontherapeutic human experimentation. After reviewing the evidence, the court determined that the university researcher, despite exercising diligence in staying abreast of developments in the field, was unaware of any risk of brain damage being associated with the experiments. The court therefore concluded that since the risk of brain damage was not reasonably foreseeable, the standard of disclosure for informed consent to nontherapeutic human experimentation was satisfied. The participant's suit against Duke University was dismissed. *Whitlock v. Duke University*, 637 F.Supp. 1463 (M.D.N.C.1986).

A thirty-five-year-old woman in Iowa began receiving treatments from a chiropractor who graduated from Palmer College of Chiropractic, a private chiropractic college. On the day of the injury, she went to the chiropractor's office and underwent a cervical manipulation. Shortly after the treatment she was transported to a hospital and treated for a cerebral stroke. Her sons, the plaintiffs in the present case, brought suit against the school from which the chiropractor received his degree. The plaintiffs sought damages for the permanent bodily and emotional impairment that the woman suffered since her stroke. The plaintiffs alleged that the school failed to properly research and teach the risks of stroke caused by a cervical manipulation.

The trial court dismissed the plaintiffs' claim against the private chiropractic college. On appeal of that decision, the plaintiffs asserted that a chiropractic degree constitutes an express warranty to the public that the chiropractor is competent. They asserted the literature on chiropractic medicine sent out by the college supported their claim. The Supreme Court of

Iowa rejected their assertions. Express warranties apply to goods that are sold, not services. Further, the diploma alone did not give the chiropractor a right to practice in Iowa. He had to be licensed by the state; therefore the state, not the school, was responsible for giving the public an expression of competency in the form of license. The woman testified that she had no idea where the doctor had received his diploma and that this had not influenced her in choosing him as her doctor.

The plaintiffs also alleged the college was negligent under an educational malpractice theory because the college had failed to teach the chiropractor properly. The supreme court held that educational malpractice suits would not be recognized in the state. The court found it would be difficult to determine a standard for satisfactory educational instruction. The court also expressed concern that a suit brought against an educator would consume an excessive amount of resources in terms of the time and money spent by an educational institution on litigation. Finally, the supreme court stated that it was reluctant to interfere in the state's licensing process. The plaintiffs' suit against the college was dismissed. *Moore v. Vanderloo*, 386 N.W.2d 108 (Iowa 1986).

B. Dram Shop/Social Host Liability

The following two cases involve tort liability arising from the serving of intoxicating alcoholic beverages. In a typical case involving social host liability, a college or its agents have served alcohol to a guest. The intoxicated guest then injures a third person who attempts to hold the college liable. Under the common law, such lawsuits were usually unsuccessful. The courts reasoned that a college had no "duty of care" with respect to an injured third person. This result has led a number states to enact dram shop or social host laws allowing such lawsuits to be maintained.

A student from St. Mary of the Woods College, an all female college in Terre Haute, Indiana, brought suit against the Board of Trustees of Wabash College in Crawfordsville, Indiana, the Sigma Chi Fraternity, Inc., and the fraternity's Delta Chi Chapter, to recover damages for injuries she sustained in an accident involving an automobile driven by a male student of Wabash. In the hours prior to the early morning mishap, the two were together in the male student's room at the fraternity consuming alcoholic beverages (which he had purchased). Neither had attended a college or fraternity sponsored event during the time period involved. Later, when he attempted to take her back to St. Mary of the Woods College, he lost control of his automobile and drove into a ditch causing her serious injuries. His blood alcohol level exceeded the legal limit and he was arrested. A state superior court subsequently dismissed her personal injury lawsuit.

On appeal, the student argued that her lawsuit should not have been dismissed because Wabash College and the fraternity had a duty to control the consumption of alcohol on the premises. The Indiana Court of Appeals explained the current state of the law in Indiana regarding the liability of third parties for the acts of drunk drivers. When determining the duty of a third party to control the conduct of others, the court stated that the relationship must fit into one of the following categories: 1) parent and child, 2) employer and employee, 3) landlord and licensee, 4) those in charge of persons having dangerous tendencies, and 5) persons having custody of others. Because the facts of the case did not fit into any of these categories, the court ruled that the college and fraternity were not liable for their failure to control the male student's drinking. Except for a few exceptions, stated the court, college students are "adult citizens, ready, able, and willing to be responsible for their own actions. Colleges and fraternities are not expected to assume a role anything akin to [a parent] or a general insurer." The court of appeals therefore upheld the superior court's dismissal of the female student's lawsuit. *Campbell v. Board of Trustees of Wabash College*, 495 N.E.2d 227 (Ind.App.1st Dist.1986).

In September, 1982, two minor females attended a fraternity party at the Villanova University chapter of Delta Cappa Epsilon. The girls left the party with a man who allegedly consumed a large quantity of alcohol at the party. The trio was involved in an auto accident in which one of the girls was killed and the other was left a quadriplegic. The injured girl and the estate of the deceased girl sued the fraternity and several other parties seeking to hold them liable for damages. When a U.S. district court ruled in favor of the fraternity the girls appealed to the U.S. Court of Appeals, Third Circuit. The question before the court was whether Pennsylvania's social host liability law was so limited in scope that the girls had failed to state a valid claim against the fraternity. The district court had concluded that Pennsylvania would impose social host liability only on individuals who physically handed alcoholic beverages to minors (the drinking age in Pennsylvania was twenty-one). The court of appeals agreed with the district court in concluding that Pennsylvania would permit intoxicated minors and third parties injured by them to maintain a cause of action against persons (including minors) who have made alcohol available to the minors. However, the court of appeals disagreed with the district court by concluding that Pennsylvania would extend liability under the social host doctrine to cover accomplices or civil conspirators. It concluded that two criteria must be established to hold a defendant civilly liable as an accomplice: 1) the alleged accomplice must have had an intention to promote the consumption of alcohol by a minor, and 2) the alleged accomplice must have aided, agreed, or attempted to aid in the minor's consumption of alcohol.

The fraternity contended that a "furnisher" of alcohol should be limited to those who physically hand alcohol to a minor and that any person who was one or more steps removed from that furnishing should not be liable. The court of appeals rejected this argument, stating that when assistance rendered by an accomplice is substantial, that person's actions will give rise to liability. "Substantiality," reasoned the court, is determined by the defendant's relation to the injured party, the defendant's presence or absence at the time of the injury, the amount of assistance given by the defendant, the nature of the encouraged act, the defendant's state of mind and the foreseeability of the harm that occurred. In reversing the district court's decision, the court of appeals noted that the fraternity and its officers and members had organized the party, financed the party, and knowingly allowed the premises to be used for the purpose of serving intoxicants to minors. The case was remanded to the district court for further proceedings to determine the liability of the fraternity and other defendants. *Fassett v. Delta Kappa Epsilon (New York)*, 807 F.2d 1150 (3d Cir.1986).

C. Wrongful Death

A sixteen-year-old cadet at a private military school threatened suicide with a hunting rifle which had been a gift from his mother. School authorities thereupon locked the rifle in a cabinet in the school's storage facilities. The cadet was placed in a psychiatric hospital for the remainder of the school year and reenrolled in the school for the following year on the condition that he continue to receive psychiatric help. The student arrived at the school one day before registration, accompanied by his mother, but was caught smoking marijuana in his dormitory room and was not allowed to register the following day. He and his mother left the school to go to their hotel but the boy, on the pretext of having to retrieve personal items from the school, returned without his mother to get his rifle. The rifle and ammunition were released to the boy and subsequently used by him to commit suicide. The mother sued the school alleging that the school had been negligent in handling the readmission of a student with her son's particular problems, that the school had negligently handled the marijuana incident and that there had been failure to exercise reasonable care in releasing the firearms to the boy. A U.S. district court in Virginia held in favor of the school, saying that there had been contributory negligence by the boy's sister in making a gift to him of the marijuana involved in the smoking incident. The mother appealed to the U.S. Court of Appeals, Fourth Circuit, which affirmed the district court's ruling. *Seidman v. Fishburne-Hudgins Educ. Foundation*, 724 F.2d 413 (4th Cir.1984).

In the summer of 1980, a twelve-year-old boy was a camper enrolled in a private summer camp in Maine. While at the camp the boy went sailing with a camp counselor and three other campers in a sailboat owned by one of the camp directors. The boat capsized after a gust of wind caught the sail and the boy was stranded at the capsized boat. Fifty-five minutes later the boy was pulled into a rescue boat and was pronounced dead of hypothermia. The boy's parents sued the summer camp in a New York trial court seeking damages for his conscious pain and suffering, funeral expenses and wrongful death. An expert witness for the parents testified that Red Cross regulations required that every passenger aboard a sail boat wear a life preserver and that proper safety procedures require that a spotter be posted on shore to observe the sailboat in order to render immediate help if necessary. The jury was faced with three questions: first, whether any employee of the camp had been negligent; second, whether such negligence was the cause of the boy's death; and third, whether the owners of the sailboat had constructive knowledge of the negligent acts which the jury found to be the cause of the boy's death. The trial court jury answered yes to all three questions and awarded the parents $350,000 for the boy's conscious pain and suffering and $3,574 for funeral expenses. It refused, however, to make any monetary award for wrongful death. Both the parents and the camp appealed the decision to the New York Supreme Court, Appellate Division. The appellate court ruled that the evidence presented at trial was sufficient to support the jury's finding that the camp's employees had failed to exercise reasonable care for providing for the safety of the camper. The court also observed that there was sufficient evidence at the jury trial to find that the owners of the boat had personal knowledge of the camp's failure to adhere to proper safety standards. According to New York law the vessel owner is personally liable for the negligence of a person who uses the vessel with his permission, if the owner has knowledge of the acts of negligence which caused the accident. The court concluded that the parents were only entitled to $200,000 for the boy's conscious pain and suffering. *Pollock v. Collipp*, 508 N.Y.S.2d 34 (A.D.2d Dept.1986).

III. ATHLETIC INJURIES

Under the common law, athletes were held to assume the risks inherent in participating in school athletics; consequently most lawsuits by injured individuals were unsuccessful. However, in many states the doctrine of assumption of risk has been eliminated or replaced with comparative negligence, which allows at least partial recovery of damages if negligence is proven.

A. Participants

A student in Oregon was rendered a quadriplegic as a result of a neck injury he suffered at a school football practice. He brought suit against a private organization connected with his school's competitive sports program alleging that a contact scrimmage was conducted notwithstanding an advisory recommendation of the district against such contact during the first week of practice. An Oregon trial court held in favor of the student, but it found that he was forty percent at fault and reduced the amount of the judgment awarded after the fault was determined by the amount of a pretrial settlement. Both parties appealed. The Court of Appeals of Oregon held that the mere fact that the private organization may have lacked the authority to regulate a public school's conduct of football activities did not absolve it of liability under the limited liability provisions of the Oregon Tort Claims Act for failure to implement the safety recommendations of the national high school association. The court was persuaded that the damages were correctly computed and affirmed the trial court's holding. *Peterson v. Multnomah County School Dist. No. 1*, 668 P.2d 385 (Or.App.1983).

A fifteen-year-old female student at the Pomfret School in Rhode Island was injured while she was practicing with the school's rowing crew. She and several others girls were performing an exercise called the "Harvard Step" in which they divide equally on opposite sides of a sixteen inch high bench, then step quickly up and down from the bench to the ground for approximately two minutes. A photograph introduced as evidence at trial showed that the ground was uneven, causing the bench to wobble during the exercise. the team's coach testified that he could not remember if the bench was on level ground when the exercise began. Also, there were no spotters and the coach was not watching the girls at the time of the injury. At the conclusion of the trial, the federal district judge ruled that the evidence was insufficient to prove either that the bench had been improperly positioned by the coach or that the students had been inadequately supervised. The district judge removed the case from the jury and ruled that, as a matter of law, Pomfret School was not liable for the girl's injuries. On appeal, the U.S. Court of

Appeals, First Circuit, reversed the district court's decision and ordered a new trial. It was error to take the case from the jury since ample evidence had been presented to allow a jury to make a reasonable decision as to whether the coach or the school had been negligent. The court stated the rule as follows: "it is enough that [a plaintiff] introduce[] evidence from which reasonable men may conclude that it is more probable that the event was caused by the defendant than that it was not." The case was remanded for retrial with instructions that a new jury be allowed to determine whether the school was liable. *Hornyak v. Pomfret School*, 783 F.2d 284 (1st Cir.1986).

On May 2, 1980, a student at Loyola Academy High School in Illinois was severely injured in a rugby game between Loyola and Gordon Technical High School. The student sued the Loyola and Gordon schools contending that his injuries were the result of their alleged negligence and wilful and wanton misconduct. He also sued all fourteen Catholic high schools comprising the Chicago Catholic High School Athletic League because of their association with Loyola and Gordon, which were member schools. This case involved only the student's action against the Catholic League; his case against Loyola and Gordon was heard separately. In his complaint, the student alleged that 1) the Catholic League failed to require protective equipment in rugby competition even though it knew, or should have known, that such equipment was necessary for the safety of the athletes in the member schools; 2) it failed to inform member schools of the incidence of serious injuries in rugby; 3) it allowed Gordon Technical High School to employ coaches with little or no rugby experience; and 4) it failed to provide adequate training for the coaches at Gordon. The Appellate Court of Illinois stated the applicable law in such a case:

A complaint for negligence must set out the existence of a duty owed by the defendant to the plaintiff, a breach of that duty and an injury proximately resulting from the breach.... The issue of duty is a question of law to be decided by the court, and it encompasses the question of whether [the Catholic League] and [the student] stand in such a relationship to one another that the law imposes upon the defendant an obligation to act with reasonable care for the plaintiff's benefit.

The court explained that in Illinois, the constitution and bylaws of an unincorporated athletic association constitute a contract between the association and its members. This "contract" defined the Catholic League's assumption of responsibilities in sports activities and, in turn, defined the legal duty that the Catholic League owed to the student. The scope of the Catholic League's duty of care must be determined by the terms of the contract, said the court. In reviewing the constitution and bylaws of the Catholic League, the court determined that rugby was not a Catholic League sport and was not regulated by the league. Although the league attempted to regulate competition among its member schools, it did not assume responsibility in any of the areas that the student had listed in his complaint. For this reason, the court held that no duty could be imposed on the Catholic League in this case and the student's lawsuit against it was dismissed. *Perkaus v. Chicago Catholic High School Athletic League*, 488 N.E.2d 623 (Ill.App.1st Dist.1986).

An athlete sustained severe injuries while playing in a lacrosse game between Ashland University and Ohio State University (OSU) at the Ashland playing field. The athlete, an OSU player, was thrown to the ground by an Ashland player. As a result of his head striking the ground, the athlete was rendered a quadriplegic. The athlete filed suit against Ashland maintaining that the Ashland player was acting as Ashland's agent, making Ashland liable for his injuries. He also alleged that Ashland was negligent for failing to have an ambulance or emergency vehicle on the premises and in permitting the main entrance to the playing field to be blocked, delaying an ambulance when it arrived. Although a court of common pleas ruled in favor of Ashland, the Ohio Court of Appeals reversed in favor of the athlete. On appeal, the Ohio Supreme Court disagreed with the athlete's contention that the Ashland player was an agent of Ashland. Citing past cases, the court determined that the relationship between a university and its students is contractual rather than a principal-agent relationship. According to the court, a student who attends a university of his choice, who receives no compensation or scholarships and who voluntarily becomes a member of a private university lacrosse team to engage in competition with other universities, is participating in "part of his total educational experience while attending school" rather than working for the university as its agent. With regard to the athlete's allegation of negligence, the court noted that expert trial testimony showed that the athlete suffered no further injury as a result of the delay in treatment. Therefore, Ashland could not be held negligent for failing to have an ambulance or emergency vehicle on the premises or for permitting the main entrance to the playing filed to be blocked delaying the ambulance when it arrived. The court reversed the holding of the court of appeals and ruled in favor of Ashland University. *Hanson v. Kynast*, 494 N.E.2d 1091 (Ohio 1986).

B. Spectators

During a baseball game held at a Fort Wayne, Indiana, high school, a spectator was injured. The incident involved a player from a neighboring high school who was taking warm-up swings with his bat. On the end of the bat was a practice weight referred to as a "doughnut." During one of the swings the doughnut flew off the end of the bat and into the stands, hitting the spectator. The spectator brought a personal injury suit against East Noble School Corp. and the player, but a superior court dismissed the case. The spectator appealed. The Court of Appeals of Indiana observed that the general rule in Indiana is that spectators attending baseball games are presumed to know that bats and baseballs are occasionally hit or thrown into unscreened spectator areas. By choosing to attend the game, they agree to accept the ordinary risks inherent in the game. The court also observed that when the doughnut flew off the bat, the player was where he was entitled to be and was using a regular practice bat and swing weight generally authorized for baseball teams. The only duty that the player owed, stated the court, was to not "wilfully or wantonly" injure any spectators or bystanders. Since nothing in the record suggested that the player's actions were wilful or wanton, the court of appeals ruled in favor of East Noble School Corp. and the player, holding that the superior court properly dismissed the case. *Sprunger v. East Noble School Corp.*, 495 N.E.2d 250 (Ind.App.3d Dist.1986).

IV. INSURANCE

In many cases a private educational institution will possess liability insurance which may provide coverage for injury claims. Unless an exclusion in the policy specifically exempts a type of injury from coverage, an insurer will be bound to defend and indemnify the school in any lawsuit arising from an injury. If an insurance policy is applicable, such insurance may in many states constitute a waiver by the school of any charitable immunity defenses.

An eleven-year-old girl who was enrolled in a Virginia parochial school alleged that she fell off her stool in class and that in helping her get up, the teacher squeezed her buttocks in a sexually suggestive manner. She and her mother alleged that the school administrator failed to investigate the incident and that they were humiliated in a private meeting and again in a schoolwide assembly by public remarks about the incident by school personnel. The mother and girl sued the school in a state circuit court for assault and battery and intentional infliction of emotional distress. The mother and girl amended the original lawsuit to include the allegations of improper sexual contact and negligent infliction of emotional distress. The parochial school's liability insurer asked a U.S. district court for a declaration that it owed no duty to defend or indemnify the school because there was:

(1) [f]ailure of a condition precedent to coverage under the policy, claiming Church Schools had failed to provide notice of the occurrence "as soon as practicable"; (2) lack of coverage under the policy provision covering "bodily injury...caused by an occurrence"; (3) lack of coverage under the provision covering "personal injury" arising out of a "publication or utterance...of a libel or slander or other defamatory or disparaging material, or...in violation of an individual's right of privacy."

The issue before the court was whether the personal and bodily injury provision of the policy covered the allegations. If the allegations were within the policy the insurer had a duty to defend the school. The court observed that coverage is determined by examining whether the allegations of the suit, whether proved or unproved, fall within the scope of the policy's coverage. The school claimed that because the girl and her mother alleged a battery, which requires some type of bodily contact, the allegation fit within the definition of bodily injury and therefore the school was covered under the policy. The court concluded that bodily injury is not the same as bodily contact and therefore the insurer did not have to defend the assault and battery allegation. The court ruled that the allegations of negligence did state a claim for an "occurrence" under the policy but that because there was no allegation of bodily injury, the negligence claim still fell outside the scope of the policy's liability coverage. The court further ruled that the insurer did not have to defend the school for the intentional or negligent infliction of emotional distress resulting from the comments in the schoolwide assembly since these allegations could only result from libel, slander, defamation or disparagement claims, and such claims were not made in the suit. The court observed that the only contention by the mother and girl was that the school assembly remarks humiliated and embarrassed the girl. The mother and girl raised no substantive claim for invasion of privacy. The allegations of humiliation and embarrassment did not necessitate coverage under the broad form personal injury provision of the policy. The school had to defend itself in the lawsuit. *American & Foreign Ins. Co. v. Church Schools in the Diocese of Virginia*, 645 F.Supp. 628 (E.D.Va.1986).

An Illinois preschool nursery had a liability insurance policy which covered bodily injury to persons injured on the school premises. The policy provided coverage for such injuries up to $1 million per occurrence with a $2,000 deductible per claim. When a boy at the preschool was injured, he brought a claim of liability against the preschool. After conducting an investigation, the insurer settled the claim for $1,800 and requested reimbursement from the preschool. When the preschool refused payment, the insurer sued the preschool in a state circuit court. The court ruled for the insurance company. The preschool appealed to the Appellate Court of Illinois. The preschool maintained that because the insurer's claims adjuster allegedly informed its attorney that the preschool was not liable for the child's injuries, a question of good faith arose when the insurer proceeded to settle the claim. The preschool further emphasized that the insurer settled the claim at no cost to itself, which raised a factual issue as to whether it acted in a self-serving manner without considering the interests of the school. The court ruled that the terms of the policy were clear and enforceable. The policy provided that the "insured's duties in the event of the occurrence apply irrespective of the application of the deductible amount." The policy further provided that "the company may pay any part or all of the deductible amount and, upon notification of the action taken, the named insured shall promptly reimburse the company for such part of the deductible amount as has been paid by the company." The insurer had the right to settle the case within the policy limits and its duty of good faith was not a material fact issue. The preschool was held liable for the $1,800 personal injury claim. *Casualty Ins. Co. v. Town & Country Preschool Nursery*, 498 N.E.2d 1177 (Ill.App.1st Dist.1986).

CHAPTER FOUR
STATE AID TO PRIVATE SCHOOLS

                                                                      Page

  I. FIRST AMENDMENT 90

 II. TEXTBOOK LOANS 90

III. BUS TRANSPORTATION 92

 IV. COOPERATIVE EFFORTS BETWEEN
      PUBLIC AND PRIVATE SCHOOLS 95
      A. Release Time Programs 95
      B. Public School Personnel on Parochial School Grounds 98
      C. Instruction Offered on Public School Grounds 100
      D. Leasing of Public or Private School Facilities 102

  V. STATE FUNDING OF INSTRUCTIONAL
      AND OTHER SERVICES 103
      A. Instructional Services 104
      B. Classroom Equipment 106
      C. Diagnostic and Therapeutic Services 107

 VI. STUDENT AID 107
      A. Tuition Assistance 107
      B. Tax Deductions and Credits 110
      C. Tax Refunds 111

VII. FEDERAL AID TO SCHOOLS 111

VIII. BUILDING CONSTRUCTION, MAINTENANCE
      AND DISPOSAL 112
      A. Construction and Maintenance Programs 112
      B. Zoning 113
      C. Disposal of Federal Property 114

 IX. TAXATION OF PRIVATE SCHOOLS 114
      A. Federal Income Taxation 114
      B. Local Property Taxation 116

I. FIRST AMENDMENT

The First Amendment to the U.S. Constitution provides in part that "Congress shall make no law respecting an establishment of religion, or prohibiting the free exercise thereof...." The courts have consistently held that this constitutional provision requires the separation of church and state at all levels of government.

In *Lemon v. Kurtzman*, 403 U.S. 602 (1971), the U.S. Supreme Court established a three-part test for determining whether government aid to religious schools (and religion in general) violates the First Amendment. The elements of the "Lemon" test are as follows: "First, the statute must have a secular legislative purpose; second, its principal or primary effect must be one that neither advances nor inhibits religion, ... finally, the statute must not foster 'an excessive government entanglement with religion.'" If a statute or government program fails any of these three tests, it will be declared unconstitutional.

II. TEXTBOOK LOANS

Under the First Amendment, the provision of textbooks by the state to private and parochial school students is permissible.

In *Cochran v. Louisiana State Board of Education*, 281 U.S. 370 (1930), the U.S. Supreme Court upheld a state law which authorized the purchasing and supplying of textbooks to all school children, including parochial school children, on the basis of what is now called the "child benefit" doctrine. The Court held that the textbook loan statute was constitutional because the legislature's purpose in enacting the statute was to benefit *children* (and their parents), not religious schools.

Nearly forty years later, the Supreme Court reaffirmed the validity of the child benefit doctrine in a case involving a New York textbook loan statute. This statute required local school districts to lend textbooks free of charge to all children in grades seven through twelve. Parochial school students were included. The Court observed that the textbooks loaned to parochial school children were the same nonreligious textbooks used in the public schools. The loaning of textbooks was permissible here because the parochial school students used them for secular study. Thus there was no state involvement in religious training. The state of New York was merely providing a secular benefit to all school children, explained the Court. *Board of Education v. Allen*, 392 U.S. 236 (1968).

Although a state's textbook loan program might be permissible under the U.S. Constitution, such programs are nevertheless subject to attack under state constitutional provisions. As the following cases illustrate, some state constitutions contain separation of church and state clauses which are more restrictive than that found in the First Amendment.

A group of South Dakota taxpayers brought suit in U.S. district court contending that a state statute authorizing loans of textbooks by public school districts to "all persons," including parochial school children, violated both the South Dakota and U.S. constitutions. The taxpayers argued that their right to religious freedom was being infringed by the use of textbooks purchased at public expense for religious purposes. The district court asked the South Dakota Supreme Court to rule on the issue of whether the textbook loan statute violated the state constitution. After examining the strictures of the South Dakota Constitution against public assistance to religion, the state supreme court struck down the textbook loan statute. The legislature's attempt to word the statute so as to ostensibly benefit all students was unsuccessful in light of the inevitable result that parochial school students would be its primary beneficiaries. The court noted that under the U.S. Supreme Court's "child benefit" doctrine, the statute may have passed muster under the federal constitution. However, the mandates of the South Dakota Constitution were at issue here. Accordingly, the textbook loan statute was declared unconstitutional. *In re Cert. of Question: Elbe v. Yankton Indep. School Dist. No. 63-3*, 372 N.W.2d 113 (S.D.1985).

The Supreme Court of Kentucky also ruled that a statute allowing the supplying of textbooks to children in nonpublic schools violated the establishment clauses of both the U.S. and Kentucky consitutions. The Kentucky Constitution provides that taxes should be levied and collected for public purposes only, and the court found that the textbook statute benefited nonpublic schools by appropriating public money to aid private education. This was a violation of the state constitution, which requires that no tax revenues be used to aid any church, sectarian, or denominational school. Because the state of Kentucky was constitutionally proscribed from providing aid to furnish a private education, the state textbook commission was enjoined from distributing textbooks to private schools. *Fannin v. Williams*, 655 S.W.2d 480 (Ky.1983).

Likewise, California statutes authorizing the Superintendent of Public Instruction to lend public school textbooks without charge to students attending nonprofit nonpublic schools and providing funds for that purpose were held by the Supreme Court of California to be unconstitutional. The record in the case showed that most of the schools participating in the textbook loan program were religious schools. The court utilized the traditional three-pronged test to make its determinations: whether the aid program had a secular legislative purpose, whether the primary effect neither advanced nor inhibited religion, and whether the program fostered an excessive government entanglement with religion. The court also considered the "child benefit" theory, which states that if the benefit involved is directed toward the child and if the benefit to the school is indirect, remote or incidental then the statutes are constitutional. Here the court said the benefits to the pupils and the schools were inseparable and it was impossible to characterize one as remote and the other as direct. Therefore, the "child benefit" theory was rejected which, in effect, meant that the statutes were unable to pass the three-pronged test. The statutes were thus held unconstitutional. *California Teachers Ass'n v. Riles*, 176 Cal.Rptr. 300 (1981).

In *Norwood v. Harrison*, the U.S. Supreme Court ruled that private schools with racially discriminatory admissions policies may not benefit from textbook loan programs. This ruling was based on the principle that the state may not give assistance to acts of racial discrimination. Textbooks were "a basic educational tool," said the Court, and to permit racially discriminatory private schoools to benefit from state textbook loans would be to allow the state to accomplish indirectly what it could not accomplish directly: a state-funded racially segregated school system. *Norwood v. Harrison*, 413 U.S. 455 (1973).

III. BUS TRANSPORTATION

Under the U.S. Constitution a state may permissibly provide bus transportation to and from school for parochial school children. Although the Constitution does not *require* that such transportation be provided, some states have enacted statutes which grant this benefit to all students regardless of where they attend school.

The principle that transportation may be provided to parochial school students without violating the First Amendment was established in the 1947 U.S. Supreme Court case *Everson v. Board of Education*. This case involved a New Jersey law which allowed reimbursement to parents of children attending nonprofit religious schools for costs incurred by the children in using public transportation to travel to and from school. The law's purpose was to provide transportation expenses for all school children regardless of where they attended school, as long as the school was nonprofit. The Supreme Court's analysis was as follows:

[1.] New Jersey cannot consistently with the "establishment of religion" clause of the First Amendment contribute tax-raised funds to the support of an institution which teaches the tenets and faith of any church. [2.] On the other hand, other language of the amendment commands that New Jersey cannot hamper its citizens in the free exercise of their own religion. [3.] Consequently, it cannot exclude individual Catholics, Lutherans, Mohammedans, Baptists, Jews, Methodists, Non-believers, Presbyterians, or the members of any other faith, *because of their faith, or lack of it*, from receiving the benefits of public welfare legislation. While we do not mean to intimate that a state could not provide transportation only to children attending public schools, we must be careful to be sure that we do not inadvertently prohibit New Jersey from extending its general state law benefits to all citizens without regard to their religious belief. [¶] Measured by these standards, we cannot say that the First Amendment prohibits New Jersey from spending tax-raised funds to pay the bus fares of parochial school pupils as a part of a general program under which it pays the fares of pupils attending public and other schools.

The Supreme Court analogized free transportation to other state benefits such as police and fire protection, connections for sewage disposal, and public roads and sidewalks, which also benefited parochial school children. It was not the purpose of the First Amendment to cut off religious institutions from all government benefits. Rather, the state was only required to be neutral toward religion. *Everson v. Board of Education*, 330 U.S. 1 (1947).

However, use of state funds to reimburse for transportation for field trips was declared unconstitutional by the U.S. Supreme Court in *Wolman v. Walter*, 433 U.S. 229 (1977). There was no way public officials could monitor the field trips to assure that the trips had a secular purpose, said the Court. Even if monitoring by the state *was* feasible, the monitoring would be so extensive that the state would become entangled in religion to an impermissible degree.

Most of the state legislation which provides for public transportation of nonpublic school students includes some limitations. For example, in a New York case, a school district was required by law to provide busing to the nearest parochial school of the children's denomination. When the district refused to bus the children to another school because there was a parochial school of the same denomination nearer than the school the parents requested, the parents sued the school district claiming an abridgement of their constitutional rights. The New York Supreme Court, Appellate Division, held that absent a claim by the parents that the nearest parochial school could not accommodate their children, the district was under no obligation to transport the children to a more distant school. *Rackmyer v. Gates-Chili Cent. School Dist.*, 368 N.Y.S.2d 636 (A.D.4th Dept.1975).

In a Wisconsin case, a public school district provided bus service to a number of Lutheran and Catholic schools in the area, pursuant to state statutes. During Holy Week the public, Lutheran and Catholic high schools closed, but five Catholic grade schools remained open. These schools requested busing service but this was refused on a cost and administrative difficulty basis. The Wisconsin Court of Appeals said that the law clearly indicated that busing shall be provided to all students within the state to insure the safety and welfare of the students. It was the court's opinion that the objective of this requirement was to prevent discriminatory treatment in the transportation provided to pupils attending private schools. The fact that the district would save money by not transporting private school pupils during a week when the public schools were closed was of no consequence since this bore no relationship to the safety and welfare of parochial school pupils. *Hahner v. Bd. of Educ.*, 278 N.W.2d 474 (Wis.App.1978).

In a Pennsylvania case, children attending nonpublic schools in Delaware brought suit seeking to compel the public school district in Pennsylvania in which they resided to provide free transportation to and from school and to reimburse parents for expenses already incurred in providing such transportation. Pennsylvania law states that a school district may provide free transportation to resident pupils attending schools not operated for profit and located within district boundaries or within ten miles of district boundaries. The law states no requirement that the ten-mile limitation be confined to transporting children within the confines of Pennsylvania. The school district, while busing students to nonpublic schools within Pennsylvania, refused to bus them into Delaware even though the students in this lawsuit attended school within the ten-mile limitation. The Commonwealth Court of Pennsylvania held in favor of the students and ordered the school district to pay for the cost of transportation and to reimburse parents for amounts already expended in providing their own transportation for the students. *Garnet Valley School Dist. v. Hanlon*, 327 A.2d 215 (Pa.Cmwlth.1974).

The Attorney General of the Comonwealth of Massachusetts brought suit against a town school committee to enforce the provisions of a Massachusetts statute which required school committees to provide to residents attending private schools the same rights as are provided for residents attending public schools. The school committee claimed the statute requiring such transportation was unconstitutional because of an amendment to the state constitution known as the "anti-aid amendment." The Massachusetts Supreme Judicial Court examined the facts and determined that the statute violated no constitutional mandates. The statute only required transportation to any approved private school that is the same distance or closer than the public school which the students would normally attend. A lower court's ruling in favor of the Attorney General was upheld. *Attorney General v. School Comm. of Essex*, 439 N.E.2d 770 (Mass.1982).

A holding contrary to most court decisions in this area occurred in Rhode Island, but the decision was reversed by a federal appeals court. In this case, a Rhode Island statute provided bus transportation for sectarian school pupils. The statute divided the state into five regions. It required each local school district to provide bus transportation to public or private school students to the school the student attended, as long as the school was within the student's region. An exception would be made for students who desired to attend a school outside the region if there was "no similar school within the region" and if the school was within fifteen miles of the student's home town. However, a public school student could attend a school outside his or her town only if the local school board determined that the school provided a curriculum not available in the local school district. This resulted in school districts paying considerably more for the transportation of the sectarian pupils. A lawsuit was brought by several board members of districts where transportation of sectarian children was costing many times as much as transportation for public school children. The statute was declared unconstitutional as violative of the Establishment Clause by a U.S. district court.

In making its decision, the district court used the standard three-part test to determine whether a statute violates the Establishment Clause: 1) Does the statute have a secular legislative purpose? 2) Is its principal or primary effect one that neither advances not inhibits religion? 3) Is there a fostering of an excessive government entanglement with religion? The statute in this case passed the first part of the test because its purpose obviously was the providing of safe transportation for all pupils. However, the district court felt the primary effect of the statute was the aiding of religion. It also felt the plaintiffs had successfully shown the statute caused an excessive entanglement of church and state. Hence, the statute was found to be unconstitutional.

On appeal, however, the U.S. Court of Appeals, First Circuit, reversed this decision and held that most of the statute was constitutional. The U.S. Supreme Court in *Everson v. Board of Education* (see above) held that states may pay for bus transportation for parochial school students in a case where the cost of busing public and private school students was approximately the same. Here, the court of appeals found that although apparently the cost of busing private school students was greater than the costs associated with public school students, the difference was not constitutionally significant. Strict equality of cost was not required. The court of appeals, however, found that the portion of the Rhode Island statute allowing exceptions for private school students to be bused outside their regions was unconstitutional. This was because the state education department, in deciding whether to grant exceptions, had to inquire into the curricula of area private schools to see whether there was a "similar" private school in the student's region. Excessive government entanglement would be the result. With the exception of this variance provision, the court of appeals upheld the busing statute. *Members of Jamestown School Committee v. Schmidt*, 699 F.2d 1 (1st Cir.1983).

In another federal court case, the question was whether the state of Missouri, once it determined to provide bus transportation only to public school students, was compelled by the U.S. Constitution to also provide like transportation to parochial school students. A U.S. district court answered in the negative, saying that the state could provide such transportation but that it was not required to do so. *Luetkemeyer v. Kaufmann*, 364 F.Supp. 376 (W.D.Mo.1973).

IV. COOPERATIVE EFFORTS BETWEEN PUBLIC AND PRIVATE SCHOOLS

Any cooperation between public school systems and parochial schools must pass stringent constitutional examination. Cooperative efforts, such as leasing of public or private school classrooms, must avoid the appearance of government approval of religion and must not constitute government aid to, or excessive government entanglement with, religious schools or organizations.

A. Release Time Programs

The courts generally will uphold release time programs only where the religious education takes place off public school grounds.

The first type of release time program to be declared unconstitutional by the U.S. Supreme Court was a Champaign, Illinois, program in which public school students were given religious instruction in the public schools. In this 1948 case Jewish, Catholic and Protestant community leaders formed the Champaign Council on Religious Education and obtained permission to offer classes to students in grades four through nine. The three religious groups each taught their own classes. The classes were conducted in public school classrooms and were composed of pupils whose parents had given permission for them to attend. Each religious group offered one 30-45 minute class per week. Although the council supplied the religious education teachers at no cost to the school district, the superintendent of schools exercised supervisory powers over them. Only students whose parents released them for religious study attended the religion classes held at the public school. Attendance was monitored by the religion teachers and absences were reported to the public school authorities. Students in the religious education program were released from regular class study while they attended the religion classes. However, the students not released for religious study were not released from regular class study.

A taxpayer in the Champaign school district sued the school board claiming that the release time program violated the Establishment Clause of the First Amendment. The U.S. Supreme Court agreed. It noted that public school authorities engaged in close cooperation with the religious council and its religious education program and that taxpayer-supported public school buildings were made available for various religions to propagate their faiths. Further, the Illinois compulsory attendance law helped provide a captive audience of pupils for the religious education classes. "This is beyond all question a utilization of the tax-established and tax-supported public school system to aid religious groups," said the Court. "[T]he First Amendment has erected a wall between Church and State which must be kept high and impregnable." According to the Court, it was irrelevant whether the Champaign release time program aided only one religion or aided all religions. The critical fact was that the program aided *religion*, and that was unacceptable. *McCollum v. Board of Education*, 333 U.S. 203 (1948).

However, four years later the U.S. Supreme Court upheld a different kind of release time program. In this New York program students could be released from public school classes during the school day for a few hours in order to attend religious education classes. However, unlike the program in the *McCollum* case, students in the New York release time program received their religious instruction off the public school grounds. Church officials made out weekly attendance reports and sent the reports to public school officials, who then checked to assure that the released students had actually reported for their off-school grounds religious instruction. The Supreme Court approved the New York program largely because the religious instruction took place off school grounds. There was no religious indoctrination taking place in the public school buildings nor was there any expenditure of public funds on behalf of religious training. Also, there was no evidence of any subtle or overt coercion exerted by any public school officials to induce students to attend the religious classes. The public schools were merely accommodating religion, not aiding it. The Court declined to invalidate the New York release time program, saying, "We cannot read into the Bill of Rights such a philosophy of hostility to religion." *Zorach v. Clauson*, 343 U.S. 306 (1952).

A lawsuit was brought in Virginia challenging a release time program for religious instruction. A religious organization obtained school enrollment lists and mailed cards to parents asking their consent to their children's participation in the program. The cards were deposited at the school and picked up by the religious organization. The school was then notified which children should be released for the program. Those children not participating in the religious program remained in the classroom but no formal instruction was provided. In upholding the release time program, the U.S. Court of Appeals, Fourth Circuit, cited the U.S. Supreme Court's three-part test regarding establishment of religion, which provides that state action is valid 1) if it has a secular purpose, 2) if its primary effect neither advances nor inhibits religion, and 3) if it does not excessively entangle the state with religion. The lower court held that this release time program was unconstitutional because its effect was to advance religious training. The court of appeals disagreed, citing recent cases holding that not all programs which provide indirect or incidental benefit to religious institutions are prohibited by the Constitution. The court said that the public school's cooperation with a religious organization did not constitute advancing or inhibiting religion. *Smith v. Smith*, 523 F.2d 121 (4th Cir.1975).

The U.S. Court of Appeals, Tenth Circuit, ruled that a Utah public school release time program was in part unconstitutional because certain elements of the program violate the Establishment Clause of the First Amendment. While holding that a release time program *per se* does not violate the First Amendment, the court found that this particular program ran afoul of constitutional prohibitions by excessively entangling the state in religion. One aspect of the program which the court objected to was the public school sending a student to the religious school to gather attendance slips. The court agreed with the parents who complained that this violated the Constitution. The court felt that a less entangling alternative was available to the school to achieve the state's purpose of keeping attendance records. Such an alternative would be to require the personnel of the religious school to gather the attendance slips and bring them to the public school. Also found to be unconstitutional was the practice of granting credits toward graduation to students who successfully completed the release time Bible studies. In this phase of the program the state had to determine if the release time courses were "mainly denominational" in content. For the state to make such a determination, the court concluded, caused it to become too closely entangled with religious matters. *Lanner v. Wimmer*, 662 F.2d 1349 (10th Cir.1981).

In another case upholding the validity of a release time program, a lawsuit was brought challenging a Wisconsin law which provided for release time from school for religious instruction. The Supreme Court of Wisconsin found that since the religious instruction was not taking place in public school buildings, and since such instruction was voluntary on the part of students, there was no state establishment of religion as prohibited by the Constitution. *State v. Thompson*, 225 N.W.2d 678 (Wis.1975).

Shared time programs usually involve cooperative agreements between public school districts and private school officials which involve the sharing of school facilities. An example of permissible shared time instruction is found in a recent Michigan case. Here a sixth grade girl who was a full-time student at a private school sought to enroll in a band course at her local public school. She was refused enrollment because she was a full-time student at the private school and the public school's regulations required that all of its students attend full-time. Public school authorities cited the regulation as prohibiting the girl from enrolling in only one public school course. The girl's parents sued the school district seeking to compel it to enroll their daughter in the band course. The Michigan Supreme Court ordered that the girl be allowed to take the single band course at the public school while she attended the private school full-time. The court held that to prevent the girl from enrolling in the band course would penalize her for having exercised her religious freedom by attending a private school. Thus, the Free Exercise

Clause of the First Amendment mandated that shared time instruction be allowed. *Snyder v. Charlotte Public School District*, 365 N.W.2d 151 (Mich.1984).

B. Public School Personnel on Parochial School Grounds

Recent court decisions indicate that most, if not all, programs in which public school personnel offer instruction on the grounds of religious schools will be deemed unconstitutional.

In 1985, the U.S. Supreme Court invalidated programs in Michigan and New York aimed at providing supplementary educational services to children attending private religious schools. In the first case a Michigan public school district adopted a shared time program in which full-time public school teachers offered instruction in remedial courses during the regular school day at various parochial schools. A significant number of these teachers were former parochial school employees. The district also operated a community education program where remedial courses were offered at the close of the day at parochial schools. Unlike their counterparts in the shared time program, community education teachers were full-time employees of private schools who were considered part-time public school employees. In both programs, the instruction was offered on the premises of the parochial schools and the classes were attended only by parochial school students. All religious symbols were removed from any classroom where shared time or community education programs took place. The Supreme Court held that the programs violated the Establishment Clause of the U.S. Constitution by impermissibly aiding religion in three ways. First, most teachers in the program were either former or present employees of religious schools and it was likely that they would subtly (perhaps unconsciously) allow religious indoctrination to creep into their classes. Second, the fact that the government provided such services on the premises of a religious school building threatened to convey the message of state approval of religion. Third, the programs subsidized religion by taking over a substantial portion of each school's duty to provide a comprehensive education. Thus, the programs were declared to be unconstitutional. *Grand Rapids School Dist. v. Ball*, 105 S.Ct. 3216 (1985).

In the New York case, a group of taxpayers brought suit in federal court challenging a city program in which federal funds received under Title I were used to send public school teachers into parochial schools. The teachers provided remedial educational services to underprivileged children. In this case the city had established a comprehensive supervision program to ensure that no state endorsement of religion could occur. Although the Supreme Court found that the city had succeeded in establishing a program that did not impermissibly aid religion, the very monitoring system that prevented Title I funds from aiding religion created excessive entanglement between church and state. "Agents of the state must visit and inspect the religious school regularly, alert for the subtle or overt presence of religious matter in Title I classes," said the Court. This pervasive monitoring by public authorities created a constitutionally unacceptable level of entanglement between church and state. *Aguilar v. Felton*, 105 S.Ct. 3232 (1985).

In an earlier case the U.S. Supreme Court also addressed the question of public aid to private schools under Title I. Parents of children attending nonpublic schools in Kansas City claimed that the state of Missouri had failed to provide "comparable" aid programs for public and nonpublic school students as required by Title I. Specifically, they contended that on-the-premises teacher instruction was being given public school students but denied private school students. The state of Missouri argued that the Missouri Constitution prohibited the state from providing on-the-premises instruction in private schools. The Supreme Court held that under Title I, state and local public educational officials are responsible for developing programs which are "comparable" for public and nonpublic school students, but that "comparable" did not mean identical. The Court said that if the state of Missouri determined that on-the-premises instruction violated the Missouri Constitution it would then become necessary for state education officials to devise other means of implementing "comparable," but not necessarily identical, aid programs for nonpublic school students. *Wheeler v. Barrera*, 94 S.Ct. 2274 (1974).

Students seeking education degrees at St. Cloud State University in Minnesota were required to act as student teachers for one academic quarter in schools that contracted to become student teaching sites. Participating schools were paid $96 per quarter for each student teacher placed. The student teachers began by observing a licensed teacher, then assumed more and more responsibility until eventually the students would actually teach the class under the licensed teacher's supervision. The student teachers were observed and evaluated approximately once a week by a student teaching supervisor from the university. The university permitted teachers to be placed in private and parochial schools pursuant to a written policy which provided that 1) participating private schools must meet criteria required of public schools, 2) a student teacher could be placed, at his or her option, at a participating private or parochial school, and 3) the student's participation in any religious aspect of the school was "exclusively between the parochial school's personnel and the student teacher." Under this policy three student teachers were placed at parochial schools which were members of the local Catholic diocese. The university paid the parochial schools the ordinary rate and placed no limitations on the schools' use of this money. A university professor filed a lawsuit seeking a court order that the university's policy violated the Establishment Clause of the First Amendment to the U.S. Constitution, and requested a permanent injunction against the policy. A U.S. district court decided that the university's policy had the primary effect of advancing religion and also excessively entangled the state with religion. It ruled against the university and prohibited it from further application of the policy. The university appealed. The U.S. Court of Appeals, Eighth Circuit, considered the district court's application of the second and third prongs of the Supreme Court's "Lemon" test. Addressing the second prong, the court of appeals observed that state aid has the primary effect of advancing religion when it flows to "an institution in which religion is so pervasive that a substantial portion of its functions are subsumed in their religious mission." The court referred to literature produced by one of the parochial schools stating that "God is the center of all that we do." The court concluded that the schools involved were pervasively religious institutions, and aid to those schools violated the Establishment Clause. On the third prong of the test, the court of appeals noted that "the University here makes no effort even to limit its student teachers from participating in religious events of the schools and thereby furthering the identification of church and state." The court of appeals affirmed the judgment against the university and upheld the permanent injunction against enforcement of the university's policy. *Stark v. St. Cloud State University*, 802 F.2d 1046 (8th Cir.1986).

C. Instruction Offered on Public School Grounds

The two cases in this section demonstrate that in order for religious instruction to be offered on the grounds of a public school, the state (i.e. the school board) must appear to be strictly neutral toward religion, and no excessive state entanglement with religion may result from such instruction.

In August, 1978, the board of education of the Findlay City School District in Ohio adopted a policy authorizing community use of school facilities. Two weeks later it approved the rental of elementary school buildings for one dollar per year to a private association sponsoring religious education. During the 1983-84 school year, classes were conducted weekly by the association in eight of the ten public elementary schools both before and after regular school hours. Although school district principals, teachers and administrative personnel were required to be at school between 8:00 a.m. and 4:00 p.m., the religion classes were taught by nonschool personnel. Attendance at the religion classes was voluntary and parental permission was required. During the 1983-84 school year, promotional materials for the religion classes were distributed in each elementary school. In most instances, homeroom teachers would distribute the material along with registration and parental permission slips. In several of the schools, teachers would collect the slips after the students returned them and then forward them to the religious education association. Before the beginning of the 1984-85 school year, the superintendent of schools issued a policy directive prohibiting the collection or distribution of religious materials in the schools. In addition, the directive provided that school personnel would not supervise the religion classes except in "emergency situations."

Charging that the policies of the school board violated the Establishment Clause of the First Amendment to the U.S. Constitution, taxpayers and parents of children enrolled in the Findlay public school system filed a class action lawsuit against the school board. The American Jewish Congress filed a friend-of-the-court brief in favor of the plaintiffs' position. The plaintiffs argued that the school board's policies with regard to the religion classes were in violation of the U.S. Constitution even considering the changes made by the superintendent's policy directive prior to the start of the 1984-85 school year. Pointing out that the religious program was directed toward eight- and nine-year-old children, the plaintiffs argued that the policies gave the perception of the endorsement by the schools of religious instruction to a "very impressionable age group." In addition, the plaintiffs claimed that the program caused excessive entanglement of the school board in religious matters because school personnel were required to be on the premises during the times the religion classes were held. The defendant school board argued that any involvement of public school personnel with religion classes was slight. It also emphasized that a variety of both school and nonschool-related groups including political, business and social welfare groups regularly used the school building. This policy of providing equal access to private organizations, the board argued, created a public forum for First Amendment purposes. The board contended that this policy did not violate the Establishment Clause in any respect.

The district court applied the analysis used in *Lemon v. Kurtzman*, 403 U.S. 602 (1971). In the *Lemon* case, the U.S. Supreme Court ruled that the statute or policy in dispute must pass three tests in order to be constitutionally upheld. "First, the statute must have a secular legislative purpose: second, its principal or primary effect must be one that neither advances nor inhibits religion,... finally, the statute must not foster an excessive government entanglement with religion." The Supreme Court in a later case ruled that an improper appearance of official support of religion would act as an advancement of religion and would cause the statute or policy to fail the second prong of the *Lemon* test and be held unconstitutional. Applying the principles of the *Lemon* case to the issues at hand, the district court determined that the school board policy permitting the private religious association's classes to be held in public school buildings immediately before and after regular school hours impermissibly advanced religious interests by creating, for impressionable eight- and nine-year-old children, the appearance of government endorsement of religion. In addition, since the religion classes were held immediately preceding or following public school classes, the private religious association directly benefited from the operation of Ohio's compulsory education law. Such a benefit, stated the court, rendered the school board policy unconstitutional. The court noted that its decision was based primarily on the timing and location of the religion classes, as well as the "tender and impressionable ages of the children, whether or not participants, in contact with the program." The school board was ordered to immediately discontinue its practice of allowing public school buildings to be used for religion classes closely related to the opening and closing of the regular school day. *Ford v. Manuel*, 629 F.Supp. 771 (N.D.Ohio 1985).

A recent federal appeals court case involved Chapter One of the Education Consolidation and Improvement Act of 1981, which superseded Title I of the Elementary and Secondary Education Act of 1965. Chapter One established a federally funded program to provide remedial instruction and related support services to elementary and secondary school children who are "educationally deprived" and who live in areas having a high concentration of low income families. The purpose of the program is to meet the remedial educational needs of students that cannot otherwise be met by the schools they attend. States receiving Chapter One funding are required to provide such remedial services to private as well as public school students.

Prior to 1986 the city of New York provided such remedial instruction to children attending private (including parochial) schools by sending public school teachers to the private schools to teach classes. However, in order to comply with *Aguilar v. Felton*, 105 S.Ct. 3232 (1985) (see Section IV B), which held that sending federally supported public school teachers to teach in private religious schools violated the Establishment Clause of the First Amendment, the city adopted a new plan. One aspect of the plan called for the city to conduct remedial education classes for girls from a Hasidic Jewish school on public school premises. Specifically, the plan provided for a section of the public school to be completely closed off for use by the Hasidic girls by constructing a wall in a previously open corridor. The plan also provided for the girls to be taught only by women (in accordance with Hasidic tradition) who spoke Yiddish. Before the plan was implemented, a local parents' association sued the Chancellor of the New York City School District in a U.S. district court seeking a preliminary injunction against the plan. When the injunction was denied, the parents appealed to the U.S. Court of Appeals, Second Circuit.

The parents contended that the city's plan had the primary effect of promoting religion and excessively entangling the state in religious matters. The city argued that the injunction was properly denied because the plan did not have those effects and was no more than a reasonable effort to encourage the Hasidic Jews to send their children to the remedial classes conducted in the public school. The court of appeals observed that the U.S. Supreme Court has developed a three-part test for determining whether a given state law is one that "establishes" religion. Failure to meet any of the three conditions means that the state program violates the Establishment Clause. First, the statute must have a secular legislative purpose; second, its primary effect must be one that neither advances nor inhibits religion; third, the statute must not promote an excessive government entanglement with religion.

The court of appeals stated that the issue was whether the city's plan had the primary effect of advancing the religious tenets of the Hasidic Jews and whether it fostered an excessive entanglement of the city with religion. In ruling for the parents the court of appeals observed that the city's plan seemed "plainly to create a symbolic link between the state and the Hasidic sect that is likely to have a magnified negative impact on the minds of the youngsters attending P.S. 16." The court of appeals also disagreed with the district court's observation that an injunction against the plan would hinder the free exercise of religion on the part of the Jewish girls. "The Free Exercise Clause of the First Amendment...does not prohibit a government from forcing a choice between receipt of a public benefit and a pursuit of a religious belief if it can show a compelling reason for doing so." The court of appeals ruled that avoiding a violation of the Establishment Clause that would otherwise result from an apparent endorsement of the tenets of a particular faith is ample reason for compelling that choice. The court of appeals reversed the lower court decision and held that the parents were entitled to preliminary injunctive relief on the ground that the city's plan had the primary effect of establishing religion through a federally funded program. *Parents' Association of P.S. 16 v. Quinones*, 803 F.2d 1235 (2d Cir.1986).

D. Leasing of Public or Private School Facilities

Lease agreements between public and private schools must avoid the appearance of state sponsorship of religion.

The U.S. Supreme Court invalidated a shared time program where the school district leased classrooms from religious schools and offered remedial and enriched education to the private school students. Although all religious symbols were removed from the leased classrooms, the court held that the program conveyed a message of state approval of religion and was therefore unconstitutional. The danger was also presented that public funds would be used to advance religious purposes. *Grand Rapids School Dist. v. Ball*, 105 S.Ct. 3216 (1985).

A religious organization in Kansas brought suit against a school district seeking a permanent injunction ordering the district to make its facilities available for religious purposes on the same basis as for nonreligious purposes. The school district had long made its facilities available for a fee to a wide variety of community groups. Religious groups were permitted to use the facilities only if they were used for nonreligious activities. The school district maintained that to allow religious services would violate the Establishment Clause of the First Amendment. A U.S. district court disagreed. It held that in allowing its facilities to be used by a wide variety of community organizations for diverse purposes the school district had created a public forum for nonschool groups. Having created a public forum, the school district may not prohibit groups from using the facilities on the basis of what they intend to say. Stating that the First Amendment "no more requires state governments to handicap religions than it does to favor them," the court ruled that an equal access policy toward its facilities was permissible and issued the permanent injunction. *Country Hills Christian Church v. Unified School Dist. No. 512*, 560 F.Supp. 1207 (D.Kan.1983).

A group of parents in Indiana protested the closing of an old public high school in a predominantly Protestant area and the transferring of students to a larger, newer facility which was formerly a Catholic school and which was located in a predominantly Catholic area. The parents sued to prevent the closing of the old school on grounds that the Catholic influence in the new school remained strong and that their children would be affected by the Catholic environment. The U.S. Court of Appeals upheld the closing of the old school but did order certain changes at the new school including the discontinuance of the wearing of habits by teaching nuns, a better balance of books in the library, and a lessening of the predominance of religious art in the school. The court took note of efforts by the students themselves to make the transition smooth and said it could only hope that this display of cooperation would serve to reassure parents and citizens in other school corporations in Indiana who are faced with similar problems relative to the integration of school facilities. *Buford v. Southeast Dubois County School Corp.*, 472 F.2d 890 (7th Cir.1973). See, however, *Americans United for Separation of Church & State v. Porter*, 485 F.Supp. 432 (W.D.Mich.1980), where a U.S. district court rejected a dual enrollment program involving the rental of space from Catholic schools.

V. STATE FUNDING OF INSTRUCTIONAL AND OTHER SERVICES

Lemon v. Kurtzman, Meek v. Pittenger and **Wolman v. Walter** are the three major U.S. Supreme Court cases which address government aid to religious schools. The rules which have emerged from these cases appear to be as follows: 1) state-provided salary supplements for teachers of parochial school students are forbidden, 2) state funding may be provided to parochial schools to defray the costs of preparing and administering state-required student testing and the like *if* such funds are monitored to ensure that none are diverted to religious uses, 3) state-prepared standardized student testing may be paid for by the state without any monitoring, 4) textbooks may be supplied by the state to students at racially nondiscriminatory parochial schools, 5) maps, charts and the like may not be provided by the state to parochial school students, 6) teaching and counseling services may only be provided by the state to parochial school students off the premises of the parochial schools, and 7) diagnostic and therapeutic services may be provided by the state to parochial school students at any location.

A. Instructional Services

In *Lemon v. Kurtzman*, the U.S. Supreme Court invalidated Rhode Island and Pennsylvania statutes which provided state money to finance the operation of parochial schools. The Rhode Island statute provided a fifteen percent salary supplement to parochial school teachers who taught nonreligious subjects also offered in the public schools using only public school teaching materials. The Pennsylvania statute authorized payment of state funds to parochial schools to help defray the cost of teachers' salaries, textbooks and other instructional materials. Reimbursement was limited, however, to the costs of secular subjects which were also taught in the public schools. The Supreme Court evaluated the Rhode Island and Pennsylvania programs using its three-part test: "First, the statute must have a secular legislative purpose; second, its principal or primary effect must be one that neither advances nor inhibits religion, ... finally, the statute must not foster 'an excessive government entanglement with religion.'" Applying this test to the two state programs in question, the Court held that the legislative purpose of the programs was a legitimate, secular concern with maintaining high educational standards in both public and private schools. The Court did not reach the second inquiry under the three-part test because it concluded that the state programs failed to pass muster under the third inquiry.

The Rhode Island salary supplement program excessively entangled the state with religion because of the highly religious nature of the Roman Catholic parochial schools which were the primary beneficiaries of the program. The teachers who received the salary supplements provided instruction in classrooms and buildings containing religious symbols such as crucifixes. In such an atmosphere, even a person dedicated to remaining religiously neutral would probably allow some religious content to creep into the ostensibly secular instruction. Similar defects were found in the Pennsylvania program. The Court also observed that in order to ensure that the state-funded parochial school teachers did not inject religious dogma into their instruction, the state would be forced to extensively monitor the parochial school classrooms. This would result in excessive state entanglement with religion. The Court also found the danger of a different type of entanglement in the Pennsylvania program: politics and religion would inexorably tend to be mixed. In communities with large numbers of parochial school students, candidates for political office might be elected on the basis of their degree of support for financial aid to parochial schools. "Ordinarily political debate and division, however vigorous or even partisan, are normal and healthy manifestations of our democratic system of government, but political division along religious lines was one of the principal evils against which the First Amendment was intended to protect....The potential divisiveness of such conflict is a threat to the normal political process ...." Consequently, the salary supplement programs were held to violate the First Amendment. *Lemon v. Kurtzman*, 403 U.S. 602 (1971).

One year later the U.S. Supreme Court struck down another form of state funding of instructional services. The case involved a New York program which granted annual lump-sum disbursements to parochial schools to help pay the costs of administering state-required student testing and record-keeping activities. The tests, which were prepared by parochial school personnel, were characterized by the U.S. Supreme Court as "an integral part of the teaching process." The Court concluded that it was likely that the tests would, "unconsciously or otherwise,...inculcate students in the religious precepts of the sponsoring church." *Levitt v. Committee for Public Education and Religious Liberty*, 413 U.S. 472 (1972).

However, the New York legislature responded to the *Levitt* decision by reenacting the reimbursements for teacher-prepared tests but adding a requirement that the funds be audited to ensure that no state subsidizing of religion would occur. The Supreme Court upheld the plan and found that the state audits did not excessively entangle the state in the affairs of parochial schools. *Committee for Public Education and Religious Liberty v. Regan*, 444 U.S. 646 (1980).

In *Wolman v. Walter*, 433 U.S. 229 (1977), the Supreme Court had no difficulty upholding a portion of an Ohio program which supplied all private school children with the same standardized tests as were used in the public schools. The Court held that the program merely ensured that parochial school students received adequate secular educations.

A New Hampshire case provides an example of lower courts' interpretations of the above decisions. In this case the state supreme court was asked by the governor and executive council to give its opinion on whether the New Hampshire State Board of Education guidelines in matters of aid to private school students were constitutionally permissible. The court found three distinguishable groups of aid authorized by New Hampshire law. The three groups were: 1) hot lunches, textbooks loaned to students, physician, school nurse and school health services; 2) guidance and psychological services, educational testing, health and welfare services, driver education and special programs for the handicapped; and 3) instructional materials incidental and necessary to provide the services in group two.

The court found the state board guidelines to be constitutionally permissible. Specifically, the court held that the services in group one were constitutional because they were either furnished directly to the student or, if furnished to the school, were so nonideological and unrelated to the educational program that there was no danger they could be used to foster religion. Nor, said the court, would there be any need for continuous monitoring resulting in government entanglement. Groups two and three, materials and services, were to be furnished directly to students, thus eliminating the danger of the establishment of religion and government entanglement. *Opinion of the Justices*, 345 A.2d 412 (N.H.1975).

In a Wisconsin case, a U.S. district court held that the award of CETA grants and contracts to religious institutions for the employment of teachers and other staff for parochial schools was unconstitutional on the grounds that such awards led to excessive entanglement with religion. *Decker v. U.S. Dep't of Labor*, 473 F.Supp. 770 (E.D.Wis.1979); see also *Decker v. O'Donnell*, 661 F.2d 598 (7th Cir.1980).

B. Classroom Equipment

In *Meek v. Pittenger*, the U.S. Supreme Court ruled unconstitutional most of a Pennsylvania program providing various types of state aid to parochial schools. This was a new program enacted by the state legislature after the Supreme Court in *Lemon v. Kurtzman* (see above) invalidated Pennsylvania's direct funding of parochial school operations. The state's new program provided that 1) textbooks would be loaned to private school students in grades K-12; 2) classroom equipment such as periodicals, photographs, maps, charts, tapes, records, films, projectors and lab equipment would be "loaned" to private schools; and 3) "auxiliary services" such as counseling, testing, and speech and hearing therapy would be provided on the private school premises by public school personnel.

The Supreme Court upheld the textbook loans but the remainder of the program was invalidated. The loaning of classroom equipment was found to present a danger that public funds would advance religion since there was no guarantee that the maps, projectors and the like would not be used for religious lessons. Unlike the loaned textbooks, which had a nonreligious content and presumably could not readily be used for religious indoctrination, maps and other equipment could easily be put to religious uses. Because maps and the like could be used to advance religion the state could not "loan" such items to parochial schools. The Supreme Court also struck down the "auxiliary services" on the ground of excessive entanglement. The Court once again stated that the political divisiveness of the Pennsylvania program caused politics and religion to mix, thus entangling the state in religion. It also emphasized that because the auxiliary services were to be provided by public school employees on the grounds of parochial schools, there was a danger that public employees might transmit or advance religious doctrines in the course of their employment. *Meek v. Pittenger*, 421 U.S. 349 (1975).

The state of Ohio attempted to circumvent the Supreme Court's ruling in *Meek v. Pittenger* by enacting a program which loaned classroom equipment to parochial school *students*, who would then place the equipment at the disposal of the school. The Supreme Court rejected this ploy:

Before *Meek* was decided by this Court, Ohio authorized the loan of material and equipment directly to the nonpublic schools. Then, in light of *Meek*, the state legislature decided to channel the goods through the parents and pupils. Despite the technical change...the program is in substance the same as before: the equipment is substantially the same; it will receive the same use by the students; and it may still be stored and distributed on the nonpublic school premises.

The Court thus rejected Ohio's attempt to provide instructional equipment (as opposed to textbooks) to parochial school students. *Wolman v. Walter*, 433 U.S. 229 (1977).

C. Diagnostic and Therapeutic Services

The *Wolman v. Walter* case (see the discussions above) placed major limitations on the Court's ruling in *Meek v. Pittenger* with regard to state provision of various types of counseling services to parochial school children. One part of the Ohio statute involved in *Wolman v. Walter* authorized the provision of diagnostic and therapeutic services. The diagnostic services were to consist of speech, hearing and psychological evaluations performed on the parochial school premises by public employees and physicians. Any treatment rendered as a result of the diagnostic evaluations would take place off the parochial school premises. The U.S. Supreme Court upheld this plan and distinguished diagnostic services from teaching or counseling. "The nature of the relationship between the diagnostician and the pupil," said the Court, "does not provide the same opportunity for the transmission of sectarian views as attends the relationship between teacher and student or that between counselor and student." Accordingly, it made no difference whether the diagnostic services were provided on or off the parochial school grounds.

The provision of therapeutic services, such as guidance counseling and remedial services, was also upheld because these services were provided to parochial school students off the parochial school premises. As long as the services were rendered at a "religiously neutral" site, said the Court, there was no danger of public employees transmitting religious views to the students. Although the Court conceded that some minimal level of monitoring would be necessary to ensure that religious views were not transmitted by the counselors to the students, this monitoring would not result in excessive entanglement: "It can hardly be said that the supervision of public employees performing public functions on public property creates an excessive entanglement between church and state." *Wolman v. Walter*, 433 U.S. 229 (1977).

VI. STUDENT AID

Grants, loans and tax credits or deductions are the most common forms of state financial assistance to private school students. Such financial assistance programs are constitutionally permissible as long as the state purpose underlying the program is to benefit both secular and religious educations.

A. Tuition Assistance

The U.S. Supreme Court unanimously ruled that the First Amendment to the U.S. Constitution did not prevent the state of Washington from providing financial assistance directly to a handicapped individual attending a Christian college. The plaintiff in this case, a blind person, sought vocational rehabilitation services from the Washington Commission for the Blind pursuant to state law [Wash.Rev.Code § 74.16.181 (1981)]. The law provided that visually handicapped persons were eligible for educational assistance to enable them to "overcome vocational handicaps and to obtain the maximum degree of self-support and self-care." However, because the plaintiff was a student at a Christian college intending to pursue a career of service in the church, the Commission for the Blind denied him assistance. The Washington Supreme Court upheld this decision on the ground that the First Amendment to the U.S. Constitution prohibited state funding of a student's education at a religious college. The U.S. Supreme Court took a less restrictive view of the First Amendment and reversed the Washington court. The operation of Washington's program was such that the Commission for the Blind paid money directly to students, who could then attend the schools of their choice. The fact that the student in this case chose to attend a religious college did not constitute state support of religion because "the decision to support religious education is made by the individual, not the state." The First Amendment was therefore not offended. *Witters v. Washington Dep't of Servs. for the Blind*, 106 S.Ct. 748 (1986).

In a Rhode Island case, a school district did not operate a public high school. Under state law, a school district that chooses not to operate a public high school is required to pay students' tuition to attend a high school. A parent in the school district requested that his son's tuition at a religiously affiliated academy be paid by the district, but the district refused. The father appealed the decision to the Rhode Island Commissioner of Education who approved the request. The school district and a taxpayer in the district filed suit in U.S. district court against the Commissioner of Education and claimed that the school district's payment of state tax money to a religious academy would be unconstitutional, since it violated the Establishment Clause of the First Amendment to the U.S. Constitution. The district court held that the commissioner had misconstrued Rhode Island law, and ruled that the school district should limit tuition reimbursement for students who attend public high schools in other school districts. The court also granted the school district its attorney's fees. The commissioner appealed the award of attorney's fees to the U.S. Court of Appeals, First Circuit. The court of appeals upheld the decision in favor of the school district. It also upheld the decision to award attorney's fees to the school district because it had succeeded on the merits of the case. In addition, the court of appeals found that the school district had possessed no alternative but to file a federal court lawsuit in order to rescind the commissioner's order to pay the private school tuition. *Exeter-West Greenwich Regional School District v. Pontarelli*, 788 F.2d 47 (1st Cir. 1986).

A twenty-year-old citizen of Vietnam who was a permanent resident alien in the United States graduated from a Virginia high school in 1984. He was severely handicapped as defined in the Vocational Rehabilitation Act of 1973. Subsequently, he applied to and was accepted for admission to St. Andrews Presbyterian College, a nonprofit liberal arts college affiliated with the Presbyterian Synod of North Carolina. The primary purpose of St. Andrews is to provide collegiate or graduate education and not to provide religious training through a theological education. The student and his foster father sought financial assistance from the state of Virginia under its program of financial aid to the handicapped, which is eighty percent federally financed and twenty percent Virginia financed. Virginia denied financial aid to the student to attend St. Andrews solely because it is a church-affiliated school located outside Virginia. Until 1969, Virginia law forbade the state from providing assistance to any church-affiliated schools through tuition grants to students. However, in that year the Virginia Constitution was amended to provide for loans to students attending in-state church-affiliated schools so long as the primary purpose of those schools was to provide collegiate or graduate education, not theological education.

The student sued the state of Virginia in a U.S. district court claiming that the denial of financial aid violated both the Establishment and Free Exercise Clauses of the First Amendment. He also contended that even if tuition aid to attend St. Andrews was properly denied, he should still receive payments for incidental expenses to attend the school. The district court ruled for the state and the student appealed to the U.S. Court of Appeals, Fourth Circuit. The appeals court explained that in order for a state law to be consistent with the Establishment Clause its primary effect must neither advance nor inhibit religion. The student contended that distinguishing between out-of-state and in-state schools on the basis of religious affiliation violated the primary effect standard because it disfavored church-affiliated schools. The appeals court disagreed, noting that the U.S. Supreme Court has recognized that a decision to fund religious studies, along with other post-secondary education, lies within the permissible zone of accommodation of religion. The court ruled that it was difficult to sustain an Establishment Clause challenge based on discrimination against religion when some Virginia funds were flowing to church-affiliated colleges.

The student also claimed that the Virginia policy infringed upon his right to the free exercise of religion since it forced him to forfeit attendance at an out-of-state religious institution in order to receive tuition aid. The court dismissed this allegation, observing that Virginia is not obligated to provide the student with an ideal learning situation. The state was only prohibited from forcing him to give up essential beliefs and practices in order to obtain tuition aid. The court of appeals reasoned that the student's free exercise of religion needs and physical needs could be met in Virginia schools. Further, the court of appeals noted that the Virginia Constitution did not prohibit the student's reimbursement for incidental expenses (books, transportation costs, living expenses, etc.) should he still choose to attend St. Andrews. Such subsidies would be to the student and not to the disqualified out-of-state school. Because Virginia provides tuition assistance to students in in-state church-affiliated schools where religious activities are required, the appeals court remanded the case to the district court to determine how the state determines the primary purpose of in-state church-affiliated schools and how it provides for their monitoring so as to insure that Virginia was not advancing in-state religious educational institutions at the expense of out-of-state institutions. *Phan v. Commonwealth of Virginia*, 806 F.2d 516 (4th Cir.1986).

A well-publicized Tennessee decision resulted in a federal court ordering a school district to pay private school tuition. In this case, a group of parents brought suit in a U.S. district court against their local school district claiming that the forced use of certain textbooks violated their right to free exercise of religion and their fundamental right to control the religious and moral instruction of their children. The parents alleged that the textbooks (the 1983 edition of the Holt, Rinehart and Winston basic reading series) conveyed the message that a belief in God was unnecessary and that any type of faith in the supernatural was an acceptable means of salvation. They also contended that after students read the Holt series they would be inclined to adopt feminist, humanist, pacifist, anti-Christian, vegetarian, and "pro-world government" viewpoints.

The district court ruled that the textbooks burdened the parents' and children's religious beliefs because the Holt series contained ideas inimical to the fundamentalist Christian faith. Further, several children had been suspended from school for refusing to read the textbooks. The court ordered the school district to accommodate the children's religious beliefs by allowing them to go to study hall or to the library during reading period, and further ordered that the students' parents ensure that their children made up the missed readings at home, using alternate textbooks in compliance with Tennessee's home instruction laws. Because the school district violated the children's constitutional rights, the district court held a hearing to determine the amount of damages to be paid to the children. After the hearing, the court concluded that the seven families were entitled to a total of $44,750 to compensate for 1) their expenses incurred in sending their children to private Christian schools and 2) other expenses they incurred in pursuing the lawsuit, such as lost wages and transportation costs. The court ruled that the First Amendment did not preclude it from ordering a public school district to assume these expenses. This case is currently on appeal to the U.S. Court of Appeals, and due to the lack of prior Supreme Court decisions on this question, educators should seek the advice of legal counsel before relying on the case. *Mozert v. Hawkins County Pub. Schools*, 647 F.Supp. 1194 (E.D.Tenn.1986).

B. Tax Deductions and Credits

In 1973 the U.S. Supreme Court invalidated a New York program which 1) provided $50-$100 in direct money grants to low-income parents with children in private schools and 2) authorized income tax credits of up to $1,000 for parents with children in private schools. The program had the primary effect of advancing religion and thus was constitutionally invalid. The Court characterized the tax credits as akin to tuition grants and observed that they were really cash giveaways by the state on behalf of religious schools. *Committee for Public Education & Religious Liberty v. Nyquist*, 413 U.S. 756 (1973).

However, in *Mueller v. Allen*, the U.S. Supreme Court upheld a Minnesota program which involved tax deductions (as opposed to tax credits) that were available to parents of public and private school children alike. The Minnesota program allowed state income tax deductions for tuition, nonreligious textbooks and transportation. In upholding the program the Court observed that the state had a legitimate interest in assuring that all its citizens were well educated. Also, the tax deductions in question were only a few among many other deductions such as those for medical expenses or charitable contributions. Unlike the program in the *Nyquist* case, the Minnesota program was part of a bona fide income tax deduction system available to parents of all school children. The Court held that the First Amendment was not offended by the Minnesota tax deduction program. *Mueller v. Allen*, 463 U.S. 388 (1983).

In New Jersey, a state statute allowing a $1,000 deduction per child from gross income to those having dependent children in nonpublic schools was held to be unconstitutional by the U.S. Court of Appeals, Third Circuit. The court noted that nearly all children attending private schools in New Jersey attend religious schools, and that the legislation was unquestionably supportive of religious education. *Pub. Funds for Pub. Schools of New Jersey v. Byrne*, 590 F.2d 514 (3d Cir.1979).

C. Tax Refunds

In Missouri, a taxpayer whose child attended a private religious school filed for a refund of that portion of his property tax which supported the public schools. The taxpayer claimed that payment of such tax imposed a practical economic burden which interefered with his constitutional right to send his child to a private school. The Missouri Supreme Court denied his claim for a tax refund. While the court sympathized with the financial burden of parents who choose not to send their children to public schools, the court held that such a self-imposed burden is not violative of the constitution. By analogy, the court cited the case of bachelors, childless couples, and corporations who paid taxes for the support of public schools and received no more benefit from such taxes than did the parents in this case, who chose to forego sending their children to free public schools. *McDonough v. Alyward*, 500 S.W.2d 721 (Mo.1973).

VII. FEDERAL AID TO SCHOOLS

Private schools receiving federal financial assistance are bound by several federal civil rights laws (see Chapter Six), among which is Title IX. These laws generally proscribe various types of discrimination. Schools where students pay their tuition with Basic Educational Opportunity Grants, National Direct Student Loans and other federal grants will be deemed as receiving assistance for federal law purposes.

The U.S. Supreme Court recently ruled on the issue of whether a private college whose students were receiving BEOGs (Basic Educational Opportunity Grants) was "receiving federal assistance" for purposes of compliance with Title IX prohibitions against discrimination on the basis of sex. A private college which had an "unbending policy" of refusing all forms of government assistance in order to remain independent of governmental restrictions was asked by the Department of Education (DOE) to supply "assurance of compliance" with Title IX, which the college refused to do on the ground that it was receiving no federal funding. The DOE disagreed, saying that because the school enrolled large numbers of students receiving federal BEOGs, it was receiving financial assistance for purposes of Title IX. The DOE then cut off students' financial assistance based on the college's failure to execute the assurance of compliance. Four students and the college brought suit challenging the termination of financial assistance. The Supreme Court held that the college was a recipient of federal financial assistance and thus subject to the statute prohibiting sex discrimination. This was so despite the fact that only some of the college's students received BEOG grants and even though the college did not receive any direct federal financial assistance. Thus, the college was obliged to submit assurance of compliance, but only with regard to the administration of its financial aid program, in order for students to continue to receive federal aid. The majority of the Court refused to adopt the dissenting justices' view that the entire college should be subjected to the strictures of Title IX. *Grove City College v. Bell*, 104 S.Ct. 1211 (1984) (see appendix for the text of the opinion).

VIII. BUILDING CONSTRUCTION, MAINTENANCE AND DISPOSAL

The courts have required strict governmental neutrality in the area of grants for buildings used by religiously affiliated educational institutions. The grant programs that have been upheld involved buildings used for nonreligious purposes or grants which were equally available to religious and nonreligious schools.

A. Construction and Maintenance Programs

In *Committee for Public Education v. Nyquist*, 413 U.S. 756 (1973), the U.S. Supreme Court held that a New York program authorizing direct money grants to private K-12 schools serving low-income families for maintenance and repair of buildings was unconstitutional. The primary effect of this program was to "subsidize and advance the religious mission of sectarian schools."

State aid to religion in the context of higher education has fared much better. In *Hunt v. McNair*, the Supreme Court upheld a South Carolina plan which allowed both private and public colleges to use the state's authority to borrow money at low interest rates. The case involved a Baptist college which used this money to finance the construction of a dining hall. The college had no religious test for either its faculty or students and the student body was only about sixty percent Baptist, the same percentage found in the surrounding community. The Supreme Court found that the college was not "pervaded by religion." Unlike the situation commonly found in K-12 parochial schools, religiously-affiliated colleges and universities are often not dominated by a religious atmosphere. The Court concluded that both the purpose and effect of the state's borrowing program was secular and was therefore constitutional. The argument that aid to one (secular) portion of a religious institution makes it free to spend more money on religious pursuits was rejected as unpersuasive and irrelevant. If that were the case, the Court noted that police and fire protection for religious schools would have to be cut off as well. *Hunt v. McNair*, 413 U.S. 734 (1973).

A 1971 case involved the federal Higher Education Facilities Act of 1963. This federal funding program offered assistance to both public and private colleges in constructing academic facilities. Although the program mandated that any building constructed with federal assistance be used by private colleges only for nonreligious purposes, it stated that after twenty years the buildings could be put to religious uses if the private college so desired. The U.S. Supreme Court upheld most of this program against constitutional challenges. The Court, however, invalidated the portion of the program that would have lifted the religious uses provision after twenty years. *Tilton v. Richardson*, 403 U.S. 672 (1971).

A more recent case illustrates the Supreme Court's reluctance to invalidate state aid given for secular purposes. The state of Maryland enacted a program which authorized annual, noncategorical grants to religiously affiliated colleges. The program was challenged by taxpayers who alleged that state money was being put to religious uses by the schools, which had wide discretion in spending the funds. The Supreme Court began its analysis of the Maryland program with the following observation:

> *Hunt [v. McNair]* requires (1) that no state aid at all go to institutions that are so "pervasively sectarian" that secular activities cannot be separated from sectarian ones, and (2) that if secular activities *can* be separated out, they alone may be funded.

The colleges involved in this case were not found to be pervasively sectarian even though they were affiliated with the Roman Catholic Church. The Court held that the "secular side" of the colleges could be separated from the sectarian, and found that state aid had only gone to the colleges' secular side. It was admittedly somewhat difficult to ensure that the colleges and the Maryland Council for Higher Education would take care to avoid spending state funds on religious acitivities, but the Court expressed its belief that those entities would spend the money in good faith and avoid violating the First Amendment. *Roemer v. Board of Public Works*, 426 U.S. 736 (1976).

B. Zoning

The following case discusses the ability of a private, nonreligious school to take advantage of a zoning law designed to benefit public and parochial schools.

Rhode Island law prohibits the issuance of certain types of liquor licenses to any business located within 200 feet of a public or parochial school. In September, 1983, the city of East Providence, Rhode Island, granted a class-B limited alcoholic beverage license for the sale of beer to a business located within 200 feet of the Children's Place, Ltd., a private preschool. The preschool appealed the granting of the license and a liquor control administrator reversed the grant. The would-be licensee appealed to a Rhode Island superior court which upheld the liquor control administrator's denial of licensing. The licensee appealed to the Rhode Island Supreme Court. The licensee contended that the 200-foot limit only applied to public or parochial schools. He also argued that by interpreting the law to include private nonsectarian schools, the superior court judge essentially rewrote the law. The supreme court observed that where "the language of a statute is clear and unambiguous, the statute may not be construed or extended but must be applied literally." The supreme court concluded that the preschool did not fall within the Rhode Island law. The private preschool was not established or maintained at public expense and was not associated with or sponsored by a religious denomination. Because the preschool was a privately funded, for-profit institution it was not entitled to the protection of the 200-foot limit.

The court noted that if it had not interpreted the statute in a manner consistent with the legislative intent to promote temperance, the legislature could expand the law to include private schools. The liquor license was ordered to be reinstated. *Pizza Hut of America, Inc. v. Pastore*, 519 A.2d 592 (R.I.1987).

C. Disposal of Federal Property

As the case below indicates, persons wishing to object to conveyances of federal property to religious schools must be able to demonstrate 1) that the conveyance will actually harm them, and 2) that the conveyance is unconstitutional.

The U.S. Supreme Court held that the Americans United for Separation of Church and State lacked "standing" to challenge a governmental conveyance of surplus property to a private religious school. Federal law authorizes the U.S. Secretary of Education to dispose of surplus real property for educational use. Property which was formerly used as a military hospital valued at $557,500 was conveyed to a private religious school without any financial payment. The taxpayer-citizen group challenged this conveyance on the ground that it violated the Establishment Clause of the First Amendment to the U.S. Constitution. The Court rejected that challenge since the group could show no injury to itself or its members as a consequence of the conveyance. Thus, the group had no real interest in objecting to the conveyance of federal property to the religious college. *Valley Forge Christian College v. Americans United for Separation of Church & State*, 102 S.Ct. 752 (1982).

IX. TAXATION OF PRIVATE SCHOOLS

(See also Chapter Two, Unemployment Taxation.)

There is no constitutional requirement that religious or other schools be afforded tax exemption. Such exemption is generally a question of state or federal statutory law.

A. Federal Income Taxation

Section 501(c)(3) of the Internal Revenue Code provides that "corporations...organized and operated exclusively for religious, charitable...or educational purposes" are entitled to tax exempt status. The Internal Revenue Service routinely granted tax exemption under § 501(c)(3) to private schools regardless of whether they had racially discriminatory admissions policies. In 1970, however, the IRS concluded that it could no longer grant tax exempt status to racially discriminatory private schools because such schools were not "charitable" within the meaning of § 501(c)(3). In *Bob Jones University v. United States*, two private colleges whose racial admissions policies were rooted in their interpretations of the Bible sued to prevent the IRS from interpreting the federal tax laws in this manner. The Supreme Court rejected the colleges' challenge and upheld the IRS's interpretation.

The Court's ruling was based on what it perceived as the strong public policy against racial discrimination in education. Because the colleges were operating in violation of that public policy, the colleges could not be considered to be "charitable" under § 501(c)(3). Thus they were ineligible for tax exemption. The Court held that in order to fall under the exemption of § 501(c)(3) an institution must be in harmony with the public interest. It also held that the denial of an exemption did not impermissibly burden Bob Jones' alleged religious freedom interest in practicing racial discrimination. The lone dissenting opinion in the case was filed by then-Justice Rehnquist, who accused the majority of "legislat[ing] for Congress." Justice Rehnquist argued that because no provision in the Internal Revenue Code specifically precluded racially discriminatory private schools from seeking tax exempt status, the schools should be entitled to federal tax exemption. *Bob Jones University v. United States*, 461 U.S. 574 (1983) (see appendix for the text of the opinion).

A 1984 Supreme Court case provided a sequel to the *Bob Jones* decision. Here, parents of black public school children sought a federal court order requiring the IRS to adopt more stringent standards for determining whether private schools had racially discriminatory admissions policies. The black parents claimed that the IRS standards were too lax, and that certain private schools were practicing racial discrimination and were nevertheless obtaining tax exemption. The Supreme Court dismissed the parents' claims and held that they had no right to challenge the IRS standards (i.e., they lacked "standing"). The ruling rested on the Court's perception that the parents and children had shown no injury to themselves as a result of the allegedly lax IRS standards. None of the children had sought enrollment at the private schools involved, and the abstract stigma attached to living in a community with racially discriminatory private schools was also insufficient to show actual injury. Further, the parents' theory that denial of tax exemption to such schools would result in greater white student enrollment in area public schools, and hence result in a greater degree of public school integration, was too speculative to confer standing. The Court therefore refused to allow the parents to interfere with IRS discretion in setting standards by which to evaluate the admissions policies of private schools. *Allen v. Wright*, 104 S.Ct. 3315 (1984).

The Virginia Education Fund was established to solicit funds for distribution to segregated private schools for whites desiring to avoid integration in the public schools. The IRS originally granted the fund tax exemption in 1961 when IRS policy permitted segregated schools to qualify as charitable organizations under § 501(c)(3). The IRS changed the policy in 1970 (see above) and announced that it would no longer recognize the tax exempt status of any private school that failed to show that it operated with a racially nondiscriminatory admissions policy. The IRS revoked the fund's exemptions in 1977, retroactive to 1974. The fund sued the commissioner of the IRS but the tax court upheld the IRS decision. The fund appealed to the U.S. Court of Appeals, Fourth Circuit. The appeals court upheld the tax court decision which retroactively denied tax exempt status to the fund. The court reasoned that the fund had made no effort to demonstrate that private schools receiving funds had adopted nondiscriminatory admissions policies. Acknowledging that IRS procedures are guidelines without force of law, the court observed that the fund's failure to introduce any evidence supporting its exempt status justified the decision of the IRS to revoke that status. The court further observed that there was no reason to excuse the fund from the general ongoing burden that all taxpayers bear to prove themselves tax exempt. *Virginia Education Fund v. Commissioner of Internal Revenue*, 799 F.2d 903 (4th Cir.1986).

B. Local Property Taxation

The Michigan Tax Tribunal denied exemption from property taxation as a charitable and/or educational institution to a taxpayer group which ran a camp allegedly devoted to educational purposes. The state court of appeals upheld the Tax Tribunal's determination, holding that while the group's activities focus on cooperative education and are both commendable and of benefit to the participants, it cannot be said that such programs "sufficiently relieve the government's education burden to warrant the claimed educational-institution exemption." In addition, since the group allowed its facilities to be used by outside organizations for the sole purpose of generating profit, it failed to satisfy one of the main criteria for being granted exemption. *Circle Pines Cent. v. Orangeville Township*, 302 N.W.2d 917 (Mich.App.1981).

In 1947, Middlebury College sued the town of Hancock claiming that Vermont law allowed for a tax exemption on a piece of land (the Snow Bowl) the college owned in Hancock. The law exempted from taxation "real and personal estate granted, sequestered or used for public, pious or charitable uses." Another clause exempted "lands owned by colleges." The Vermont Supreme Court, in a 1947 decision, had held that the Snow Bowl was not "owned" by the college in a beneficial sense since the college only had a trustee-type ownership of the land "and it was not for the appropriate use and benefit of the institution as a college in carrying out the purposes of its incorporation." The college was therefore required to pay property taxes to the town of Hancock. In this lawsuit the college sued claiming that because it owned the Snow Bowl and its improvements, it was entitled to an exemption as "college owned public use" land. When the lower court ruled in favor of the college, the town of Hancock appealed to the Vermont Supreme Court. In ruling against the college, the supreme court looked to a new state law which did not exist in its present form in the 1947 decision. The new law stated that the public use exemption "shall not be construed as exempting" certain properties from taxation. Among properties subject to taxation were "real and personal property of an organization used primarily for recreational purposes," unless the town voted an exemption. The supreme court concluded that although the Snow Bowl was for public use, the use was primarily recreational and it was therefore subject to taxation by the town of Hancock. *Middlebury College v. Town of Hancock*, 514 A.2d 1061 (Vt.1986).

In 1932, the trustees of Amherst College in the District of Columbia established the Folger Shakespeare Library, which was administered by Amherst in accordance with the last will and testament of Henry Clay Folger. The will provided for the maintenance, expansion and administration of the library. The main library building, which contained the Shakespeare Library collection of Folger, had previously been granted an exemption from real property taxation by the District of Columbia. The applicable statute exempted "[b]uildings belonging to and operated by schools, colleges or universities which are not organized or operated for private gain, or which embrace the generally recognized relationship of teacher and student." Amherst College was sued by the District of Columbia in a superior court for 1983-84 real property taxes. The District of Columbia argued that several library-related properties located one block from the main Shakespeare Library building did not fall within the exemption statute. When the superior court ruled for Amherst, the District of Columbia appealed to the D.C. Court of Appeals.

The library-related properties included housing for visiting library lecturers and scholars, storage areas for the Folger Library Theater and a vacant lot. The District of Columbia argued that neither the buildings nor the vacant lot belonged to Amherst College because the will of Henry Clay Folger designated Amherst as trustee of a charitable trust, giving the trustees bare legal title and no enforceable equitable interest. The District of Columbia further argued that where the title to certain property is held in trust, the right to a tax exemption is determined by the nature of the equitable interest.

In affirming the lower court decision, the court of appeals allowed tax exemption for all of the properties except the vacant lot. The exempt properties were deemed to be required and actually used for carrying on the activities of an exempt organization. The court of appeals rejected the conclusion that Amherst's status as a trustee of a charitable trust defeated the right to real property tax exemption. The court ruled that Amherst was a college which embraced "the generally recognized relationship of teacher and student" and further observed that the properties in question belonged to Amherst and that these properties were not used for gain. Any rents collected from visiting scholars and students were nominal and therefore Amherst was entitled to full tax exempt status for the library-related properties for the tax years 1983-84. The appellate court refused to allow real property tax exemption for the vacant lot because, although the vacant lot was acquired for possible future expansion, tax exemption is not allowed until such expansion has at least begun. The court affirmed the superior court decision to allow real property tax exemption on all of the library-related properties except the vacant lot. *District of Columbia v. Trustees of Amherst College*, 515 A.2d 1115 (D.C.App.1986).

Friends School, a private school in Baltimore City, Maryland, was assessed property taxes on a caretaker's residence located on school property. The residence had been built in the 1940's to specifically house the caretaker. Until the current assessment, the caretaker's residence had always been exempt from property tax. The school appealed the assessment to the Maryland Tax Court, which determined that since the residence was not used for an academic function, Friends School was not entitled to a tax exemption on the property. A circuit court reversed the decision and found that the residence was "essential and necessary" to the operation of the school and thus was exempt from taxation. The Supervisor of City Assessments appealed. The Maryland Court of Special Appeals stated that under Maryland law a three-prong test is used to determine if property is exempt from taxation. To be exempt the property must be 1) owned by the education institution or organization, 2) actually used and necessary for educational purposes of that institution or organization, and 3) used in the promotion of the general public welfare of the citizens.

The institution was owned by the school, so it easily satisfied the first prong of the test. The court observed that under the second prong, the property must be directly related to the educational uses of the institution in order to be considered "actually used" and "necessary" for education. This is determined by several factors, such as the type of institution, the needs of the student body, the location of the school, the proximity of the property to the students or campus buildings, and whether services performed on the property can be contracted out or are shared by other employees. At Friends School, the caretaker performed primarily security and maintenance functions. However, the school operated during the day and required no special care for students at night, and any possible harm to the property was protected by the school's night watchman. In addition, when the caretaker was on vacation, no one lived in the caretaker's residence. For this reason, the court held that the caretaker's duties neither directly nor indirectly furthered the educational goals of the school. The court therefore ruled that the school did not satisfy the second prong of the test. While the third prong of the test required that the exempted school property promote the "general public welfare," the only purpose the caretaker's residence served was to provide housing for the caretaker. Since the school could not meet two of the three prongs of the test, the court held that the school was required to pay the taxes assessed on the caretaker's residence. *Supervisor of Assessments of Baltimore City v. Friends School*, 508 A.2d 514 (Md.App.1986).

CHAPTER FIVE
HANDICAPPED CHILDREN

Page

I. STATES' DUTY TO EDUCATE 120

II. TUITION REIMBURSEMENT 121

III. CHANGE IN PLACEMENT 127

IV. CIVIL RIGHTS LAWSUITS ....,............127

V. PRIVATE SCHOOL ELIGIBILITY TO
EDUCATE HANDICAPPED CHILDREN 128

VI. FACILITIES AND PROGRAMS 130

VII. CONTRACT DISPUTES 131

I. STATES' DUTY TO EDUCATE

The Education for All Handicapped Children Act of 1975 (EAHCA) requires each state to provide handicapped children with a free appropriate public education (see also Chapter Six, Section V). Because public school districts and parents often turn to private schools for the special educational services required by handicapped children, the provisions of the EAHCA are of great importance to private educators.

The term *handicapped children* is defined in the EAHCA as any children who are "mentally retarded, hard of hearing, deaf, speech or language impaired, visually handicapped, seriously emotionally disturbed, orthopedically impaired, or other health impaired children, or children with specific learning disabilities, who by reason thereof require special education and related services" [20 U.S.C. § 1401(1)]. The public schools must provide all such children with a *free appropriate public education*, which means "special education and related services which (A) have been provided at public expense, under public supervision and direction, and without charge, (B) meet the standards of the State educational agency, (C) include an appropriate preschool, elementary, or secondary school education in the State involved, and (D) are provided in conformity with the individualized education program required under section 1414(a)(5) of this title" [§ 1401(18)].

The above-mentioned *related services* are in turn defined as "transportation, and such developmental, corrective, and other supportive services (including speech pathology and audiology, pyschological services, physical and occupational therapy, recreation, and medical and counseling services, except that such medical services shall be for diagnostic and evaluation purposes only) as may be required to assist a handicapped child to benefit from special education, and includes the early identification and assessment of handicapping conditions in children" [§ 1401(17)]. While medical services are excluded from the definition of related services, insofar as they may be needed by a child for diagnostic and evaluative purposes, medical services must also be provided free of charge.

Section 1401(17) states that psychological services are related services and thus are to be provided free of charge by school districts to handicapped students who require such services. While it is clear that not all services involving psychotherapy are related services, if the psychotherapy required by the child is of the type that could be provided by a social worker, school psychologist, nurse or counselor, it will be considered a related service. Where the required psychotherapy is of such a nature that it can only be competently administered by a licensed psychiatrist, then it will be considered a medical service and the school district will not be required to furnish it. Thus, a U.S. district court in New Jersey held that a school district was required to pay $25,200 for a child's stay at a day school which provided individualized psychotherapy, family therapy, group therapy, and individual and group counseling. The court held that the psychotherapy provided here was an integral part of the child's special education. See *T.G. v. Board of Education*, 576 F.Supp. 420 (D.N.J.1983). Under § 1401(17), even medical and psychiatric services must be provided free of charge if such services are required for evaluative or diagnostic purposes. See *Darlene L. v. Illinois State Board of Education*, 568 F.Supp. 1340 (N.D.Ill.1983).

Section 1415 of the EAHCA contains mandatory procedures designed to safeguard the rights of handicapped students. The safeguards emphasize, among other things, notice to parents and an opportunity for parental participation in the development of a child's special education program. Most important, the various subsections under § 1415 require that parents be informed of all available procedures and methods by which any grievances or dissatisfactions may be resolved. Written notice must be given to parents if a school proposes to change or refuses to initiate a change in a child's educational program, or if the school refuses to perform an initial evaluation and placement of the child [§ 1415(b)(1)(C)].

In case of any dispute over their child's IEP, § 1415 of the EAHCA states that parents have the right to an impartial hearing before a hearing officer who is neither an employee of the school district nor of the state education department [§ 1415(b)(2)]. If either the parents or the school are unhappy with the hearing officer's decision, an appeal may be taken to the state education department [§ 1415(c)]. During the pendency of a dispute over any aspect of a special education program, the child must remain in his or her "then current" education program [§ 1415(e)(3)]. A lawsuit may be commenced in either state or federal court after a decision has been reached by the state education department [§ 1415(e)(2)].

II. TUITION REIMBURSEMENT

One area in which the EAHCA takes on major importance is tuition reimbursement. Dissatisfied parents frequently remove their children from public school special education programs and obtain enrollment in private school programs; the parents then rely on the courts to order the public school district to pay the private school tuition and/or living expenses. In *Burlington School Committee v. Department of Education of Massachusetts*, the U.S. Supreme Court ruled that public school districts must pay private school tuition and related expenses only where the school district fails to offer an appropriate special education program to a handicapped student.

In the *Burlington* case, the father of a learning disabled third grade boy became dissatisfied with his son's lack of progress in the Burlington, Massachusetts, public school system. A new IEP was developed for the child which called for placement in a different public school. The father, however, followed the advice of specialists at Massachusetts General Hospital and unilaterally withdrew his son from the Burlington school system, placing him instead at the Carroll School, a state-approved private facility in Lincoln, Massachusetts. He then sought reimbursement for tuition and transportation expenses from the Burlington School Committee, contending that the IEP which proposed a public school placement was inappropriate.

The state Board of Special Education Appeals (BSEA) ruled that the proposed IEP was inappropriate and that, therefore, the father had been justified in placing his son at the Carroll School. The BSEA ordered the

Burlington School Committee to reimburse the father for tuition and transportation expenses, and the School Committee appealed to the federal courts. A U.S. district court held that the parents had violated the status quo provision of the EAHCA by enrolling their child in the private school without the agreement of public school officials. Thus, they were not entitled to reimbursement. The U.S. Court of Appeals, First Circuit, reversed the district court's ruling, and the Burlington School Committee appealed to the U.S. Supreme Court.

In upholding the court of appeals' decision, the Supreme Court ruled that parents who place a handicapped child in a private educational facility are entitled to reimbursement for the child's tuition and living expenses, *if* a court later determines that the school district had proposed an inappropriate individualized educational program. Reimbursement could not be ordered if the school district's proposed individualized educational program was later found to be appropriate. The Supreme Court observed that to bar reimbursement claims under all circumstances would be contrary to the EAHCA, which favors proper interim placements for handicapped children.

In addition, under the School Committee's reading of the EAHCA status quo provision, parents would be forced to leave their child in what might later be determined to be an inappropriate educational placement, or would obtain the appropriate placement only by sacrificing any claim for reimbursement. This result, found the Court, was not intended by Congress. However, the Court noted that "[t]his is not to say that [this provision] has no effect on parents." Parents who unilaterally change their children's placement during the pendency of proceedings do so at their own financial risk. If the courts ultimately determine that a child's proposed IEP was appropriate, the parents are barred from obtaining reimbursement for an unauthorized private school placement. *Burlington School Committee v. Dep't of Education of Massachusetts*, 105 S.Ct. 1996 (1985).

In a Virginia case, lack of state approval of a private school prevented parental reimbursement for tuition and related expenses. After being declared eligible for special education services, the fourteen-year-old boy involved in this case was placed by the Fairfax County public schools in the Lab School in Washington, D.C. Later, Fairfax County determined that the Lab School no longer met the boy's special needs and proposed a placement at the Little Keswick School, Inc., a Virginia residential school for handicapped children. This private facility was approved by the Virginia Department of Education.

Upon receiving Fairfax County's offer of placement at Little Keswick, the boy's mother wrote to Fairfax rejecting the proposal. She instead suggested that Fairfax fund her son's placement at the East Hill Farm and School in Andover, Vermont. Fairfax refused, stating that East Hill was not on the Virginia Department of Education's list of approved schools. The mother nonetheless placed her son at East Hill and requested a due process hearing to resolve the question of reimbursement for tuition and living expenses. The hearing officer provided by Fairfax County conducted a full and open evidentiary hearing, after which he concluded that Little Keswick was an appropriate placement. The boy's parents appealed; the state review officer affirmed. The parents then brought an action in federal district court seeking further review.

The district court reviewed the evidence and concluded that Fairfax County was not obligated to fund the East Hill placement. Two grounds were specified for the county's decision. First, the Little Keswick School was approved by the Virginia Department of Education. The EAHCA's § 1413(a)(4)(B)(ii) allows states to establish minimum educational standards as a precondition to state approval of any school. This power of approval is expressly permitted by the EAHCA. Little Keswick was therefore an appropriate placement, said the court.

Second, East Hill was not on Virginia's list of approved schools. Indeed, it was not even on Vermont's list of schools certified for special education. Only one of East Hill's ten staff members was a certified teacher. In the court's view, lack of approval by the Virginia Department of Education precluded reimbursement. "Parents of handicapped students may not, because of personal desires, select a private institution of their choice and have the school system pay for the tuition," declared the court. "While the desires of the parents may be well motivated in that they seek the best for their child, the placement decision must be made by the school system in accordance with approved standards." The court affirmed the denial of reimbursement to the parents for the costs incurred in placing their child at the East Hill School. *Schimmel v. Spillane*, 630 F.Supp. 159 (E.D.Va.1986).

A California school district was ordered to pay the tuition and related expenses for a learning disabled boy whose parents had unilaterally placed him in an out-of-state private residential facility. In November, 1976, the boy's first individualized educational program, in which he was classified as suffering from a mild learning disability, was formulated by school district officials. The boy progressed and by June, 1977, he had successfully been partially integrated into regular classes. A new IEP was formulated at this time which provided that he continue in regular classes with minimal supplementary educational services. Three months later, in September, 1977, another IEP was developed which noted the boy's progress and recommended continued regular placement with some special education assistance. However, his performance and behavior suffered greatly during the ensuing 1977-78 school year. School officials observed increased anger, hostility and rebelliousness during this period. The boy's parents were contacted in February, 1978, and a review session was held at which it was agreed that the September, 1977 IEP would remain in effect.

At the close of the 1977-78 school year, the boy was removed from school after slashing the tires on a teacher's car. He also ran away from home in August, 1978, and was consequently made a ward of the juvenile court. His behavior was described as "self-destructive" with "poor impulse control." In the fall of 1978 the boy was enrolled in the local high school where school officials, with the concurrence of his parents, tentatively decided that his September, 1977, IEP would remain in effect. He was thereafter truant from school on numerous occasions and ran away from home again for a week in September, 1978, at which time he committed the offenses of joyriding and marijuana possession. He spent the remainder of the school year in juvenile hall and various youth residential facilities. The school district made no effort to reevaluate the boy or develop a new IEP during this period.

Due to the school district's failure to properly evaluate their son, the parents decided to enroll him in a private residential facility in Utah in

March, 1979, and asked that the school district pay the cost of his placement. The district, however, stated that it would pay only educational expenses at the facility. The parents requested a due process hearing on the matter and the hearing panel found that because the parents had acted unilaterally in placing their son at the residential facility, thereby breaching the "status quo" provision of the Education for All Handicapped Children Act, the school district was not liable for the cost of the placement. The parents appealed and the California Court of Appeal held that the school district was liable under the EAHCA for the boy's educational and related expenses at the private, out-of-state residential facility.

The court based its decision on the failure of the school district to develop an IEP for the boy annually, as required by the EAHCA. An IEP had been formulated in September, 1977, but as of April, 1979, a new IEP had not been developed. The court rejected the school district's contention that because the boy had been truant and was frequently involved in the juvenile court system, it would have been difficult to properly evaluate him. The boy's status in the juvenile court system was well known to school officials and their failure to update the "manifestly inappropriate" September, 1977, IEP was characterized by the court as evidence of bad faith. The school district was therefore ordered to pay the cost of the private school placement. Attorney's fees were also awarded to the boy's parents. *In Re John K.*, 216 Cal.Rptr. 557 (App.1st Dist.1985).

A special education dispute of fourteen years' duration was recently settled by the U.S. Court of Appeals, Third Circuit. The court of appeals upheld a U.S. district court's ruling that the Westfield, New Jersey, board of education was not liable for the cost of nine years of private school placement. The child in this case was first identified as handicapped in 1968. At that time the Westfield Board of Education placed the child at the Midland School, a private facility. In 1972, further testing was performed by outside experts as well as Westfield's child study team. The child was thereafter labeled "mentally retarded-educable" by the child study team, and an IEP was formulated which called for placement at a different institution, the Tamaques School. Objecting to the label "mentally retarded-educable" (the parents felt their child was neurologically impaired), as well as the change in placement, the parents kept him at Midland and paid the tuition themselves.

In 1975, the parents filed a petition with the New Jersey Department of Education seeking review of Westfield's 1972 reclassification decision. The parents contended that during the pendency of all review proceedings, Westfield was obligated to pay for their child's tuition at Midland, since § 1415(e)(3) of the EAHCA requires that a child remain in his or her "then current" placement until review is completed. Due to the department's failure to comply with the procedural requirements of the EAHCA, a proper hearing on the merits of the parents' claim was not held until June 9, 1983.

During the period between the filing of the petition in 1975 and the 1983 hearing officer's decision, the child was evaluated many times by Westfield's child study team as well as the parents' outside experts. In 1976, the child study team changed its classification from mentally retarded-educable to "Multiply Handicapped: Primary—Mentally Retarded-Educable; Secondary—Neurologically Impaired." The child study team, however, did not change its recommendation of placement at the Tamaques School. Adhering to their view that the child study team's classifications were erroneous, the parents continued their child at the Midland School.

In 1980, the parents placed their child at the Maplebrook School. One year later, the Westfield child study team reclassified the child as "Neurologically or Perceptually Impaired: Perceptually Impaired" and agreed to fund the Maplebrook placement. An IEP was developed and agreed to, and pursuant to this IEP the child graduated from Maplebrook in the spring of 1982. The Westfield Board of Education granted a diploma to the child and contended that its responsibility for his education had terminated. The parents disagreed and enrolled him in the Summit Collegiate Studies Center in Jerusalem, Israel.

At the due process hearing in 1983, the parents claimed that they were entitled to tuition reimbursement for their child's education at the Midland school from 1972 to 1981, since they were entitled to leave their child at Midland during all review proceedings. They also claimed that the Westfield Board of Education was liable for the period their child attended school in Jerusalem. The hearing officer denied the parents' claims and they filed an action in U.S. district court, seeking review, but the court upheld the hearing officer's decision. The parents appealed their case to the U.S. Court of Appeals, Third Circuit, which similarly agreed with the hearing officer. The appeals court stated that since § 1415(e)(3) had not become effective until 1977, the Westfield Board of Education was relieved of responsibility for its 1972 decision to change the child's educational placement from Midland to Tamaques. Thus, the parents' decision to keep their child at Midland was not protected by § 1415(e)(3). The appeals court ruled that the parents should have placed the child at Tamaques in accordance with Westfield's 1972 recommendation.

The court also held that under § 1412(2)(B), the Westfield Board of Education would be responsible for the post-graduation education of the child only if the board made it a regular practice to educate children even after they had graduated. Since the board did not, and since the child had already graduated when his parents sent him to the school in Jerusalem, the board was not liable for those expenses. Noting that all the classifications and placements proposed by Westfield's child study team were appropriate under the EAHCA, the court of appeals affirmed the prior rulings against the parents. *Wexler v. Westfield Board of Education*, 784 F.2d 176 (3d Cir.1986).

Relying on the EAHCA's status quo provision, a U.S. district court ordered the New York City Board of Education to fund a handicapped child's placement at a private educational facility. The city's school system, explained the court, had been operating since 1982 under a federal court order which mandated that an offer of a public school placement must be made by the school system within sixty days of a child's identification as a handicapped individual. Under the court order, if the child is not offered such a placement within sixty days the parents have the right to place the child in a private facility at the board's expense.

The present case arose when a child was unilaterally enrolled by his parents in the Hebrew Academy for Special Children as provided by the order described above. The board agreed to pay for the placement at the academy, but at the beginning of the following school year it once again recommended public school placement. The parents, however, desired to keep their child at the academy, and he remained there during the due process hearings which ensued. The hearings culminated in an order by the state education commissioner that the board was required to fund the child's education at the academy, and the board appealed to a U.S. district court.

Ruling that the Hebrew Academy had become the child's "then current" educational placement under the EAHCA, the court upheld the commissioner's order. By initially failing to offer a placement within the required sixty days, the board had given the parents the unqualified right to place the child in a private facility at the board's expense. That placement then became the status quo, which could not be altered by the board until such time as they offered an acceptable placement. Under the EAHCA, the board then became unconditionally liable for the resulting tuition and related expenses. The court affirmed the commissioner's order of reimbursement for the parents' cost of placing the child at the Hebrew Academy. *Board of Education v. Ambach*, 628 F.Supp. 972 (E.D.N.Y.1986).

Another New York case, which also relied on New York City's sixty-day placement order, resulted in an award of tuition for private school placement. The parents of an emotionally handicapped student had sought to enroll their son in the New York City public school system in 1982. However, due to enormous delays by the Board of Education's Committee on the Handicapped (COH), the parents placed their son in a private facility. This was done pursuant to the 1982 court order, which attempted to prod New York's COH into action by granting parents of handicapped children in New York City the right to choose private school placement if the board's COH did not recommend an appropriate placement within sixty days of proposed entry of a child into the public school system. After the parents in this case enrolled their child in the private facility, the COH evaluated him and recommended public school placement. The parents disagreed with this recommendation and requested a hearing.

This hearing, which took place in March, 1983, resulted in a determination that the COH had not followed proper procedures, rendering its recommendation null and void. In May, 1983, the COH once again evaluated the child and again proposed a public school placement. The parents requested a hearing and this time an impartial hearing officer found that the COH's recommendation was proper. Appeal was taken to the state commissioner of education, who issued a decision in April, 1984, upholding the COH recommendation of public school placement. The commission also found that the board of education was liable for the child's private school tuition up until the date of the commissioner's decision. The board appealed to a U.S. district court, seeking a reversal of the award of tuition costs. The court stated that the Education for All Handicapped Children Act's status quo provision should govern, and hence upheld the award.

The court noted that the parents had placed their child in the private school pursuant to a court order intended to eliminate delay by New York's COH. This placement therefore became the child's "then current" educational placement, and the child was entitled to remain their until all review proceedings were completed. The fact that the COH later formulated an acceptable public school placement program for the child did not relieve the board of its duty to fund the child's private school placement until the COH's proposal was approved. The court then proceeded to award the parents the cost of the private school tuition, but only through April, 1984, the date of the commissioner's approval of the COH's public school placement recommendation. *Board of Education v. Ambach*, 612 F.Supp. 230 (E.D.N.Y.1985).

III. CHANGE IN PLACEMENT

Both private and public schools may not change the educational placement of a handicapped child while a court proceeding concerning the child is pending.

Two U.S. district court cases held, respectively, that a school for the blind located in New York and a Connecticut school district would not be allowed to expel handicapped students pending proceedings to determine an approprite placement for the children. *Sherry v. New York State Department of Education*, 479 F.Supp. 1328 (W.D.N.Y.1979), and *Stuart v. Nappi*, 443 F.Supp. 1235 (D.Conn.1978).

Woods Schools, an approved Pennsylvania nonprofit corporation, operates a residential private school for exceptional children. In March, 1985, an exceptional child from the Central Dauphin School District enrolled at Woods. In August, 1985, Woods requested that Central Dauphin and the child's parents find an alternate placement for the child. In October, 1985, Woods requested that Central Dauphin initiate due process proceedings leading to the child's removal since § 171.18 of the Standards of Approved Private Schools (Standards) provides that "an approved private school may not...disenroll a student...until notice and the opportunity for a hearing have been given in accordance with Chapter 13 (relative to special education)." Central Dauphin refused and in December, 1985, Woods filed a petition with the Commonwealth Court of Pennsylvania stating that Woods was not receiving the full cost of the child's program and that the child was admitted to Woods upon the express condition that Central Dauphin bear the full cost of the child's program at Woods. In ruling for Central Dauphin (represented by the Pennsylvania Department of Education) the court reasoned that it could not yet be determined what Woods' reimbursement would be and therefore it could not adjudicate the cost controversy. Woods emphasized that its primary claim was its inability to initiate due process procedures to disenroll the child. The court observed that § 171.20(a) of the Standards states that an "approved private school shall operate in accordance with this chapter" and that Woods knew of the Standards' cost restrictions when it agreed to accept the child. The court observed that Woods was bound by and limited to the steps outlined in administrative agency law in seeking additional reimbursement. The court also concluded that the best interest of the private school is irrelevant when determining the best interest of the child. Woods was required to continue serving the child until either the parent or school district determined that its program was inadequate. The court ruled that Woods must pursue a remedy as to the educational costs and replacement of the child through administrative procedures outlined by the Standards before it could look to the court for help. *Woods Schools v. Commonwealth Department of Education*, 514 A.2d 686 (Pa.Cmwlth.1986).

IV. CIVIL RIGHTS LAWSUITS

The EAHCA allows handicapped students and their parents to sue public school districts under the federal civil rights laws, regardless of whether the student is enrolled in a public or private school program.

In 1986, Congress enacted the Handicapped Children's Protection Act (P.L. 99-372), which amended the EAHCA to include awards of attorney's fees to handicapped students who prevail in special education lawsuits. The Act also provided that § 1983 of the Civil Rights Act and § 504 of the Rehabilitation Act can be utilized by handicapped students. It is likely that this action by Congress will result in a greater willingness on the part of handicapped students' parents to seek private school tuition payments from public school districts.

V. PRIVATE SCHOOL ELIGIBILITY TO EDUCATE HANDICAPPED CHILDREN

States receiving federal funding under the EAHCA are required to maintain a list of approved private schools to educate handicapped children where no public school program is available or appropriate. Disputes sometimes arise among states, private schools and students when a private school is excluded, for a particular reason or reasons, from the state's list of approved private schools.

New Jersey's department of education issued detailed regulations governing private schools which educate handicapped children. The regulations applied only to private schools to which local school boards have sent handicapped children in order to satisfy the local board's educational obligations. These private schools were required to submit detailed budgets, establish strict bookkeeping and accounting procedures, submit to annual audits by the state, and most objectionably, a school's profit was limited to 2.5% of its per pupil costs. Several private school associations sued the department seeking to have the regulations declared invalid. They claimed that the regulations were "confiscatory" and had been enacted without proper authority.

The New Jersey Superior Court, Appellate Division, upheld the regulations as within the scope of the department's powers. Especially persuasive to the court was the argument that private schools, by choosing to accept handicapped students on referral from local school boards, should expect to relinquish a degree of privacy and autonomy over their affairs. The 2.5% profit ceiling was a reasonable exercise of department authority over private schools which, said the court, had voluntarily submitted to department control. However, the court left open the possibility that in the future, if a private school were able to show that due to its financial condition the regulations were unreasonable as applied to it, then a waiver of the regulations might be justified. *Council of Private Schools for Children with Special Needs, Inc. v. Cooperman*, 501 A.2d 575 (N.J.Super.A.D.1985).

A private school in Pennsylvania alleged that it was denied due process of law after the Pennsylvania Secretary of Education denied the school's application for status as an approved private school for socially and emotionally disturbed children. A hearing examiner determined that three State Board of Education standards were not met: first, the student interns used in the school classrooms did not provide full-time supportive assistance to the classroom teachers; second, the school lacked an immediately available supervisor or other competent and trained person to handle a student in a period of crisis and to remove that student, if necessary, from the classroom; third, the school's behavior management system did not permit its classroom teachers to control classroom conduct adequately. The school appealed to the Commonwealth Court of Pennsylvania, which affirmed the hearing examiner's decision. The school then appealed to the Supreme Court of Pennsylvania, which found that the evidence was sufficient to support a finding that the school failed to provide adequate staff assistance to classroom teachers. The court concluded that the hearing examiner's findings went to the heart of the Pennsylvania regulatory scheme of insuring that approved private schools were able to provide adequate and necessary training and education to handicapped children. *Wiley House v. Scanlon*, 465 A.2d 995 (Pa.1983).

A U.S. district court in New York held that the removal by the New York Commissioner of Education of all residential schools treating learning disabled children from a list of schools approved for the treatment of handicapped children, thereby eliminating such schools as options for the placement of learning disabled children, conflicted with the EAHCA. The court observed that only a small number of learning disabled children require residential placement and that some local programs were inadequate to serve learning disabled children. Thus, the policy was declared invalid. *Riley v. Ambach*, 508 F.Supp. 1222 (E.D.N.Y.1980). However, this case was reversed by the U.S. Court of Appeals, Second Circuit, on the ground that the plaintiffs had failed to exhaust their administrative remedies prior to bringing suit in federal court. *See* 668 F.2d 635 (2d Cir.1981).

The U.S. Court of Appeals, Second Circuit, has ruled on the proper educational placement of an emotionally disturbed twenty-year-old. The child had been maintained by the state of New York at an approved institution for handicapped children. The institution later was removed from the state list of certified facilities on the grounds it was a hospital, not a school, and was therefore not appropriate for placement. Although the child continued to reside there for some time following decertification, the state ultimately determined that it was not obligated to pay the costs of maintenance (approximately $185 per day). The parents sued for the maintenance costs and to have the child remain at the institution during the interim period necessary to determine an alternative placement that satisfied the requirements of the EAHCA.

The court of appeals, basically upholding the lower court's decision, held that the state was obligated to pay for maintenance at the institution. Both sides in the case had relied on the "status quo" provisions of the EAHCA, with the parents claiming that status quo meant the child should be maintained at no cost to them, and the state claiming that status quo meant a continuation of residence at the parents' expense. The court ruled that the state could not disclaim its statutory responsibility by decertifying an institution. A free appropriate public education in a suitable institution remains the responsibility of the state, held the court. *Vander Malle v. Ambach*, 673 F.2d 49 (2nd Cir.1982).

In another New York case, the parents of several handicapped children brought suit against the state of New York, alleging that the transfer of their children from a private special education school violated the EAHCA. The children were transferred to alternate sites after the New York City school board decided not to renew its contract with the school on the ground of financial mismanagement. A U.S. district court held that "while a school board and a state do not have unfettered power in all cases to close schools and transfer students, they must be permitted to make independent determinations regarding the suitability of private institutions to fulfill the educational and fiscal needs of a school system without first according parents and guardians a due process forum." *Dima v. Macchiarola*, 513 F.Supp. 565 (E.D.N.Y.1981).

VI. FACILITIES AND PROGRAMS

The appropriateness of private school facilities and programs to the particular needs of handicapped students has been a source of dispute between schools and students, schools and parents, and schools and states.

The mother of a seriously emotionally disturbed nineteen-year-old brought suit against a Tennessee school district alleging that her son had not been placed in an appropriate facility. A hearing officer had determined that a Tennessee residential school providing psychiatric treatment was the appropriate placement for the boy. The mother, however, wanted him placed in a special school in Texas. She appealed the hearing officer's decision to a federal district court, which held for the school district. The mother then appealed to the U.S. Court of Appeals, Sixth Circuit, which reversed the district court ruling. The court of appeals was persuaded by psychiatric testimony which established that the Texas school, which offered long-term treatment and had locked wards, was a better school for the boy. The court rejected the school district's argument that because the Texas school cost $88,000 per year as compared to $55,000 per year for the school chosen by the board, placement at the Tennessee school was warranted. It stated that cost considerations, when devising programs for individual handicapped students, are only relevant when choosing between several options, all of which offer an "appropriate" education. *Clevenger v. Oak Ridge School Board*, 744 F.2d 514 (6th Cir.1984).

In the following case, which involved insurance coverage for a disabled child's placement at a residential facility, the U.S. Court of Appeals ordered an insurer to pay for the costs. Here, a child who suffered from a functional nervous disorder was admitted to the Clear Water Ranch Children's House, a residential treatment facility in California which specialized in the treatment of such disorders. The staff at the facility consisted of one registered nurse, who worked days only, child care workers who were present twenty-four hours per day, and licensed clinical social workers. A psychiatrist supervised this staff. The child's stepfather, who was issued a group medical insurance policy by his employer, submitted a claim to his insurer for the cost of the child's treatment at the facility. The insurer denied the claim and stated that the facility did not qualify as a "hospital," which was defined in the policy as "an institution...primarily engaged in providing on an in-patient basis for the medical care and treatment of sick and injured persons through medical, diagnostic and major surgical facilities, all of which must be provided on its premises under the supervision of a staff of Physicians with 24-hour a day nursing service." The U.S. Court of Appeals, Ninth

Circuit, awarded coverage. The term "nursing service" was not defined in the policy. The insurer's argument that coverage could be provided only for facilities with twenty-four hour a day registered nurses was rejected by the court, which found that the child care workers who were on duty twenty-four hours a day satisfied the policy requirements. Furthermore, the court held that the fact that the treatment facility possessed no major surgical facilities presented no bar to coverage, since it was the insurer's admitted practice to disregard this policy requirement for facilities which treat mental illnesses. *Hanson v. Prudential Insurance Co. of America*, 772 F.2d 580 (9th Cir.1985).

VII. CONTRACT DISPUTES

Private schools enjoy the unfettered ability to enter into contractual agreements with the parents of handicapped children, or school districts, to provide special education services.

The parents of a handicapped child in Illinois brought suit against a Massachusetts private school, alleging that the school violated the terms of an agreement between the parents and the school. The parents claimed the agreement provided that the school would apply for increased funding from the state of Illinois for their handicapped daughter's placement at the Massachusetts school. As a result of Massachusetts and Illinois using different criteria in setting tuition rates, and dramatic increases in tuition rates at the school, the amounts the parents received in assistance from the state of Illinois proved to be insufficient to cover the costs of the child's attendance at the school. The parents also claimed that a school official called the child's mother requesting that the child not return to school for the summer session preceding the 1979-80 school year, as well as the following school year, because of the tuition reimbursement problem, and that if the parents sent their daughter to the school on a plane, there would be no one to meet her at the airport. The child's father then negotiated an arrangement with the school whereby the child would be allowed to return for summer session, with the parents paying the full cost of her attendance and the school applying for the funds due from Illinois. When summer session ended, the school received a contract from Illinois for the child's placement for the 1980-81 school year. The school refused to sign the contract, knowing it was not going to get the tuition reimbursement it was due. Further, the school had never received a formal letter from the child's father saying he would pay the child's tuition in full.

The father then wrote a letter to the school requesting that his daughter be allowed to remain there, while the school investigated the possibility of receiving funding from Illinois. The school's investigation revealed that it was not even on the Illinois State Board of Education's (ISBE) list of approved schools; thus, even if the school had signed the contract it would not have been paid. Further, a new Illinois law would not allow Massachusetts to assess parents the difference between what Illinois would pay and what the Massachusetts school charged. The school then informed the parents that the child would be allowed to remain as a private student only; otherwise she would be requested to leave and not return after Christmas vacation of the 1980-81 school year. The child stayed at the school during Christmas because of a family disruption. Shortly thereafter, the father visited the director of the school, who signed an agreement to apply to Illinois for ISBE eligibility. Eligibility was denied by Illinois. The child remained at the school until March, with no money from any source being offered for the child's placement.

In April, with approximately $30,000 owing for the child's placement, the school threatened to return the child to Illinois. The father went to Massachusetts once again and obtained a temporary restraining order preventing the school from discharging the child. The child returned to Illinois in June and entered another school. The father sued the Massachusetts school for failing to apply for Illinois funds, and the school countersued the father for tuition, room and board owed. In the parents' lawsuit, a jury awarded the parents $4,000 in compensatory damages, $30,000 for fraud and $50,000 to the wife on her claim of intentional infliction of emotional distress resulting from the phone call she received from the school. The school appealed and both lawsuits were consolidated in a U.S. district court in Illinois, which upheld the compensatory damage award but set aside the jury's awards for fraud and emotional distress.

The parents appealed to the U.S. Court of Appeals, Seventh Circuit, which held that the parents were not entitled to damages. The child's father, a medical doctor, had not shown that on the days of his trips to Massachusetts to resolve the problems with the school he would otherwise have been in consultation with patients. Thus, the $4,000 damage award, consisting of travel and lodging costs, lost consulting fees and attorney expenses was denied. The court also found that there was no implied contract wherein the parents agreed to pay the complete tuition for the 1979-80 school year. Thus, the parents were not liable for tuition for that year. However, the parents reenrolled their child in the school the following year with the full knowledge that the school was having tuition reimbursement problems with Illinois. Thus, there was an implied contract for the 1980-81 school year for the parents to bear the tuition expenses.

Further, the telephone call to the child's mother regarding the school's request that the child not return to school did not constitute intentional infliction of emotional distress. Under Massachusetts law, only "extreme and outrageous" conduct can give rise to such a claim. Such conduct does not qualify as extreme and outrageous unless it is "beyond all bounds of decency and utterly intolerable in a civilized community." Finally, the court found no evidence of fraud as the school merely made a promise to apply for additional funding and, although not always gracious about the circumstances, intended to carry out that promise. In fact, said the court, whenever the possibility arose that the child would be requested to withdraw, the school accommodated the parents' request to reconsider its position. It did so, observed the court, because of its respect for the family situation in light of the son's illness. *Dr. Franklin Perkins School v. Freeman*, 741 F.2d 1503 (7th Cir.1984).

A breach of contract claim resulted from a New York private school's alleged misrepresentations with regard to its specialized faculty and capabilities. After the school brought an action to recover tuition expenses from the mother of a student, the mother counterclaimed against the school for breach of contract, fraudulent/negligent misrepresentation and negligent infliction of emotional distress. The school moved to dismiss the mother's counterclaim for failure to state a claim for which relief could be granted. The mother's counterclaim alleged that the school's agents represented to her that they possessed a specialized faculty that could identify and individually treat children with learning disabilities. She claimed that these representations were fraudulently and/or negligently made, and that, to her detriment, she relied on the representations in entering into her agreement with the school. She also claimed that the school did not provide the stated services and therefore breached the contract. Finally, the mother alleged that psychiatric intervention was necessary because her son received services which proved to be inappropriate and harmful when the school failed to diagnose (or misdiagnosed) his learning disability. This, she claimed, constituted negligent infliction of emotional distress.

The Civil Court of the City of New York granted a portion of the private school's motion to dismiss and denied part of the motion. The court held that the mother's breach of contract claim, alleging that the school agreed to detect her child's learning deficiencies and to provide the necessary tutorial and guidance services but failed to do so, was permissible. However, the mother could make a claim for fraudulent misrepresentation only if she could show that the school knowingly made the misrepresentations to her. Thus, she could only maintain an action based on intentional misrepresentation, not negligent misrepresentation. Finally, the mother could not recover under her claim for negligent infliction of emotional distress. The court noted that it is well established that physical contact or injury is no longer necessary for such a claim. However, the courts have unanimously held that monetary damages for educational malpractice based on a negligence theory are not recoverable. Therefore, the mother could not sue for alleged mental distress caused by negligence in educational practices. *Village Community School v. Adler*, 478 N.Y.S.2d 546 (N.Y.City Civ.Ct.1984).

In a breach of contract case, a private residential facility for the treatment of mentally handicapped adolescent boys located in Milwaukee, Wisconsin, brought suit in Illinois against the Chicago Board of Education and another local suburban school district to recover the value of services rendered to students from the defendant school districts. The dispute arose from the placement with the facility of six high school students. The facility, unfamiliar with Illinois procedures for the payment of tuition to private facilities for handicapped students, accepted the Illinois students into its program before it had received the approval from Illinois for its rate structure. Without such approval, the facility was ineligible under Illinois law to receive tuition payments from Illinois school boards. The facility ultimately received the necessary approval and then sought payment of tuition for the entire time the children were at the facility. The school districts, however, refused to pay for any treatment provided prior to the facility's approval for Illinois funds. The facility then filed suit, seeking recovery for breach of contract. A lower court held that the facts were not sufficient to prove the existence of an express or implied contract since the districts had not agreed to assume responsiblity for the tuition for services provided prior to Illinois approval of the facility, nor did the districts have authority to enter into such agreements. The case was appealed to the Appellate Court of Illinois, which affirmed the lower court.

The appellate court rejected an argument made by the facility that the Illinois statute involved here was not applicable. Said the court, "the statute on its face clearly prohibits the placement of Illinois students in a nonapproved institution," such as the one involved here. The facility also argued that, under federal law, the school districts had a duty to provide handicapped children with a free education and that, therefore, the Illinois School Code could not be construed to prohibit the school districts from contracting with the facility. The court dismissed this argument by stating that a private education facility, such as the one involved here, lacks standing to assert the rights of handicapped children to a free education. The facility, therefore, could not rely on the students' rights under federal law to advance its contract claim. Also rejected was a contention by the facility that the evidence supported a finding that it should be permitted to recover in quasi-contract. The law will not imply an agreement which would be illegal if it were express. Because the court held that Illinois law prohibited the placement of students in nonapproved private facilities such as the one here, the law could not imply a contract for the placement of the students prior to the facility's approval in Illinois. The lower court decision was affirmed. *Juneau Academy v. Chicago Board of Education*, 461 N.E.2d 597 (Ill.App.1st Dist.1984).

CHAPTER SIX
FEDERAL STATUTORY REQUIREMENTS

Page

I. OVERVIEW 136

II. CIVIL RIGHTS ACT OF 1964 136
   A. Title VI: Racial Discrimination 136
   B. Title VII: Employment Discrimination 138

III. EQUAL PAY ACT 144

IV. TITLE IX 145

V. REHABILITATION ACT OF 1973 157

VI. AGE DISCRIMINATION 165
   A. Age Discrimination in Employment Act 165
   B. Age Discrimination Act 167

VII. BUCKLEY AMENDMENT 169

VIII. RECONSTRUCTION CIVIL RIGHTS STATUTES 189
   A. Section 1981 189
   B. Section 1983 189

I. OVERVIEW

The federal civil rights statutes may be viewed as covering three general kinds of institutions: 1) institutions which have programs or activities receiving federal funding, 2) institutions which have such extensive contact with state or local governments that they are deemed "state actors," and 3) all other institutions.

Private educational institutions which fall into the first category must comply with Title VI, Title IX, the Rehabilitation Act, the Age Discrimination Act, and the Buckley Amendment. Institutions falling into the second category (see the discussion of "state action" in *Rendell-Baker v. Kohn*, Chapter Two) are held to the same constitutional standards of due process, equal protection and the like as are government entities, under the 1871 Civil Rights Act (42 U.S.C. § 1983). The third category refers to private educational institutions which are subject to laws of general applicability, such as Title VII, the Age Discrimination in Employment Act, and the 1866 Civil Rights Act (42 U.S.C. § 1981).

II. CIVIL RIGHTS ACT OF 1964

Of primary relevance to private schools, the Civil Rights Act of 1964 included Title VI, which outlawed racial discrimination in federally funded programs, and Title VII, the general employment discrimination statute.

A. Title VI: Racial Discrimination

Private school programs and activities which receive federal funding may not discriminate on the basis of race. U.S. Department of Education regulations implementing Title VI (see below) make it clear that this nondiscrimination mandate extends to admissions, financial aid and virtually every aspect of the federally-assisted program. The standards for determining whether unlawful racial discrimination under Title VI has occurred are generally the same standards applied to government entities under the Fourteenth Amendment's Equal Protection Clause.

A major exception to the nondiscrimination mandate of Title VI involves affirmative action programs. Federal regulations adopted pursuant to Title VI require public or private schools that have had a history of racial discrimination to adopt affirmative action programs as a prerequisite to federal funding.

Nondiscriminatory public or private schools are not required to engage in affirmative action but they may do so if they desire. Racial quotas as part of an affirmative action program are, however, not permitted, as *Regents of University of California v. Bakke*, 438 U.S. 265 (1978), points out. Decided under Title VI, the *Bakke* case held that while quotas were illegal, race could legitimately be considered as "one of the many factors" in deciding whether to admit a student, if such consideration of race was done as part of an affirmative action program.

The relevant portion of Title VI, 42 U.S.C. § 2000d, reads as follows:

§ **2000d. Prohibition against exclusion from participation in, denial of benefits of, and discrimination under Federally assisted programs on ground of race, color, or national origin**

No person in the United States shall, on the ground of race, color, or national origin, be excluded from participation in, be denied the benefits of, or be subjected to discrimination under any program or activity receiving Federal financial assistance.

Relevant federal regulations implementing Title VI, found at 34 CFR Part 100, include the following:

* * *

§ **100.3 Discrimination prohibited.**

(a) *General.* No person in the United States shall, on the ground of race, color, or national origin be excluded from participation in, be denied the benefits of, or be otherwise subjected to discrimination under any program to which this part applies.

(b) *Specific discriminatory actions prohibited.* (1) A recipient under any program to which this part applies may not, directly or through contractual or other arrangements, on ground of race, color, or national origin:

(i) Deny an individual any service, financial aid, or other benefit provided under the program;

(ii) Provide any service, financial aid, or other benefit to an individual which is different, or is provided in a different manner, from that provided to others under the program;

(iii) Subject an individual to segregation or separate treatment in any matter related to his receipt of any service, financial aid, or other benefit under the program;

(iv) Restrict an individual in any way in the enjoyment of any advantage or privilege enjoyed by others receiving any service, financial aid, or other benefit under the program;

(v) Treat an individual differently from others in determining whether he satisfies any admission, enrollment, quota, eligibility, membership or other requirement or condition which individuals must meet in order to be provided any service, financial aid, or other benefit provided under the program;

(vi) Deny an individual an opportunity to participate in the program through the provision of services or otherwise or afford him an opportunity to do so which is different from that afforded others under the program (including the opportunity to participate in the program as an employee but only to the extent set forth in paragraph (c) of this section).

(vii) Deny a person the opportunity to participate as a member of a planning or advisory body which is an integral part of the program.

(2) A recipient, in determining the types of services, financial aid, or other benefits, or facilities which will be provided under any such program, or the class of individuals to whom, or the situations in which, such services, financial aid, other benefits, or facilities will be provided under any such program, or the class of individuals to be afforded an opportunity to participate in any such program, may not, directly or through contractual or other arrangements, utilize criteria or methods of administration which have the effect of subjecting individuals to discrimination because of their race, color, or national origin, or have the effect of defeating or substantially impairing accomplishment of the objectives of the program as respect individuals of a particular race, color, or national origin.

(3) In determining the site or location of a facilities, an applicant or recipient may not make selections with the effect of excluding individuals from, denying

them the benefits of, or subjecting them to discrimination under any programs to which this regulation applies, on the ground of race, color, or national origin; or with the purpose or effect of defeating or substantially impairing the accomplishment of the objectives of the Act or this regulation.

(4) As used in this section, the services, financial aid, or other benefits provided under a program receiving Federal financial assistance shall be deemed to include any service, financial aid, or other benefits provided in or through a facility provided with the aid of Federal financial assistance.

(5) The enumeration of specific forms of prohibited discrimination in this paragraph and paragraph (c) of this section does not limit the generality of the prohibition in paragraph (a) of this section.

(6) (i) In administering a program regarding which the recipient has previously discriminated against persons on the ground of race, color, or national origin, the recipient must take affirmative action to overcome the effects of prior discrimination.

(ii) Even in the absence of such prior discrimination, a recipient in administering a program may take affirmative action to overcome the effects of conditions which resulted in limiting participation by persons of a particular race, color, or national origin.

*   *   *

§ 100.5 Illustrative application.

The following examples will illustrate the programs aided by Federal financial assistance of the Department. (In all cases the discrimination prohibited is discrimination on the ground of race, color, or national origin prohibited by Title VI of the Act and this regulation, as a condition of the receipt of Federal financial assistance).

*   *   *

(h) In some situations, even though past discriminatory practices attributable to a recipient or applicant have been abandoned, the consequences of such practices continue to impede the full availability of a benefit. If the efforts required of the applicant or recipient under § 100.6(d), to provide information as to the availability of the program or activity and the rights of beneficiaries under this regulation, have failed to overcome these consequences, it will become necessary under the requirement stated in paragraph (1) of § 100.3(b)(6) for such applicant or recipient to take additional steps to make the benefits fully available to racial and nationality groups previously subject to discrimination. This action might take the form, for example, of special arrangements for obtaining referrals or making selections which will insure that groups previously subjected to discrimination are adequately served.

(i) Even though an applicant or recipient has never used discriminatory policies, the services and benefits of the program or activity it administers may not in fact be equally available to some racial or nationality groups. In such circumstances, an applicant or recipient may properly give special consideration to race, color, or national origin to make the benefits of its program more widely available to such groups, not then being adequately served. For example, where a university is not adequately serving members of a particular racial or nationality group, it may establish special recruitment policies to make its program better known and more readily available to such group, and take other steps to provide that group with more adequate service.

*   *   *

B. Title VII: Employment Discrimination

Title VII applies to any institution which has fifteen or more employees.

Its coverage is limited to employment discrimination based upon race, color, sex, religion or national origin. The U.S. Equal Employment Opportunity Commission (EEOC) is empowered to enforce Title VII through investigation and/or federal court lawsuits. Indeed, a private individual alleging discrimination must pursue administrative remedies within the EEOC before the individual will be allowed to file suit against an employer under Title VII. Plaintiffs who prevail in an employment discrimination lawsuit will be entitled, where appropriate, to back pay, front pay, accumulated seniority and other benefits, and attorney's fees.

Title VII lawsuits may be divided into two categories: *disparate treatment* and *disparate impact*. In a disparate treatment lawsuit an individual usually claims that he or she was not hired, was fired, or was denied a promotion simply because of his or her race, color, sex, religion or national origin. Such lawsuits proceed in three stages. *First*, the plaintiff must show a) that he or she belongs to a protected class (male, female, black, white, Jew, Catholic, etc.); b) that he or she was qualified for the position; c) that despite the plaintiff's qualifications, he or she was rejected; and d) that after rejection the position remained open (i.e. the position was not abolished). *Second*, the burden then shifts to the defendant to "articulate" a legitimate, nondiscriminatory reason (such as incompetence or lack of qualifications) for rejecting the plaintiff. *Third*, the plaintiff must show that the reason given by the employer in step two is a pretext for unlawful discrimination. As illustrated by *Board of Trustees of Keene State College v. Sweeney*, 439 U.S. 25 (1978), such cases often become credibility disputes in which a court must decide whether it believes the employer or the plaintiff.

The bona fide occupational qualification (BFOQ) exception [see 42 U.S.C. § 2000e-2(e)(1), below] allows employers (especially religiously-affiliated private schools) to use sex, religion or national origin as a hiring criteria if one of those three characteristics is a "bona fide occupational qualification necessary to the normal operation of that particular business or enterprise." However, the BFOQ exception is narrowly construed by the courts. While being female can be a BFOQ for counseling high school girls [see *Stone v. Belgrade School District No. 44*, 703 P.2d 136 (Mont.1984)], numerous other cases have indicated that BFOQ defenses will fail unless the qualification at issue is a matter of "necessity," not merely employer convenience. In any case, successful assertion of a BFOQ defense will result in dismissal of a disparate treatment claim. See *Dothard v. Rawlinson*, 433 U.S. 321 (1977).

Disparate impact lawsuits differ from disparate treatment in that claims of the former type do not allege overt discriminatory actions. Instead, disparate impact lawsuits claim that a facially neutral employer policy (e.g., high school diplomas or I.Q. testing as a condition of employment) has an adverse or disparate impact on minorities. If such a policy does have an adverse impact, it will constitute a violation of Title VII unless the policy is "necessary" to the operation of the employer's business. Simply put, the policy must be related to job performance. (See Chapter Two for cases involving Title VII issues in private education.)

A separate issue under Title VII is affirmative action. Generally, an affirmative action in employment plan voluntarily adopted by a private school will not result in unlawful reverse discrimination under Title VII if 1) there exists a statistical disparity between the races or sexes in a given job category, or if the institution was guilty of discrimination in the past, 2) the affirmative action plan does not "unnecessarily trammel" the rights of nonminority employees, 3) the plan does not stigmatize nonminority employees, and 4) the plan is temporary in nature and is scheduled to terminate upon the achievement of a racially or sexually integrated work force. See *United Steelworkers of America v. Weber*, 443 U.S. 193 (1979), and *Johnson v. Transportation Agency*, 107 S.Ct. 1442 (1987).

The operative provisions of Title VII, 42 U.S.C. § 2000e *et seq.*, are as follows:

§ 2000e. Definitions

For the purposes of this subchapter—
(a) The term "person" includes one or more individuals, governments, governmental agencies, political subdivisions, labor unions, partnerships, associations, corporations, legal representatives, mutual companies, joint-stock companies, trusts, unincorporated organizations, trustees, trustees in cases under title 11, or receivers.
(b) The term "employer" means a person engaged in an industry affecting commerce who has fifteen or more employees for each working day in each of twenty or more calendar weeks in the current or preceding calendar year, and any agent of such a person, but such term does not include (1) the United States, a corporation wholly owned by the Government of the United States, an Indian tribe, or any department or agency of the District of Columbia subject by statute to procedures of the competitive service (as defined in section 2102 of title 5), or (2) a bona fide private membership club (other than a labor organization) which is exempt from taxation under section 501(c) of title 26, except that during the first year after March 24, 1972, persons having fewer than twenty-five employees (and their agents) shall not be considered employers.

* * *

(f) The term "employee" means an individual employed by an employer, except that the term "employee" shall not include any person elected to public office in any State or political subdivision of any State by the qualified voters thereof, or any person chosen by such officer to be on such officer's personal staff, or an appointee on the policy making level or an immediate adviser with respect to the exercise of the constitutional or legal powers of the office. The exemption set forth in the preceding sentence shall not include employees subject to the civil service laws of a State government, governmental agency or political subdivision.
(g) The term "commerce" means trade, traffic, commerce, transportation, transmission, or communication among the several States; or between a State and any place outside thereof; or within the District of Columbia, or a possession of the United States; or between points in the same State but through a point outside thereof.
(h) The term "industry affecting commerce" means any activity, business, or industry in commerce or in which a labor dispute would hinder or obstruct commerce or the free flow of commerce and includes any activity or industry "affecting commerce" within the meaning of the Labor-Management Reporting and Disclosure Act of 1959 [29 U.S.C. 401 et seq.], and further includes any governmental industry, business, or activity.

* * *

(j) The term "religion" includes all aspects of religious observance and practice, as well as belief, unless an employer demonstrates that he is unable to reasonably accommodate to an employee's or prospective employee's religious observance or practice without undue hardship on the conduct of the employer's business.

(k) The terms "because of sex" or "on the basis of sex" include, but are not limited to, because of or on the basis of pregnancy, childbirth, or related medical conditions; and women affected by pregnancy, childbirth, or related medical conditions shall be treated the same for all employment-related purposes, including receipt of benefits under fringe benefit programs, as other persons not so affected but similar in their ability or inability to work, and nothing in section 2000e-2(h) of this title shall be interpreted to permit otherwise. This subsection shall not require an employer to pay for health insurance benefits for abortion, except where the life of the mother would be endangered if the fetus were carried to term, or except where medical complications have arisen from an abortion: *Provided*, That nothing herein shall preclude an employer from providing abortion benefits or otherwise affect bargaining agreements in regard to abortion.

* * *

§ 2000e-2. Unlawful employment practices

(a) Employer practices

It shall be an unlawful employment practice for an employer—
(1) to fail or refuse to hire or to discharge any individual, or otherwise to discriminate against any individual with respect to his compensation, terms, conditions, or privileges of employment, because of such individual's race, color, religion, sex, or national origin; or
(2) to limit, segregate, or classify his employees or applicants for employment in any way which would deprive or tend to deprive any individual of employment opportunities or otherwise adversely affect his status as an employee, because of such individual's race, color, religion, sex, or national origin.

* * *

(e) Businesses or enterprises with personnel qualified on basis of religion, sex, or national origin; educational institutions with personnel of particular religion

Notwithstanding any other provision of this subchapter, (1) it shall not be an unlawful employment practice for an employer to hire and employ employees, for an employment agency to classify, or refer for employment any individual, for a labor organization to classify its membership or to classify or refer for employment any individual, or for an employer, labor organization or joint labor-management committee controlling apprenticeship or other training or retraining programs to admit or employ any individual in any such program, on the basis of his religion, sex, or national origin in those certain instances where religion, sex, or national origin is a bona fide occupational qualification reasonably necessary to the normal operation of that particular business or enterprise, and (2) it shall not be an unlawful employment practice for a school, college, university, or other educational institution or institution of learning to hire and employ employees of a particular religion if such a school, college, university, or other educational institution or institution of learning is, in whole or in substantial part, owned, supported, controlled, or managed by a particular religion or by a particular religious corporation, association, or society, or if the curriculum of such school, college, university, or other educational institution or institution of learning is directed toward the propagation of a particular religion.

(f) Members of Communist Party or Communist-action or Communist-front organizations

As used in this subchapter, the phrase "unlawful employment practice" shall not be deemed to include any action or measure taken by an employer, labor organization, joint labor-management committee, or employment agency with respect to an individual who is a member of the Communist Party of the United States or of any other organization required to register as a Communist-action or Communist-front organization by final order of the Subversive Activities Control Board pursuant to the Subversive Activities Control Act of 1950 [50 U.S.C. 781 et seq.].

(g) National security

Notwithstanding any other provision of this subchapter, it shall not be an unlawful employment practice for an employer to fail or refuse to hire and employ any individual for any position, for an employer to discharge any individual from any position, or for an employment agency to fail or refuse to refer any individual for employment in any position, or for a labor organization to fail or refuse to refer any individual for employment in any position, if—

(1) the occupancy of such position, or access to the premises in or upon which any part of the duties of such position is performed or is to be performed, is subject to any requirement imposed in the interest of the national security of the United States under any security program in effect pursuant to or administered under any statute of the United States or any Executive order of the President; and

(2) such individual has not fulfilled or has ceased to fulfill that requirement.

(h) Seniority or merit system; quantity or quality of production; ability tests; compensation based on sex and authorized by minimum wage provisions

Notwithstanding any other provision of this subchapter, it shall not be an unlawful employment practice for an employer to apply different standards of compensation, or different terms, conditions, or privileges of employment pursuant to a bona fide seniority or merit system, or a system which measures earnings by quantity or quality of production or to employees who work in different locations, provided that such differences are not the result of an intention to discriminate because of race, color, religion, sex, or national origin, nor shall it be an unlawful employment practice for an employer to give and to act upon the results of any professionally developed ability test provided that such test, its administration or action upon the results is not designed, intended or used to discriminate because of race, color, religion, sex, or national origin. It shall not be an unlawful employment practice under this subchapter for any employer to differentiate upon the basis of sex in determining the amount of the wages or compensation paid or to be paid to employees of such employer if such differentiation is authorized by the provisions of section 206(d) of title 29.

(i) Businesses or enterprises extending preferential treatment to Indians

Nothing contained in this subchapter shall apply to any business or enterprise on or near an Indian reservation with respect to any publicly announced employment practice of such business or enterprise under which a preferential treatment is given to any individual because he is an Indian living on or near a reservation.

(j) Preferential treatment not to be granted on account of existing number or percentage imbalance

Nothing contained in this subchapter shall be interpreted to require any employer, employment agency, labor organization or joint labor-management committee subject to this subchapter to grant preferential treatment to any individual or to any group because of the race, color, religion, sex, or national origin of such individual or group on account of an imbalance which my exist with respect to the total number or percentage of persons of any race, color, religion, sex, or national origin employed by any employer, referred or classified for employment by any employment agency or labor organization, admitted to membership or classified by any labor organization, or admitted to, or employed in, any apprenticeship or other training program, in comparison with the total number or percentage of persons of such race, color, religion, sex, or national origin in any community, State, section, or other area, or in the available work force in any community, State, section, or other area.

§ 2000e-3. Other unlawful employment practices

(a) Discrimination for making charges, testifying, assisting, or participating in enforcement proceedings

It shall be an unlawful employment practice for an employer to discriminate against any of his employees or applicants for employment for an employment agency, or joint labor-management committee controlling apprenticeship or other training or retraining, including on-the-job training programs, to discriminate against any individual, or for a labor organization to discriminate against any member thereof or applicant for membership, because he has opposed any practice made an unlawful employment practice by this subchapter, or because he has made a charge, testified, assisted, or participated in any manner in an investigation, proceeding, or hearing under this subchapter.

(b) Printing or publication of notices or advertisements indicating prohibited preference, limitation, specification, or discrimination; occupational qualification exception

It shall be an unlawful employment practice for an employer, labor organization, employment agency or joint labor-management committee controlling apprenticeship or other training or retraining, including on-the-job training programs, to print or publish or cause to be printed or published any notice or advertisement relating to employment by such an employer or membership in or any classification or referral for employment by such a labor organization, or relating to any classification or referral for employment by such an employment agency, or relating to admission to, or employment in, any program established to provide apprenticeship or other training by such a joint labor-management committee, indicating any preference, limitation, specification, or discrimination, based on race, color, religion, sex, or national origin, except that such a notice or advertisement may indicate a preference, limitation, specification, or discrimination based on race, color, religion, sex, or national origin when religion, sex, or national origin is a bona fide occupational qualification for employment.

* * *

§ 2000e-5. Enforcement provisions

* * *

(g) Injunctions; appropriate affirmative action; equitable relief; accrual of back pay; reduction of back pay, limitations on judicial orders

If the court finds that the respondent has intentionally engaged in or is intentionally engaging in an unlawful employment practice charged in the complaint, the court may enjoin the respondent from engaging in such unlawful employment practice, and order such affirmative action as may be appropriate, which may include, but is not limited to, reinstatement or hiring of employees, with or without back pay (payable by the employer, employment agency, or labor organization, as the case may be, responsible for the unlawful employment practice), or any other equitable relief as the court deems appropriate. Back pay liability shall not accrue from a date more than two years prior to the filing of a charge with the Commission. Interim earnings or amounts earnable with reasonable diligence by the person or persons discriminated against shall operate to reduce the back pay otherwise allowable. No order of the court shall require the admission or reinstatement of an individual as a member of a union, or the hiring, reinstatement, or promotion of an individual as an employee, or the payment to him of any back pay, if such individual was refused admission, suspended, or expelled, or was refused employment or advancement or was suspended or discharged for any reason other than discrimination on account of race, color, religion, sex, or national origin or in violation of section 2000e-3(a) of this title.

* * *

(k) Attorney's fee; liability of Commission and United States for costs

In any action or proceeding under this subchapter the court, in its discretion, may allow the prevailing party, other than the Commission or the United States, a reasonable attorney's fee as part of the costs, and the Commission and the United States shall be liable for costs the same as a private person.

* * *

§ 2000e-11. Veterans' special rights or preference

Nothing contained in this subchapter shall be construed to repeal or modify any Federal, State, territorial, or local law creating special rights or preference for veterans.

* * *

III. EQUAL PAY ACT

Enacted by Congress in 1963, the Equal Pay Act requires that employers pay males and females the same wages for equal work. As such, the Act applies only to sexual discrimination in pay, and thus racially-based equal pay claims must be litigated under the more general provisions of Title VII. Because the Equal Pay Act is part of the Fair Labor Standards Act, employees are protected by the Act as long as the employer is engaged in an industry affecting interstate commerce (contrast Title VII's fifteen-employee minimum for triggering coverage). The courts have consistently interpreted the "interstate commerce" requirement in a liberal fashion in favor of finding

Equal Pay Act coverage. See, e.g., *Usery v. Columbia University,* **568 F.2d 953 (2d Cir.1977). The employee's burden of proof under the Act has been interpreted by the courts to require only that the jobs under comparison be "substantially" equal. Strict equality of the jobs under comparison is not required.**

The Equal Pay Act, 29 U.S.C. § 206(d), provides in relevant part as follows:

(d) Prohibition of sex discrimination

(1) No employer having employees subject to any provisions of this section shall discriminate, within any establishment in which such employees are employed, between employees on the basis of sex by paying wages to employees in such establishment at a rate less than the rate at which he pays wages to employees of the opposite sex in such establishment for equal work on jobs the performance of which requires equal skill, effort, and responsibility, and which are performed under similar working conditions, except where such payment is made pursuant to (i) a seniority system; (ii) a merit system; (iii) a system which measures earnings by quantity or quality of production; or (iv) a differential based on any other factor other than sex: *Provided,* That an employer who is paying a wage rate differential in violation of this subsection shall not, in order to comply with the provisions of this subsection, reduce the wage rate of any employee.

IV. TITLE IX

Enacted as part of the Education Amendments of 1972, Title IX prohibits sexual discrimination in any public or private school program or activity receiving federal financial assistance. While the U.S. Supreme Court has given an expansive reading to the term "federal financial assistance," it has given a narrow reading to the term "program or activity" (see Chapter Four).

The relevant provisions of Title IX, 20 U.S.C. § 1681 *et seq.*, are as follows:

§ 1681. Sex

(a) Prohibition against discrimination; exceptions

No person in the United States shall, on the basis of sex, be excluded from participation in, be denied the benefits of, or be subjected to discrimination under any education program or activity receiving Federal financial assistance, except that:

(1) Classes of educational institutions subject to prohibition

in regard to admissions to educational institutions, this section shall apply only to institutions of vocational education, professional education, and graduate higher education, and to public institutions of undergraduate higher education;

(2) Educational institutions commencing planned change in admissions

in regard to admissions to educational institutions, this section shall not apply (A) for one year from June 23, 1972, nor for six years after June 23, 1972, in the case of an educational institution which has begun the process of changing from being an institution which admits only students of one sex to being an institution which admits students of both sexes, but only if it is carrying out a plan for such a change which is approved by the Secretary of Education or (B) for seven years from the date an educational institution begins the process of changing from being an institution which admits only students of one sex to being an institution which admits students of both sexes, but only if it is carrying out a plan for such a change which is approved by the Secretary of Education, whichever is the later;

(3) Educational institutions of religious organizations with contrary religious tenets

this section shall not apply to an educational institution which is controlled by a religious organization if the application of this subsection would not be consistent with the religious tenets of such organization;

(4) Educational institutions training individuals for military services or merchant marine

this section shall not apply to an educational institution whose primary purpose is the training of individuals for the military services of the United States, or the merchant marine;

(5) Public educational institutions with traditional and continuing admissions policy

in regard to admissions this section shall not apply to any public institution of undergraduate higher education which is an institution that traditionally and continually from its establishment has had a policy of admitting only students of one sex;

(6) Social fraternities or sororities; voluntary youth service organizations

this section shall not apply to membership practices—
(A) of a social fraternity or social sorority which is exempt from taxation under section 501(a) of title 26, the active membership of which consists primarily of students in attendance at an institution of higher education, or
(B) of the Young Men's Christian Association, Young Women's Christian Association, Girl Scouts, Boy Scouts, Camp Fire Girls, and voluntary youth service organizations which are so exempt, the membership of which has traditionally been limited to persons of one sex and principally to persons of less than nineteen years of age;

(7) Boy or Girl conferences

this section shall not apply to—
(A) any program or activity of the American Legion undertaken in connection with the organization or operation of any Boys State conference, Boys Nation conference, Girls State conference, or Girls Nation conference; or
(B) any program or activity of any secondary school or educational institution specifically for—
(i) the promotion of any Boys State conference, Boys Nation conference, Girls State conference, or Girls Nation conference; or
(ii) the selection of students to attend any such conference;

(8) Father-son or mother-daughter activities at educational institutions

this section shall not preclude father-son or mother-daughter activities at an educational institution, but if such activities are provided for students of one sex, opportunities for reasonably comparable activities shall be provided for students of the other sex; and

(9) Institution of higher education scholarship awards in "beauty" pageants

this section shall not apply with respect to any scholarship or other financial assistance awarded by an institution of higher education to any individual because such individual has received such award in any pageant in which the attainment of such award is based upon a combination of factors related to the personal appearance, poise, and talent of such individual and in which participation is limited to individuals of one sex only, so long as such pageant is in compliance with other nondiscrimination provisions of Federal law.

(b) Preferential or disparate treatment because of imbalance in participation or receipt of Federal benefits; statistical evidence of imbalance

Nothing contained in subsection (a) of this section shall be interpreted to require any educational institution to grant preferential or disparate treatment to the members of one sex on account of an imbalance which may exist with respect to the total number or percentage of persons of that sex participating in or receiving the benefits of any federally supported program or activity, in comparison with the total number or percentage of persons of that sex in any community, State, section, or other area: *Provided*, That this subsection shall not be construed to prevent the consideration in any hearing or proceeding under this chapter of statistical evidence tending to show that such an imbalance exists with respect to the participation in, or receipt of the benefits of, any such program or activity by the members of one sex.

(c) "Educational institution" defined

For purposes of this chapter an educational institution means any public or private preschool, elementary, or secondary school, or any institution of vocational, professional, or higher education, except that in the case of an educational institution composed of more than one school, college, or department which are administratively separate units, such term means such school, college, or department.

* * *

§ 1684. Blindness or visual impairment; prohibition against discrimination

No person in the United States shall, on the ground of blindness or severely impaired vision, be denied admission in any course of study by a recipient of Federal financial assistance for any education program or activity, but nothing herein shall be construed to require any such institution to provide any special services to such person because of his blindness or visual impairment.

* * *

§ 1686. Interpretation with respect to living facilities

Notwithstanding anything to the contrary contained in this chapter, nothing contained herein shall be construed to prohibit any educational institution from receiving funds under this Act, from maintaining separate living facilities for the different sexes.

The U.S. Department of Education has issued detailed regulations interpreting the requirements of Title IX. The most important of these regulations, found at 34 CFR Part 106, are reproduced below. These regulations, especially §§ 106.2(g) and 106.2(h), should be read in light of *Grove City College v. Bell*, 104 S.Ct. 1211 (1984) (see Chapter Four, Section VII; see also appendix).

Subpart A—Introduction

§ 106.1 Purpose and effective date.

The purpose of this part is to effectuate title IX of the Education Amendments of 1972, as amended by Pub. L. 93-568, 88 Stat. 1855 (except sections 904 and 906 of those Amendments) which is designed to eliminate (with certain exceptions) discrimination on the basis of sex in any education program or activity receiving Federal financial assistance, whether or not such program or activity is offered or sponsored by an educational institution as defined in this part. This part is also intended to effectuate section 844 of the Education Amendments of 1974, Pub. L. 93-380, 88 Stat. 484. The effective date of this part shall be July 21, 1975.

§ 106.2 Definitions.

As used in this part, the term—

* * *

(g) *"Federal financial assistance"* means any of the following, when authorized or extended under a law administered by the Department:

(1) A grant or loan of Federal financial assistance, including funds made available for:

(i) The acquisition, construction, renovation, restoration, or repair of a building or facility or any portion thereof; and

(ii) Scholarships, loans, grants, wages or other funds extended to any entity for payment to or on behalf of students admitted to that entity, or extended directly to such students for payment to that entity.

(2) A grant of Federal real or personal property or any interest therein, including surplus property, and the proceeds of the sale or transfer of such property, if the Federal share of the fair market value of the property is not, upon such sale or transfer, properly accounted for to the Federal Government.

(3) Provision of the services of Federal personnel.

(4) Sale or lease of Federal property or any interest therein at nominal consideration, or at consideration reduced for the purpose of assisting the recipient or in recognition of public interest to be served thereby, or permission to use Federal property or any interest therein without consideration.

(5) Any other contract, agreement, or arrangement which has as one of its purposes the provision of assistance to any education program or activity, except a contract of insurance or guaranty.

(h) *"Recipient"* means any State or political subdivision thereof, or any instrumentality of a State or political subdivision thereof, any public or private agency, institution, or organization, or other entity, or any person, to whom Federal financial assistance is extended directly or through another recipient and which operates an education program or activity which receives or benefits from such assistance, including any subunit, successor, assignee, or transferee thereof.

(i) *"Applicant"* means one who submits an application, request, or plan required to be approved by a Department official, or by a recipient, as a condition to becoming a recipient.

(j) *"Educational institution"* means a local educational agency (LEA) as defined by section 1001(f) of the Elementary and Secondary Education Act of 1965 (20 U.S.C. 3381), a preschool, a private elementary or secondary school, or an applicant or recipient of the type defined by paragraph (k), (l), (m), or (n) of this section.

(k) *"Institution of graduate higher education"* means an institution which:

(1) Offers academic study beyond the bachelor of arts or bachelor of science degree, whether or not leading to a certificate of any higher degree in the liberal arts and sciences; or

(2) Awards any degree in a professional field beyond the first professional degree (regardless of whether the first professional degree in such field is awarded by an institution of undergraduate higher education or professional education); or

(3) Awards no degree and offers no further academic study, but operates ordinarily for the purpose of facilitating research by persons who have received the highest graduate degree in any field of study.

(l) *"Institution of undergraduate higher education"* means:

(1) An institution offering at least two but less than four years of college level study beyond the high school level, leading to a diploma or an associate degree, or wholly or principally creditable toward a baccalaureate degree; or

(2) An institution offering academic study leading to a baccalaureate degree; or

(3) An agency or body which certifies credentials or offers degrees, but which may or may not offer academic study.

(m) *"Institution of professional education"* means an institution (except any institution of undergraduate higher education) which offers a program of academic study that leads to a first professional degree in a field for which there is a national specialized accrediting agency recognized by the Secretary.

(n) *"Institution of vocational education"* means a school or institution (except an institution of professional or graduate or undergraduate higher education) which has as its primary purpose preparation of students to pursue a technical, skilled, or semi-skilled occupation or trade, or to pursue study in a technical field, whether or not the school or institution offers certificates, diplomas, or degrees and whether or not it offers fulltime study.

(o) *"Administratively separate unit"* means a school, department or college of an educational institution (other than a local educational agency) admission to which is independent of admission to any other component of such institution.

(p) *"Admission"* means selection for part-time, full-time, special, associate, transfer, exchange, or any other enrollment, membership, or matriculation in or at an education program or activity operated by a recipient.

(q) *"Student"* means a person who has gained admission.

* * *

§ 106.3 Remedial and affirmative action and self-evaluation.

(a) *Remedial action.* If the Assistant Secretary finds that a recipient has discriminated against persons on the basis of sex in an education program or activity, such recipient shall take such remedial action as the Assistant Secretary deems necessary to overcome the effects of such discrimination.

(b) *Affirmative action.* In the absence of a finding of discrimination on the basis of sex in an education program or activity, a recipient may take affirmative action to overcome the effects of conditions which resulted in limited participation therein by persons of a particular sex. Nothing herein shall be interpreted to alter any affirmative action obligations which a recipient may have under Executive Order 11246.

* * *

§ 106.6 Effect of other requirements.

* * *

(b) *Effect of State or local law or other requirements.* The obligation to comply with this part is not obviated or alleviated by any State or local law or other requirement which would render any applicant or student ineligible, or limit the eligibility of any applicant or student, on the basis of sex, to practice any occupation or profession.

(c) *Effect of rules or regulations of private organizations.* The obligation to comply with this part is not obviated or alleviated by any rule or regulation of any organization, club, athletic or other league, or association which would render any applicant or student ineligible to participate or limit the eligibility or participation of any applicant or student, on the basis of sex, in any education program or activity operated by a recipient and which receives or benefits from Federal financial assistance.

§ 106.7 Effect of employment opportunities.

The obligation to comply with this part is not obviated or alleviated because employment opportunities in any occupation or profession are or may be more limited for members of one sex than for members of the other sex.

* * *

§ 106.9 Dissemination of policy.

* * *

(b) *Publications.* (1) Each recipient shall prominently include a statement of the policy described in paragraph (a) of this section in each announcement, bulletin, catalog, or application form which it makes available to any person of a type, described in paragraph (a) of this section, or which is otherwise used in connection with the recruitment of students or employees.

(2) A recipient shall not use or distribute a publication of the type described in this paragraph which suggests, by text or illustration, that such recipient treats applicants, students, or employees differently on the basis of sex except as such treatment is permitted by this part.

(c) *Distribution.* Each recipient shall distribute without discrimination on the basis of sex each publication described in paragraph (b) of this section, and shall apprise each of its admission and employment recruitment representatives of the policy of nondiscrimination described in paragraph (a) of this section, and require such representatives to adhere to such policy.

Subpart B—Coverage

§ 106.11 Application.

Except as provided in this subpart, this Part 106 applies to every recipient and to each education program or activity operated by such recipient which receives or benefits from Federal financial assistance.

§ 106.12 Educational institutions controlled by religious organizations.

(a) *Application.* This part does not apply to an educational institution which is controlled by a religious organization to the extent application of this part would not be consistent with the religious tenets of such organization.

(b) *Exemption.* An educational institution which wishes to claim the exemption set forth in paragraph (a) of this section, shall do so by submitting in writing to the Assistant Secretary a statement by the highest ranking official of the institution, identifying the provisions of this part which conflict with a specific tenet of the religious organization.

§ 106.13 Military and merchant marine educational institutions.

This part does not apply to an educational institution whose primary purpose is the training of individuals for a military service of the United States or for the merchant marine.

§ 106.14 Membership practices of certain organizations.

(a) *Social fraternities and sororities.* This part does not apply to the membership practices of social fraternities and sororities which are exempt from taxation under section 501(a) of the Internal Revenue Code of 1954, the active membership of which consists primarily of students in attendance at institutions of higher education.

(b) *YMCA, YWCA, Girl Scouts, Boy Scouts and Camp Fire Girls.* This part does not apply to the membership practices of the Young Men's Christian Association, the Young Women's Christian Association, the Girl Scouts, the Boy Scouts, and Camp Fire Girls.

(c) *Voluntary youth service organizations.* This part does not apply to the membership practices of voluntary youth service organizations which are exempt from taxation under section 501(a) of the Internal Revenue Code of 1954 and the membership of which has been traditionally limited to members of one sex and principally to persons of less than nineteen years of age.

§ 106.15 Admissions.

(a) Admissions to educational institutions prior to June 24, 1973, are not covered by this part.

(b) *Administratively separate units.* For the purposes only of this section, §§ 106.16 and 106.17, and Subpart C, each administratively separate unit shall be deemed to be an educational institution.

(c) *Application of Subpart C.* Except as provided in paragraphs (d) and (e) of this section, Subpart C applies to each recipient. A recipient to which Subpart C applies shall not discriminate on the basis of sex in admission or recruitment in violation of that subpart.

(d) *Educational institutions.* Except as provided in paragraph (e) of this section as to recipients which are educational institutions, Subpart C applies only to institutions of vocational education, professional education, graduate higher education, and public institutions of undergraduate higher education.

(e) *Public institutions of undergraduate higher education.* Subpart C does not apply to any public institution of undergraduate higher education which traditionally and continually from its establishment has had a policy of admitting only students of one sex.

* * *

Subpart C—Discrimination on the Basis of Sex in Admission and Recruitment Prohibited

§ 106.21 Admission.

(a) *General.* No person shall, on the basis of sex, be denied admission, or be subjected to discrimination in admission, by any recipient to which this subpart applies, except as provided in §§ 106.16 and 106.17 [relating to transition plans].

(b) *Specific prohibitions.* (1) In determining whether a person satisfies any policy or criterion for admission, or in making any offer of admission, a recipient to which this subpart applies shall not:

(i) Give preference to one person over another on the basis of sex, by ranking applicants separately on such basis, or otherwise;

(ii) Apply numerical limitations upon the number or proportion of persons of either sex who may be admitted; or

(iii) Otherwise treat one individual differently from another on the basis of sex.

* * *

Subpart D—Discrimination on the Basis of Sex in Education Programs and Activities Prohibited

§ 106.31 Education programs and activities.

(a) *General.* Except as provided elsewhere in this part, no person shall, on the basis of sex, be excluded from participation in, be denied the benefits of, or be subjected to discrimination under any academic, extracurricular, research, occupational training, or other education program or activity operated by a recipient which receives or benefits from Federal financial assistance. This subpart does not apply to actions of a recipient in connection with admission of its students to an education program or activity of (1) a recipient to which Subpart C does not apply, or (2) an entity, not a recipient, to which Subpart C would not apply if the entity were a recipient.

(b) *Specific prohibitions.* Except as provided in this subpart, in providing any aid, benefit, or service to a student, a recipient shall not, on the basis of sex:

(1) Treat one person differently from another in determining whether such person satisfies any requirement or condition for the provision of such aid, benefit, or service;

(2) Provide different aid, benefits, or services or provide aid, benefits, or services in a different manner;

(3) Deny any person any such aid, benefit, or service;

(4) Subject any person to separate or different rules of behavior, sanctions, or other treatment;

(5) Apply any rule concerning the domicile or residence of a student or applicant, including eligibility for in-state fees and tuition;

(6) Aid or perpetuate discrimination against any person by providing significant assistance to any agency, organization, or person which discriminates on' the basis of sex in providing any aid, benefit or service to students or employees;

(7) Otherwise limit any person in the enjoyment of any right, privilege, advantage, or opportunity.

(c) *Assistance administered by a recipient educational institution to study at a foreign institution.* A recipient educational institution may administer or assist in the administration of scholarships, fellowships, or other awards established by foreign or domestic wills, trusts, or similar legal instruments, or by acts of foreign governments and restricted to members of one sex, which are designed to provide opportunities to study abroad, and which are awarded to students who are already matriculating at or who are graduates of the recipient institution; *Provided*, a recipient educational institution which administers or assists in the administration of such scholarships, fellowships, or other awards which are restricted to members of one sex provides, or otherwise makes available reasonable opportunities for similar studies for members of the other sex. Such opportunities may be derived from either domestic or foreign sources.

(d) *Programs not operated by recipient.* (1) This paragraph applies to any recipient which requires participation by any applicant, student, or employee in any education program or activity not operated wholly by such recipient, or which facilitates, permits, or considers such participation as part of or equivalent to an education program or activity operated by such recipient, including participation in educational consortia and cooperative employment and student-teaching assignments.

(2) Such recipient;

(i) Shall develop and implement a procedure designed to assure itself that the operator or sponsor of such other education program or activity takes no action affecting any applicant, student, or employee of such recipient which this part would prohibit such recipient from taking; and

(ii) Shall not facilitate, require, permit or consider such participation if such action occurs.

§ 106.32 Housing.

(a) *Generally.* A recipient shall not, on the basis of sex, apply different rules or regulations, impose different fees or requirements, or offer different services or benefits related to housing, except as provided in this section (including housing provided only to married students).

(b) *Housing provided by recipient.* (1) A recipient may provide separate housing on the basis of sex.

(2) Housing provided by a recipient to students of one sex, when compared to that provided to students of the other sex, shall be as a whole:

(i) Proportionate in quantity to the number of students of that sex applying for such housing; and

(ii) Comparable in quality and cost to the student.

(c) *Other housing.* (1) A recipient shall not, on the basis of sex, administer different policies or practices concerning occupancy by its students of housing other than provided by such recipient.

(2) A recipient which, through solicitation, listing, approval of housing, or otherwise, assists any agency, organization, or person in making housing available to any of its students, shall take such reasonable action as may be necessary to assure itself that such housing as is provided to students of one sex, when compared to that provided to students of the other sex, is as a whole:

(i) Proportionate in quantity and (ii) comparable in quality and cost to the student. A recipient may render such assistance to any agency, organization, or person which provides all or part of such housing to students only of one sex.

§ 106.33 Comparable facilities.

A recipient may provide separate toilet, locker room, and shower facilities on the basis of sex, but such facilities provided for students of one sex shall be comparable to such facilities provided for students of the other sex.

§ 106.34 Access to course offerings.

A recipient shall not provide any course or otherwise carry out any of its education program or activity separately on the basis of sex, or require or refuse participation therein by any of its students on such basis, including health, physical education, industrial, business, vocational, technical, home economics, music, and adult education courses.

(a) With respect to classes and activities in physical education at the elementary school level, the recipient shall comply fully with this section as expeditiously as possible but in no event later than one year from the effective date of this regulation. With respect to physical education classes and activities at the secondary and post-secondary levels, the recipient shall comply fully with this section as expeditiously as possible but in no event later than three years from the effective date of this regulation.

(b) This section does not prohibit grouping of students in physical education classes and activities by ability as assessed by objective standards of individual performance developed and applied without regard to sex.

(c) This section does not prohibit separation of students by sex within physical education classes or activities during participation in wrestling, boxing, rugby, ice hockey, football, basketball and other sports the purpose or major activity of which involves bodily contact.

(d) Where use of a single standard of measuring skill or progress in a physical education class has an adverse effect on members of one sex, the recipient shall use appropriate standards which do not have such effect.

(e) Portions of classes in elementary and secondary schools which deal exclusively with human sexuality may be conducted in separate sessions for boys and girls.

(f) Recipients may make requirements based on vocal range or quality which may result in a chrous or choruses of one or predominantly one sex.

* * *

§ 106.36 Counseling and use of appraisal and counseling materials.

(a) *Counseling.* A recipient shall not discriminate against any person on the basis of sex in the counseling or guidance of students or applicants for admission.

* * *

§ 106.37 Financial assistance.

(a) *General.* Except as provided in paragraphs (b) and (c) of this section, in providing financial assistance to any of its students, a recipient shall not:

(1) On the basis of sex, provide different amount or types of such assistance, limit eligibility for such assistance which is of any particular type or source, apply different criteria, or otherwise discriminate; (2) through solicitation, listing, approval, provision of facilities or other services, assist any foundation, trust, agency, organization, or person which provides assistance to any of such recipient's students in a manner which discriminates on the basis of sex; or (3) apply any rule or assist in application of any rule concerning eligibility for such assistance which treats persons of one sex differently from persons of the other sex with regard to marital or parental status.

(b) *Financial aid established by certain legal instruments.* (1) A recipient may administer or assist in the administration of scholarships, fellowships, or other forms of financial assistance established pursuant to domestic or foreign wills, trusts, bequests, or similar legal instruments or by acts of a foreign government which requires that awards be made to members of a particular sex specified therein; *Provided,* That the overall effect of the award of such sex-restricted scholarships, fellowships and other forms of financial assistance does not discriminate on the basis of sex.

(2) To ensure nondiscriminatory awards of assistance as required in paragraph (b)(1) of this section, recipients shall develop and use procedures under which:

(i) Students are selected for award of financial assistance on the basis of nondiscriminatory criteria and not on the basis of availability of funds restricted to members of a particular sex;

(ii) An appropriate sex-restricted scholarship, fellowship, or other form of financial assistance is allocated to each student selected under paragraph (b)(2)(i) of this section; and

(iii) No student is denied the award for which he or she was selected under paragraph (b)(2)(i) of this section because of the absence of a scholarship, fellowship, or other form of financial assistance designated for a member of that student's sex.

(c) *Athletic scholarships.* (1) To the extent that a recipient awards athletic scholarships or grants-in-aid, it must provide reasonable opportunities for such awards for members of each sex in proportion to the number of students of each sex participating in interscholastic or intercollegiate athletics.

(2) Separate athletic scholarships or grants-in-aid for members of each sex may be provided as part of separate athletic teams for members of each sex to the extent consistent with this paragraph and § 106.41.

* * *

§ 106.40 Marital or parental status.

(a) *Status generally.* A recipient shall not apply any rule concerning a student's actual or potential parental, family, or marital status which treats students differently on the basis of sex.

(b) *Pregnancy and related conditions.* (1) A recipient shall not discriminate against any student, or exclude any student from its education program or activity, including any class or extracurricular activity, on the basis of such student's pregnancy, childbirth, false pregnancy, termination of pregnancy or recovery therefrom, unless the student requests voluntarily to participate in a separate portion of the program or activity of the recipient.

(2) A recipient may require such a student to obtain the certification of a physician that the student is physically and emotionally able to continue participation in the normal education program or activity so long as such a certification is required of all students for other physical or emotional conditions requiring the attention of a physician.

(3) A recipient which operates a portion of its education program or activity separately for pregnant students, admittance to which is completely voluntary on the part of the student as provided in paragraph (b)(1) of this section shall ensure that the instructional program in the separate program is comparable to that offered to non-pregnant students.

(4) A recipient shall treat pregnancy, childbirth, false pregnancy, termination of pregnancy and recovery therefrom in the same manner and under the same policies as any other temporary disability with respect to any medical or hospital benefit, service, plan or policy which such recipient administers, operates, offers, or participates in with respect to students admitted to the recipient's educational program or activity.

(5) In the case of a recipient which does not maintain a leave policy for its students, or in the case of a student who does not otherwise qualify for leave under such a policy, a recipient shall treat pregnancy, childbirth, false pregnancy, termination of pregnancy and recovery therefrom as a justification for a leave of absence for so long a period of time as is deemed medically necessary by the student's physician, at the conclusion of which the student shall be reinstated to the status which she held when the leave began.

§ 106.41 Athletics.

(a) *General.* No person shall, on the basis of sex, be excluded from participation in, be denied the benefits of, be treated differently from another person or otherwise be discriminated against in any interscholastic, intercollegiate, club or intramural athletics offered by a recipient, and no recipient shall provide any such athletics separately on such basis.

(b) *Separate teams.* Notwithstanding the requirements of paragraph (a) of this section, a recipient may operate or sponsor separate teams for members of each sex where selection for such teams is based upon competitive skill or the activity involved is a contact sport. However, where a recipient operates or sponsors a team in a particular sport for members of one sex but operates or sponsors no such team for members of the other sex, and athletic opportunities for members of that sex have previously been limited, members of the excluded sex must be allowed to try-out for the team offered unless the sport involved is a contact sport. For the purposes of this part, contact sports include boxing, wrestling, rugby, ice hockey, football, basketball and other sports the purpose or major activity of which involves bodily contact.

(c) *Equal opportunity.* A recipient which operates or sponsors interscholastic, intercollegiate, club or intramural athletics shall provide equal athletic opportunity for members of both sexes. In determining whether equal opportunities are available the Director will consider, among other factors:

(1) Whether the selection of sports and levels of competition effectively accommodate the interests and abilities of members of both sexes;

(2) The provision of equipment and supplies;

(3) Scheduling of games and practice time;

(4) Travel and per diem allowance;

(5) Opportunity to receive coaching and academic tutoring;

(6) Assignment and compensation of coaches and tutors;

(7) Provision of locker rooms, practice and competitive facilities;

(8) Provision of medical and training facilities and services;

(9) Provision of housing and dining facilities and services;

(10) Publicity.

Unequal aggregate expenditures for members of each sex or unequal expenditures for male and female teams if a recipient operates or sponsors separate teams will not constitute noncompliance with this section, but the Assistant Secretary may consider the failure to provide necessary funds for teams for one sex in assessing equality of opportunity for members of each sex.

*   *   *

§ 106.42 Textbooks and curricular material.

Nothing in this regulation shall be interpreted as requiring or prohibiting or abridging in any way the use of particular textbooks or curricular materials.

Subpart E—Discrimination on the Basis of Sex in Employment in Education Programs and Activities Prohibited

§ 106.51 Employment.

(a) *General.* (1) No person shall, on the basis of sex, be excluded from participation in, be denied the benefits of, or be subjected to discrimination in employment, or recruitment, consideration, or selection therefor, whether full-time or part-time, under any education program or activity operated by a recipient which receives or benefits from Federal financial assistance.

*   *   *

§ 106.59 Advertising.

A recipient shall not in any advertising related to employment indicate preference, limitation, specification, or discrimination based on sex unless sex is a *bona-fide* occupational qualification for the particular job in question.

§ 106.60 Pre-employment inquiries.

(a) *Marital status.* A recipient shall not make pre-employment inquiry as to the marital status of an applicant for employment, including whether such applicant is "Miss or Mrs."

(b) *Sex.* A recipient may make pre-employment inquiry as to the sex of an applicant for employment, but only if such inquiry is made equally of such applicants of both sexes and if the results of such inquiry are not used in connection with discrimination prohibited by this part.

§ 106.61 Sex as a bona-fide occupational qualification.

A recipient may take action otherwise prohibited by this subpart provided it is shown that sex is a bona-fide occupational qualification for that action, such that consideration of sex with regard to such action is essential to successful operation of the employment function concerned. A recipient shall not take action pursuant to this section which is based upon alleged comparative employment characteristics or stereotyped characterizations of one or the other sex, or upon preference based on sex of the recipient, employees, students, or other persons, but nothing contained in this section shall prevent a recipient from considering an employee's sex in relation to employment in a locker room or toilet facility used only by members of one sex.

V. REHABILITATION ACT OF 1973

Like Title VI and Title IX, § 504 of the Rehabilitation Act of 1973 only applies to public or private institutions receiving federal financial assistance. Section 504 prohibits discrimination based upon handicap (see Chapter One, Section III, and Chapter Two, Section II).

Section 504, which is codified at 29 U.S.C. § 794, provides as follows:

§ 794. Nondiscrimination under Federal grants and programs; promulgation of rules and regulations

No otherwise qualified handicapped individual in the United States, as defined in section 706(7) of this title, shall, solely by reason of his handicap, be excluded from the participation in, be denied the benefits of, or be subjected to discrimination under any program or activity receiving Federal financial assistance or under any program or activity conducted by any Executive agency or by the United States Postal Service. The head of each such agency shall promulgate such regulations as may be necessary to carry out the amendments to this section made by the Rehabilitation, Comprehensive Services, and Developmental Disabilities Act of 1978. Copies of any proposed regulation shall be submitted to appropriate authorizing committees of the Congress, and such regulation may take effect no earlier than the thirtieth day after the date on which such regulation is so submitted to such committees.

The major U.S. Department of Education regulations interpreting § 504, found at 34 CFR Part 104, are as follows:

Subpart A—General Provisions

§ 104.1 Purpose.

The purpose of this part is to effectuate section 504 of the Rehabilitation Act of 1973, which is designed to eliminate discrimination on the basis of handicap in any program or activity receiving Federal financial assistance.

§ 104.2 Application.

This part applies to each recipient of Federal financial assistance from the Department of Education and to each program or activity that receives or benefits from such assistance.

§ 104.3 Definitions.

*   *   *

(j) "Handicapped person." (1) "Handicapped persons" means any person who (i) has a physical or mental impairment which substantially limits one or more major life activities, (ii) has a record of such an impairment, or (iii) is regarded as having such an impairment.

(2) As used in paragraph (j)(1) of this section, the phrase:

(i) "Physical or mental impairment" means (A) any physiological disorder or condition, cosmetic disfigurement, or anatomical loss affecting one or more of the following body systems: neurological; musculoskeletal; special sense organs; respiratory, including speech organs; cardiovascular; reproductive, digestive, genito-urinary; hemic and lymphatic; skin; and endocrine; or (B) any mental or psychological disorder, such as mental retardation, organic brain syndrome, emotional or mental illness, and specific learning disabilities.

(ii) "Major life activities" means functions such as caring for one's self, performing manual tasks, walking, seeing, hearing, speaking, breathing, learning, and working.

*   *   *

(k) "Qualified handicapped person" means:

(1) With respect to employment, a handicapped person who, with reasonable accommodation, can perform the essential functions of the job in question;

(2) With respect to public preschool elementary, secondary, or adult educational services, a handicapped person (i) of an age during which nonhandicapped persons are provided such services, (ii) of any age during which it is mandatory under state law to provide such services to handicapped persons, or (iii) to whom a state is required to provide a free appropriate public education under section 612 of the Education of the Handicapped Act; and

(3) With respect to postsecondary and vocational education services, a handicapped person who meets the academic and technical standards requisite to admission or participation in the recipient's education program or activity;

(4) With respect to other services, a handicapped person who meets the essential eligibility requirements for the receipt of such services.

(l) "Handicap" means any condition or characteristic that renders a person a handicapped person as defined in paragraph (j) of this section.

*   *   *

Subpart B—Employment Practices

§ 104.11 Discrimination prohibited.

(a) *General.* (1) No qualified handicapped person shall, on the basis of handicap, be subjected to discrimination in employment under any program or activity to which this part applies.

*   *   *

§ 104.12 Reasonable accommodation.

(a) A recipient shall make reasonable accommodation to the known physical or mental limitations of an otherwise qualified handicapped applicant or employee unless the recipient can demonstrate that the accommodation would impose an undue hardship on the operation of its program.

(b) Reasonable accommodation may include: (1) Making facilities used by employees readily accessible to and usable by handicapped persons, and (2) job restructuring, part-time or modified work schedules, acquisition or modification of equipment or devices, the provision of readers or interpreters, and other similar actions.

(c) In determining pursuant to paragraph (a) of this section whether an accommodation would impose an undue hardship on the operation of a recipient's program, factors to be considered include:

(1) The overall size of the recipient's program with respect to number of employees, number and type of facilities, and size of budget;

(2) The type of the recipient's operation, including the composition and structure of the recipient's workforce; and

(3) The nature and cost of the accommodation needed.

(d) A recipient may not deny any employment opportunity to a qualified handicapped employee or applicant if the basis for the denial is the need to make reasonable accommodation to the physical or mental limitations of the employee or applicant.

* * *

Subpart C—Program Accessibility

§ 104.21 Discrimination prohibited.

No qualified handicapped person shall, because a recipient's facilities are inaccessible to or unusable by handicapped persons, be denied the benefits of, be excluded from participation in, or otherwise be subjected to discrimination under any program or activity to which this part applies.

* * *

Subpart D—Preschool, Elementary, and Secondary Education

§ 104.31 Application of this subpart.

Subpart D applies to preschool, elementary, secondary, and adult education programs and activities that receive or benefit from Federal financial assistance and to recipients that operate, or that receive or benefit from Federal financial assistance for the operation of, such programs or activities.

* * *

§ 104.33 Free appropriate public education.

(a) *General.* A recipient that operates a public elementary or secondary education program shall provide a free appropriate public education to each qualified handicapped person who is in the recipient's jurisdiction, regardless of the nature or severity of the person's handicap.

(b) *Appropriate education.* (1) For the purpose of this subpart, the provision of an appropriate education is the provision of regular or special education and related aids and services that (i) are designed to meet individual educational needs of handicapped persons as adequately as the needs of nonhandicapped persons are met and (ii) are based upon adherence to procedures that satisfy the requirements of §§ 104.34, 104.35, and 104.36.

(2) Implementation of an individualized education program developed in accordance with the Education of the Handicapped Act is one means of meeting the standard established in paragraph (b)(1)(i) of this section.

(3) A recipient may place a handicapped person in or refer such person to a program other than the one that it operates as its means of carrying out the

requirements of this subpart. If so, the recipient remains responsible for ensuring that the requirements of this subpart are met with respect to any handicapped person so placed or referred.

(c) *Free education*—(1) *General.* For the purpose of this section, the provision of a free education is the provision of educational and related services without cost to the handicapped person or to his or her parents or guardian, except for those fees that are imposed on non-handicapped persons or their parents or guardian. It may consist either of the provision of free services or, if a recipient places a handicapped person in or refers such person to a program not operated by the recipient as its means of carrying out the requirements of this subpart, of payment for the costs of the program. Funds available from any public or private agency may be used to meet the requirements of this subpart. Nothing in this section shall be construed to relieve an insurer or similar third party from an otherwise valid obligation to provide or pay for services provided to a handicapped person.

(2) *Transportation.* If a recipient places a handicapped person in or refers such person to a program not operated by the recipient as its means of carrying out the requirements of this subpart, the recipient shall ensure that adequate transportation to and from the program is provided at no greater cost than would be incurred by the person of his or her parents or guardian if the person were placed in the program operated by the recipient.

(3) *Residential placement.* If placement in a public or private residential program is necessary to provide a free appropriate public education to a handicapped person because of his or her handicap, the program, including non-medical care and room and board, shall be provided at no cost to the person or his or her parents or guardian.

(4) *Placement of handicapped persons by parents.* If a recipient has made available, in conformance with the requirements of this section and § 104.34, a free appropriate public education to a handicapped person and the person's parents or guardian choose to place the person in a private school, the recipient is not required to pay for the person's education in the private school. Disagreements between a parent or guardian and a recipient regarding whether the recipient has made such a program available or otherwise regarding the question of financial responsibility are subject to the due process procedures of § 104.36.

(d) *Compliance.* A recipient may not exclude any qualified handicapped person from a public elementary or secondary education after the effective date of this part. A recipient that is not, on the effective date of this regulation, in full compliance with the other requirements of the preceding paragraphs of this section shall meet such requirements at the earliest practicable time and in no event later than September 1, 1978.

§ 104.34 Educational setting.

(a) *Academic setting.* A recipient to which this subpart applies shall educate, or shall provide for the education of, each qualified handicapped person in its jurisdiction with persons who are not handicapped to the maximum extent appropriate to the needs of the handicapped person. A recipient shall place a handicapped person in the regular educational environment operated by the recipient unless it is demonstrated by the recipient that the education of the person in the regular environment with the use of supplementary aids and services cannot be achieved satisfactorily. Whenever a recipient places a person in a setting other than the regular educational environment pursuant to this paragraph, it shall take into account the proximity of the alternate setting to the person's home.

(b) *Nonacademic settings.* In providing or arranging for the provision of nonacademic and extracurricular services and activities, including meals, recess periods, and the services and activities set forth in § 104.37(a)(2), a recipient shall ensure that handicapped persons participate with nonhandicapped persons in such activities and services to the maximum extent appropriate to the needs of the handicapped person in question.

(c) *Comparable facilities.* If a recipient, in compliance with paragraph (a) of this section, operates a facility that is identifiable as being for handicapped persons, the recipient shall ensure that the facility and the services and activities provided therein are comparable to the other facilities, services, and activities of the recipient.

§ 104.35 Evaluation and placement.

(a) *Preplacement evaluation.* A recipient that operates a public elementary or secondary education program shall conduct an evaluation in accordance with the requirements of paragraph (b) of this section of any person who, because of handicap, needs or is believed to need special education or related services before taking any action with respect to the initial placement of the person in a regular or special education program and any subsequent significant change in placement.

(b) *Evaluation procedures.* A recipient to which this subpart applies shall establish standards and procedures for the evaluation and placement of persons who, because of handicap, need or are believed to need special education or related services which ensure that:

(1) Tests and other evaluation materials have been validated for the specific purpose for which they are used and are administered by trained personnel in conformance with the instructions provided by their producer;

(2) Tests and other evaluation materials include those tailored to assess specific areas of educational need and not merely those which are designed to provide a single general intelligence quotient; and

(3) Tests are selected and administered so as best to ensure that, when a test is administered to a student with impaired sensory, manual, or speaking skills, the test results accurately reflect the student's aptitude or achievement level or whatever other factor the test purports to measure, rather than reflecting the student's impaired sensory, manual, or speaking skills (except where those skills are the factors that the test purports to measure).

(c) *Placement procedures.* In interpreting evaluation data and in making placement decisions, a recipient shall (1) draw upon information from a variety of sources, including aptitude and achievement tests, teacher recommendations, physical condition, social or cultural background, and adaptive behavior, (2) establish procedures to ensure that information obtained from all such sources is documented and carefully considered, (3) ensure that the placement decision is made by a group of persons, including persons knowledgeable about the child, the meaning of the evaluation data, and the placement options, and (4) ensure that the placement decision is made in conformity with § 104.34.

(d) *Reevaluation.* A recipient to which this section applies shall establish procedures, in accordance with paragraph (b) of this section, for periodic reevaluation of students who have been provided special education and related services. A reevaluation procedure consistent with the Education for the Handicapped Act is one means of meeting this requirement.

§ 104.36 Procedural safeguards.

A recipient that operates a public elementary or secondary education program shall establish and implement, with respect to actions regarding the identification, evaluation, or education placement of persons who, because of handicap, need or are believed to need special instruction or related services, a system of procedural safeguards that includes notice, an opportunity for the parents or guardian of the person to examine relevant records, an impartial hearing with opportunity for participation by the person's parents or guardian and representation by counsel, and a review procedure. Compliance with the procedural safeguards of section 615 of the Education of the Handicapped Act is one means of meeting this requirement.

§ 104.37 Nonacademic services.

(a) *General.* (1) A recipient to which this subpart applies shall provide nonacademic and extracurricular services and activities in such manner as is necessary to afford handicapped students an equal opportunity for participation in such services and activities.

(2) Nonacademic and extracurricular services and activities may include counseling services, physical recreational athletics, transportion, health services, recreational activities, special interest groups or clubs sponsored by the recipients, referrals to agencies which provide assistance to handicapped persons, and employment of students, including both employment by the recipient and assistance in making available outside employment.

(b) *Counseling services.* A recipient to which this subpart applies that provides personal, academic, or vocational counseling, guidance, or placement services to its students shall provide these services without discrimination on the basis of handicap. The recipient shall ensure that qualified handicapped students are not counseled toward more restrictive career objectives than are nonhandicapped students with similar interests and abilities.

(c) *Physical education and athletics.* (1) In providing physical education courses and athletics and similar programs and activities to any of its students, a recipient to which this subpart applies may not discriminate on the basis of handicap. A recipient that offers physical education courses or that operates or sponsors interscholastic, club or intramural athletics shall provide to qualified handicapped students an equal opportunity for participation in these activities.

(2) A recipient may offer to handicapped students physical education and athletic activities that are separate or different from those offered to nonhandicapped students only if separation or differentiation is consistent with the requirements of § 104.34 and only if no qualified handicapped student is denied the opportunity to compete for teams or to participate in courses that are not separate or different.

§ 104.38 Preschool and adult education programs.

A recipient to which this subpart applies that operates a preschool education or day care program or activity or an adult education program or activity may not, on the basis of handicap, exclude qualified handicapped persons from the program or activity and shall take into account the needs of such persons in determining the aid, benefits, or services to be provided under the program or activity.

§ 104.39 Private education programs.

(a) A recipient that operates a private elementary or secondary education program may not, on the basis of handicap, exclude a qualified handicapped person from such program if the person can, with minor adjustments, be provided an appropriate education, as defined in § 104.33(b)(1), within the recipient's program.

(b) A recipient to which this section applies may not charge more for the provision of an appropriate education to handicapped persons than to nonhandicapped persons except to the extent that any additional charge is justified by a substantial increase in cost to the recipient.

* * *

Subpart E—Postsecondary Education

* * *

§ 104.42 Admissions and recruitment.

(a) *General.* Qualified handicapped persons may not, on the basis of handicap, be denied admission or be subjected to discrimination in admission or recruitment by a recipient to which this subpart applies.

* * *

§ 104.43 Treatment of students; general.

(a) No qualified handicapped student shall, on the basis of handicap, be excluded from participation in, be denied the benefits of, or otherwise be subjected to discrimination under any academic, research, occupational training, housing, health insurance, counseling, financial aid, physical education, athletics, recreation, transportation, other extracurricular, or other postsecondary education program or activity to which this subpart applies.

* * *

(d) A recipient to which this subpart applies shall operate its programs and activities in the most integrated setting appropriate.

§ 104.44 Academic adjustments.

(a) *Academic requirements.* A recipient to which this subpart applies shall make such modifications to its academic requirements as are necessary to ensure that such requirements do not discriminate or have the effect of discriminating, on the basis of handicap, against a qualified handicapped applicant or student. Academic requirements that the recipient can demonstrate are essential to the program of instruction being pursued by such student or to any directly related licensing requirement will not be regarded as discriminatory within the meaning of this section. Modifications may include changes in the length of time permitted for the completion of degree requirements, substitution of specific courses required for the completion of degree requirements, and adaptation of the manner in which specific courses are conducted.

(b) *Other rules.* A recipient to which this subpart applies may not impose upon handicapped students other rules, such as the prohibition of tape recorders in classrooms or of dog guides in campus buildings, that have the effect of limiting the participation of handicapped students in the recipient's education program or activity.

(c) *Course examinations.* In its course examinations or other procedures for evaluating students' academic achievement in its program, a recipient to which this subpart applies shall provide such methods for evaluating the achievement of students who have a handicap that impairs sensory, manual, or speaking skills as will best ensure that the results of the evaluation represents the student's achievement in the course, rather than reflecting the student's impaired sensory, manual, or speaking skills (except where such skills are the factors that the test purports to measure).

(d) *Auxiliary aids.* (1) A recipient to which this subpart applies shall take such steps as are necessary to ensure that no handicapped student is denied the benefits of, excluded form participation in, or otherwise subjected to discrimination under the education program or activity operated by the recipient because of the absence of educational auxiliary aids for students with impaired sensory, manual, or speaking skills.

(2) Auxiliary aids may include taped texts; interpreters or other effective methods of making orally delivered materials available to students with hearing impairments, readers in libraries for students with visual impairments, classroom equipment adapted for use by students with manual impairments, and other similar services and actions. Recipients need not provide attendants, individually prescribed devices, readers for personal use or study, or other devices or services of a personal nature.

§ 104.45 Housing.

(a) *Housing provided by the recipient.* A recipient that provides housing to its nonhandicapped students shall provide comparable, convenient, and accessible housing to handicapped students at the same cost as to others. At the end of the transition period provided for in Subpart C, such housing shall be available in sufficient quantity and variety so that the scope of handicapped students' choice of living accommodations is, as a whole, comparable to that of nonhandicapped students.

(b) *Other housing.* A recipient that assists any agency, organization, or person in making housing available to any of its students shall take such action as may be necessary to assure itself that such housing is, as a whole, made available in a manner that does not result in discrimination on the basis of handicap.

§ 104.46 Financial and employment assistance to students.

(a) *Provision of financial assistance.* (1) In providing financial assistance to qualified handicapped persons, a recipient to which this subpart applies may not (i), on the basis of handicap, provide less assistance than is provided to nonhandicapped persons, limit eligibility for assistance, or otherwise discriminate or (ii) assist any entity or person that provides assistance to any of the recipient's student's in a manner that discriminates against qualified handicapped persons on the basis of handicap.

(2) A recipient may administer or assist in the administration of scholarships, fellowships, or other forms of financial assistance established under wills, trusts, bequests, or similar legal instruments that require awards to be made on the basis of factors that discriminate or have the effect of discriminating on the basis of handicap only if the overall effect of the award of scholarships, fellowships, and other forms of financial assistance is not discriminatory on the basis of handicap.

* * *

§ 104.47 Nonacademic services.

(a) *Physical education and athletics.* (1) In providing physical education courses and athletics and similar programs and activities to any of its students, a recipient to which this subpart applies may not discriminate on the basis of handicap. A recipient that offers physical education courses or that operates or sponsors intercollegiate, club, or intramural athletics shall provide to qualified handicapped students an equal opportunity for participation in these activities.

(2) A recipient may offer to handicapped students physical education and athletic activities that are separate or different only if separation or differentiation is consistent with the requirements of § 104.43(d) and only if no qualified handicapped student is denied the opportunity to compete for teams or to participate in courses that are not separate or different.

(b) *Counseling and placement services.* A recipient to which this subpart applies that provides personal, academic, or vocational counseling, guidance, or placement services to its students shall provide these services without discrimination on the basis of handicap. The recipient shall ensure that qualified handicapped students are not counseled toward more restrictive career objectives than are nonhandicapped students with similar interests and abilities. This requirement does not preclude a recipient from providing factual information about licensing and certification requirements that may present obstacles to handicapped persons in their pursuit of particular careers.

(c) *Social organizations.* A recipient that provides significant assistance to fraternities, sororities, or similar organizations shall assure itself that the membership practices of such organizations do not permit discrimination otherwise prohibited by this subpart.

[Subparts F and G are omitted.]

VI. AGE DISCRIMINATION

The use of an individual's age as a criteria for employment generally is forbidden by federal law. In the nonemployment context, age discrimination is forbidden in public or private school "programs or activities" receiving federal financial assistance.

A. Age Discrimination in Employment Act

Like the Equal Pay Act, the Age Discrimination in Employment Act of 1967 (ADEA) (29 U.S.C. § 621 *et seq.*) is part of the Fair Labor Standards Act. It applies to institutions which have twenty or more employees and which affect interstate commerce (see Section III). Prior to January 1, 1987, the ADEA protected individuals between the ages of forty and seventy. However, a 1986 amendment to the ADEA removed the upper age limit and extended protection to any individual forty years of age or older. As indicated below in § 631(d), the 1986 amendment also added a special sunset provision with respect to public and private colleges. Section 631(d) automatically expires on December 31, 1993 [P.L. 99-592 § 6(b)].

Relevant provisions of the ADEA are as follows:

§ 623. Prohibition of age discrimination

(a) Employer practices

It shall be unlawful for an employer—
(1) to fail or refuse to hire or to discharge any individual or otherwise discriminate against any individual with respect to his compensation, terms, conditions, or privileges of employment, because of such individual's age;
(2) to limit, segregate, or classify his employees in any way which would deprive or tend to deprive any individual of employment opportunities or otherwise adversely affect his status as an employee, because of such individual's age; or
(3) to reduce the wage rate of any employee in order to comply with this chapter.

* * *

(f) Lawful practices; age an occupational qualification; other reasonable factors; seniority system; employee benefit plans; discharge or discipline for good cause

It shall not be unlawful for an employer, employment agency, or labor organization—

(1) to take any action otherwise prohibited under subsections (a), (b), (c), or (e) or this section where age is a bona fide occupational qualification reasonably necessary to the normal operation of the particular business, or where the differentiation is based on reasonable factors other than age;

(2) to observe the terms of a bona fide seniority system or any bona fide employee benefit plan such as a retirement, pension, or insurance plan, which is not a subterfuge to evade the purposes of this chapter, except that no such employee benefit plan shall excuse the failure to hire any individual, and no such seniority system or employee benefit plan shall require or permit the involuntary retirement of any individual specified by section 631(a) of this title because of the age of such individual; or

(3) to discharge or otherwise discipline an individual for good cause.

* * *

§ 631. Age limits

(a) Individuals at least 40 years of age

The prohibitions in this chapter (except the provisions of section 623(g) of this title) shall be limited to individuals who are at least 40 years of age.

* * *

(c) Bona fide executives or high policymakers

(1) Nothing in this chapter shall be construed to prohibit compulsory retirement of any employee who has attained 65 years of age and who, for the 2-year period immediately before retirement, is employed in a bona fide executive or a high policymaking position, if such employee is entitled to an immediate nonforfeitable annual retirement benefit from a pension, profit-sharing, savings, or deferred compensation plan, or any combination of such plans, of the employer of such employee, which equals, in the aggregate, at least $27,000.

(2) In applying the retirement benefit test of paragraph (1) of this subsection, if any such retirement benefit is in a form other than a straight life annuity (with no ancillary benefits), or if employees contribute to any such plan or make rollover contributions, such benefit shall be adjusted in accordance with regulations prescribed by the Equal Employment Opportunity Commission, after consultation with the Secretary of the Treasury, so that the benefit is the equivalent of a straight life annuity (with no ancillary benefits) under a plan to which employees do not contribute and under which no rollover contributions are made.

(d) Tenured employee at institution of higher education

Nothing in this Act shall be construed to prohibit compulsory retirement of any employee who has attained 70 years of age, and who is serving under a contract of unlimited tenure (or similar arrangement providing for unlimited tenure) at an institution of higher education (as defined by section 1201(a) of the Higher Education Act of 1965).

B. Age Discrimination Act

The Age Discrimination Act of 1975 (ADA) (42 U.S.C. § 6101 *et seq.*) is a more general age discrimination statute. It primarily addresses age discrimination outside the employment context. Unlike the ADEA, the ADA applies only to programs or activities receiving federal funds. The ADA provides as follows:

*   *   *

§ 6102. Prohibition of discrimination

Pursuant to regulations prescribed under section 6103 of this title, and except as provided by section 6103(b) and section 6103(c) of this title, no person in the United States shall, on the basis of age, be excluded from participation in, be denied the benefits of, or be subjected to discrimination under, any program or activity receiving Federal financial assistance.

§ 6103. Regulations

*   *   *

(b) Nonviolative actions; program or activity exemption

(1) It shall not be a violation of any provision of this chapter, or of any regulation issued under this chapter, for any person to take any action otherwise prohibited by the provisions of section 6102 of this title if, in the program or activity involved—

(A) such action reasonably takes into account age as a factor necessary to the normal operation or the achievement of any statutory objective of such program or activity; or

(B) the differentiation made by such action is based upon reasonable factors other than age.

(2) The provisions of this chapter shall not apply to any program or activity established under authority of any law which (A) provides any benefits or assistance to persons based upon the age of such persons; or (B) establishes criteria for participation in age-related terms or describes intended beneficiaries or target groups in such terms.

U.S. Department of Health and Human Services (HHS) regulations interpreting the ADA are found at 45 CFR Part 90. The regulatory provisions most relevant to private education are as follows:

§ 90.12 Rules against age discrimination.

The rules stated in this section are limited by the exceptions contained in §§ 90.14, and 90.15 of these regulations.

(a) *General rule:* No person in the United States shall, on the basis of age, be excluded from participation in, be denied the benefits of, or be subjected to discrimination under, any program or activity receiving Federal financial assistance.

(b) *Specific rules:* A recipient may not, in any program or activity receiving Federal financial assistance, directly or through contractual, licensing, or other arrangements use age distinctions or take any other actions which have the effect, on the basis of age, of:

(1) Excluding individuals from, denying them the benefits of, or subjecting them to discrimination under, a program or activity receiving Federal financial assistance, or

(2) Denying or limiting individuals in their opportunity to participate in any program or activity receiving Federal financial assistance.

(c) The specific forms of age discrimination listed in paragraph (b) of this section do not necessarily constitute a complete list.

§ 90.13 Definitions of "normal operation" and "statutory objective."

For purposes of §§ 90.14 and 90.15, the terms "normal operation" and "statutory objective" shall have the following meaning:

(a) "Normal operation" means the operation of a program or activity without significant changes that would impair its ability to meet its objectives.

(b) "Statutory objective" means any purpose of a program or activity expressly stated in any Federal statute, State statute, or local statute or ordinance adopted by an elected, general purpose legislative body.

§ 90.14 Exceptions to the rules against age discrimination. Normal operation or statutory objective of any program or activity.

A recipient is permitted to take an action, otherwise prohibited by § 90.12, if the action reasonably takes into account age as a factor necessary to the normal operation or the achievement of any statutory objective of a program or activity. An action reasonably takes into account age as a factor necessary to the normal operation or the achievement of any statutory objective of a program or activity, if:

(a) Age is used as a measure or approximation of one or more other characteristics; and

(b) The other characteristic(s) must be measured or approximated in order for the normal operation of the program or activity to continue, or to achieve any statutory objective of the program or activity; and

(c) The other characteristic(s) can be reasonably measured or approximated by the use of age; and

(d) The other characteristic(s) are impractical to measure directly on an individual basis.

§ 90.15 Exceptions to the rules against age discrimination. Reasonable factors other than age.

A recipient is permitted to take an action otherwise prohibited by § 90.12 which is based on a factor other than age, even though that action may have a disproportionate effect on persons of different ages. An action may be based on a factor other than age only if the factor bears a direct and substantial relationship to the normal operation of the program or activity or to the achievement of a statutory objective.

§ 90.16 Burden of proof.

The burden of proving that an age distinction or other action falls within the exceptions outlined in §§ 90.14 and 90.15 is on the recipient of Federal financial assistance.

The above regulations were promulgated by HHS along with the following official comments [found at 44 Fed. Reg. 33773-74 (June 12, 1979)], which provide further guidance as to how the federal government will interpret them:

1. A medical school receiving federal financial assistance generally does not admit anyone over 35 years of age, even though this results in turning away highly qualified applicants over 35. The school claims it has an objective, the teaching of qualified medical students who, upon graduation, will practice as long as possible. The school believes that this objective requires it to select younger applicants over older ones. The use of such an age distinction *is not necessary* to.normal operation of the recipient's program because it does not meet the requirement of Section 90.14(b). Age of the applicant may be a reasonable measure of a nonage characteristic (longevity of practice). This characteristic may be impractical to measure directly on an individual basis. Nevertheless, achieving a high average of longevity of practice cannot be considered a program objective for a medical school within the meaning of the Act. The "normal operation" exception is not intended to permit a recipient to use broad notions of efficiency or cost-benefit analysis to justify exclusion from a program on the basis of age. The basic objectives of the medical school involve training competent and qualified medical school graduates. These objectives are not impaired if the average length its graduates practice medicine is lowered by a fraction of a year (or even more) by the admission of qualified applicants over 35 years of age.

2. A federally assisted training program uses a physical fitness test as a factor for selecting participants to train for a certain job. The job involves frequent heavy lifting and other demands for physical strength and stamina. Even though older persons might fail the test more frequently than younger persons, the physical fitness test measures a characteristic that is *directly and substantially* related to the job for which persons are being trained and is, therefore, permissible under the Act.

VII. BUCKLEY AMENDMENT

The Family Education Rights and Privacy Act of 1974 (20 U.S.C. § 1232g), also called the Buckley Amendment, establishes student and parent rights with regard to student records. The Amendment applies only to records pertaining to individuals who have been admitted as students at private or public educational institutions. Like Title VI, Title IX, § 504 and the ADA, the Buckley Amendment applies only to schools receiving federal funding. Unlike the other statutes, however, the Amendment applies to the entire institution and not only to the "program or activity" receiving federal funding.

Relevant provisions of the Buckley Amendment are as follows:

§ 1232g. Family educational and privacy rights

(a) Conditions for availability of funds to educational agencies or institutions; inspection and review of education records; specific information to be made available; procedure for access to education records; reasonableness of time for such access; hearings; written explanations by parents; definitions

(1)(A) No funds shall be made available under any applicable program to any educational agency or institution which has a policy of denying, or which effectively prevents, the parents of students who are or have been in attendance at a school of such agency or at such institution, as the case may be, the right to inspect and review the education records of their children. If any material or document in the education record of a student includes information on more than one student, the parents of one of such students shall have the right to inspect and review only such part of such material or document as relates top such student or to be informed of the specific information contained in such part of such material. Each educational agency or institution shall establish appropriate procedures for the granting of a request by parents for access to the education records of their children within a reasonable period of time, but in no case more than forty-five days after the request has been made.

(B) The first sentence of subparagraph (A) shall not operate to make available to students in institutions of postsecondary education the following materials:

(i) financial records of the parents of the student or any information contained therein;

(ii) confidential letters and statements of recommendation, which were placed in the education records prior to January 1, 1975, if such letters or statements are not used for purposes other than those for which they were specifically intended;

(iii) if the student has signed a waiver of the student's right of access under this subsection in accordance with subparagraph (C), confidential recommendations—

(I) respecting admission to any educational agency or institution,

(II) respecting an application for employment, and

(III) respecting the receipt of an honor or honorary recognition.

(C) A student or a person applying for admission may waive his right of access to confidential statements described in clause (iii) of subparagraph (B), except that such waiver shall apply to recommendations only if (i) the student is, upon request, notified of the names of all persons making confidential recommendations and (ii) such recommendations are used solely for the purpose for which they were specifically intended. Such waivers may not be required as a condition for admission to, receipt of financial aid from, or receipt of any other services or benefits from such agency or institution.

(2) No funds shall be made available under any applicable program to any educational agency or institution unless the parents of students who are or have been in attendance at a school of such agency or at such institution are provided an opportunity for a hearing by such agency or institution, in accordance with regulations of the Secretary, to challenge the content of such student's education records in order to insure that the records are not inaccurate, misleading, or otherwise in violation of the privacy or other rights of students, and to provide an opportunity for the correction or deletion of any such inaccurate, misleading or otherwise inappropriate data contained therein and to insert into such records a written explanation of the parents respecting the content of such records.

(3) For the purposes of this section the term "educational agency or institution" means any public or private agency or institution which is the recipient of funds under any applicable program.

(4)(A) For the purposes of this section the term, "education records" means, except as may be provided otherwise in subparagraph (B), those records, files, documents, and other materials which—

(i) contain information directly related to a student; and

(ii) are maintained by an educational agency or institution or by a person acting for such agency or institution.

(B) The term "education records" does not include—

(i) records of instructional, supervisory, and administrative personnel and educational personnel ancillary thereto which are in the sole possession of the maker thereof and which are not accessible or revealed to any other person except a substitute;

(ii) if the personnel of a law enforcement unit do not have access to education records under subsection (b)(1) of this section, the records and documents of such law enforcement unit which (I) are kept apart from records described in subparagraph (A), (II) are maintained solely for law enforcement purposes, and

(III) are not made available to persons other than law enforcement officials of the same jurisdiction;

(iii) in the case of persons who are employed by an educational agency or institution but who are not in attendance at such agency or institution, records made and maintained in the normal course of business which relate exclusively to such person in that person's capacity as an employee and are not available for use for any other purpose; or

(iv) records on a student who is eighteen years of age or older, or is attending an institution of postsecondary education, which are made or maintained by a physician, psychiatrist, psychologist, or other recognized professional or para-professional acting in his professional or paraprofessional capacity, or assisting in that capacity, and which are made, maintained, or used only in connection with the provision of treatment to the student, and are not available to anyone other than persons providing such treatment, except that such records can be personally reviewed by a physician or other appropriate professional of the student's choice.

(5)(A) For the purposes of this section the term "directory information" relating to a student includes the following: the student's name, address, telephone listing, date and place of birth, major field of study, participation in officially recognized activities and sports, weight and height of members of athletic teams, dates of attendance, degrees and awards received, and the most recent previous educational agency or institution attended by the student.

(B) Any educational agency or institution making public directory information shall give public notice of the categories of information which it has designated as such information with respect to each student attending the institution or agency and shall allow a reasonable period of time after such notice has been given for a parent to inform the institution or agency that any or all of the information designated should not be released without the parent's prior consent.

(6) For the purposes of this section, the term, "student" includes any person with respect to whom an educational agency or institution maintains education records or personally identifiable information, but does not include a person who has not been in attendance at such agency or institution.

(b) Release of education records; parental consent requirement; exceptions; compliance with judicial orders and subpoenas; audit and evaluation of federally-supported education programs; recordkeeping

(1) No funds shall be made available under any applicable program to any educational agency or institution which has a policy or practice of permitting the release of education records (or personally identifiable information contained therein other than directory information, as defined in paragraph (5) of subsection (a) of this section) of students without the written consent of their parents to any individual, agency, or organization, other than to the following—

(A) other school officials, including teachers within the educational institution or local educational agency, who have been determined by such agency or institution to have legitimate educational interest;

(B) officials of other schools or school systems in which the student seeks or intends to enroll, upon condition that the student's parents be notified of the transfer, receive a copy of the record if desired, and have an opportunity for a hearing to challenge the content of the record;

(C) authorized representatives of (i) the Comptroller General of the United States, (ii) the Secretary, (iii) an administrative head of an education agency (as defined in section 1221e-3(c) of this title), or (iv) State educational authorities under the conditions set forth in paragraph (3) of this subsection;

(D) in connection with a student's application for, or receipt of, financial aid;

(E) State and local officials or authorities to whom such information is specifically required to be reported or disclosed pursuant to State statute adopted prior to November 19, 1974;

(F) organizations conducting studies for, or on behalf of, educational agencies or institutions for the purpose of developing, validating, or administering predictive tests, administering student aid programs, and improving instruction, if such studies are conducted in such a manner as will not permit the personal identification of students and their parents by persons other than representatives of such organizations and such information will be destroyed when no longer needed for the purpose for which it is conducted;

(G) accrediting organizations in order to carry out their accrediting functions;

(H) parents of a dependent student of such parents, as defined in section 152 of title 26; and

(I) subject to regulations of the Secretary, in connection with an emergency, appropriate persons if the knowledge of such information is necessary to protect the health or safety of the student or other persons.

Nothing in clause (E) of this paragraph shall prevent a State from further limiting the number or type of State or local officials who will continue to have access thereunder.

(2) No funds shall be made available under any applicable program to any educational agency or institution which has a policy or practice of releasing, or providing access to, any personally identifiable information in education records other than directory information, or as is permitted under paragraph (1) of this subsection unless—

(A) there is written consent from the student's parents specifying records to be released, the reasons for such release, and to whom, and with a copy of the records to be released to the student's parents and the student if desired by the parents, or

(B) such information is furnished in compliance with judicial order, or pursuant to any lawfully issued subpoena, upon condition that parents and the students are notified of all such orders or subpoenas in advance of the compliance therewith by the educational institution or agency.

(3) Nothing contained in this section shall preclude authorized representatives of (A) the Comptroller General of the United States, (B) the Secretary, (C) an administrative head of an education agency or (D) State educational authorities from having access to student or other records which may be necessary in connection with the audit and evaluation of a Federally-supported education program, or in connection with the enforcement of the Federal legal requirements which relate to such programs: *Provided*, That except when collection of personally identifiable information is specifically authorized by Federal law, any data collected by such officials shall be protected in a manner which will not permit the personal identification of students and their parents by other than those officials, and such personally identifiable data shall be destroyed when no longer needed for such audit, evaluation, and enforcement of Federal legal requirements.

(4)(A) Each educational agency or institution shall maintain a record, kept with the education records of each student, which will indicate all individuals (other than those specified in paragraph (1)(A) of this subsection), agencies, or organizations which have requested or obtained access to a student's education records maintained by such educational agency or institution, and which will indicate specifically the legitimate interest that each such person, agency, or organization has in obtaining this information. Such record of access shall be available only to parents, to the school official and his assistants who are responsible for the custody of such records, and to persons or organizations authorized in, and under the conditions of, clauses (A) and (C) of paragraph (1) as a means of auditing the operating of the system.

(B) With respect to this subsection, personal information shall only be transferred to a third party on the condition that.such party will not permit any other party to have access to such information without the written consent of the parents of the student.

(5) Nothing in this section shall be construed to prohibit State and local educational officials from having access to student or other records which may be necessary in connection with the audit and evaluation of any federally or State supported education program or in connection with the enforcement of the Federal legal requirements which relate to any such program, subject to the conditions specified in the proviso in paragraph (3).

(c) Surveys or data-gathering activities; regulations

The Secretary shall adopt appropriate regulations to protect the rights of privacy of students and their families in connection with any surveys or data-gathering activities conducted, assisted, or authorized by the Secretary or an administrative head of an education agency. Regulations established under his subsection shall include provisions controlling the use, dissemination, and protection of such data. No survey or data-gathering activities shall be conducted by the Secretary, or an administrative head of an education agency under an applicable program, unless such activities are authorized by law.

(d) Students' rather than parents' permission or consent

For the purposes of this section, whenever a student has attained eighteen years of age, or is attending an institution or postsecondary education the permission or consent required of and the rights accorded to the parents of the student shall thereafter only be required of and accorded to the student.

(e) Informing parents or students of rights under this section

No funds shall be made available under any applicable program to any educational agency or institution unless such agency or institution informs the parents of students, or the students, if they are eighteen years of age or older, or are attending an institution of postsecondary education, of the rights accorded them by this section.

* * *

The federal regulations implementing the Buckley Amendment, found at 34 CFR Part 99, are reprinted below in their entirety.

PART 99—PRIVACY RIGHTS OF PARENTS AND STUDENTS

Subpart A—General

Sec.
99.1 Applicability of part.
99.2 Purpose.
99.3 Definitions.
99.4 Student Rights.
99.5 Formulation of institutional policy and procedures.
99.6 Annual notification of rights.

Sec.
99.7   Limitations on waivers.
99.8   Fees.

Subpart B—Inspection and Review of Education Records

99.11   Right to inspect and review education records.
99.12   Limitations on right to inspect and review education records at the postsecondary level.
99.13   Limitation on destruction of education records.

Subpart C—Amendment of Education Records

99.20   Request to amend education records.
99.21   Right to a hearing.
99.22   Conduct of the hearing.

Subpart D—Disclosure of Personally Identifiable Information From Education Records

99.30   Prior consent for disclosure required.
99.31   Prior consent for disclosure not required.
99.32   Record of requests and disclosures required to be maintained.
99.33   Limitation on redisclosure.
99.34   Conditions for disclosure to officials of other schools and school systems.
99.35   Disclosure to certain Federal and State officials for Federal program purposes.
99.36   Conditions for disclosure in health and safety emergencies.
99.37   Conditions for disclosure of directory information.

Subpart E—Enforcement

99.60   Office and review board.
99.61   Conflict with State or local law.
99.62   Reports and records.
99.63   Complaint procedure.
99.64   Termination of funding.
99.65   Hearing procedures.
99.66   Hearing before Panel or a Hearing Officer.
99.67   Initial decision; final decision.

AUTHORITY: Sec. 438, Pub. L. 90-247, Title IV, as amended, 88 Stat. 571-574 (20 U.S.C. 1232g), unless otherwise noted.

SOURCE: 45 FR 30911, May 9, 1980, unless otherwise noted.

Subpart A—General

§ 99.1 Applicability of part.

(a) This part applies to all educational agencies or institutions to which funds are made available under any Federal program for which the Secretary of the U.S. Department of Education has administrative responsibility, as specified by law or by delegation of authority pursuant to law.

(Authority: 20 U.S.C. 1230, 1232g)

(b) This part does not apply to an educational agency or institution solely because students attending that non-monetary agency or institution receive benefits under one or more of the Federal programs referenced in paragraph (a) of this section, if no funds under those programs are made available to the agency or institution itself.

(c) For the purposes of this part, funds will be considered to have been made available to an agency or institution when funds under one or more of the programs referenced in paragraph (a) of this section:

(1) Are provided to the agency or institution by grant, contract, subgrant, or subcontract, or (2) are provided to students attending the agency or institution and the funds may be paid to the agency or institution by those students for educational purposes, such as under the Basic Educational Opportunity Grants Program and the Guaranteed Student Loan Program (Titles IV-A-1 and IV-B, respectively, of the Higher Education Act of 1965, as amended).

(Authority: 20 U.S.C. 1232g)

(d) Except as otherwise specifically provided, this part applies to education records of students who are or have been in attendance at the educational agency or institution which maintains the records.

NOTE: This section is based on a provision in the General Education Provisions Act (GEPA). Section 427 of the Department of Education Organization Act (DEOA), 20 U.S.C. 3487, provides that except to the extent inconsistent with the DEOA, the GEPA "shall apply to functions tranferred by this Act to the extent applicable on the day preceding the effective date of this Act." Although standardized nomenclature is used in this section to reflect the creation of the Department of Education, there is no intent to extend the coverage of the GEPA beyond that authorized under Section 427 or other applicable law.)

(Authority: 20 U.S.C. 1232g)

[45 FR 30911, May 9, 1980, as amended at 45 FR 86296, Dec. 30, 1980]

§ 99.2 Purpose.

The purpose of this part is to set forth requirements governing the protection of privacy of parents and students under section 438 of the General Education Provisions Act, as amended.

(Authority: 20 U.S.C. 1232g)

§ 99.3 Definitions.

As used in this part:
"Act" means the General Education Provisions Act, Title IV of Pub. L. 90-247 as amended.
"Attendance" at an agency or institution includes, but is not limited to: (a) Attendance in person and by correspondence, and (b) the period during which a person is working under a work-study program.

(Authority: 20 U.S.C. 1232g)

"Directory information" includes the following information relating to a student: The student's name, address, telephone number, date and place of birth, major field of study, participation in officially recognized activities and sports, weight and height of members of athletic teams, dates of attendance, degrees and awards received, the most recent previous educational agency or institution attended by the student, and other similar information.

(Authority: 20 U.S.C. 1232g(a)(5)(A))

"Disclosure" means permitting access or the release, transfer, or other communication of education records of the student or the personally identifiable information contained therein, orally or in writing, or by electronic means, or by any other means to any party.

(Authority: 20 U.S.C. 1232g(b)(1))

"Educational institution" or "educational agency or institution" means any public or private agency or institution which is the recipient of funds under any Federal program referenced in § 99.1(a). The term refers to the agency or institution recipient as a whole, including all of its components (such as schools or departments in a university) and shall not be read to refer to one or more of these components separate from that agency or institution.

(Authority: 20 U.S.C. 1232g(a)(3))

"Education records" (a) means those records which: (1) Are directly related to a student, and (2) are maintained by an educational agency or institution or by a party acting for the agency or institution.

(b) The term does not include:

(1) Records of instructional, supervisory, and administrative personnel and educational personnel ancillary thereto which:

(i) Are in the sole possession of the maker thereof, and

(ii) Are not accessible or revealed to any other person except a substitute. For the purpose of this definition, a "substitute" means an individual who performs on a temporary basis the duties of the individual who made the record, and does not refer to an individual who permanently succeeds the maker of the record in his or her position.

(2) Records of a law enforcement unit of an educational agency or institution which are:

(i) Maintained apart from the records described in paragraph (a) of this definition;

(ii) Maintained solely for law enforcement purposes, and

(iii) Not disclosed to individuals other than law enforcement officials of the same jurisdiction; *Provided*, That education records maintained by the educational agency or institution are not disclosed to the personnel of the law enforcement unit.

(3) (i) Records relating to an individual who is employed by an educational agency or institution which:

(A) Are made and maintained in the normal course of business;

(B) Relate exclusively to the individual in that individual's capacity as an employee, and

(C) Are not available for use for any other purpose.

(ii) This paragraph does not apply to records relating to an individual in attendance at the agency or institution who is employed as a result of his or her status as a student.

(4) Records relating to an eligible student which are:

(i) Created or maintained by a physician, psychiatrist, psychologist, or other recognized professional or paraprofessional acting in his or her professional or paraprofessional capacity, or assisting in that capacity;

(ii) Created, maintained, or used only in connection with the provision of treatment to the student, and

(iii) Not disclosed to anyone other than inidividuals providing the treatment; *Provided*, That the records can be personally reviewed by a physician or other appropriate professional of the student's choice. For the purpose of this definition, "treatment" does not include remedial educational activities or activities which are part of the program of instruction at the educational agency or institution.

(5) Records of an educational agency or institution which contain only information relating to a person after that person was no longer a student at the educational agency or institution. An example would be information collected by an educational agency or institution pertaining to the accomplishments of its alumni.

(Authority: 20 U.S.C. 1232g(a)(4))

"Eligible student" means a student who has attained eighteen years of age, or is attending an institution of postsecondary education.

(Authority: 20 U.S.C. 1232g(d))

"Financial Aid", as used in § 99.31(a)(4), means a payment of funds provided to an individual (or a payment in kind of tangible or intangible property to the individual) which is conditioned on the individual's attendance at an educational agency or institution.

(Authority: 20 U.S.C. 1232g(b)(1)(D))

"Institution of postsecondary education" means an institution which provides education to students beyond the secondary school level; "secondary school level" means the education level (not beyond grade 12) at which secondary education is provided, as determined under State law.

(Authority: 20 U.S.C. 1232g(d))

"Panel" means the body which will adjudicate cases under procedures set forth in §§ 99.65-99.67.

"Parent" includes a parent, a guardian, or an individual acting as a parent of a student in the absence of a parent or guardian. An educational agency or institution may presume the parent has the authority to exercise the rights inherent in the Act unless the agency or institution has been provided with evidence that there is a State law or court order governing such matters as divorce, separation or custody, or a legally binding instrument which provides to the contrary.

"Party" means an individual, agency, institution or organization.

(Authority: 20 U.S.C. 1232g(b)(4)(A))

"Personally identifiable" means that the data or information includes (a) the name of a student, the student's parent, or other family member, (b) the address of the student, (c) a personal identifier, such as the student's social security number or student number, (d) a list of personal characteristics which would make the student's identity easily traceable, or (e) other information which would make the student's identity easily traceable.

(Authority: 20 U.S.C. 1232g)

"Record" means any information or data recorded in any medium, including, but not limited to: handwriting, print, tapes, film, microfilm and microfiche.

(Authority: 20 U.S.C. 1232g)

"Secretary" means the Secretary of the U.S. Department of Education.

(Authority: 20 U.S.C. 1232g)

"Student" (a) includes any individual with respect to whom an educational agency or institution maintains education records.

(b) The term does not include an individual who has not been in attendance at an educational agency or institution. A person who has applied for admission to, but has never been in attendance at a component unit of an institution of postsecondary education (such as the various colleges or schools which comprise a university), even if that individual is or has been in attendance at another component unit of that institution of postsecondary education, is not considered to be a student with respect to the component to which an application for admission has been made.

(Authority: 20 U.S.C. 1232g(a)(5))

§ 99.4 Student rights.

(a) For the purposes of this part, whenever a student has attained eighteen years of age, or is attending an institution of postsecondary education, the rights accorded to and the consent required of the parent of the student shall thereafter only be accorded to and required of the eligible student.

(b) The status of an eligible student as a dependent of his or her parents for the purposes of § 99.31(a)(8) does not otherwise affect the rights accorded to and the consent required of the eligible student by paragraph (a) of this section.

(Authority: 20 U.S.C. 1232g(d))

(c) Section 438 of the Act and the regulations in this part shall not be construed to preclude educational agencies or institutions from according to students rights in addition to those accorded to parents of students.

§ 99.5 Formulation of institutional policy and procedures.

(a) Each educational agency or institution shall, consistent with the minimum requirements of section 438 of the Act and this part, formulate and adopt a policy of—

(1) Informing parents of students or eligible students of their rights under § 99.6;

(2) Permitting parents of students or eligible students to inspect and review the education records of the student in accordance with § 99.11, including at least:

(i) A statement of the procedure to be followed by a parent or an eligible student who requests to inspect and review the education records of the student;

(ii) With an understanding that it may not deny access to an education record, a description of the circumstances in which the agency or institution feels it has a legitimate cause to deny a request for a copy of such records;

(iii) A schedule of fees for copies, and

(iv) A listing of the types and locations of education records maintained by the educational agency or institution and the titles and addresses of the officials responsible for those records;

(3) Not disclosing personally identifiable information from the education records of a student without the prior written consent of the parent of the student or the eligible student, except as otherwise permitted by §§ 99.31 and 99.37; the policy shall include, at least: (i) A statement of whether the educational agency or institution will disclose personally identifiable information from the education records of a student under § 99.31(a)(1) and, if so, a specification of the criteria for determining which parties are "school officials" and what the educational agency or institution considers to be a "legitimate educational interest", and (ii)

a specification of the personally identifiable information to be designated as directory information under § 99.37;

(4) Maintaining the record of disclosures of personally identifiable information from the education records of a student required to be maintained by § 99.32, and permitting a parent or an eligible student to inspect that record;

(5) Providing a parent of the student or an eligible student with an opportunity to seek the correction of education records of the student through a request to amend the records or a hearing under Subpart C, and permitting the parent of a student or an eligible student to place a statement in the education records of the student as provided in § 99.21(c);

(b) The policy required to be adopted by paragraph (a) of this section shall be in writing and copies shall be made available upon request to parents of students and to eligible students.

(Authority: 20 U.S.C. 1232g(e) and (f))

§ 99.6 Annual notification of rights.

(a) Each educational agency or institution shall give parents of students in attendance or eligible students in attendance at the agency or institution annual notice by such means as are reasonably likely to inform them of the following:

(1) Their rights under section 438 of the Act, the regulations in this part, and the policy adopted under § 99.5; the notice shall also inform parents of students or eligible students of the locations where copies of the policy may be obtained; and

(2) The right to file complaints under § 99.63 concerning alleged failures by the educational agency or institution to comply with the requirements of section 438 of the Act and this part.

(b) Agencies and institutions of elementary and secondary education shall provide for the need to effectively notify parents of students identified as having a primary or home language other than English.

(Authority: 20 U.S.C. 1232g(e))

§ 99.7 Limitations on waivers.

(a) Subject to the limitations in this section and § 99.12, a parent of a student or a student may waive any of his or her rights under section 438 of the Act or this part. A waiver shall not be valid unless in writing and signed by the parent or student, as appropriate.

(b) An educational agency or institution may not require that a parent of a student or student waive his or her rights under section 438 of the Act or this part. This paragraph does not preclude an educational agency or institution from requesting such a waiver.

(c) An individual who is an applicant for admission to an institution of post-secondary education or is a student in attendance at an institution of postsecondary education may waive his or her right to inspect and review confidential letters and confidential statements of recommendation described in § 99.12(a)(3) except that the waiver may apply to confidential letters and statements only if:

(1) The applicant or student is, upon request, notified of the names of all individuals providing the letters or statements; (2) the letters or statements are used only for the purpose for which they were originally intended, and (3) such waiver is not required by the agency or institution as a condition of admission to or receipt of any other service or benefit from the agency or institution.

(d) All waivers under paragraph (c) of this section must be executed by the individual, regardless of age, rather than by the parent of the individual.

(e) A waiver under this section may be made with respect to specified classes of: (1) Education records, and (2) persons or institutions.

(f) (1) A waiver under this section may be revoked with respect to any actions occurring after the revocation.

(2) A revocation under this paragraph must be in writing.

(3) If a parent of a student executes a waiver under this section, that waiver may be revoked by the student at any time after he or she becomes an eligible student.

(Authority: 20 U.S.C. 1232g(a)(1) (B) and (C))

§ 99.8 Fees.

(a) An educational agency or institution may charge a fee for copies of education records which are made for the parents of students, students, and eligible students under section 438 of the Act and this part; *Provided*, That the fee does not effectively prevent the parents and students from exercising their right to inspect and review those records.

(b) An educational agency or institution may not charge a fee to search for or to retrieve the education records of a student.

(Authority: 20 U.S.C. 1232g(a)(1))

Subpart B—Inspection and Review of Education Records

§ 99.11 Right to inspect and review education records.

(a) Each educational agency or institution, except as may be provided by § 99.12, shall permit the parent of a student or an eligible student who is or has been in attendance at the agency or institution, to inspect and review the education records of the student. The agency or institution shall comply with a request within a reasonable period of time, but in no case more than 45 days after the request has been made.

(b) The right to inspect and review education records under paragraph (a) of this section includes:

(1) The right to a response from the educational agency or institution to reasonable requests for explanations and interpretations of the records; and

(2) The right to obtain copies of the records from the educational agency or institution where failure of the agency or institution to provide the copies would effectively prevent a parent or eligible student from exercising the right to inspect and review the education records.

(c) An educational agency or institution may presume that either parent of the student has authority to inspect and review the education records of the student unless the agency or institution has been provided with evidence that there is a legally binding instrument, or a State law or court order governing such matters as divorce, separation or custody, which provides to the contrary.

§ 99.12 Limitations on right to inspect and review education records at the post-secondary level.

(a) An institution of postsecondary education is not required by section 438 of the Act or this part to permit a student to inspect and review the following records:

(1) Financial records and statements of their parents or any information contained therein;

(2) Confidential letters and confidential statements of recommendation which were placed in the education records of a student prior to January 1, 1975; *Provided*, That:

(i) The letters and statements were solicited with a written assurance of confidentiality, or sent and retained with a documented understanding of confidentiality, and

(ii) The letters and statements are used only for the purposes for which they were specifically intended;

(3) Confidential letters of recommendation and confidential statements of recommendation which were placed in the education records of the student after January 1, 1975:

(i) Respecting admission to an educational institution;

(ii) Respecting an application for employment, or

(iii) Respecting the receipt of an honor or honorary recognition; *Provided*, That the student has waived his or her right to inspect and review those letters and statements of recommendation under § 99.7(c).

(Authority: 20 U.S.C. 1232g(a)(1)(B))

(b) If the education records of a student contain information on more than one student, the parent of the student or the eligible student may inspect and review or be informed of only the specific information which pertains to that student.

(Authority: 20 U.S.C. 1232g(a)(1)(A))

§ 99.13 Limitation on destruction of education records.

An educational agency or institution is not precluded by section 438 of the Act or this part from destroying education records, subject to the following exceptions:

(a) The agency or institution may not destroy any education records if there is an outstanding request to inspect and review them under § 99.11;

(b) Explanations placed in the education record under § 99.21 shall be maintained as provided in § 99.21(d), and

(c) The record of access required under § 99.32 shall be maintained for as long as the education record to which it pertains is maintained.

(Authority: 20 U.S.C. 1232g(f))

Subpart C—Amendment of Education Records

§ 99.20 Request to amend education records.

(a) The parent of a student or an eligible student who believes that information contained in the education records of the student is inaccurate or misleading or violates the privacy or other rights of the student may request that the educational agency or institution which maintains the records amend them.

(b) The educational agency or institution shall decide whether to amend the education records of the student in accordance with the request within a reasonable period of time of receipt of the request.

(c) If the educational agency or institution decides to refuse to amend the education records of the student in accordance with the request it shall so inform the parent of the student or the eligible student of the refusal, and advise the parent or the eligible student of the right to a hearing under § 99.21.

(Authority: 20 U.S.C. 1232g(a)(2))

§ 99.21 Right to a hearing.

(a) An educational agency or institution shall, on request, provide an opportunity for a hearing in order to challenge the content of a student's education records to insure that information in the education records of the student is not inaccurate, misleading or otherwise in violation of the privacy or other rights of students. The hearing shall be conducted in accordance with § 99.22.

(b) If, as a result of the hearing, the educational agency or institution decides that the information is inaccurate, misleading or otherwise in violation of the privacy or other rights of the students, it shall amend the education records of the student accordingly and so inform the parent of the student or the eligible student in writing.

(c) If, as a result of the hearing, the educational agency or institution decides that the information is not inaccurate, misleading or in violation of the privacy or other rights of the students, it shall inform the parent or eligible student of the right to place in the education records of the student a statement commenting upon the information in the education records and/or setting forth any reasons for disagreeing with the decision of the agency or institution.

(d) Any explanation placed in the education records of the student under paragraph (c) of this section shall:

(1) Be maintained by the educational agency or institution as part of the education records of the student as long as the record or contested portion thereof is maintained by the agency or institution, and

(2) If the education records of the student or the contest portion thereof is disclosed by the educational agency or institution to any party, the explanation shall also be disclosed to that party.

(Authority: 20 U.S.C. 1232g(a)(2))

§ 99.22 Conduct of the hearing.

The hearing required to be held by § 99.21(a) shall be conducted according to procedures which shall include at least the following elements:

(a) The hearing shall be held within a reasonable period of time after the educational agency or institution has received the request, and the parent of the student or the eligible student shall be given notice of the date, place and time reasonably in advance of the hearing;

(b) The hearing may be conducted by any party, including an official of the educational agency or institution, who does not have a direct interest in the outcome of the hearing;

(c) The parent of the student or the eligible student shall be afforded a full and fair opportunity to present evidence relevant to the issues raised under § 99.21, and may be assisted or represented by individuals of his or her choice at his or her own expense, including an attorney;

(d) The educational agency or institution shall make its decision in writing within a reasonable period of time after the conclusion of the hearing; and

(e) The decision of the agency or institution shall be based solely upon the evidence presented at the hearing and shall include a summary of the evidence and the reasons for the decision.

(Authority: 20 U.S.C. 1232g(a)(2))

Subpart D—Disclosure of Personally Identifiable Information From Education Records

§ 99.30 Prior consent for disclosure required.

(a)(1) An educational agency or institution shall obtain the written consent of the parent of a student or the eligible student before disclosing personally identifiable information from the education records of a student, other than directory information, except as provided in § 99.31.

(2) Consent is not required under this section where the disclosure is to (i) the parent of a student who is not an eligible student, or (ii) the student himself or herself.

(b) Whenever written consent is required, an educational agency or institution may presume that the parent of the student or the eligible student giving consent has the authority to do so unless the agency or institution has been provided with evidence that there is a legally binding instrument, or a State law or court order governing such matters as divorce, separation or custody, which provides to the contrary.

(c) The written consent required by paragraph (a) of this section must be signed and dated by the parent of the student or the eligible student giving the consent and shall include:

(1) A specification of the records to be disclosed,

(2) The purpose or purposes of the disclosure, and

(3) The party or class of parties to whom the disclosure may be made.

(d) When a disclosure is made pursuant to paragraph (a) of this section, the educational agency or institution shall, upon request, provide a copy of the record which is disclosed to the parent of the student or the eligible student, and to the student who is not an eligible student if so requested by the student's parents.

(Authority: 20 U.S.C. 1232g(b)(1) and (b)(2)(A))

§ 99.31 Prior consent for disclosure not required.

(a) An educational agency or institution may disclose personally identifiable information from the education records of a student without the written consent of the parent of the student or the eligible student if the disclosure is—

(1) To other school officials, including teachers, within the educational institution or local educational agency who have been determined by the agency or institution to have legitimate educational interests;

(2) To officials of another school or school system in which the student seeks or intends to enroll, subject to the requirements set forth in § 99.34;

(3) Subject to the conditions set forth in § 99.35, to authorized representatives of:

(i) The Comptroller General of the United States,

(ii) The Secretary, or

(iii) State educational authorities;

(4) In connection with financial aid for which a student has applied or which a student has received; *Provided*, That personally identifiable information from the education records of the student may be disclosed only as may be necessary for such purposes as:

(i) To determine the eligibility of the student for financial aid,

(ii) To determine the amount of the financial aid,

(iii) To determine the conditions which will be imposed regarding the financial aid, or

(iv) To enforce the terms or conditions of the financial aid;

(5) To State and local officials or authorities to whom information is specifically required to be reported or disclosed pursuant to State statute adopted prior to November 19, 1974. This paragraph applies only to statutes which require that specific information be disclosed to State or local officials and does not apply to statutes which permit but do not require disclosure. Nothing in this paragraph shall prevent a State from further limiting the number or type of State or local officials to whom disclosures are made under this paragraph;

(6) To organizations conducting studies for, or on behalf of, educational agencies or institutions for the purpose of developing, validating, or administering

predictive tests, administering student aid programs, and improving instruction; *Provided*, That the studies are conducted in a manner which will not permit the personal identification of students and their parents by individuals other than representatives of the organization and the information will be destroyed when no longer needed for the purposes for which the study was conducted; the term "organizations" includes, but is not limited to, Federal, State and local agencies, and independent organizations;

(7) To accrediting organizations in order to carry out their accrediting functions;

(8) To parents of a dependent student, as defined in section 152 of the Internal Revenue Code of 1954;

(9) To comply with a judicial order or lawfully issued subpoena; *Provided*, That the educational agency or institution makes a reasonable effort to notify the parent of the student or the eligible student of the order or subpoena in advance of compliance therewith; and

(10) To appropriate parties in a health or safety emergency subject to the conditions set forth in § 99.36.

(b) This section shall not be construed to require or preclude disclosure of any personally identifiable information from the education records of a student by an educational agency or institution to the parties set forth in paragraph (a) of this section.

(Authority: 20 U.S.C. 1232g(b)(1))

§ 99.32 Record of requests and disclosures required to be maintained.

(a) An educational agency or institution shall for each request for and each disclosure of personally identifiable information from the education records of a student, maintain a record kept with the education records of the student which indicates:

(1) The parties who have requested or obtained personally identifiable information from the education records of the student, and

(2) The legitimate interests these parties had in requesting or obtaining the information.

(b) Paragraph (a) of this section does not apply:

(1) To requests by or disclosure to a parent of a student or an eligible student;

(2) To requests by or disclosures to school officials under § 99.31(a)(1);

(3) If there is written consent of a parent of a student or an eligible student; or

(4) To requests for or disclosure of directory information under § 99.37.

(c) The record of requests and disclosures may be inspected:

(1) By the parent of the student or the eligible student,

(2) By the school official and his or her assistants who are responsible for the custody of the records, and

(3) For the purpose of auditing the recordkeeping procedures of the educational agency or institution by the parties authorized in, and under the conditions set forth in § 99.31(a) (1) and (3).

(Authority: 20 U.S.C. 1232g(b)(4)(A))

§ 99.33 Limitation on redisclosure.

(a) An educational agency or institution may disclose personally identifiable information from the education records of a student only on the condition that the party to whom the information is disclosed will not disclose the information to any other party without the prior written consent of the parent of the student or the eligible student, except that the personally identifiable information which is disclosed to an institution, agency or organization may be used by its officers, employees and agents, but only for the purposes for which the disclosure was made.

(b) Paragraph (a) of this section does not preclude an agency or institution from disclosing personally identifiable information under § 99.31 with the understanding that the information will be redisclosed to other parties under that section; *Provided*, That the recordkeeping requirements of § 99.32 are met with respect to each of those parties.

(c) An educational agency or institution shall, except for the disclosure of directory information under § 99.37, inform the party to whom a disclosure is made of the requirement set forth in paragraph (a) of this section.

(Authority: 20 U.S.C. 1232g(b)(4)(B))

§ 99.34 Conditions for disclosure to officials of other schools and school systems.

(a) An educational agency or institution transferring the education records of a student pursuant to § 99.31(a)(2) shall:

(1) Make a reasonable attempt to notify the parent of the student or the eligible student of the transfer of the records at the last known address of the parent or eligible student, except:

(i) When the transfer of the records is initiated by the parent or eligible student at the sending agency or institution, or

(ii) When the agency or institution includes a notice in its policies and procedures formulated under § 99.5 that it forwards education records on request to a school in which a student seeks or intends to enroll; the agency or institution does not have to provide any further notice of the transfer;

(2) Provide the parent of the student or the eligible student, upon request, with a copy of the education records which have been transferred; and

(3) Provide the parent of the student or the eligible student, upon request, with an opportunity for a hearing under Subpart C of this part.

(b) If a student is enrolled in more than one school, or receives services from more than one school, the schools may disclose information from the education records of the student to each other without obtaining the written consent of the parent of the student or the eligible student; *Provided*, That the disclosure meets the requirements of paragraph (a) of this section.

(Authority: 20 U.S.C. 1232g(b)(1)(B))

§ 99.35 Disclosure to certain Federal and State officials for Federal program purposes.

(a) Nothing in section 438 of the Act or this part shall preclude authorized representatives of officials listed in § 99.31(a)(3) from having access to student and other records which may be necessary in connection with the audit and evaluation of Federally supported education programs, or in connection with the enforcement of or compliance with the Federal legal requirements which relate to these programs.

(b) Except when the consent of the parent of a student or an eligible student has been obtained under § 99.30, or when the collection of personally identifiable information is specifically authorized by Federal law, any data collected by officials listed in § 99.31(a)(3) shall be protected in a manner which will not permit the personal identification of students and their parents by other than those officials, and personally identifiable data shall be destroyed when no longer needed for such audit, evaluation, or enforcement of or compliance with Federal legal requirements.

(Authority: 20 U.S.C. 1232g(b)(3)).

§ 99.36 Conditions for disclosure in health and safety emergencies.

(a) An educational agency or institution may disclose personally identifiable information from the education records of a student to appropriate parties in connection with an emergency if knowledge of the information is necessary to protect the health or safety of the student or other individuals.

(b) The factors to be taken into account in determining whether personally identifiable information from the education records of a student may be disclosed under this section shall include the following:

(1) The seriousness of the threat to the health or safety of the student or other individuals;

(2) The need for the information to meet the emergency;

(3) Whether the parties to whom the information is disclosed are in a position to deal with the emergency; and

(4) The extent to which time is of the essence in dealing with the emergency.

(c) Paragraph (a) of this section shall be strictly construed.

(Authority: 20 U.S.C. 1232g(b)(1)(I))

§ 99.37 Conditions for disclosure of directory information.

(a) An educational agency or institution may disclose personally identifiable information from the education records of a student who is in attendance at the institution or agency if that information has been designated as directory information (as defined in § 99.3) under paragraph (c) of this section.

(b) An educational agency or institution my disclose directory information from the education records of an individual who is no longer in attendance at the agency or institution without following the procedures under paragraph (c) of this section.

(c) An educational agency or institution which wishes to designate directory information shall give public notice of the following:

(1) The categories of personally identifiable information which the institution has designated as directory information;

(2) The right of the parent of the student or the eligible student to refuse to permit the designation of any or all of the categories of personally identifiable information with respect to that student as directory information; and

(3) The period of time within which the parent of the student or the eligible student must inform the agency or institution in writing that such personally identifiable information is not to be designated as directory information with respect to that student.

(Authority: 20 U.S.C. 1232g(a)(5) (A) and (B))

Subpart E—Enforcement

§ 99.60 Office and review board.

(a) The Secretary is required to establish or designate an office and a review board under section 438(g) of the Act. The office will investigate, process, and review violations, and complaints which may be filed concerning alleged violations of the provisions of section 438 of the Act and the regulations in this part. The review board will adjudicate cases referred to it by the office under the procedures set forth in §§ 99.65-99.67.

(b) The following is the address of the office which has been designated under paragraph (a) of this section: The Family Educational Rights and Privacy Act

Office (FERPA), Department of Education, 400 Maryland Avenue, S.W., Washington, D.C. 20202.

(Authority: 20 U.S.C. 1232g(g))

§ 99.61 Conflict with State or local law.

An educational agency or institution which determines that it cannot comply with the requirements of section 438 of the Act or of this part because a State or local law conflicts with the provisions of section 438 of the Act or the regulations in this part shall so advise the office designated under § 99.60(b) within 45 days of any such determination, giving the text and legal citation of the conflicting law.

(Authority: 20 U.S.C. 1232g(f))

§ 99.62. Reports and records.

Each educational agency or institution shall (a) submit reports in the form and containing such information as the Office of the Review Board may require to carry out their functions under this part, and (b) keep the records and afford access thereto as the Office or the Review Board may find necessary to assure the correctness of those reports and compliance with the provisions of sections 438 of the Act and this part.

(Authority: 20 U.S.C. 1232g (f) and (g))

§ 99.63 Complaint procedure.

(a) Complaints regarding violations of rights accorded parents and eligible students by section 438 of the Act or the regulations in this part shall be submitted to the Office in writing.

(b)(1) The Office will notify each complainant and the educational agency or institution against which the violation has been alleged, in writing, that the complaint has been received.

(2) The notification to the agency or institution under paragraph (b)(1) of this section shall include the substance of the alleged violation and the agency or institution shall be given an opportunity to submit a written response.

(c)(1) The Office will investigate all timely complaints received to determine whether there has been a failure to comply with the provisions of section 438 of the Act or the regulations in this part, and may permit further written or oral submissions by both parties.

(2) Following its investigation the Office will provide written notification of its findings and the basis for such findings, to the complainant and the agency or institution involved.

(3) If the Office finds that there has been a failure to comply, it will include in its notification under paragraph (c)(2) of this section, the specific steps which must be taken by the agency or educational institution to bring the agency or institution into compliance. The notification shall also set forth a reasonable period of time, given all of he circumstances of the case, for the agency or institution to voluntarily comply.

(d) If the educational agency or institution does not come into compliance within the period of time set under paragraph (c)(3) of this section, the matter will be referred to the Review Board for a hearing under §§ 99.64-99.67, inclusive.

(Authority: 20 U.S.C. 1232g(f))

§ 99.64. Termination of funding.

If the Secretary, after reasonable notice and opportunity for a hearing by the Review Board, (a) finds that an educational agency or institution has failed to comply with the provisions of section 438 of the Act, or the regulations in this part, and (b) determines that compliance cannot be secured by voluntary means, he shall issue a decision, in writing, that no funds under any of the Federal programs referenced in § 99.1(a) shall be made available to that educational agency or institution, (or at the Secretary's discretion, to the unit of the educational agency or institution affected by the failure to comply) until there is no longer any such failure to comply.

(Authority: 20 U.S.C. 1232g(f))

§ 99.65 Hearing procedures.

(a) *Panels.* The Chairman of the Review Board shall designate Hearing Panels to conduct one or more hearings under § 99.64. Each Panel shall consist of not less than three members of the Review Board. The Review Board may, at its discretion, sit for any hearing or class of hearings. The Chairman of the Review Board shall designate himself or any other member of a Panel to serve as Chairman.

(b) *Procedural rules.* (1) With respect to hearings involving, in the opinion of the Panel, no dispute as to a material fact the resolution of which would be materially assisted by oral testimony, the Panel shall take appropriate steps to afford each party to the proceeding an opportunity for presenting his case at the option of the Panel (i) in whole or in part in writing or (ii) in an informal conference before the Panel which shall afford each party:

(A) Sufficient notice of the issues to be considered (where such notice has not previously been afforded); and (B) an opportunity to be represented by counsel.

(2) With respect to hearings involving a dispute as to a material fact the resolution of which would be materially assisted by oral testimony, the Panel shall afford each party an opportunity, which shall include, in addition to provisions required by paragraph (1)(ii) of this paragraph (b), provisions designed to assure to each party the following:

(i) An opportunity for a record of the proceedings;

(ii) An opportunity to present witnesses on the party's behalf; and

(iii) An opportunity to cross-examine other witnesses either orally or through written interrogatories.

(Authority: 20 U.S.C. 1232g(g))

§ 99.66 Hearing before Panel or a Hearing Officer.

A hearing pursuant to § 99.65(b)(2) shall be conducted, as determined by the Panel Chairman, either before the Panel or a hearing officer. The hearing officer may be (a) one of the members of the Panel or (b) a nonmember who is appointed as a hearing examiner under 5 U.S.C. 3105.

(Authority: 20 U.S.C. 1232g(g))

§ 99.67 Initial decision; final decision.

(a) The Panel shall prepare an initial written decision, which shall include findings of fact and conclusions based thereon. When a hearing is conducted before a hearing officer alone, the hearing officer shall separately find and state the facts and conclusions which shall be incorporated in the initial decision prepared by the Panel.

(b) Copies of the initial decision shall be mailed promptly by the Panel to each party (or to the party's counsel), and to the Secretary with a notice affording the party an opportunity to submit written comments thereon to the Secretary within a specified reasonable time.

(c) The initial decision of the Panel transmitted to the Secretary shall become the final decision of the Secretary, unless, within 25 days after the expiration of the time for receipt of written comments, the Secretary advises the Review Board in writing of his determination to review the decision.

(d) In any case in which the Secretary modifies or reverses the initial decision of the Panel, he shall accompany that action with a written statement of the grounds for the modification or reversal, which shall promptly be filed with the Review Board.

(e) Review of any initial decision by the Secretary shall be based upon the decision, the written record, if any, of the Panel's proceedings, and written comments or oral arguments by the parties, or by their counsel, to the proceedings.

(f) No decision under this section shall become final until it is served upon the educational agency or institution involved or its attorney.

(Authority: 20 U.S.C. 1232g(g))

VIII. RECONSTRUCTION CIVIL RIGHTS STATUTES

In an effort to safeguard the rights of newly freed slaves, immediately after the Civil War Congress enacted a series of laws known as the Reconstruction Civil Rights Statutes. Most of these laws fell into disuse and languished in the statute books until the modern-day civil rights movement. Two of these statutes, 42 U.S.C. § 1981 and § 1983, have become relevant to private educational institutions.

A. Section 1981

Section 1 of the Civil Rights Act of 1866, which is codified as 42 U.S.C. § 1981, prohibits racial discrimination in the making and enforcement of contracts. In *Runyon v. McCrary* the U.S. Supreme Court applied this statute in the private school context, holding that it outlawed racially discriminatory private schools (see Chapter One, Section III; see appendix for the text of the opinion). Section 1981 provides as follows:

§ 1981. Equal rights under the law

All persons within the jurisdiction of the United States shall have the same right in every State and Territory to make and enforce contracts, to sue, be parties, give evidence, and to the full and equal benefit of all laws and proceedings for the security of persons and property as is enjoyed by white citizens, and shall be subject to like punishment, pains, penalties, taxes, licenses, and exactions of every kind, and to no other.

B. Section 1983

Section 1 of the Civil Rights Act of 1871, which is codified as 42 U.S.C. § 1983, is the most frequently used civil rights provision. Section 1983 provides the basis for a federal court lawsuit to any individual whose constitutional rights, or federal statutory rights, have been violated by the government or its officials. Compensatory damages, punitive damages, injunctions and attorney's fees may be awarded under § 1983. Two elements are required for a successful § 1983 lawsuit: 1) action by the state or by a person or institution acting "under color of" state law, which 2) deprives an individual of federally guaranteed rights. Section VII of Chapter Two discusses the applicability of § 1983 to private schools receiving state funding or which are controlled by or involved with the government to a substantial degree. Section 1983 provides as follows:

§ 1983. Civil action for deprivation of rights

Every person who, under color of any statute, ordinance, regulation, custom, or usage, of any State or Territory or the District of Columbia, subjects, or causes to be subjected, any citizen of the United States or other person within the jurisdiction thereof to the deprivation of any rights, privileges, or immunities secured by the Constitution and laws, shall be liable to the party injured in an action at law, suit in equity, or other proper proceeding for redress. For the purposes of this section, any Act of Congress applicable exclusively to the District of Columbia shall be considered to be a statute of the District of Columbia.

APPENDIX A

UNITED STATES CONSTITUTION

Provisions of Interest to Private Educators

ARTICLE I

Section 1. All legislative Powers herein granted shall be vested in a Congress of the United States, which shall consist of a Senate and House of Representatives.

* * *

Section 8. The Congress shall have Power To lay and collect Taxes, Duties, Imposts and Excises, to pay the Debts and provide for the common Defence and general Welfare of the United States; but all Duties, Imposts and Excises shall be uniform throughout the United States;

To borrow money on the credit of the United States;

To regulate Commerce with foreign Nations, and among the several States, and with the Indian Tribes;

To establish an uniform Rule of Naturalization, and uniform Laws on the subject of Bankruptcies throughout the United States;

* * *

To promote the Progress of Science and useful Arts, by securing for limited Times to Authors and Inventors the exclusive Right to their respective Writings and Discoveries;

* * *

To make all Laws which shall be necessary and proper for carrying into Execution for the foregoing Powers, and all other Powers vested by this Constitution in the Government of the United States, or in any Department or Officer thereof.

* * *

Section 9. * * * No Bill of Attainder or ex post facto Law shall be passed.

* * *

Section 10. No State shall * * * pass any Bill of Attainder, ex post facto Law, or Law impairing the Obligation of Contracts, or grant any Title of Nobility.

* * *

ARTICLE II

Section 1. The executive Power shall be vested in a President of the United States of America. * * *

ARTICLE III

Section 1. The judicial Power of the United States, shall be vested in one supreme Court, and in such inferior Courts as the Congress may from time to time ordain and establish. The Judges, both of the supreme and inferior Courts, shall hold their Offices during good Behaviour, and shall, at stated Times, receive for their Services a Compensation, which shall not be diminished during their Continuance in Office.

Section 2. The judicial Power shall extend to all Cases, in Law and Equity, arising under this Constitution, the Laws of the United States, and Treaties made, or which shall be made, under their Authority;—to all Cases affecting Ambassadors, other public Ministers and Consuls;—to all Cases of admiralty and maritime Jurisdiction,—to Controversies to which the United States shall be a Party;—to Controversies between two or more States;—between a State and Citizens of another State;—between Citizens of different States;—between Citizens of the same State claiming Lands under the Grants of different States, and between a State, or the Citizens thereof, and foreign States, Citizens or Subjects.

* * *

ARTICLE IV

Section 1. Full Faith and Credit shall be given in each State to the public Acts, Records, and judicial Proceedings of every other State. * * *

Section 2. The Citizens of each State shall be entitled to all Privileges and Immunities of Citizens in the several States.

* * *

Section 4. The United States shall guarantee to every State in this Union a Republican Form of Government, and shall protect each of them against Invasion; and on Application of the Legislature, or of the Executive (when the Legislature cannot be convened) against domestic Violence.

ARTICLE V

The Congress, whenever two thirds of both Houses shall deem it necessary, shall propose Amendments to this Constitution, or, on the Application of the Legislatures of two thirds of the several States, shall call a Convention for proposing Amendments, which, in either Case, shall be valid to all Intents and Purposes, as part of this Constitution, when ratified by the Legislatures of three fourths of the several States, or by Conventions in three fourths thereof, as the one or the other Mode of Ratification may be proposed by the Congress; Provided that no Amendment which may be made prior to the Year One thousand eight hundred and eight shall in any Manner affect the first and fourth Clauses in the Ninth Section of the first Article; and that no State, without its Consent, shall be deprived of its equal Suffrage in the Senate.

ARTICLE VI

* * *

This Constitution, and the Laws of the United States which shall be made in Pursuance thereof; and all Treaties made, or which shall be made, under the Authority of the United States, shall be the supreme Law of the Land; and the Judges in every State shall be bound thereby, any Thing in the Constitution or Laws of any State to the Contrary notwithstanding.

The Senators and Representatives before mentioned, and the Members of the several State Legislatures, and all executive and judicial Officers, both of the United States and of the several States, shall be bound by Oath or Affirmation, to support this Constitution; but no religious Test shall ever be required as a Qualification to any Office or public Trust under the United States.

* * *

AMENDMENT I

Congress shall make no law respecting an establishment of religion, or prohibiting the free exercise thereof; or abridging the freedom of speech, or of the press; or the right of the people peaceably to assemble, and to petition the Government for a redress of grievances.

* * *

AMENDMENT IV

The right of the people to be secure in their persons, houses, papers, and effects, against unreasonable searches and seizures, shall not be violated, and no Warrants shall issue, but upon probable cause, supported by Oath or affirmation, and particularly describing the place to be searched, and the persons or things to be seized.

AMENDMENT V

No person shall be held to answer for a capital, or otherwise infamous crime, unless on a presentment or indictment of a Grand Jury, except in cases arising in the land or naval forces, or in the Militia, when in actual service in time of War or public danger; nor shall any person be subject for the same offence to be twice put in jeopardy of life or limb; nor shall be compelled in any criminal case to be a witness against himself, nor be deprived of life, liberty, or property, without due process of law; nor shall private property be taken for public use, without just compensation.

AMENDMENT VI

In all criminal prosecutions, the accused shall enjoy the right to a speedy and public trial, by an impartial jury of the State and district wherein the crime shall have been committed, which district shall have been previously ascertained by law, and to be informed of the nature and cause of the accusation; to be confronted with the witnesses against him; to have compulsory process for obtaining witnesses in his favor, and to have the Assistance of Counsel for his defence.

AMENDMENT VII

In Suits at common law, where the value in controversy shall exceed twenty dollars, the right of trial by jury shall be preserved, and no fact tried by jury, shall be otherwise re-examined in any Court of the United States, than according to the rules of the common law.

AMENDMENT VIII

Excessive bail shall not be required, nor excessive fines imposed, nor cruel and unusual punishments inflicted.

AMENDMENT IX

The enumeration in the Constitution, of certain rights, shall not be construed to deny or disparage others retained by the people.

AMENDMENT X

The powers not delegated to the United States by the Constitution, nor prohibited by it to the States, are reserved to the States respectively, or to the people.

AMENDMENT XI

The Judicial power of the United States shall not be construed to extend to any suit in law or equity, commenced or prosecuted against one of the United States by Citizens of another State, or by Citizens or Subjects of any Foreign State.

*   *   *

AMENDMENT XIII

Section 1. Neither slavery nor involuntary servitude, except as a punishment for crime whereof the party shall have been duly convicted, shall exist within the United States, or any place subject to their jurisdiction.

Section 2. Congress shall have power to enforce this article by appropriate legislation.

AMENDMENT XIV

Section 1. All persons born or naturalized in the United States, and subject to the jurisdiction thereof, are citizens of the United States and of the State wherein they reside. No State shall make or enforce any law which shall abridge the privileges or immunities of citizens of the United States; nor shall any State deprive any person of life, liberty, or property, without due process of law; nor deny to any person within its jurisdiction the equal protection of the laws.

*   *   *

Section 5. The Congress shall have power to enforce, by appropriate legislation, the provisions of this article.

APPENDIX B

SUBJECT MATTER TABLE
OF RECENT LAW REVIEW ARTICLES

Academic Freedom
Bosmajian, Haig. *The judiciary's use of metaphors, metonymies and other tropes to give First Amendment protection to students and teachers.* 15 J.L. & Educ. 439 (1986).
Heckling: a protected right or disorderly conduct? 60 S.Cal. L.Rev. 215 (1986).
Professing Law: a Colloquy on critical legal studies. 31 St. Louis U.L.J. 1 (1986).
Ramirez, M. Christina. *The balance of interests between national security controls and First Amendment interests in academic freedom.* 13 J.Col. & Univ.L. 179 (1986).

Athletics
Antitrust—price fixing—NCAA may not establish price and output level of televised college football games. [NCAA v. Board of Regents, 104 S.Ct. 2948 (1984)] 16 Seton Hall L.Rev. 170 (1986).
Graves, Judson. *Coaches in the courtroom: recovery in actions for breach of employment contracts.* 12 J.C. & U.L. 545 (1986).
Hickman, William. *The NCAA and televised college football: does economic efficiency score points?* 11 Okla.Cty.U.L.Rev. 323 (1986).
Lee, Robert W. *The taxation of athletic scholarships: an uneasy tension between benevolence and consistency.* 37 U.Fla.L.Rev. 591 (1985).
Martin, Gordon A., Jr. *The NCAA and its student-athlete: is there still state action?* 21 New Eng.L.Rev. 49 (1986).
Title IX and the future of private education: backdoor regulation of a private entity. 22 Tulsa L.J. 109 (1986).
Tokarz, Karen L. *Separate but unequal educational sports programs: the need for a new theory of equality.* 1 Berkeley Women's L.J. 201 (1985).
Where the boys are: can separate be equal in school sports? 58 S.Cal.L.Rev. 1425 (1985).
Wong, Glenn M., and Richard J. Ensor. *Recent developments in amateur athletics: the organization's responsibility to the public.* 2 E. & S.L.J. 123 (1984).

197

Athletics (continued)

Wong, Glenn M., and Richard J. Ensor. *Sex discrimination in athletics: a review of two decades of accomplishments and defeats.* 21 Gonz.L.Rev. 345 (1985-86).

Charitable Contributions

Kruger, Steven R. *The enforceability of charitable pledges in Minnesota: issues of consideration.* 9 Hamline L. Rev. 365 (1986).

Steele, Athornia. *Regulation of charitable solicitation: a review and proposal.* 13 J.Legis. 149 (1986).

The implications of changing the current law on charitable deductions—maintaining incentives for donating art to museums. 47 Ohio St.L.J. 773 (1986).

Copyright

Gemignani, Michael. *A college's liability for unauthorized copying of microcomputer software by students.* 15 J.L. & Educ. 421 (1986).

Olson, Dale P. *Copyright and fair use: implications of national enterprises for higher education.* 12 J.C. & U.L. 489 (1986).

Sorenson, Gail Paulus. *Impact of the copyright law on college teaching.* 12 J.C. & U.L. 509 (1986).

Defamation

Eades, Ronald W. *The school counselor or psychologist and problems of defamation.* 15 J.L. & Educ. 117 (1986).

Tidwell, James A. *Educators' liability for negative letters of recommendation.* 15 J.L. & Educ. 479 (1986).

Desegregation

Federal practice: clarifying the desegregation process. 39 Okla. L.Rev. 519 (1986).

Participation and Department of Justice school desegregation consent decrees. 95 Yale L.J. 1811 (1986).

Discrimination

AIDS and employment: an epidemic strikes the workplace and the law. 8 Whittier L.Rev. 651 (1986).

Balancing the free religious exercise right against government interests. [State v. Sports & Health Club, Inc., 370 N.W.2d 844 (Minn.1985)] 9 Hamline L.Rev. 649 (1986).

Educating through the law: the Los Angeles AIDS discrimination ordinance. 33 UCLA L.Rev. 1410 (1986).

Eglit, Howard. *The Age Discrimination in Employment Act's forgotten affirmative defense: the reasonable factors other than age exception.* 66 B.U.L.Rev. 155 (1986).

Groves, Harry E. and Albert Broderick. *Affirmative action goals under Title VII: statute, legislative history, and policy.* 11 T.Marshall L.J. 327 (1986).

Law, Social Policy, and contagious disease: a Symposium on Acquired Immune Deficiency Syndrome (AIDS). 14 Hofstra L.Rev. 1 (1986).

Reportability of exposure to the AIDS virus: an equal protection analysis. 7 Cardozo L.Rev. 1103 (1986).

Discrimination (continued)

Symposium: Civil Rights issues in the Eighties. 5 Rev.Lit. 1 (1986).

Teacher competency exams in Texas: are they legal? Are they constitutional? 11 T.Marshall L.J. 381 (1986).

The weakening of Title IX. [Grove City College v. Bell, 104 S.Ct. 1211 (1984)] 20 N.E.L.Rev. 425 (1985).

Title IX and the future of private education: backdoor regulation of a private entity. 22 Tulsa L.J. 109 (1986).

Title IX and the outer limits of the spending powers. [Grove City College v. Bell, 104 S.Ct. 1211 (1984)] 61 Chi.-Kent L.Rev. 711 (1985).

Tokarz, Karen L. *Separate but unequal educational sports programs: the need for a new theory of equality.* 1 Berkeley Women's L.J. 201 (1985).

Waiver of rights under the Age Discrimination in Employment Act of 1967. 86 Colum.L.Rev. 1067 (1986).

What's a handicap anyway? Analyzing handicap claims under the Rehabilitation Act of 1973 and analogous state statutes. 22 Willamette L.Rev. 529 (1986).

Wong, Glenn M., and Richard J. Ensor. *Sex discrimination in athletics: a review of two decades of accomplishments and defeats.* 21 Gonz.L.Rev. 345 (1985-86).

Education Generally

Educational malpractice update. 14 Cap.U.L.Rev. 609 (1985).

Louisiana Constitution: Article VIII: Education. 46 La.L.Rev. 1137 (1986).

Paschall, Samuel S. *Expanding educational objectives through the undergraduate business law course.* 19 Akron L.Rev. 615 (1986).

Popvich, Peter S., Donald W. Niles and Michael T. Miller. *Recent developments in Minnesota educational law.* 13 Wm. Mitchell L.Rev. 1 (1987).

Rossell, Christine H. and J. Michael Ross. *The social science evidence on bilingual education.* 15 J.L. & Educ. 385 (1986).

Smith, Steven R. *Privacy, dangerousness and counselors.* 15 J.L. & Educ. 121 (1986).

Worona, Jay and Norman H. Gross. *Education law (Survey).* 37 Syracuse L.Rev. 441 (1986).

Employment

AIDS and employment: an epidemic strikes the workplace and the law. 8 Whittier L.Rev. 651 (1986).

Balancing the free religious exercise right against government interests. [State v. Sports & Health Club, Inc., 370 N.W.2d 844 (Minn.1985)] 9 Hamline L.Rev. 649 (1986).

Constitutional law—free exercise clause permits church to fire homosexual employee. [Madsen v. Erwin, 395 Mass. 715, 481 N.E.2d 1160 (1985)] 20 Suffolk U.L.Rev. 119 (1986).

Educating through the law: the Los Angeles AIDS discrimination ordinance. 33 UCLA L.Rev. 1410 (1986).

Employment (continued)

Eglit, Howard. *The Age Discrimination in Employment Act's forgotten affirmative defense: the reasonable factors other than age exception.* 66 B.U.L.Rev. 155 (1986).

Graves, Judson. *Coaches in the courtroom: recovery in actions for breach of employment contracts.* 12 J.C. & U.L. 545 (1986).

Groves, Harry E. and Albert Broderick. *Affirmative action goals under Title VII: statute, legislative history, and policy.* 11 T.Marshall L.J. 327 (1986).

Land, Janet L. *Teacher collective bargaining (Survey).* 19 Ind. L.Rev. 235 (1986).

State unemployment tax and the interdenominational school—the lions win again. [Salem College & Academy v. Employment Division, 695 P.2d 25 (Or.App.1985)] 21 Willamette L.Rev. 937 (1985).

Teacher competency exams in Texas: are they legal? Are they constitutional? 11 T.Marshall L.J. 381 (1986).

The Martin Luther King, Jr. Holiday: a misstep in the right direction. [In the Matter of Arbitration Between: American Fed'n of State, County and Mun. Employees, Council 75, and State of Oregon (Or.Exec.Dept.1986)] 22 Willamette L.J. 614 (1986).

Tidwell, James A. *Educators' liability for negative letters of recommendation.* 15 J.L. & Educ. 479 (1986).

Torts—charitable immunity—Charitable Immunity Act bars claim by a beneficiary of a charitable institution based on the charity's alleged negligence in hiring. N.J.Stat.Ann. § 2A:53A-7 to -11. [Schultz v. Roman Catholic Archdiocese of Newark, 472 A.2d 531 (1984)] 16 Rutgers L.J. 393 (1985).

Waiver of rights under the Age Discrimination in Employment Act of 1967. 86 Colum.L.Rev. 1067 (1986).

Weeks, Kent M. and Jerry Organ. *Educational institutions and comparable worth: a doctrine in search of application.* 15 J.L. & Educ. 207 (1986).

What's a handicap anyway? Analyzing handicap claims under the Rehabilitation Act of 1973 and analogous state statutes. 22 Willamette L.Rev. 529 (1986).

Finance

Divestiture as a remedy in private actions brought under section 16 of the Clayton Act. 84 Mich.L.Rev. 1579 (1986).

Johnson, Edward A. and Kent M. Weeks. *To save a college: independent college trustees and decisions on financial exigency, endowment use, and closure.* 12 J.C. & U.L. 455 (1986).

Schneider, Carl E. *Free speech and corporate freedom: a comment on First National Bank of Boston v. Bellotti.* 59 S.Cal. L.Rev. 1227 (1986).

The South African divestment debate: factoring "political risk" into the prudent investor rule. 55 U.Cin.L.Rev. 201 (1986).

First Amendment

A new twist on the old lemon? [Wallace v. Jaffree, 105 S.Ct. 2479 (1985)] 13 W.St.U.L.Rev. 659 (1986).

Beschle, Donald L. *The conservative as liberal: the religion clauses, liberal neutrality, and the approach of Justice O'Connor.* 62 Notre Dame L.Rev. 151 (1987).

Bosmajian, Haig. *The judiciary's use of metaphors, metonymies and other tropes to give First Amendment protection to students and teachers.* 15 J.L. & Educ. 439 (1986).

Bradley, Gerald V. *Dogmatomachy—a "privatization" theory of the religion clause cases.* 30 St. Louis U.L.J. 275 (1986).

Braveman, Daan. *The establishment clause and the course of religious neutrality.* 45 Md.L.Rev. 352 (1986).

Church and state—moment of silence in public schools for meditation or voluntary prayer is unconstitutional. [Wallace v. Jaffree, 105 S.Ct. 2479 (1985)] 1985 S.Ill.U.L.J. 585.

Church tort liability in spite of First Amendment protection. 12 S.U.L.Rev. 37 (1985).

Civil religion and the establishment clause. 95 Yale L.J. 1237 (1986).

Constitutional Fiction: an analysis of the Supreme Court's interpretation of the religion clauses. 47 La.L.Rev. 169 (1986).

Constitutional law—First Amendment—establishment clause—the United States Supreme Court has held that state educational programs providing remedial and enrichment courses within leased parochial school facilities violate the establishment clause of the First Amendment. [Grand Rapids School District v. Ball. 105 S.Ct. 3216 (1985)] 24 Duq.L.Rev. 1237 (1986).

Constitutional law—free exercise clause permits church to fire homosexual employee. [Madsen v. Erwin, 395 Mass. 715, 481 N.E.2d 1160 (1985)] 20 Suffolk U.L.Rev. 119 (1986).

Constitutional law: the conflict of First Amendment rights and the motive requirement in selective enforcement cases. 39 Okla. L.Rev. 498 (1986).

Dellinger, Walter. *The sound of silence: an epistle on prayer and the constitution.* 95 Yale L.J. 1631 (1986).

Esbeck, Carl H. *Tort claims against churches and ecclesiastical officers: the First Amendment considerations.* 89 W.Va.L.Rev. 1 (1986).

Establishment clause analysis: an apology for the Lemon test in the wake of Wallace v. Jaffree. 30 S.D.L.Rev. 599 (1985).

Federal taxation—exempt organizations—constitutional law— First Amendment—right to free exercise of religion. [Bob Jones University v. United States, 461 U.S. 574 (1983)] 30 N.Y. L.Sch.L.Rev. 825 (1985).

First Amendment restrictions on Title I programs in private schools. [Aguilar v. Felton, 105 S.Ct. 3232 (1985)] 30 Wash.U. J.Urb. & Contemp.L. 295 (1986).

First Amendment (continued)

Garvey, John H. *A comment on religious convictions and law making.* 84 Mich.L.Rev. 1288 (1986).

Gibney, Mark P. *State aid to religious-affiliated schools: a political analysis.* 28 Wm. & Mary L.Rev. 119 (1986).

Heckling: a protected right or disorderly conduct? 60 S.Cal. L.Rev. 215 (1986).

Invoking the presence of God at public high school graduation ceremonies. [Graham v. Central Community School District, 608 F.Supp. 531 (S.D.Iowa 1985)] 71 Iowa L.Rev. 1247 (1986).

Kobylka, Joseph F. and David M. Debnel. *Toward a structuralist understanding of First and Sixth Amendment guarantees.* 21 Wake Forest L.Rev. 363 (1986).

Lacey, Linda J. *Gay Rights Coalition v. Georgetown University* [496 A.2d 567 (D.C.App.1985)]: *constitutional values on a collision course.* 64 Or.L.Rev. 409 (1986).

Moment of silence statutes: an improper relation between church and state in public schools. 54 UMKC L.Rev. 488 (1986).

Mueller, Lori Leff. *Religious rights of children: a gallery of judicial visions.* 14 N.Y.U.R.L. & Soc. Change 277 (1986).

Oaks, Dallin H. *Separation, accommodation and the future of church and state.* 35 De Paul L.Rev. 1 (1986).

Of crosses and creches: the establishment clause and publicly sponsored displays of religious symbols. [Lynch v. Donnelly, 104 S.Ct. 1355 (1984)] 35 Am.U.L.Rev. 477 (1986).

Ramirez, M. Christina. *The balance of interests between national security controls and First Amendment interests in academic freedom.* 13 J.Col. & Univ.L. 179 (1986).

Schools and Colleges—church and state—"entanglement" or relinquishment of our religious and governmental aims. [Aguilar v. Felton, 105 S.Ct. 3232 (1986)] 11 T.Marshall L.J. 449 (1986).

Secular humanism as religion within the meaning of the First Amendment. [Grove v. Mead School District, 753 F.2d 1528 (9th Cir.1985); cert. denied, 106 S.Ct. 85 (1986)] 61 Tul. L.Rev. 453 (1986).

Smith, Rodney K. *Now is the time for reflection: Wallace v. Jaffree and its legislative aftermath.* 37 Ala.L.Rev. 345 (1986).

State regulation of private education: Ohio law in the shadow of the United States Supreme Court decisions. 54 U.Cin.L.Rev. 1003 (1986).

Symposium: The tension between the Free Exercise Clause and the Establishment Clause of the First Amendment. 47 Ohio St.L.J. 289 (1986).

Teitel, Ruti G. *The unconstitutionality of equal access policies and legislation allowing organized student-initiated religious activities in the public high schools: a proposal for a unitary First Amendment forum analysis.* 12 Hastings Const.L.Q. 529 (1985).

First Amendment (continued)

The constitutionality of home education statutes. 55 UMKC
L.Rev. 69 (1986).

*The Second Circuit and the establishment clause: shoring up a
crumbling wall (Survey).* [Felton v. Secretary, U.S. Dep't of
Education, 739 F.2d 48 (2d Cir.1984)] 51 Brooklyn L.Rev. 642
(1985).

The secular humanism ban and Equal Access Act. 43 Wash. &
Lee L.Rev. 265 (1986).

*The Solomon Amendment, Department of Defense Authorization
Act of 1983, and the Secretary of Education's authority to
implement.* [Alexander v. Trustees of Boston University, 584
F.Supp. 282 (D.Mass.1984)] 11 T.Marshall L.Rev. 161 (1985).

West, Ellis M. *The free exercise clause and the Internal Revenue
Code's restrictions on the political activity of tax-exempt organizations.* 21 Wake Forest L.Rev. 395 (1986).

Freedom of Speech

Bosmajian, Haig. *The judiciary's use of metaphors, metonymies
and other tropes to give First Amendment protection to students
and teachers.* 15 J.L. & Educ. 439 (1986).

Clarke, Desmond M. *Freedom of thought in schools: a comparative study.* 35 Int'l & Comp.L.Q. 271 (1986).

*Constitutional law: the conflict of First Amendment rights and the
motive requirement in selective enforcement cases.* 39 Okla.
L.Rev. 498 (1986).

Heckling: a protected right or disorderly conduct? 60 S.Cal.
L.Rev. 215 (1986).

Schneider, Carl E. *Free speech and corporate freedom: a comment on First National Bank of Boston v. Bellotti.* 59 S.Cal.
L.Rev. 1227 (1986).

Handicapped Students

*Equal educational opportunity: the visually impaired and Public
Law 94-142.* 33 UCLA L.Rev. 549 (1985).

Hartog-Rapp, Fay. *The legal standards for determining the relationship between a child's handicapping condition and misconduct charged in a school disciplinary proceeding.* 1985 S.Ill.
U.L.J. 243.

*The Burlington decision: a vehicle to enforce free appropriate
public education for the handicapped.* [Burlington School
Comm. v. Department of Education, 105 S.Ct. 1996 (1985)] 19
Akron L.Rev. 311 (1985).

Home Instruction

Constitutional law: Roemhild v. State [308 S.E.2d 154 (Ga.1983)]
and State v. Popanz [332 N.W.2d 750 (Wis.1983)]: *their effect
on the constitutionality of Oklahoma's compulsory education
statute.* 38 Okla.L.Rev. 741 (1985).

The constitutionality of home education statutes. 55 UMKC
L.Rev. 69 (1986).

Injuries

Church tort liability in spite of First Amendment protection. 12
S.U.L.Rev. 37 (1985).

Injuries (continued)

Cross, Frank B. *Asbestos in schools: a remonstrance against panic.* 11 Colum.J.Envtl.L. 1 (1986).

Esbeck, Carl H. *Tort claims against churches and ecclesiastical officers: the First Amendment considerations.* 89 W.Va.L.Rev. 1 (1986).

Smith, Steven R. *Privacy, dangerousness and counselors.* 15 J.L. & Educ. 121 (1986).

Torts—charitable immunity—Charitable Immunity Act bars claim by a beneficiary of a charitable institution based on the charity's alleged negligence in hiring. N.J.Stat.Ann. § 2A:53A-7 to -11. [Schultz v. Roman Catholic Archdiocese of Newark, 472 A.2d 531 (1984)] 16 Rutgers L.J. 393 (1985).

Instructional Methods

Rossell, Christine H. and J. Michael Ross. *The social science evidence on bilingual education.* 15 J.L. & Educ. 385 (1986).

Labor Relations

Constitutional law—jurisdiction over religious colleges and universities—the need for substantive constitutional analysis. [Universidad Central de Bayamon v. NLRB, 793 F.2d 383 (1st Cir.1986)] 62 Notre Dame L.Rev. 255 (1987).

Land, Janet L. *Teacher collective bargaining (Survey).* 19 Ind. L.Rev. 235 (1986).

The Martin Luther King, Jr. Holiday: a misstep in the right direction. [In the Matter of Arbitration Between: American Fed'n of State, County and Mun. Employees, Council 75, and State of Oregon (Or.Exec.Dept.1986)] 22 Willamette L.J. 614 (1986).

Legal Education

Baumberger, Clinton. *Debilitating conformity in "local" law schools.* 17 Rutgers L.J. 215 (1986).

Byse, Clark. *Fifty years of legal education.* 71 Iowa L.Rev. 1063 (1986).

Chretien, David M. & Doris Chretien. *Reconsidering nontraditional factors in law school admissions.* 11 S.U.L.Rev. 31 (1985).

Ely, James W., Jr. *Through a crystal ball: legal education—its relation to the bench, bar and university community.* 21 Tulsa L.J. 650 (1986).

Greenstein, Richard K. *Teaching case synthesis.* 2 Ga.St.U. L.Rev. 1 (1985-86).

Lee, Rex E. *The role of the religious law school.* 30 Vill.L.Rev. 1175 (1985).

Menkel-Meadow, Carrie. *Two contradictory criticisms of clinical education: dilemmas and directions in lawyering education.* 4 Antioch L.J. 287 (1986).

Professing Law: a Colloquy on critical legal studies. 31 St. Louis U.L.J. 1 (1986).

Transforming legal education: a symposium of provocative thought. 10 Nova L.J. 255 (1986).

Student Rights
Chretien, David M. & Doris Chretien. *Reconsidering nontraditional factors in law school admissions.* 11 S.U.L.Rev. 31 (1985).
Constitutional law: the conflict of First Amendment rights and the motive requirement in selective enforcement cases. 39 Okla. L.Rev. 498 (1986).
Draft cards and report cards: financial aid remains contingent upon draft registration under Selective Service System v. Minnesota Public Interest Research Group [104 S.Ct. 3348 (1984)]. 5 N.Ill.L.Rev. 307 (1985).
Eades, Ronald W. *The school counselor or psychologist and problems of defamation.* 15 J.L. & Educ. 117 (1986).
Hartog-Rapp, Fay. *The legal standards for determining the relationship between a child's handicapping condition and misconduct charged in a school disciplinary proceeding.* 1985 S.Ill. U.L.J. 243.
In support of education: an examination of the parental obligation to provide postsecondary education in California. 18 Pac.L.J. 377 (1987).
Lacey, Linda J. *Gay Rights Coalition v. Georgetown University* [496 A.2d 567 (D.C.App.1985)]: *constitutional values on a collision course.* 64 Or.L.Rev. 409 (1986).
Mueller, Lori Leff. *Religious rights of children: a gallery of judicial visions.* 14 N.Y.U.R.L. & Soc. Change 277 (1986).
New Jersey v. T.L.O.—closing the schoolhouse gate on the Fourth Amendment. 14 N.Y.U.R.L. & Soc.Change 455 (1986).
School search—the Supreme Court's adoption of a "reasonable suspicion" standard in New Jersey v. T.L.O. and the heightened need for extension of the exclusionary rule to school search cases. 1985 S.Ill.U.L.J. 263.
Search and seizure—the Supreme Court abandons probable cause as a requirement for student searches in favor of a reasonableness standard. [New Jersey v. T.L.O., 105 S.Ct. 733 (1985)] 19 Suffolk U.L.Rev. 1023 (1985).
Stenger, Robert L. *The school counselor and the law: new developments.* 15 J.L. & Educ. 105 (1986).
The Fourth Amendment applied to school searches. [New Jersey v. T.L.O., 105 S.Ct. 733 (1985)] 11 Okla.City U.L.Rev. 225 (1986).
The 1978 Hatch Amendment: attempted applications are failing to protect pupil rights. 19 Ind.L.Rev. 589 (1986).
The Solomon Amendment, Department of Defense Authorization Act of 1983, and the Secretary of Education's authority to implement. [Alexander v. Trustees of Boston University, 584 F.Supp. 282 (D.Mass.1984)] 11 T.Marshall L.Rev. 161 (1985).
The Supreme Court sanctions the conditioning of financial aid for college on draft registration. [Selective Service System v. Minnesota Public Interest Research Group, 104 S.Ct. 3348 (1984)] 26 B.C.L.Rev. 1063 (1985).

Student Rights (continued)

> *What's a handicap anyway? Analyzing handicap claims under the Rehabilitation Act of 1973 and analogous state statutes.* 22 Willamette L.Rev. 529 (1986).

Taxation

> *Collaboration between nonprofit universities and commercial enterprises: the rationale for exempting nonprofit universities from federal income taxation.* 95 Yale L.J. 1857 (1986).

> *Federal taxation—exempt organizations—constitutional law— First Amendment—right to free exercise of religion.* [Bob Jones University v. United States, 461 U.S. 574 (1983)] 30 N.Y. L.Sch.L.Rev. 825 (1985).

> Friedland, Jerold A. *Constitutional issues in revoking religious tax exemptions: Church of Scientology of California v. Commissioner.* 37 U.Fla.L.Rev. 565 (1985).

> Lee, Robert W. *The taxation of athletic scholarships: an uneasy tension between benevolence and consistency.* 37 U.Fla.L.Rev. 591 (1985).

> Mangrum, R. Collin. *Naming religion (and eligible cognates) in tax exemption cases (Survey).* 19 Creighton L.Rev. 821 (1985-86).

> *Real property tax exemptions for religious institutions in Ohio: Bishop ordains a faulty progeny.* [Bishop v. Kinney, 2 Ohio St.3d 52, 442 N.E.2d 764 (1982)] 47 Ohio St.L.J. 535 (1986).

> West, Ellis M. *The free exercise clause and the Internal Revenue Code's restrictions on the political activity of tax- exempt organizations.* 21 Wake Forest L.Rev. 395 (1986).

Tuition

> *In support of education: an examination of the parental obligation to provide postsecondary education in California.* 18 Pac.L.J. 377 (1987).

APPENDIX C

SUBJECT MATTER TABLE OF
UNITED STATES SUPREME COURT CASES
AFFECTING PRIVATE EDUCATION

Subject   Title & Citation

Academic Freedom
Epperson v. Arkansas, 393 U.S. 97 (1968).
Meyer v. Nebraska, 262 U.S. 390 (1923).

Civil Rights
Grove City College v. Bell, 465 U.S. 555 (1984).
Rendell-Baker v. Kohn, 457 U.S. 830 (1982).

Compulsory Attendance
Wisconsin v. Yoder, 406 U.S. 205 (1972).
Pierce v. Society of Sisters, 268 U.S. 510 (1925).

Federal Aid
Bennett v. Kentucky Department of Education, 470 U.S. 656 (1985).
Bennett v. New Jersey, 470 U.S. 632 (1985).
Selective Service System v. MPIRG, 468 U.S. 841 (1984).
Grove City College v. Bell, 465 U.S. 555 (1984).
Bell v. New Jersey and Pennsylvania, 461 U.S. 773 (1984).
Valley Forge Christian College v. Americans United for Separation of Church and State, 454 U.S. 464 (1982).
Wheeler v. Barrera, 417 U.S. 402 (1974).
Tilton v. Richardson, 403 U.S. 672 (1971).

Free Speech
Wayte v. U.S., 470 U.S. 598 (1985).

Handicapped Students
Burlington School Committee v. Department of Education, 471 U.S. 359 (1985).
Smith v. Robinson, 468 U.S. 992 (1984).
Irving Independent School District v. Tatro, 468 U.S. 883 (1984).
Board of Education v. Rowley, 458 U.S. 176 (1982).
Southeastern Community College v. Davis, 442 U.S. 397 (1979).

Labor Relations
NLRB v. Yeshiva University, 444 U.S. 672 (1980).
NLRB v. Catholic Bishop of Chicago, 440 U.S. 490 (1979).

Racial Discrimination
Runyon v. McCrary, 427 U.S. 160 (1976).
Lau v. Nichols, 414 U.S. 563 (1974).
Norwood v. Harrison, 413 U.S. 455 (1973).

Rehabilitation Act
>   School Board of Nassau County v. Arline, 107 S.Ct. 1123 (1987).
>   Southeastern Community College v. Davis, 442 U.S. 397 (1979).

Release Time
>   Zorach v. Clauson, 343 U.S. 306 (1952).
>   McCollum v. Board of Education, 333 U.S. 203 (1948).

Religious Activities in Public Schools
>   Bender v. Williamsport Area School District, 106 S.Ct. 1326 (1986).
>   Wallace v. Jaffree, 472 U.S. 38 (1985).
>   Widmar v. Vincent, 454 U.S. 263 (1981).
>   Stone v. Graham, 449 U.S. 39 (1980).
>   Chamberlin v. Dade County Board of Public Instruction, 377 U.S. 402 (1964).
>   Abington School District v. Schempp, 374 U.S. 203 (1963).
>   Engel v. Vitale, 370 U.S. 421 (1962).
>   West Virginia Board of Education v. Barnette, 319 U.S. 624 (1943).

Sex Discrimination
>   Ohio Civil Rights Commission v. Dayton Christian Schools, 106 S.Ct. 2718 (1986).
>   Mississippi University for Women v. Hogan, 458 U.S. 718 (1982).

State Funding of Private Education
>   Witters v. Washington Department of Services for the Blind, 106 S.Ct. 748 (1986).
>   Aguilar v. Felton, 105 S.Ct. 3232 (1985).
>   Grand Rapids School District v. Ball, 105 S.Ct. 3216 (1985).
>   Committee for Public Education and Religious Liberty v. Regan, 444 U.S. 646 (1980).
>   New York v. Cathedral Academy, 434 U.S. 125 (1977).
>   Wolman v. Walter, 433 U.S. 229 (1977).
>   Roemer v. Board of Public Works, 426 U.S. 736 (1976).
>   Meek v. Pittenger, 421 U.S. 349 (1975).
>   Sloan v. Lemon, 413 U.S. 825 (1973).
>   Committee for Public Education and Religious Liberty v. Nyquist, 413 U.S. 756 (1973).
>   Hunt v. McNair, 413 U.S. 734 (1973).
>   Levitt v. Committee for Public Education and Religious Liberty, 413 U.S. 472 (1973).
>   Lemon v. Kurtzman, 403 U.S. 602 (1971).

Taxation
>   Allen v. Wright, 468 U.S. 737 (1984).
>   Mueller v. Allen, 463 U.S. 388 (1983).
>   Bob Jones University v. United States, 461 U.S. 574 (1983).

Textbooks
>   Norwood v. Harrison, 413 U.S. 455 (1973).
>   Board of Education v. Allen, 392 U.S. 236 (1968).
>   Cochran v. Louisiana State Board of Education, 281 U.S. 370 (1930).

Transportation

Wolman v. Walter, 433 U.S. 229 (1977).

Everson v. Board of Education, 330 U.S. 1 (1947).

Unemployment Taxation

St. Martin's Evangelical Lutheran Church v. South Dakota, 451 U.S. 772 (1981).

APPENDIX D

TEXT OF SELECTED UNITED STATES SUPREME COURT CASES

Runyon v. McCrary, 427 U.S. 160, 96 S.Ct. 2586 (1976):
Nonsectarian private schools open to the public may not
exclude qualified black children solely because of race 212

Bob Jones University v. United States, 461 U.S. 574, 103 S.Ct.
2017 (1983):
Private schools practicing racial discrimination are not
entitled to federal income tax exemptions 232

Grove City College v. Bell, 465 U.S. 555, 104 S.Ct. 1211 (1984):
Private schools enrolling students receiving BEOGs are
recipients of federal financial aid for Title IX purposes; Title
IX coverage applicable only to schools' administration of
financial aid programs 257

211

Runyon v. McCrary

United States Supreme Court, 427 U.S. 160, 96 S.Ct. 2586 (1976)

Syllabus*

Title 42 U.S.C. § 1981 provides in part that "[a]ll persons within the jurisdiction of the United States shall have the same right in every State...to make and enforce contracts...as is enjoyed by white citizens...." After they had been denied admission to petitioner private schools in Virginia for the stated reason that the schools were not integrated, two Negro children (hereafter respondents), by their parents, brought actions against the schools, alleging that they had been prevented from attending the schools because of the schools' admitted policies of denying admission to Negroes, in violation of § 1981, and seeking declaratory and injunctive relief and damages. The District Court, finding that respondents had been denied admission on racial grounds, held that § 1981 makes illegal the schools' racially discriminatory admissions policies and accordingly enjoined the schools and the member schools of petitioner private school association (which had intervened as a party defendant) from discriminating against applicants for admission on the basis of race. The court also awarded compensatory relief to both children and to the parents of one and assessed attorneys' fees against each school, but held that the damages claim of the parents of the other child was barred by Virginia's two-year statute of limitations for "personal injury" actions, "borrowed" for § 1981 suits filed in that State. The Court of Appeals, while reversing the award of attorneys' fees, affirmed the grant of equitable and compensatory relief and the ruling as to the applicable statute of limitations, holding that § 1981 is a "limitation upon private discrimination, and its enforcement in the context of this case is not a deprivation of any right of free association or of privacy of the defendants, of the intervenor, or of their pupils or patrons." *Held:*

1. Section 1981 prohibits private, commercially operated, non-sectarian schools from denying admission to prospective students because they are Negroes. Pp. 216-220.

(a) Section 1 of the Civil Rights Act of 1866, from which § 1981 is derived, prohibits racial discrimination in the making and enforcing of private contracts. See *Johnson v. Railway Express Agency*, 421 U.S. 454, 459-460; *Tillman v. Wheaton-Haven Recreation Assn.*, 410 U.S. 431, 439-440. Cf. *Jones v. Alfred H. Mayer Co.*, 392 U.S. 409, 441-443, n. 78. Pp. 216-218.

(b) The racial discrimination practiced by petitioner schools amounts to a classic violation of § 1981: Respondents' parents sought to enter into a contractual relationship with petitioner schools, but neither school offered services on an equal basis to white and nonwhite students. Pp. 218-219.

2. Section 1981, as applied in this case, does not violate constitutionally protected rights of free association and privacy, or a parent's right to direct the education of his children. Pp. 220-222.

(a) While under the principle that there is a First Amendment right "to engage in association for the advancement of beliefs and ideas," *NAACP v. Alabama*, 357 U.S. 449, 460, it may be assumed that parents have a right to send their children to schools that promote the belief that racial segregation is desirable and that the children have a right to attend such schools, it does not follow that the *practice* of excluding racial minorities from such schools is also protected by the same principle. The Constitution places no value on discrimination, and while "[i]nvidious private discrimination may be characterized as

---

*The syllabus constitutes no part of the opinion of the Court but has been prepared by the Reporter of Decisions for the convenience of the reader.

212

a form of exercising freedom of association protected by the First Amendment... it has never been accorded affirmative constitutional protections." *Norwood v. Harrison*, 413 U.S. 455, 470. P. 220.

(b) The application of § 1981 in this case infringed no parental right such as was recognized in *Meyer v. Nebraska*, 262 U.S. 390; *Pierce v. Society of Sisters*, 268 U.S. 510; *Wisconsin v. Yoder*, 406 U.S. 205; or *Norwood v. Harrison, supra,* since no challenge is made to petitioner schools' right to operate, to parents' right to send their children to a particular private school rather than a public school, or to the subject matter that is taught at any private school. Pp. 220-221.

(c) While parents have a constitutional right to send their children to private schools and to select private schools that offer specialized instruction, they have no constitutional right to provide their children with private school education unfettered by reasonable government regulation. Section 1981, as applied to the conduct at issue here, constitutes an exercise of federal legislative power under § 2 of the Thirteenth Amendment "to enforce [that Amendment] by appropriate legislation," fully consistent with *Meyer v. Nebraska, supra; Pierce v. Society of Sisters, supra,* and the cases that followed in their wake, such power including "the power to enact laws 'direct and primary, operating upon the acts of individuals, whether sanctioned by State legislation or not.'" *Jones v. Alfred H. Mayer Co., supra,* at 438. Pp. 221-222.

3. Absent a federal statute of limitations for § 1981 actions or Virginia statute of limitations specifically governing civil rights actions, the Court of Appeals applied the appropriate statute of limitations to bar the damages claim in question, particularly where it appears that the Court of Appeals, as well as the Federal District Courts in Virginia, had considered the question in previous federal civil rights litigation, and that the phrase "personal injuries" in the Virginia two-year statute of limitations can reasonably be construed to apply to the sort of injuries claimed here and not only to "physical injuries" as one respondent's parents contend. Pp. 222-224.

4. Absent any federal statute expressly providing for attorneys' fees in § 1981 cases or any bad faith on petitioner schools' part in contesting the actions, the Court of Appeals properly reversed the award of such fees. Nor is implied authority for such an award furnished by the generalized command of 42 U.S.C. § 1988 "to furnish suitable remedies" to vindicate the rights conferred by the various Civil Rights Acts. Pp. 224-225.

515 F.2d 1082, affirmed.

STEWART, J., delivered the opinion of the Court, in which BURGER, C.J., and BRENNAN, MARSHALL, BLACKMUN, POWELL, and STEVENS, JJ., joined. POWELL, J., *post,* p. 225, and STEVENS, J., *post,* p. 227, filed concurring opinions. WHITE, J., filed a dissenting opinion, in which REHNQUIST, J., joined, *post,* p. 229.

MR. JUSTICE STEWART delivered the opinion of the Court.

The principal issue presented by these consolidated cases is whether a federal law, namely 42 U.S.C. § 1981, prohibits private schools from excluding qualified children solely because they are Negroes.

I

The respondents in No. 75-62, Michael McCrary and Colin Gonzales, are Negro children. By their parents, they filed a class action against the petitioners in No. 75-62, Russell and Katheryne Runyon, who are the proprietors of Bobbe's School in Arlington, Va. Their complaint alleged that they had been prevented from attending the school because of the petitioners' policy of denying admission to Negroes, in violation of 42 U.S.C. § 1981[1] and Title II of the Civil Rights Act of 1964, 78 Stat. 243, 42 U.S.C. § 2000a *et seq.*[2] They sought declaratory and injunctive relief and damages. On the same day Colin Gonzales, the respondent in No. 75-66, filed a similar complaint by his parents against the petitioner in No. 75-66, Fairfax-Brewster School, Inc., located in Fairfax County, Va. The petitioner in No. 75-278, the Southern Independent School Association, sought and was granted permission to intervene as a party defendant in the suit against the Runyons. That organization is a nonprofit association composed of six state private school associations, and represents 395 private schools. It is stipulated that many of these schools deny admission to Negroes.

The suits were consolidated for trial. The findings of the District Court, which were left undisturbed by the Court of Appeals, were as follows. Bobbe's School opened in 1958 and grew from an initial enrollment of five students to 200 in 1972. A day camp was begun in 1967 and has averaged 100 children per year. The Fairfax-Brewster School commenced operations in 1955 and opened a summer day camp in 1956. A total of 223 students were enrolled at the school during the 1972-1973 academic year, and 236 attended the day camp in the summer of 1972. Neither school has ever accepted a Negro child for any of its programs.

In response to a mailed brochure addressed "resident" and an advertisement in the "Yellow Pages" of the telephone directory, Mr. and Mrs. Gonzales telephoned and then visited the Fairfax-Brewster School in May 1969. After the visit, they submitted an application for Colin's admission to the day camp. The school responded with a form letter, which stated that the school was "unable to accommodate [Colin's] application." Mr. Gonzales telephoned the school. Fairfax-Brewster's Chairman of the Board explained that the reason for Colin's rejection was that the school was not integrated. Mr. Gonzales then telephoned Bobbe's School, from which the family had also received in the mail a brochure addressed to "resident." In response to a question concerning that school's admission policies, he was told that only members of the Caucasian race were accepted. In August 1972, Mrs. McCrary telephoned Bobbe's School in response to an advertisement in the telephone book. She inquired about nursery school facilities for her son Michael. She also asked if the school was integrated. The answer was no.

Upon these facts, the District Court found that the Fairfax-Brewster School had rejected Colin Gonzales' application on account of his race and that Bobbe's School had denied both children admission on racial grounds. The court held that 42 U.S.C. § 1981 makes illegal the schools' racially discriminatory admissions policies. It therefore enjoined Fairfax-Brewster School and Bobbe's School and the member schools of the Southern Independent

---

[1]Title 42 U.S.C. § 1981 provides:

"All persons within the jurisdiction of the United States shall have the same right in every State and Territory to make and enforce contracts, to sue, be parties, give evidence, and to the full and equal benefit of all laws and proceedings for the security of persons and property as is enjoyed by white citizens, and shall be subject to like punishment, pains, penalties, taxes, licenses, and exactions of every kind, and to no other."

The respondents withdrew their Title II claim before trial.

School Association³ from discriminating against applicants for admission on the basis of race. The court awarded compensatory relief to Mr. and Mrs. McCrary, Michael McCrary, and Colin Gonzales.⁴ In a previous ruling the court had held that the damages claim of Mr. and Mrs. Gonzales was barred by Virginia's two-year statute of limitations for personal injury actions, "borrowed" for § 1981 suits filed in that State. Finally, the court assessed attorneys' fees of $1,000 against each school. 363 F.Supp. 1200 (ED Va. 1973).

The Court of Appeals for the Fourth Circuit, sitting en banc, affirmed the District Court's grant of equitable and compensatory relief and its ruling as to the applicable statute of limitations, but reversed its award of attorneys' fees. 515 F.2d 1082 (1975). Factually, the court held that there was sufficient evidence to support the trial court's finding that the two schools had discriminated racially against the children. On the basic issue of law, the court agreed that 42 U.S.C. § 1981'is a "limitation upon private discrimination, and its enforcement in the context of this case is not a deprivation of any right of free association or of privacy of the defendants, of the intervenor, or of their pupils or patrons." 515 F.2d, at 1086. The relationship the parents had sought to enter into with the schools was in the court's view undeniably contractual in nature, within the meaning of § 1981, and the court rejected the schools' claim that § 1981 confers no right of action unless the contractual relationship denied to Negroes is available to all whites. 515 F.2d, at 1087. Finally, the appellate court rejected the schools' contention that their racially discriminatory policies are protected by a constitutional right of privacy. "When a school holds itself open to the public... or even to those applicants meeting established qualifications, there is no perceived privacy of the sort that has been given constitutional protection." *Id.*, at 1088.

We granted the petitions for certiorari filed by the Fairfax-Brewster School, No. 75-66; Bobbe's School, No. 75-62; and the Southern Independent School Association, No. 75-278, to consider whether 42 U.S.C. § 1981 prevents private schools from discriminating racially among applicants. 423 U.S. 945. We also granted the cross-petition of Michael McCrary, Colin Gonzales, and their parents, No. 75-306, to determine the attorneys' fees and statute of limitations issues. *Ibid.*

II

It is worth noting at the outset some of the questions that these cases do not present. They do not present any question of the right of a private social organization to limit its membership on racial or any other grounds.⁵ They do not present any question of the right of a private school to limit its student body to boys, to girls, or to adherents of a particular religious faith, since 42 U.S.C. § 1981 is in no way addressed to such categories of selectivity. They do not even present the application of § 1981 to private sectarian schools

---

³The District Court determined that the suit could not be maintained as a class action.

⁴For the embarrassment, humiliation, and mental anguish which the parents and children suffered, the Court awarded Colin Gonzales $2,000 against the Fairfax-Brewster School and $500 against Bobbe's School. Michael McCrary was awarded damages of $1,000, and Mr. and Mrs. McCrary $2,000, against Bobbe's School.

⁵See generally *Tillman v. Wheaton-Haven Recreation Assn.*, 410 U.S. 431, 439-440; *Moose Lodge No. 107 v. Irvis*, 407 U.S. 163.

that practice *racial* exclusion on religious grounds.[6] Rather, these cases present only two basic questions:[7] whether § 1981 prohibits private, commercially operated, nonsectarian schools from denying admission to prospective students because they are Negroes, and, if so, whether that federal law is constitutional as so applied.

A. *Applicability of § 1981*

It is now well established that § 1 of the Civil Rights Act of 1866, 14 Stat. 27, 42 U.S.C. § 1981, prohibits racial discrimination in the making and enforcement of private contracts.[8] See *Johnson v. Railway Express Agency,*

---

[6]Nothing in this record suggests that either the Fairfax-Brewster School or Bobbe's Private School excludes applicants on religious grounds, and the Free Exercise Clause of the First Amendment is thus in no way here involved.

[7]Apart, of course, from the statute of limitations and attorneys' fees issues involved in No. 75-306, and dealt with in Part III of this opinion.

[8]The historical note appended to the portion of the Civil Rights Act of 1866, presently codified in 42 U.S.C. § 1981, indicates that § 1981 is derived solely from § 16 of the Act of May 31, 1870, 16 Stat. 144. The omission from the historical note of any reference to § 18 of the 1870 Act, which re-enacted § 1 of the 1866 Act, or to the 1866 Act itself reflects a similar omission from the historical note that was prepared in connection with the 1874 codification of federal statutory law. The earlier note was appended to the draft version of the 1874 revision prepared by three commissioners appointed by Congress.

On the basis of this omission, at least one court has concluded, in an opinion that antedated *Johnson v. Railway Express Agency,* 421 U.S. 454, that § 1981 is based exclusively on the Fourteenth Amendment and does not, therefore, reach private action. *Cook v. Advertiser Co.,* 323 F.Supp. 1212 (MD Ala.), aff'd on other grounds, 458 F.2d 1119 (CA5). But the holding in that case ascribes an inappropriate significance to the historical note presently accompanying § 1981, and thus implicitly to the earlier revisers' note.

The commissioners who prepared the 1874 draft revision were appointed pursuant to the Act of June 27, 1866, 15 Stat. 74, re-enacted by the Act of May 4, 1870, c. 72, 16 Stat. 96. They were given authority to "revise, simplify, arrange, and consolidate all statutes of the United States," Act of June 27, 1866, § 1, 14 Stat. 74, by "bring[ing] together all statutes and parts of statutes which, from similarity of subject, ought to be brought together, *omitting redundant or obsolete enactments. . . ."* § 2, 14 Stat. 75 (emphasis added). The commissioners also had the authority under § 3 of the Act of June 27, 1866, to "designate such statutes or parts of statutes as, in their judgment, ought to be repealed, with their reasons for such repeal." 14 Stat. 75.

It is clear that the commissioners did not intend to recommend to Congress, pursuant to their authority under § 3 of the Act of June 27, 1866, that any portion of § 1 of the Civil Rights Act of 1866 be repealed upon the enactment of the 1874 revision. When the commissioners were exercising their § 3 power of recommendation, they so indicated, in accordance with the requirements of § 3. See 1 Draft Revision of the United States Statutes, Title XXVI, §§ 8, 13 (1872). No indication of a recommended change was noted with respect to the section of the draft which was to become § 1981. It is thus most plausible to assume that the revisers omitted a reference to § 1 of the 1866 Act or § 18 of the 1870 Act either inadvertently or on the assumption that the relevant language in § 1 of the 1866 Act was superfluous in light of the closely parallel language in § 16 of the 1870 Act.

We have, in past decisions, expressed the view that § 16 of the 1870 Act was merely a re-enactment, with minor changes, of certain language in § 1 of the 1866 Act. *E. g., Georgia v. Rachel,* 384 U.S. 780, 790-791. If this is so, then an assumption on the part of the revisers that the language of the 1866 Act was superfluous was perfectly

421 U.S. 454, 459-460; *Tillman v. Wheaton-Haven Recreation Assn.*, 410
U.S. 431, 439-440. Cf. *Jones v. Alfred H. Mayer Co.*, 392 U.S. 409, 441-443,
n. 78.

In *Jones* the Court held that the portion of § 1 of the Civil Rights Act of
1866 presently codified as 42 U.S.C. § 1982 prohibits private racial discrimination in the sale of rental of real or personal property. Relying on the
legislative history of § 1, from which both § 1981 and § 1982 derive, the Court
concluded that Congress intended to prohibit "all racial discrimination, private and public, in the sale...of property," 392 U.S., at 437, and that this
prohibition was within Congress' power under § 2 of the Thirteenth Amendment "rationally to determine what are the badges and the incidents of
slavery, and...to translate that determination into effective legislation." 392
U.S., at 440.

As the Court indicated in *Jones, supra*, at 441-443, n. 78, that holding
necessarily implied that the portion of § 1 of the 1866 Act presently codified
as 42 U.S.C. § 1981 likewise reaches purely private acts of racial discrimination. The statutory holding in *Jones* was that the "[1866] Act was designed
to do just what its terms suggest: to prohibit all racial discrimination, whether
or not under color of law, with respect to the rights enumerated therein—
including the right to purchase or lease property," 392 U.S., at 436. One of
the "rights enumerated" in § 1 is the "the same right...to make and enforce
contracts...as is enjoyed by white citizens ... ." 14 Stat. 27. Just as in *Jones*
a Negro's § 1 right to purchase property on equal terms with whites was
violated when a private person refused to sell to the prospective purchaser
solely because he was a Negro, so also a Negro's § 1 right to "make and
enforce contracts" is violated if a private offeror refuses to extend to a Negro,
solely because he is a Negro, the same opportunity to enter into contracts
as he extends to white offerees.[9]

---

accurate. But even assuming that the purpose behind the enactment of § 16 of the
1870 Act was narrower than that behind the enactment of relevant language in § 1
of the 1866 Act—and thus that the revisers' hypothetical assumption was wrong—
there is still no basis for inferring that Congress did not understand the draft legislation which eventually became 42 U.S.C. § 1981 to be drawn from both § 16 of the
1870 Act and § 1 of the 1866 Act.

To hold otherwise would be to attribute to Congress an intent to repeal a major
piece of Reconstruction legislation on the basis of an unexplained omission from the
revisers' marginal notes. Such an inference would be inconsistent with Congress'
delineation in § 3 of the Act of June 27, 1866, of specific procedures to be followed
in connection with the submission of substantive proposals by the revisers. It would
also conflict with the square holding of this Court in *Johnson v. Railway Express
Agency, supra*, that § 1981 reaches private conduct.

[9]The petitioning schools and school association rely on a statement in *Norwood v.
Harrison*, 413 U.S. 455, 469, that "private bias [in the admission of students to private
schools] is not barred by the Constitution, *nor does it invoke any sanction of laws*,
but neither can it call on the Constitution for material aid from the State." (Emphasis
added.) They argue that this statement supports their contention that § 1981 does
not proscribe private racial discrimination that interferes with the formation of contracts for educational services. But *Norwood* involved no issue concerning the applicability of § 1981 to such discrimination. The question there was rather whether a
state statute providing free textbooks to students attending private segregated schools
violated the Equal Protection Clause of the Fourteenth Amendment. Indeed, *Norwood*, expressly noted that "some private discrimination is subject to special remedial

The applicability of the holding in *Jones* to § 1981 was confirmed by this Court's decisions in *Tillman v. Wheaton-Haven Recreation Assn.*, *supra*, and *Johnson v. Railway Express Agency, Inc.*, *supra*. In *Tillman* the petitioners urged that a private swimming club had violated 42 U.S. C. §§ 1981, 1982, and 2000a *et seq.* by enforcing a guest policy that discriminated against Negroes. The Court noted that "[t]he operative language of both § 1981 and § 1982 is traceable to the Act of April 9, 1866, c. 31, § 1, 14 Stat. 27." 410 U.S., at 439. Referring to its earlier rejection of the respondents' contention that Wheaton-Haven was exempt from § 1982 under the private-club exception of the Civil Rights Act of 1964, the Court concluded: "In light of the historical inter-relationship between § 1981 and § 1982 [there is] no reason to construe these sections differently when applied on these facts to the claim of Wheaton-Haven that it is a private club." 410 U.S., at 440. Accordingly the Court remanded the case to the District Court for further proceedings "free of the misconception that Wheaton-Haven is exempt from §§ 1981, 1982 and 2000a." *Ibid.* In *Johnson v. Railway Express Agency, supra*, the Court noted that § 1981 "relates primarily to racial discrimination in the making and enforcement of contracts," 421 U.S., at 459, and held unequivocally "that § 1981 affords a federal remedy against discrimination in private employment on the basis of race." *Id.*, at 459-460.

It is apparent that the racial exclusion practiced by the Fairfax-Brewster School and Bobbe's Private School amounts to a classic violation of § 1981. The parents of Colin Gonzales and Michael McCrary sought to enter into contractual relationships with Bobbe's School for educational services. Colin Gonzales' parents sought to enter into similar relationship with the Fairfax-Brewster School. Under those contractual relationships, the schools would have received payments for services rendered, and the prospective students would have received instruction in return for those payments. The educational services of Bobbe's School and the Fairfax-Brewster School were advertised and offered to members of the general public.[10] But neither school

---

legislation in certain circumstances under § 2 of the Thirteenth Amendment...." 413 U.S., at 470.

[10]These cases do not raise the issue of whether the "private club or other [private] establishment" exemption in § 201 (e) of the Civil Rights Act of 1964, 42 U.S.C. § 2000a (e), operates to narrow § 1 of the Civil Rights Act of 1866. As the Court of Appeals implied, that exemption, if applicable at all, comes into play only if the establishment is "not in fact open to the public...." 42 U.S.C. § 2000a (e). See 515 F.2d 1082, 1088-1089. Both Bobbe's School and the Fairfax-Brewster School advertised in the "Yellow Pages" of the telephone directory and both used mass mailings in attempting to attract students. As the Court of Appeals observed, these "schools are private only in the sense that they are managed by private persons and they are not direct recipients of public funds. Their actual and potential constituency, however, is more public than private. They appeal to the parents of all children in the area who can meet their academic and other admission requirements. This is clearly demonstrated in this case by the public advertisements." *Id.*, at 1089.

The pattern of exclusion is thus directly analogous to that at issue in *Sullivan v. Little Hunting Park, Inc.*, 396 U.S. 229, and *Tillman v. Wheaton-Haven Recreation Assn.*, 410 U.S. 431, where the so-called private clubs were open to all objectively qualified whites—*i.e.*, those living within a specified geographic area.

Moreover, it is doubtful that a plausible "implied repeal" argument could be made in this context in any event. Implied repeals occur if two Acts are in irreconcilable

offered services on an equal basis to white and nonwhite students. As the Court of Appeals held, "there is ample evidence in the record to support the trial judge's factual determinations...[that] Colin [Gonzales] and Michael [McCrary] were denied admission to the schools because of their race." 515 F.2d, at 1086. The Court of Appeals' conclusion that § 1981 was thereby violated follows inexorably from the language of that statute, as construed in *Jones, Tillman,* and *Johnson.*

The petitioning schools and school association argue principally that § 1981 does not reach private acts of racial discrimination. That view is wholly inconsistent with *Jones'* interpretation of the legislative history of § 1 of the Civil Rights Act of 1866, an interpretation that was reaffirmed in *Sullivan v. Little Hunting Park, Inc.,* 396 U.S. 229, and again in *Tillman v. Wheaton-Haven Recreation Assn., supra.* And this consistent interpretation of the law necessarily requires the conclusion that § 1981, like § 1982, reaches private conduct. See *Tillman v. Wheaton-Haven Recreation Assn.,* 410 U.S., at 439-440; *Johnson v. Railway Express Agency,* 421 U.S., at 459-460.

It is noteworthy that Congress in enacting the Equal Employment Opportunity Act of 1972, 86 Stat. 103, as amended, 42 U.S.C. § 2000e *et seq.* (1970 ed., Supp. IV), specifically considered and rejected an amendment that would have repealed the Civil Rights Act of 1866, as interpreted by this Court in *Jones,* insofar as it affords private-sector employees a right of action based on racial discrimination in employment. See *Johnson v. Railway Express Agency, supra,* at 459.[11] There could hardly be a clearer indication of

---

conflict. *Radzanower v. Touche Ross & Co.,* 426 U.S. 148, 154-155. Title II of the Civil Rights Act of 1964, of which the "private club" exemption is a part, does not by its terms reach private schools. Since there would appear to be no potential for overlapping application of § 1981 and Title II of the 1964 Act with respect to racial discrimination practiced by private schools, there would also appear to be no potential for conflict between § 1981 and Title II's "private club" exemption in this context. See Note, The Desegregation of Private Schools: Is Section 1981 the Answer?, 48 N.Y.U.L. Rev. 1147, 1159 (1973).

[11]Senator Hruska proposed an amendment which would have made Title VII of the Civil Rights Act of 1964 and the Equal Pay Act the exclusive sources of federal relief for employment discrimination. 118 Cong. Rec. 3371 (1972). Senator Williams, the floor manager of the pending bill and one of its original sponsors, argued against the proposed amendment on the ground that "[i]t is not our purpose to repeal existing civil rights laws" and that to do so "would severely weaken our overall effort to combat the presence of employment discrimination." *Ibid.* Senator Williams specifically noted: "The law against employment discrimination did not begin with title VII and the EEOC, nor is it intended to end with it. The right of individuals to bring suits in Federal courts to redress individual acts of discrimination, including employment discrimination was first provided by the Civil Rights Acts of 1866 and 1871, 42 U.S.C. sections 1981, 1983. It was recently stated by the Supreme Court in the case of Jones v. Mayer, that these acts provide fundamental constitutional guarantees. In any case, the courts have specifically held that title VII and the Civil Rights Acts of 1866 and 1871 are not mutually exclusive, and must be read together to provide alternative means to redress individual grievances. Mr. President, the amendment of the Senator from Nebraska will repeal the first major piece of civil rights legislation in this Nation's history. We cannot do that." *Ibid.* The Senate was persuaded by Senator Williams' entreaty that it not "strip from [the] individual his rights that have been established, going back to the first Civil Rights law of 1866, *id.,* at 3372, and Senator Hruska's proposed amendment was rejected. *Id.,* at 3372-3373.

congressional agreement with the view that § 1981 *does* reach private acts of racial discrimination. Cf. *Flood v. Kuhn*, 407 U.S. 258, 269-285; *Joint Industry Board v. United States*, 391 U.S. 224, 228-229. In these circumstances there is no basis for deviating from the well-settled principles of *stare decisis* applicable to this Court's construction of federal statutes. See *Edelman v. Jordan*, 415 U.S. 651, 671 n. 14.[12]

B. *Constitutionality of § 1981 as Applied*

The question remains whether § 1981, as applied, violates constitutionally protected rights of free association and privacy, or a parent's right to direct the education of his children.[13]

1. *Freedom of Association*

In *NAACP v. Alabama*, 357 U.S. 449, and similar decisions, the Court has recognized a First Amendment right "to engage in association for the advancement of beliefs and ideas...." *Id.*, at 460. That right is protected because it promotes and may well be essential to the "[e]ffective advocacy of both public and private points of view, particularly controversial ones" that the First Amendment is designed to foster. *Ibid.* See *Buckley v. Valeo*, 424 U.S. 1, 15; *NAACP v. Button*, 371 U.S. 415.

From this principle it may be assumed that parents have a First Amendment right to send their children to educational institutions that promote the belief that racial segregation is desirable, and that the children have an equal right to attend such institutions. But it does not follow that the *practice* of excluding racial minorities from such institutions is also protected by the same principle. As the Court stated in *Norwood v. Harrison*, 413 U.S. 455, "the Constitution...places no value on discrimination," *id.*, at 469, and while "[i]nvidious private discrimination may be characterized as a form of exercising freedom of association protected by the First Amendment...it has never been accorded affirmative constitutional protections. And even some private discrimination is subject to special remedial legislation in certain circumstances under § 2 of the Thirteenth Amendment; Congress has made such discrimination unlawful in other significant contexts." *Id.*, at 470. In any event, as the Court of Appeals noted, "there is no showing that discontinuance of [the] discriminatory admission practices would inhibit in any way the teaching in these schools of any ideas or dogma." 515 F.2d, at˙ 1087.

2. *Parental Rights*

In *Meyer v. Nebraska*, 262 U.S. 390, the Court held that the liberty protected by the Due Process Clause of the Fourteenth Amendment includes the right "to acquire useful knowledge, to marry, establish a home and bring up children," *id.*, at 399, and, concomitantly, the right to send one's children

---

[12]The Court in *Edelman* stated as follows:

"In the words of Mr. Justice Brandeis: '*Stare decisis* is usually the wise policy, because in most matters it is more important that the applicable rule of law be settled than that it be settled right.... This is commonly true even where the error is a matter of serious concern, provided correction can be had by legislation....' " 415 U.S., at 671 n. 14 (citation omitted).

[13]It is clear that the schools have standing to assert these arguments on behalf of their patrons. See *Pierce v. Society of Sisters*, 268 U.S. 510, 535-536.

to a private school that offers specialized training—in that case, instruction in the German language. In *Pierce v. Society of Sisters*, 268 U.S. 510, the Court applied "the doctrine of *Meyer v. Nebraska*," *id.*, at 534, to hold unconstitutional an Oregon law requiring the parent, guardian, or other person having custody of a child between 8 and 16 years of age to send that child to public school on pain of criminal liability. The Court thought it "entirely plain that the [statute] unreasonably interferes with the liberty of parents and guardians to direct the upbringing and education of children under their control." *Id.*, at 534-535. In *Wisconsin v. Yoder*, 406 U.S. 205, the Court stressed the limited scope of *Pierce*, pointing out that it lent "no support to the contention that parents may replace state educational requirements with their own idiosyncratic views of what knowledge a child needs to be a productive and happy member of society" but rather "held simply that while a State may posit [educational] standards, it may not pre-empt the educational process by requiring children to attend public schools." *Id.*, at 239 (WHITE, J., concurring). And in *Norwood v. Harrison*, 413 U.S. 455, the Court once again stressed the "limited scope of *Pierce*," *id.*, at 461, which simply "affirmed the right of private schools to exist and operate...." *Id.*, at 462.

It is clear that the present application of § 1981 infringes no parental right recognized in *Meyer, Pierce, Yoder,* or *Norwood*. No challenge is made to the petitioner schools' right to operate or the right of parents to send their children to a particular private school rather than a public school. Nor do these cases involve a challenge to the subject matter which is taught at any private school. Thus, the Fairfax-Brewster School and Bobbe's School and members of the intervenor association remain presumptively free to inculcate whatever values and standards they deem desirable. *Meyer* and its progeny entitle them to no more.

3. *The Right of Privacy*

The Court has held that in some situations the Constitution confers a right of privacy. See *Roe v. Wade*, 410 U.S. 113, 152-153; *Eisenstadt v. Baird*, 405 U.S. 438, 453; *Stanley v. Georgia*, 394 U.S. 557, 564-565; *Griswold v. Connecticut*, 381 U.S. 479, 484-485. See also *Loving v. Virginia*, 388 U.S. 1, 12; *Skinner v. Oklahoma ex rel. Williamson*, 316 U.S. 535, 541.

While the application of § 1981 to the conduct at issue here—a private school's adherence to a racially discriminatory admissions policy—does not represent governmental intrusion into the privacy of the home or a similarly intimate setting,[14] it does implicate parental interests. These interests are related to the procreative rights protected in *Roe v. Wade, supra*, and *Griswold v. Connecticut, supra*. A persons' decision whether to bear a child and a parent's decision concerning the manner in which his child is to be educated may fairly be characterized as exercises of familial rights and responsibilities. But it does not follow that because government is largely or even entirely precluded from regulating the child-bearing decision, it is similarly restricted by the Constitution from regulating the implementation of parental decisions concerning a child's education.

The Court has repeatedly stressed that while parents have a constitutional right to send their children to private schools and a constitutional right to

---

[14]See n. 10, *supra*.

select private schools that offer specialized instruction, they have no constitutional right to provide their children with private school education unfettered by reasonable government regulation. See *Wisconsin v. Yoder, supra,*
at 213; *Pierce v. Society of Sisters, supra,* at 534; *Meyer v. Nebraska,* 262
U.S., at 402.[15] Indeed, the Court in *Pierce* expressly acknowledged "the
power of the State reasonably to regulate all schools, to inspect, supervise
and examine them, their teachers and pupils...." 268 U.S., at 534. See also
Prince v. Massachusetts, 321 U.S. 158, 166.

Section 1981, as applied to the conduct at issue here, constitutes an exercise of federal legislative power under § 2 of the Thirteenth Amendment
fully consistent with *Meyer, Pierce,* and the cases that followed in their wake.
As the Court held in *Jones v. Alfred H. Mayer Co., supra,* "It has never
been doubted...'that the power vested in Congress to enforce [the Thirteenth Amendment] by appropriate legislation' ... includes the power to
enact laws 'direct and primary, operating upon the acts of individuals, whether
sanctioned by State legislation or not.' " 392 U.S., at 438 (citation omitted).
The prohibition of racial discrimination that interferes with the making and
enforcement of contacts for private educational services furthers goals closely
analogous to those served by § 1981's elimination of racial discrimination in
the making of private employment contracts[16] and, more generally, by §
1982's guarantee that "a dollar in the hands of a Negro will purchase the
same thing as a dollar in the hands of a white man." 392 U.S., at 443.

III

A. *Statute of Limitations*

The District Court held that the damages suit of the petitioners in No. 75-
306, Mr. and Mrs. Gonzales, which was initiated 3-1/2 years after their cause
of action accrued, was barred by the statute of limitations. This ruling was
affirmed by the Court of Appeals. The petitioners contend that both courts
erred in "borrowing" the wrong Virginia statute of limitations.

Had Congress placed a limit upon the time for bringing an action under §
1981, that would, of course, end the matter. But Congress was silent. And
"[a]s to actions at law," which a damages suit under § 1981 clearly is, "the
silence of Congress has been interpreted to mean that it is federal policy to
adopt the local law of limitation." *Holmberg v. Armbrecht,* 327 U.S. 392,
395. See *Johnson v. Railway Express Agency,* 421 U.S., at 462; *Rawlings v.
Ray,* 312 U.S. 96; *O'Sullivan v. Felix,* 233 U.S. 318; *Chattanooga Foundry
v. Atlanta,* 203 U.S. 390. As the Court stated in *Holmberg, supra,* at 395:
"The implied absorption of State statutes of limitation within the interstices
of the federal enactments is a phase of fashioning remedial details where
Congress has not spoken but left matters for judicial determination within
the general framework of familiar legal principles."

---

[15]The *Meyer-Pierce-Yoder* "parental" right and the privacy right, while dealt with
separately in this opinion, may be no more than verbal variations of a single constitutional right. See *Roe v. Wade,* 410 U.S. 113, 152-153 (citing *Meyer v. Nebraska*
and *Pierce v. Society of Sisters* for the proposition that this Court has recognized a
constitutional right of privacy).

[16]The Court has recognized in similar contexts the link between equality of opportunity to obtain an education and equality of employment opportunity. See *McLaurin
v. Oklahoma State Regents,* 339 U.S. 637; *Sweatt v. Painter,* 339 U.S. 629.

At the time of this litigation Virginia had not enacted a statute that specifically governed civil rights suits. In the absence of such a specific statute, the District Court and the Court of Appeals held that the first sentence of Va. Code Ann. § 8-24 (1957) provides the relevant limitations period for a § 1981 action: "Every action for personal injuries shall be brought within two years next after the right to bring the same shall have accrued." The petitioners assert that this provision applies only to suits predicated upon actual physical injury, and that the correct limitation period is five years, by virtue of the second sentence of § 8-24, which comprehends all other "personal" actions:

> "Every personal action, for which no limitation is otherwise prescribed, shall be brought within five years next after the right to bring the same shall have accrued, if it be for a matter of such nature that in case a party die it can be brought by or against his representative; and, if it be for a matter not of such nature, shall be brought within one year next after the right to bring the same shall have accrued."

The petitioners' contention is certainly a rational one, but we are not persuaded that the Court of Appeals was mistaken in applying the two-year state statute. The issue was not a new one for that court, for it had given careful consideration to the question of the appropriate Virginia statute of limitations to be applied in federal civil rights litigation on at least two previous occasions. *Allen v. Gifford*, 462 F.2d 615; *Almond v. Kent*, 459 F.2d 200. We are not disposed to displace the considered judgment of the Court of Appeals on an issue whose resolution is so heavily contingent upon an analysis of state law, particularly when the established rule has been relied upon and applied in numerous suits filed in the Federal District Courts in Virginia.[17] In other situations in which a federal right has depended upon the interpretation of state law, "the Court has accepted the interpretation of state law in which the District Court and the Court of Appeals have concurred even if an examination of the state-law issue without such guidance might have justified a different conclusion." *Bishop v. Wood*, 426 U.S. 341, 346, and n. 10, citing, *inter alia*, *United States v. Durham Lumber Co.*, 363 U.S. 522; *Propper v. Clark*, 337 U.S. 472; *Township of Hillsborough v. Cromwell*, 326 U.S. 620.

Moreover, the petitioners have not cited any Virginia court decision to the effect that the term "personal injuries" in § 8-24 means only "physical injuries." It could be argued with at least equal force that the phrase "personal injuries" was designed to distinguish those causes of action involving torts against the person from those involving damage to property. And whether the damages claim of the Gonzaleses by properly characterized as involving "injured feelings and humiliation," as the Court of Appeals held, 515 F.2d, at 1097, or the indication of constitutional rights, as the petitioners contend, there is no dispute that the damage was to their persons, not to their realty

---

[17]See, *e.g.*, *Van Horn v. Lukhard*, 392 F.Supp. 384, 391 (ED Va.); *Edgerton v. Puckett*, 391 F.Supp. 463 (WD Va.); *Wilkinson v. Hamel*, 381 F.Supp. 768, 769 (WD Va.); *Cradle v. Superintendent, Correctional Field Unit #7*, 374 F.Supp. 435, 437 n. 3 (WD Va.); *Taliaferro v. State Council of Higher Education*, 372 F.Supp. 1378, 1383 (ED Va.); *Landman v. Brown*, 350 F.Supp. 303, 306 (ED Va.); *Sitwell v. Burnette*, 349 F.Supp. 83, 85-86 (WD Va.).

or personalty. Cf. *Carva Food Corp. v. Dawley*, 202 Va. 543, 118 E. 2d 664; *Travelers Ins. Co. v. Turner*, 211 Va. 552, 178 S.E. 2d 503.

B. *Attorneys' Fees*

The District Court, without explanation or citation of authority, awarded attorneys' fees of $1,000 against each of the two schools. The Court of Appeals reversed this part of the District Court's judgment. Anticipating our decision in *Alyeska Pipeline Service Co. v. Wilderness Society*, 421 U.S. 240, the appellate court refused to adopt the so-called private attorney general theory under which attorneys' fees could be awarded to any litigant who vindicates an important public interest. And it could find no other ground for the award: no statute explicitly provides for attorneys' fees in § 1981 cases,[18] and neither school had evinced " 'obstinate obduracy' " or bad faith in contesting the action. 515 F.2d, at 1089-1090.

Mindful of this Court's *Alyeska* decision, the petitioners do not claim that their vindication of the right of Negro children to attend private schools alone entitles them to attorneys' fees. They make instead two other arguments.

First, the petitioners claim that the schools exhibited bad faith, not by litigating the legal merits of their racially discriminatory admissions policy, but by denying that they in fact had discriminated. To support this claim, the petitioners cite a number of conflicts in testimony between the McCrarys, the Gonzaleses, and other witnesses, on the one hand, and the officials of the schools, on the other, which the District Court resolved against the schools in finding racial discrimination. Indeed, the trial court characterized as "unbelievable" the testimony of three officials of the Fairfax-Brewster School. 363 F.Supp., at 1202. By stubbornly contesting the facts, the petitioners assert, the schools attempted to deceive the court and, in any event, needlessly prolonged the litigation.

We cannot accept this argument. To be sure, the Court has recognized the "inherent power" of the federal courts to assess attorneys' fees when the losing party has "acted in bad faith, vexatiously, wantonly, or for oppressive reasons...." *F.D. Rich Co. v. United States ex rel. Industrial Lumber Co.*, 417 U.S. 116, 129. See *Alyeska, supra*, at 258-259; *Vaughan v. Atkinson*, 369 U.S. 527. But in this case the factual predicate to a finding of bad faith is absent. Simply because the facts were found against the schools does not by itself prove that threshold of irresponsible conduct for which a penalty assessment would be justified. Whenever the facts in a case are disputed, a court perforce must decide that one party's version is inaccurate. Yet it would be untenable to conclude *ipso facto* that that party had acted in bad faith. As the Court of Appeals stated, 515 F.2d, at 1090: "Faults in perception or memory often account for differing trial testimony, but that has not yet been thought a sufficient ground to shift the expense of litigation." We find no warrant for disturbing the holding of the Court of Appeals that no bad faith permeated the defense by the schools of this lawsuit.

The petitioners' second argument is that while 42 U.S.C. § 1981 contains no authorization for the award of attorneys' fees, 42 U.S.C. § 1988 implicitly does. In relevant part, that section reads:

"The jurisdiction in civil...matters conferred on the district courts by the provisions of this chapter and Title 18, for the protection of all

---

[18]Cf., *e.g.*, Title II of the Civil Rights Act of 1964, 42 U.S.C. § 2000a-3 (b). See *Alyeska Pipeline Serv. Co. v. Wilderness Society*, 421 U.S. 240, 260-262, and n. 33.

persons in the United States in their civil rights, and for their vindication, shall be exercised and enforced in conformity with the laws of the United States, so far as such laws are suitable to carry the same into effect; but in all cases where they are not adapted to the object, or are deficient in the provisions necessary to furnish suitable remedies and punish offenses against law, the common law, as modified and changed by the constitution and statutes of the State wherein the court having jurisdiction of such civil or criminal cause is held, so far as the same is not inconsistent with the Constitution and laws of the United States, shall be extended to and govern the said courts in the trial and disposition of the cause...."

The petitioners assert, in the words of their brief, that § 1988 "embodies a uniquely broad commission to the federal courts to search among federal and state statutes and common law for the remedial devices and procedures which best enforce the substantive provisions of Sec. 1981 and other civil rights statutes." As part of that "broad commission" the federal courts are obligated, the petitioners say, to award attorneys' fees whenever such fees are needed to encourage private parties to seek relief against illegal discrimination.

This contention is without merit. It is true that in order to vindicate the rights conferred by the various Civil Rights Acts, § 1988 "authorize[s] federal courts, where federal law is unsuited or insufficient 'to furnish suitable remedies,' to look to principles of the common law, as altered by state law...." *Moor v. County of Alameda*, 411 U.S. 693, 702-703. See *Sullivan v. Little Hunting Park Inc.*, 396 U.S., at 239-240. But the Court has never interpreted § 1988 to warrant the award of attorneys' fees. And nothing in the legislative history of that statute suggests that such a radical departure from the long-established American rule forbidding the award of attorneys' fees was intended.

More fundamentally, the petitioners' theory would require us to overlook the penultimate clause of § 1988: "so far as the same is not inconsistent with the Constitution and laws of the United States." As the Court recounted in some detail in *Alyeska, supra*, at 247, *passim*, the law of the United States, but for a few well-recognized exceptions not present in these cases,[19] has always been that absent explicit congressional authorization, attorneys' fees are not a recoverable cost of litigation. Hence, in order to "furnish" an award of attorneys' fees, we would have to find that at least as to cases brought under statutes to which § 1988 applies, Congress intended to set aside this longstanding American rule of law. We are unable to conclude, however, from the generalized commands of § 1988, that Congress intended any such result.

For the reasons stated in this opinion, the judgment of the Court of Appeals is in all respects affirmed.

It is so ordered.

MR. JUSTICE POWELL, concurring.

If the slate were clean I might well be inclined to agree with MR. JUSTICE WHITE that § 1981 was not intended to restrict private contractual choices.

---

[19]See, *e.g.*, *Trustees v. Greenough*, 105 U.S. 527 (allowance of attorneys' fees out of a common fund); *Toledo Scale Co. v. Computing Scale Co.*, 261 U.S. 399 (assessment of fees as part of the fine for willful disobedience of a court order); *F.D. Rich Co. v. United States ex rel. Industrial Lumber Co.*, 417 U.S. 116 (assessment of attorneys' fees against party acting in bad faith).

Much of the review of the history and purpose of this statute set forth in his dissenting opinion is quite persuasive. It seems to me, however, that it comes too late.

The applicability of § 1981 to private contracts has been considered maturely and recently, and I do not feel free to disregard these precedents.* As they are reviewed in the Court's opinion, I merely cite them: *Johnson v. Railway Express Agency*, 421 U.S. 454, 459-460 (1975), an opinion in which I joined; *Tillman v. Wheaton-Haven Recreation Assn.*, 410 U.S. 431, 439-440 (1973), another opinion in which I joined; *Sullivan v. Little Hunting Park, Inc.*, 396 U.S. 229, 236-237 (1969); and particularly and primarily, *Jones v. Alfred H. Mayer Co.*, 392 U.S. 409, 420-437 (1968). Although the latter two cases involved § 1982, rather than § 1981, I agree that their considered holdings with respect to the purpose and meaning of § 1982 necessarily apply to both statutes in view of their common derivation.

Although the range of consequences suggested by the dissenting opinion, *post*, at 212, goes far beyond what we hold today, I am concerned that our decision not be construed more broadly than would be justified.

By its terms § 1981 necessarily imposes some restrictions on those who would refuse to extend to Negroes "the same right ... to make and enforce contracts...as is enjoyed by white citizens." But our holding that this restriction extends to certain actions by private individuals does not imply the intrusive investigation into the motives of every refusal to contract by a private citizen that is suggested by the dissent. As the Court of Appeals suggested, some contracts are so personal "as to have a discernible rule of exclusivity which is inoffensive to § 1981." 515 F.2d 1082, 1088 (1975).

In *Sullivan v. Little Hunting Park*, *supra*, we were faced with an association in which "[t]here was no plan or purpose of exclusiveness." Participation was "open to every white person within the geographic area, there being no selective element other than race." 396 U.S., at 236. See also *Tillman v. Wheaton-Haven Recreation Assn.*, *supra*, at 438. In certain personal contractual relationships, however, such as those where the offeror selects those with whom he desires to bargain on an individualized basis, or where the contract is the foundation of a close association (such as, for example, that between an employer and a private tutor, babysitter, or housekeeper), there is reason to assume that, although the choice made by the offeror is selective, it reflects "a purpose of exclusiveness" other than the desire to bar members of the Negro race. Such a purpose, certainly in most cases, would invoke associational rights long respected.

The case presented on the record before us does not involve this type of personal contractual relationship. As the Court of Appeals said, the petitioning "schools are private only in the sense that they are managed by private persons and they are not direct recipients of public funds. Their actual and potential constituency, however, is more public than private." 515 F.2d,

---

*In some instances the Court has drifted almost accidentally into rather extreme interpretations of the post-Civil War Acts. The most striking example is the proposition, now often accepted uncritically, that 42 U.S.C. § 1983 does not require exhaustion of administrative remedies under any circumstances. This far-reaching conclusion was arrived at largely without the benefit of briefing and argument. See, e.g., *Wilwording v. Swenson*, 404 U.S. 249 (1971); *Houghton v. Shafer*, 392 U.S. 639 (1968); *Damico v. California*, 389 U.S. 416 (1967). I consider the posture of §§ 1981 and 1982 in the jurisprudence of this Court to be quite different from that of § 1983.

at 1089. The schools extended a public offer open, on its face, to any child
meeting certain minimum qualifications who chose to accept. They advertised in the "Yellow Pages" of the telephone directories and engaged extensively in general mail solicitations to attract students. The schools are operated
strictly on a commercial basis, and one fairly could construe their open-end
invitations as offers that matured into binding contracts when accepted by
those who met the academic, financial, and other racially neutral specified
conditions as to qualifications for entrance. There is no reason to assume
that the schools had any special reason for exercising an option of personal
choice among those who responded to their public offers. A small kindergarten or music class, operated on the basis of personal invitations extended
to a limited number of preidentified students, for example would present a
far different case.

I do not suggest that a "bright line" can be drawn that easily separates the
type of contract offer within the reach of § 1981 from the type without. The
case before us is clearly on one side of the line, however defined, and the
kindergarten and music school examples are clearly on the other side. Close
questions undoubtedly will arise in the gray area that necessarily exists in
between. But some of the applicable principles and considerations, for the
most part identified by the Court's opinion, are clear: § 1981, as interpreted
by our prior decisions, does reach certain acts of racial discrimination that
are "private" in the sense that they involve no *state* action. But choices,
including those involved in entering into a contract, that are "private" in the
sense that they are not part of a commercial relationship offered generally
or widely, and that reflect the selectivity exercised by an individual entering
into a personal relationship, certainly were never intended to be restricted
by the 19th century Civil Rights Acts. The open offer to the public generally
involved in the cases before us is simply not a "private" contract in this
sense. Accordingly, I join the opinion of the Court.

MR. JUSTICE STEVENS, concurring.

For me the problem in these cases is whether to follow a line of authority
which I firmly believe to have been incorrectly decided.

Jones v. Alfred H. Mayer Co., 392 U.S. 409, and its progeny have unequivocally held that § 1 of the Civil Rights Act of 1866 prohibits private racial
discrimination. There is no doubt in my mind that that construction of the
statute would have amazed the legislators who voted for it. Both its language
and the historical setting in which it was enacted convince me that Congress
intended only to guarantee all citizens the same legal capacity to make and
enforce contracts, to obtain, own, and convey property, and to litigate and
give evidence. Moreover, since the legislative history discloses an intent not
to outlaw segregated public schools at that time,[1] it is quite unrealistic to

---

[1]The sponsor of the bill in the House, Representative Wilson of Iowa, disclaimed
any effect of the bill upon segregated schools. Cong. Globe, 39th Cong., 1st Sess.,
1117, 1294 (1866). Opponents of the bill raised this point as an objection to a provision
in the bill that "there shall be no discrimination in civil rights or immunities among
the citizens of the United States in any State or Territory of the United States on
account of race, color, or previous condition of slavery...." *Id.*, at 1122 (remarks

assume that Congress intended the broader result of prohibiting segregated private schools. Were we writing on a clean slate, I would therefore vote to reverse.

But *Jones* has been decided and is now an important part of the fabric of our law. Although I recognize the force of MR. JUSTICE WHITE'S argument that the construction of § 1982 does not control § 1981, it would be most incongruous to give those two sections a fundamentally different construction. The net result of the enactment in 1866, the re-enactment in 1870, and the codification in 1874 produced, I believe, a statute resting on the constitutional foundations provided by both the Thirteenth and Fourteenth Amendments. An attempt to give a fundamentally different meaning to two similar provisions by ascribing one to the Thirteenth and the other to the Fourteenth Amendment cannot succeed. I am persuaded, therefore, that we must either apply the rationale of *Jones* or overrule that decision.

There are two reasons which favor overruling. First, as I have already stated, my conviction that *Jones* was wrongly decided is firm. Second, it is extremely unlikely that reliance upon *Jones* has been so extensive that this Court is foreclosed from overruling it. Cf. *Flood v. Kuhn* 407 U.S. 258, 273-274, 278-279, 283. There are, however, opposing arguments of greater force.

The first is the interest in stability and orderly development of the law. As Mr. Justice Cardozo remarked, with respect to the routine work of the judiciary: "The labor of judges would be increased almost to the breaking point if every past decision could be reopened in every case, and one could not lay one's own course of bricks on the secure foundation of the courses laid by others who had gone before him."[2] Turning to the exceptional case, Mr. Justice Cardozo noted: "[W]hen a rule, after it has been duly tested by experience, has been found to be inconsistent with the sense of justice or with the social welfare, there should be less hesitation in frank avowal and full abandonment.... If judges have woefully misinterpreted the *mores* of their day, or if the *mores* of their day are no longer those of ours, they ought not to tie, in helpless submission, the hands of their successors."[3] In this case, those admonitions favor adherence to, rather than departure from, precedent. For even if *Jones* did not accurately reflect the sentiments of the Reconstruction Congress, it surely accords with the prevailing sense of justice today.

The policy of the Nation as formulated by the Congress in recent years has moved constantly in the direction of eliminating racial segregation in all sectors of society.[4] This Court has given a sympathetic and liberal construction to such legislation.[5] For the Court now to overrule *Jones* would be a

---

of Rep. Rogers); *id.*, at 1268 (remarks of Rep. Kerr); *id.*, at 1271-1272 (remarks of Rep. Bingham); see *id.*, at 500 (remarks of Sen. Cowan). The provision was deleted in part for this reason. See *id.*, at 1366 (remarks of Rep. Wilson). In that form the bill was enacted into law.

[2]B. Cardozo, The Nature of the Judicial Process 149 (1921).

[3]*Id.*, at 150-152.

[4]See, *e.g.*, the Civil Rights Act of 1964, 78 Stat. 241, as added and as amended, 28 U.S.C. § 1447 (d), 42 U.S.C. §§ 1971, 1975a-1975d, 2000a-2000h-6 (1970 ed. and Supp. IV); the Voting Rights Act of 1965, 79 Stat. 437, as added and as amended, 42 U.S.C. §§ 1973-1973bb-4; the Civil Rights Act of 1968, Titles VIII, IX, 82 Stat. 81, 89, as amended, 42 U.S.C. §§ 3601-3631 (1970 ed. and Supp. IV).

[5]See, *e.g.*, *Trafficante v. Metropolitan Life Ins. Co.*, 409 U.S. 205; *Griggs v. Duke*

significant step backwards, with effects that would not have arisen from a correct decision in the first instance. Such a step would be so clearly contrary to my understanding of the mores of today that I think the Court is entirely correct in adhering to *Jones*.

With this explanation, I join the opinion of the Court.

MR. JUSTICE WHITE, with whom MR. JUSTICE REHNQUIST joins, dissenting.

We are urged here to extend the meaning and reach of 42 U.S.C. § 1981 so as to establish a general prohibition against a private individual's or institution's refusing to enter into a contract with another person because of that person's race. Section 1981 has been on the books since 1870 and to so hold for the first time[1] would be contrary to the language of the section, to its legislative history, and to the clear dictum of this Court in the *Civil Rights Cases*, 109 U.S. 3, 16-17 (1883), almost contemporaneously with the passage of the statute, that the section reaches only discriminations imposed by state law. The majority's belated discovery of a congressional purpose which escaped this Court only a decade after the statute was passed and which escaped all other federal courts for almost 100 years is singularly unpersuasive.[2] I therefore respectfully dissent.

* * *

Title 42 U.S.C. § 1981, captioned "Equal rights under the law,"[3] provides in pertinent part:

Power Co., 401 U.S. 424; *Daniel v. Paul*, 395 U.S. 298; *Allen v. State Board of Elections*, 393 U.S. 544.

[1] The majority and two concurring Justices assert that this Court has already considered the issue in this litigation and resolved it in favor of a right of action for private racially motivated refusals to contract. They are wrong. As is set forth more fully below, the only time the issue has been previously addressed by this Court it was addressed in a case in which the Court had issued a limited grant of certiorari, not including the issue involved here; in which the issue involved here was irrelevant to the decision; and in which the parties had not briefed the issue and the Court had not canvassed the relevant legislative history.

[2] I do not question at this point the power of Congress or a state legislature to ban racial discrimination in private school admissions decisions. But as I see it Congress has not yet chosen to exercise that power.

[3] Title 42 U.S.C. § 1981 provides in full:

"§ 1981. *Equal rights under the law*.

"All persons within the jurisdiction of the United State shall have the same right in every State and Territory to make and enforce contracts, to sue, be parties, give evidence, and to the full and equal benefit of all laws and proceedings for the security of persons and property as is enjoyed by white citizens, and shall be subject to like punishment, pains, penalties, taxes, licenses, and exactions of every kind, and to no other."

The title to § 1981 was placed there originally by the Revisers who compiled the Revised Statutes of 1874. They did so under a statute defining their responsibilities in part, as follows: to "arrange the [statutes] under titles, chapters, and sections, or other suitable divisions and subdivisions with *head-notes briefly expressive of the*

"All persons within the jurisdiction of the United States shall have the same right in every State and Territory to make and enforce contracts, to sue, be parties, give evidence, and to the full and equal benefit of all laws and proceedings for the security of persons and property as is enjoyed by white citizens...."

On its face the statute gives "[a]ll persons" (plainly including Negroes) the "*same right*...*to make*...*contracts*...*as is enjoyed by white citizens*." (Emphasis added.) The words "right...enjoyed by white citizens" clearly refer to rights existing apart from this statute. Whites had at the time when § 1981 was first enacted, and have (with a few exceptions mentioned below), no right to make a contract with an unwilling private person, no matter what that person's motivation for refusing to contract. Indeed it is and always has been central to the very concept of a "contract" that there be "assent by the parties who form the contract to the terms thereof," Restatement of Contracts § 19 (b) (1932); see also 1 S. Williston, Law of Contracts § 18 (3) (3d ed., 1957). The right to make contracts, enjoyed by white citizens, was therefore always a right to enter into binding agreements only with willing second parties. Since the statute only gives Negroes the "same rights" to contract as is enjoyed by whites, the language of the statute confers no right on Negroes to enter into a contract with an unwilling person no matter what that person's motivation for refusing to contract. What is conferred by 42 U.S.C. § 1981 is the *right*—which was enjoyed by whites—"to make contracts" with other willing parties and to "enforce" those contracts in court. Section 1981 would thus invalidate any state statute or court-made rule of law which would have the effect of disabling Negroes or any other class of persons from making contracts or enforcing contractual obligations or otherwise giving less weight to their obligations than is given to contractual obligations running to whites.[4] The statute by its terms does not require any private individual or institution to enter into a contract or perform any other act under any circumstances; and it consequently fails to supply a cause of action by respondent students against petitioner schools based on the latter's racially motivated decision not to contract with them.[5]

[The remaining portion of Justice White's dissent is omitted.]

---

matter contained in such divisions." 14 Stat. 75. (Emphasis added.) The headnote to what is now § 1981 was before Congress when it enacted the Revised Statutes into positive law. It may properly be considered as an aid to construction, if the statutory language is deemed unclear. *E.g., Patterson v. Bark Eudora,* 190 U.S. 169, 172 (1903); *FTC v. Mandel Bros.,* 359 U.S. 385, 389 (1959); *Knowlton v. Moore,* 178 U.S. 41, 65 (1900); *Maguire v. Commissioner,* 313 U.S. 1, 9 (1941).

[4]The statute also removes any state-law-created legal disabilities enacted by the Southern States—see E. McPherson, The Political History of the United States of America During the Period of Reconstruction 29, 33, 35 (1871)—preventing Negroes or any other class of persons from suing, being parties, and giving evidence; and provides that all persons shall have full and equal benefit of all laws.

[5]One of the major issues in this case plainly is whether the construction in *Jones v. Alfred H. Mayer Co.,* 392 U.S. 409 (1968), placed on similar language contained in 42 U.S.C. § 1982 granting all citizens the "same rights to...purchase...real...property" as is enjoyed by white citizens prevents this Court from independently construing the language in 42 U.S.C. § 1981. * * * *Jones v. Alfred H. Mayer Co.* does not so constrict

this Court. First, the legislative history of § 1981 is very different from the legislative history of § 1982 so heavily relied on by the Court in *Jones v. Alfred H. Mayer Co.* Second, notwithstanding the dictum in *Jones v. Alfred H. Mayer Co.*, quoted by the majority, *ante*, at 170, even the majority does not contend that the grant of the other rights enumerated in § 1981, *i.e.*, the rights "to sue, be parties, give evidence," and *"enforce* contracts" accomplishes anything other than the removal of *legal* disabilities to sue, be a party, testify or enforce a contract. Indeed it is impossible to give such language any other meaning. Thus, even accepting the *Jones v. Alfred H. Mayer Co.* dictum as applicable to § 1981, the question still would remain whether the right to "make contracts" is to be construed in the same vein as the other "right[s]" included in § 1981 or rather in the same vein as the right to "purchase...real property" under § 1982 involved in *Jones v. Alfred H. Mayer Co., supra.*

Bob Jones University v. United States†

United States Supreme Court, 461 U.S. 574, 103 S.Ct. 2017 (1983).

Syllabus*

Section 501(c)(3) of the Internal Revenue Code of 1954 (IRC) provides that
"[c]orporations...organized and operated exclusively for religious, charitable...or educational purposes" are entitled to tax exemption. Until 1970, the
Internal Revenue Service (IRS) granted tax-exempt status under § 501(c)(3) to
private schools, independent of racial admissions policies, and granted charitable deductions for contributions to such schools under § 170 of the IRC. But
in 1970, the IRS concluded that it could no longer justify allowing tax-exempt
status under § 501(c)(3) to private schools that practiced racial discrimination,
and in 1971 issued Revenue Ruling 71-447 providing that a private school not
having a racially nondiscriminatory policy as to students is not "charitable"
within the common-law concepts reflected in §§ 170 and 501(c)(3). In No. 81-3,
petitioner Bob Jones University, while permitting unmarried Negroes to enroll
as students, denies admission to applicants engaged in an interracial marriage
or known to advocate interracial marriage or dating. Because of this admissions
policy, the IRS revoked the University's tax-exempt status. After paying a
portion of the federal unemployment taxes for a certain taxable year, the University filed a refund action in Federal District Court, and the Government
counterclaimed for unpaid taxes for that and other taxable years. Holding that
the IRS exceeded its powers in revoking the University's tax-exempt status and
violated the University's rights under the Religion Clauses of the First Amendment, the District Court ordered the IRS to refund the taxes paid and rejected
the counterclaim. The Court of Appeals reversed. In No. 81-1, petitioner Goldsboro Christian Schools maintains a racially discriminatory admissions policy
based upon its interpretation of the Bible, accepting for the most part only
Caucasian students. The IRS determined that Goldsboro was not an organization described in § 501(c)(3) and hence was required to pay federal social
security and unemployment taxes. After paying a portion of such taxes for
certain years, Goldsboro filed a refund suit in Federal District Court, and the
IRS counterclaimed for unpaid taxes. The District Court entered summary
judgment for the IRS, rejecting Goldsboro's claim to tax-exempt status under
§ 501(c)(3) and also its claim that the denial of such status violated the Religion
Clauses of the First Amendment. The Court of Appeals affirmed.

Held: Neither petitioner qualifies as a tax-exempt organization under § 501(c)(3).
Pp. 238-250.

   (a) An examination of the IRC's framework and the background of congressional purposes reveals unmistakable evidence that underlying all relevant parts
of the IRC is the intent that entitlement to tax exemption depends on meeting
certain common-law standards of charity—namely, that an institution seeking
tax-exempt status must serve a public purpose and not be contrary to established
public policy. Thus, to warrant exemption under § 501(c)(3), an institution must
fall within a category specified in that section and must demonstrably serve and
be in harmony with the public interest, and the institution's purpose must not
be so at odds with the common community conscience as to undermine any
public benefit that might otherwise be conferred. Pp. 238-243.

---

†Together with No. 81-1, *Goldsboro Christian Schools, Inc. v. United States*, also
on certiorari to the same court.

*The syllabus constitutes no part of the opinion of the Court but has been prepared
by the Reporter of Decisions for the convenience of the reader.

(b) The IRS's 1970 interpretation of § 501(c)(3) was correct. It would be wholly incompatible with the concepts underlying tax exemption to grant tax-exempt status to racially discriminatory private educational entities. Whatever may be the rationale for such private schools' policies, racial discrimination in education is contrary to public policy. Racially discriminatory educational institutions cannot be viewed as conferring a public benefit within the above "charitable" concept or within the congressional intent underlying § 501(c)(3). Pp. 243-245.

(c) The IRS did not exceed its authority when it announced its interpretation of § 501(c)(3) in 1970 and 1971. Such interpretation is wholly consistent with what Congress, the Executive, and the courts had previously declared. And the actions of Congress since 1970 leave no doubt that the IRS reached the correct conclusion in exercising its authority. Pp. 245-248.

(d) The Government's fundamental, overriding interest in eradicating racial discrimination in education substantially outweighs whatever burden denial of tax benefits places on petitioners' exercise of their religious beliefs. Petitioners' asserted interests cannot be accommodated with the compelling governmental interest, and no less restrictive means are available to achieve the governmental interest. Pp. 248-250.

(e) The IRS properly applied its policy to both petitioners. Goldsboro admits that it maintains racially discriminatory policies, and, contrary to Bob Jones University's contention that it is not racially discriminatory, discrimination on the basis of racial affiliation and association is a form of racial discrimination. P. 250.

No. 81-1, 644 F.2d 879, and No. 81-3, 639 F.2d 147, affirmed.

BURGER, C.J. delivered the opinion of the Court, in which BRENNAN, WHITE, MARSHALL, BLACKMUN, STEVENS, AND O'CONNOR, JJ., joined, and in Part III of which POWELL, J., joined. POWELL, J., filed an opinion concurring in part and concurring in the judgment, *post*, p. 250. REHNQUIST, J., filed a dissenting opinion, *post*, p. 251.

CHIEF JUSTICE BURGER delivered the opinion of the Court.

We granted certiorari to decide whether petitioners, nonprofit private schools that prescribe and enforce racially discriminatory admissions standards on the basis of religious doctrine, qualify as tax-exempt organizations under § 501(c)(3) of the Internal Revenue Code of 1954.

I

A

Until 1970, the Internal Revenue Service granted tax-exempt status to private schools, without regard to their racial admissions policies, under §

501(c)(3) of the Internal Revenue Code, 26 U.S.C. § 501(c)(3),[1] and granted charitable deductions for contributions to such schools under § 170 of the Code, 26 U.S.C. § 170.[2]

On January 12, 1970, a three-judge District Court for the District of Columbia issued a preliminary injunction prohibiting the IRS from according tax-exempt status to private schools in Mississippi that discriminated as to admissions on the basis of race. *Green v. Kennedy*, 309 F.Supp. 1127, appeal dism'd *sub nom. Cannon v. Green*, 398 U.S. 956 (1970). Thereafter, in July 1970, the IRS concluded that it could "no longer legally justify allowing tax-exempt status [under § 501(c)(3)] to private schools which practice racial discrimination." IRS News Release, July 7, 1970, reprinted in App. in No. 81-3, p. A235. At the same time, the IRS announced that it could not "treat gifts to such schools as charitable deductions for income tax purposes [under § 170]." *Ibid.* By letter dated November 30, 1970, the IRS formally notified private schools, including those involved in this litigation, of this change in policy, "applicable to all private schools in the United States at all levels of education." See *id.*, at A232.

On June 30, 1971, the three-judge District Court issued its opinion on the merits of the Mississippi challenge. *Green v. Connally*, 330 F.Supp. 1150, summarily aff'd *sub nom. Coit v. Green*, 404 U.S. 997 (1971). That court approved the IRS's amended construction of the Tax Code. The court also held that racially discriminatory private schools were not entitled to exemption under § 501(c)(3) and that donors were not entitled to deductions for contributions to such schools under § 170. The court permanently enjoined the Commissioner of Internal Revenue from approving tax-exempt status for any school in Mississippi that did not publicly maintain a policy of nondiscrimination.

The revised policy on discrimination was formalized in Revenue Ruling 71-447, 1971-2 Cum. Bull. 230:

> "Both the courts and the Internal Revenue Service have long recognized that the statutory requirement of being 'organized and operated exclusively for religious, charitable,...or educational purposes' was intended to express the basic common law concept [of 'charity'].... All charitable

---

[1]Section 501(c)(3) lists the following organizations, which, pursuant to § 501(a), are exempt from taxation unless denied tax exemptions under other specified sections of the Code:

"Corporations, and any community chest, fund, or foundation, *organized and operated exclusively for religious, charitable*, scientific, testing for public safety, literary, *or educational purposes*, or to foster national or international amateur sports competition (but only if no part of its activities involve the provision of athletic facilities or equipment), or for the prevention of cruelty to children or animals, no part of the net earnings of which inures to the benefit of any private shareholder or individual, no substantial part of the activities of which is carrying on propaganda, or otherwise attempting, to influence legislation..., and which does not participate in, or intervene in (including the publishing or distributing of statements), any political campaign on behalf of any candidate for public office." (Emphasis added.)

[2]Section 170(a) allows deductions for certain "charitable contributions." Section 170(c)(2)(B) includes within the definition of "charitable contribution" a contribution or gift to or for the use of a corporation "organized and operated exclusively for religious, charitable, scientific, literary, or educational purposes...."

trusts, educational or otherwise, are subject to the requirement that the purpose of the trust may not be illegal or contrary to public policy."

Based on the "national policy to discourage racial discrimination in education," the IRS ruled that "a [private] school not having a racially nondiscriminatory policy as to students is not 'charitable' within the common law concepts reflected in sections 170 and 501(c)(3) of the Code." *Id.*, at 231.[3]

The application of the IRS construction of these provisions to petitioners, two private schools with racially discriminatory admissions policies, is now before us.

B

No. 81-3, Bob Jones University v. United States

Bob Jones University is a nonprofit corporation located in Greenville, S.C.[4] Its purpose is "to conduct an institution of learning..., giving special emphasis to the Christian religion and the ethics revealed in the Holy Scriptures." Certificate of Incorporation, Bob Jones University, Inc., of Greenville, S.C., reprinted in App. in No. 81-3, p. A119. The corporation operates a school with an enrollment of approximately 5,000 students, from kindergarten through college and graduate school. Bob Jones University is not affiliated with any religious denomination, but is dedicated to the teaching and propagation of its fundamentalist Christian religious beliefs. It is both a religious and educational institution. Its teachers are required to be devout Christians, and all courses at the University are taught according to the Bible. Entering students are screened as to their religious beliefs, and their public and private conduct is strictly regulated by standards promulgated by University authorities.

The sponsors of the University genuinely believe that the Bible forbids interracial dating and marriage. To effectuate these views, Negroes were completely excluded until 1971. From 1971 to May 1975, the University accepted no applications from unmarried Negroes,[5] but did accept applications from Negroes married within their race.

Following the decision of the United States Court of Appeals for the Fourth Circuit in *McCrary v. Runyon*, 515 F.2d 1082 (1975), aff'd. 427 U.S. 160 (1976), prohibiting racial exclusion from private schools, the University revised its policy. Since May 29, 1975, the University has permitted unmarried Negroes to enroll; but a disciplinary rule prohibits interracial dating and marriage. That rule reads:

---

[3]Revenue Ruling 71-447, 1971-2 Cum. Bull. 230, defined "racially nondiscriminatory policy as to students" as meaning that "the school admits the students of any race to all the rights, privileges, programs, and activities generally accorded or made available to students at that school and that the school does not discriminate on the basis of race in administration of its educational policies, admissions policies, scholarship and loan programs, and athletic and other school-administered programs."

[4]Bob Jones University was founded in Florida in 1927. It moved to Greenville, S.C., in 1940, and has been incorporated as an eleemosynary institution in South Carolina since 1952.

[5]Beginning in 1973, Bob Jones University instituted an exception to this rule, allowing applications from unmarried Negroes who had been members of the University staff for four years or more.

"There is to be no interracial dating.

"1. Students who are partners in an interracial marriage will be expelled.

"2. Students who are members of or affiliated with any group or organization which holds as one of its goals or advocates interracial marriage will be expelled.

"3. Students who date outside of their own race will be expelled.

"4. Students who espouse, promote, or encourage others to violate the University's dating rules and regulations will be expelled." App. in No. 81-3, p. A197.

The University continues to deny admission to applicants engaged in an interracial marriage or known to advocate interracial marriage or dating. *Id.*, at A277.

Until 1970, the IRS extended tax-exempt status to Bob Jones University under § 501(c)(3). By the letter of November 30, 1970, that followed the injunction issued in *Green v. Kennedy*, 309 F.Supp. 1127 (DC 1970), the IRS formally notified the University of the change in IRS policy, and announced its intention to challenge the tax-exempt status of private schools practicing racial discrimination in their admissions policies.

After failing to obtain an assurance of tax exemption through administrative means, the University instituted an action in 1971 seeking to enjoin the IRS from revoking the school's tax-exempt status. That suit culminated in *Bob Jones University v. Simon*, 416 U.S. 725 (1974), in which this Court held that the Anti-Injunction Act of the Internal Revenue Code, 26 U.S.C. § 7421(a), prohibited the University from obtaining judicial review by way of injunctive action before the assessment or collection of any tax.

Thereafter, on April 16, 1975, the IRS notified the University of the proposed revocation of its tax-exempt status. On January 19, 1976, the IRS officially revoked the University's tax-exempt status, effective as of December 1, 1970, the day after the University was formally notified of the change in IRS policy. The University subsequently filed returns under the Federal Unemployment Tax Act for the period from December 1, 1970, to December 31, 1975, and paid a tax totalling $21 on one employee for the calendar year of 1975. After its request for a refund was denied, the University instituted the present action, seeking to recover the $21 it had paid to the IRS. The Government counterclaimed for unpaid federal unemployment taxes for the taxable years 1971 through 1975, in the amount of $489,675.59, plus interest.

The United States District Court for the District of South Carolina held that revocation of the University's tax-exempt status exceeded the delegated powers of the IRS, was improper under the IRS rulings and procedures, and violated the University's rights under the Religion Clauses of the First Amendment. 468 F.Supp. 890, 907 (1978). The court accordingly ordered the IRS to pay the University the $21 refund it claimed and rejected the IRS's counterclaim.

The Court of Appeals for the Fourth Circuit, in a divided opinion, reversed. 639 F.2d 147 (1980). Citing *Green v. Connally*, 330 F.Supp. 1150 (DC 1971), with approval, the Court of Appeals concluded that § 501(c)(3) must be read against the background of charitable trust law. To be eligible for any exemption under that section, an institution must be "charitable" in the common-law sense, and therefore must not be contrary to public policy.

In the court's view, Bob Jones University did not meet this requirement, since its "racial policies violated the clearly defined public policy, rooted in our Constitution, condemning racial discrimination and, more specifically, the government policy against subsidizing racial discrimination in education, public or private." 639 F.2d, at 151. The court held that the IRS acted within its statutory authority in revoking the University's tax-exempt status. Finally, the Court of Appeals rejected petitioner's arguments that the revocation of the tax exemption violated the Free Exercise and Establishment Clauses of the First Amendment. The case was remanded to the District Court with instructions to dismiss the University's claim for a refund and to reinstate the IRS's counterclaim.

C

No. 81-1, Goldsboro Christian Schools, Inc. v. United States

Goldsboro Christian Schools is a nonprofit corporation located in Goldsboro, N.C. Like Bob Jones University, it was established "to conduct an institution or institutions of learning..., giving special emphasis to the Christian religion and the ethics revealed in the Holy scriptures." Articles of Incorporation ¶ 3(a); see Complaint ¶ 6, reprinted in App. in No. 81-1, pp. 5-6. The school offers classes from kindergarten through high school, and since at least 1969 has satisfied the State of North Carolina's requirements for secular education in private schools. The school requires its high school students to take Bible-related courses, and begins each class with prayer.

Since its incorporation in 1963, Goldsboro Christian Schools has maintained a racially discriminatory admissions policy based upon its interpretation of the Bible.[6] Goldsboro has for the most part accepted only Caucasians. On occasion, however, the school has accepted children from racially mixed marriages in which one of the parents is Caucasian.

Goldsboro never received a determination by the IRS that it was an organization entitled to tax exemption under § 501(c)(3). Upon audit of Goldsboro's records for the years 1969 through 1972, the IRS determined that Goldsboro was not an organization described in § 501(c)(3), and therefore was required to pay taxes under the Federal Insurance Contribution Act and the Federal Unemployment Tax Act.

Goldsboro paid the IRS $3,459.93 in withholding, social security, and unemployment taxes with respect to one employee for the years 1969 through 1972. Thereafter, Goldsboro filed a suit seeking refund of that payment, claiming that the school had been improperly denied § 501(c)(3) exempt status.[7] The IRS counterclaimed for $160,073.96 in unpaid social security

---

[6]According to the interpretation espoused by Goldsboro, race is determined by descendance from one of Noah's three sons—Ham, Shem, and Japheth. Based on this interpretation, Orientals and Negroes are Hamitic, Hebrews are Shemitic, and Caucasians are Japhethic. Cultural or biological mixing of the races is regarded as a violation of God's command. App. in No. 81-1, pp. 40-41.

[7]Goldsboro also asserted that it was not obliged to pay taxes on lodging furnished to its teachers. It does not ask this court to review the rejection of that claim.

and unemployment taxes for the years 1969 through 1972, including interest and penalties.[8]

The District Court for the Eastern District of North Carolina decided the action on cross-motions for summary judgment. 436 F.Supp. 1314 (1977). In addressing the motions for summary judgment, the court assumed that Goldsboro's racially discriminatory admissions policy was based upon a sincerely held religious belief. The court nevertheless rejected Goldsboro's claim to tax-exempt status under § 501(c)(3), finding that "private schools maintaining racially discriminatory admissions policies violate clearly declared federal policy and, therefore, must be denied the federal tax benefits flowing from qualification under Section 501(c)(3)." *Id.*, at 1318. The court also rejected Goldsboro's arguments that denial of tax-exempt status violated the Free Exercise and Establishment Clauses of the First Amendment. Accordingly, the court entered summary judgment for the IRS on its counterclaim.

The Court of Appeals for the Fourth Circuit affirmed, 644 F.2d 879 (1981) (*per curiam*). That court found an "identity for present purposes" between the *Goldsboro* case and the *Bob Jones University* case, which had been decided shortly before by another panel of that court, and affirmed for the reasons set forth in *Bob Jones University*.

We granted certiorari in both cases, 454 U.S. 892 (1981),[9] and we affirm in each.

II

A

In Revenue Ruling 71-447, the IRS formalized the policy, first announced in 1970, that § 170 and § 501(c)(3) embrace the common-law "charity" concept. Under that view, to qualify for a tax exemption pursuant to § 501(c)(3), an institution must show, first, that it falls within one of the eight categories expressly set forth in that section, and second, that its activity is not contrary to settled public policy.

Section 501(c)(3) provides that "[c]orporations ... organized and operated exclusively for religious, charitable ... or educational purposes" are entitled to tax exemption. Petitioners argue that the plain language of the statute

---

[8]By stipulation, the IRS agreed to abate its assessment for 1969 and most of 1970 to reflect the fact that the IRS did not begin enforcing its policy of denying tax-exempt status to racially discriminatory private schools until November 30, 1970. As a result, the amount of the counterclaim was reduced to $116,190.99. *Id.*, at 104, 110.

[9]After the Court granted certiorari, the Government filed a motion to dismiss, informing the Court that the Department of Treasury intended to revoke Revenue Ruling 71-447 and other pertinent rulings and to recognize § 501(c)(3) exemptions for petitioners. The Government suggested that these actions were therefore moot. Before this Court ruled on that motion, however, the United States Court of Appeals for the District of Columbia Circuit enjoined the Government from granting § 501(c)(3) tax-exempt status to any school that discriminates on the basis of race. *Wright v. Regan*, No. 80-1124 (Feb. 18, 1982) (*per curiam* order). Thereafter, the Government informed the Court that it would not revoke the Revenue Rulings and withdrew its request that the actions be dismissed as moot. The Government continues to assert that the IRS lacked authority to promulgate Revenue Ruling 71-447, and does not defend that aspect of the rulings below.

guarantees them tax-exempt status. They emphasize the absence of any language in the statute expressly requiring all exempt organizations to be "charitable" in the common-law sense, and they contend that the disjunctive "or" separating the categories in § 501(c)(3) precludes such a reading. Instead, they argue that if an institution falls within one or more of the specified categories it is automatically entitled to exemption, without regard to whether it also qualifies as "charitable." The Court of Appeals rejected that contention and concluded that petitioners' interpretation of the statute "tears section 501(c)(3) from its roots." 639 F.2d, at 151.

It is a well-established canon of statutory construction that a court should go beyond the literal language of a statute if reliance on that language would defeat the plain purpose of the statute:

> "The general words used in the clause..., taken by themselves, and literally construed, without regard to the object in view, would seem to sanction the claim of the plaintiff. But this mode of expounding a statute has never been adopted by an enlightened tribunal—because it is evident that in many cases it would defeat the object which the Legislature intended to accomplish. And it is well settled that, in interpreting a statute, the court will not look merely to a particular clause in which general words may be used, *but will take in connection with it the whole statute... and the objects and policy of the law....*" *Brown v. Duchesne,* 19 How. 183, 194 (1857) (emphasis added).

Section 501(c)(3) therefore must be analyzed and construed within the framework of the Internal Revenue Code and against the background of the congressional purposes. Such an examination reveals unmistakable evidence that, underlying all relevant parts of the Code, is the intent that entitlement to tax exemption depends on meeting certain common-law standards of charity—namely, that an institution seeking tax-exempt status must serve a public purpose and not be contrary to established public policy.

This "charitable" concept appears explicitly in § 170 of the Code. That section contains a list of organizations virtually identical to that contained in § 501(c)(3). It is apparent that Congress intended that list to have the same meaning in both sections.[10] In § 170, Congress used the list of organizations in defining the term "charitable contributions." On its face, therefore, § 170 reveals that Congress' intention was to provide tax benefits to organizations serving charitable purposes.[11] The form of § 170 simply makes plain what

---

[10][Omitted.]

[11]The dissent suggests that the Court "quite adeptly avoids the statute it is construing," *post,* 612, and "seeks refuge...by turning to § 170," *post,* at 613. This assertion dissolves when one sees that § 501(c)(3) and § 170 are construed together, as they must be. The dissent acknowledges that the two sections are "mirror" provisions; surely there can be no doubt that the Court properly looks to § 170 to determine the meaning of § 501(c)(3). It is also suggested that § 170 is "at best of little usefulness in finding the meaning of § 501(c)(3)," since "§ 170(c) simply tracks the requirements set forth in § 501(c)(3)," *post,* at 614. That reading loses sight of the fact that § 170(c) defines the term "charitable contribution." The plain language of § 170 reveals that Congress' objective was to employ tax exemptions and deductions to promote certain *charitable* purposes. While the eight categories of institutions specified in the statute are indeed presumptively charitable in nature, the IRS prop-

common sense and history tell us: in enacting both § 170 and § 501(c)(3), Congress sought to provide tax benefits to charitable organizations, to encourage the development of private institutions that serve a useful public purpose or supplement or take the place of public institutions of the same kind.

Tax exemptions for certain institutions thought beneficial to the social order of the country as a whole, or to a particular community, are deeply rooted in our history, as in that of England. The origins of such exemptions lie in the special privileges that have long been extended to charitable trusts.[12]

More than a century ago, this Court announced the caveat that is critical in this case:

> "[I]t has now become an established principle of American law, that courts of chancery will sustain and protect...a gift ... to public charitable uses, *provided the same is consistent with local laws and public policy....*" *Perin v. Carey*, 24 How. 465, 501 (1861) (emphasis added).

Soon after that, in 1877, the Court commented:

> "A charitable use, *where neither law nor public policy forbids*, may be applied to almost any thing *that tends to promote the well-doing and well-being of social man.*" *Ould v. Washington Hospital for Foundlings*, 95 U.S. 303, 311 (emphasis added).

See also, *e.g.*, *Jackson v. Phillips*, 96 Mass. 539, 556 (1867). In 1891, in a restatement of the English law of charity[13] which has long been recognized as a leading authority in this country, Lord MacNaghten stated:

> " 'Charity' in its legal sense comprises four principal divisions: trusts for the relief of poverty; *trusts for the advancement of education*; trusts for the advancement of religion; and trusts for *other purposes beneficial to the community*, not falling under any of the preceding heads." *Commissioners v. Pemsel*, [1891] A.C. 531, 583 (emphasis added).

---

erly considered principles of charitable trust law in determining whether the institutions in question may truly be considered "charitable" for purposes of entitlement to the tax benefits conferred by § 170 and § 501(c)(3).

[12]The form and history of the charitable exemption and deduction sections of the various income tax Acts reveal that Congress was guided by the common law of charitable trusts. See Simon, The Tax-Exempt Status of Racially Discriminatory Religious Schools, 36 Tax L. Rev. 477, 485-489 (1981) (hereinafter Simon). Congress acknowledged as much in 1969. The House Report on the Tax Reform Act of 1969, Pub. L. 91-172, 83 Stat. 487, stated that the § 501(c)(3) exemption was available only to institutions that served "the specified charitable purposes," H.R. Rep. No. 91-413, pt. 1, p. 35 (1969), and described "charitable" as "a term that has been used in the law of trusts for hundreds of years." *Id.*, at 43. We need not consider whether Congress intended to incorporate into the Internal Revenue Code any aspects of charitable trust law other than the requirements of public benefit and a valid public purpose.

[13]The draftsmen of the 1894 income tax law, which included the first charitable exemption provision, relied heavily on English concepts of taxation; and the list of exempt organizations appears to have been patterned upon English income tax statutes. See 26 Cong. Rec. 584-588, 6612-6615 (1894).

See, *e.g.*, 4 A. Scott, Law of Trusts § 368, pp. 2853-2854 (3d ed. 1967) (hereinafter Scott). These statements clearly reveal the legal background against which Congress enacted the first charitable exemption statute in 1894:[14] charities were to be given preferential treatment because they provide a benefit to society.

What little floor debate occurred on the charitable exemption provision of the 1894 Act and similar sections of later statutes leaves no doubt that Congress deemed the specified organizations entitled to tax benefits because they served desirable public purposes. See, *e.g.*, 26 Cong. Rec. 585-586 (1894); *id.*, at 1727. In floor debate on a similar provision in 1917, for example, Senator Hollis articulated the rationale:

> "For every dollar that a man contributes for these public charities, educational, scientific, or otherwise, the public gets 100 percent." 55 Cong. Rec. 6728.

See also, *e.g.*, 44 Cong. Rec. 4150 (1909); 50 Cong. Rec. 1305-1306 (1913). In 1924, this Court restated the common understanding of the charitable exemption provision:

> "Evidently the exemption is made in recognition of the benefit which the public derives from corporate activities of the class named, and is intended to aid them when not conducted for private gain." *Trinidad v. Sagrada Orden*, 263 U.S. 578, 581.[15]

In enacting the Revenue Act of 1938, ch. 289, 52 Stat. 447, Congress expressly reconfirmed this view with respect to the charitable deduction provision:

> "The exemption from taxation of money or property devoted to charitable and other purposes is based upon the theory that the Government is compensated for the loss of revenue by its relief from financial burdens which would otherwise have to be met by appropriations from other

---

[14]Act of Aug. 27, 1894, ch. 349 § 32, 28 Stat. 556-557. The income tax system contained in the 1894 Act was declared unconstitutional. *Pollock v. Farmers' Loan & Trust Co.*, 158 U.S. 601 (1895), for reasons unrelated to the charitable exemption provision. The terms of that exemption were in substance included in the corporate income tax contained in the Payne Aldrich Tariff Act of 1909, ch. 6, § 38, 36 Stat. 112. A similar exemption has been included in every income tax Act since the adoption of the Sixteenth Amendment, beginning with the Revenue Act of 1913, ch. 16, § II(G), 38 Stat. 172. See generally Reiling, Federal Taxation: What Is a Charitable Organization?, 44 A.B.A.J. 525 (1958); Liles & Blum.

[15]That same year, the Bureau of Internal Revenue expressed a similar view of the charitable deduction section of the estate tax contained in the Revenue Act of 1918, ch. 18, § 403(a)(3), 40 Stat. 1098. The Solicitor of Internal Revenue looked to the common law of charitable trusts in construing that provision, and noted that "generally bequests for the benefit and advantage of the general public are valid as charities." Sol.Op. 159, III-1 Cum. Bull. 480, 482 (1924).

public funds, and by the benefits resulting from the promotion of the general welfare." H.R. Rep. No. 1860, 75th Cong., 3d Sess., 19 (1938).[16]

A corollary to the public benefit principle is the requirement, long recognized in the law of trusts, that the purpose of a charitable trust may not be illegal or violate established public policy. In 1861, this Court stated that a public charitable use must be "consistent with local laws and public policy," *Perin v. Carey*, 24 How., at 501. Modern commentators and courts have echoed that view. See, *e.g.*, Restatement (Second) of Trusts § 377, Comment *c* (1959); 4 Scott § 377, and cases cited therein; Bogert § 378, at 191-192.[17]

When the Government grants exemptions or allows deductions all taxpayers are affected; the very fact of the exemption or deduction for the donor means that other taxpayers can be said to be indirect and vicarious "donors." Charitable exemptions are justified on the basis that the exempt entity confers a public benefit—a benefit which the society or the community may not itself choose or be able to provide, or which supplements and advances the work of public institutions already supported by tax revenues.[18] History buttresses logic to make clear that, to warrant exemption under § 501(c)(3), an

---

[16]The common-law requirement of public benefit is universally recognized by commentators on the law of trusts. For example, the Bogerts state:

"In return for the favorable treatment accorded charitable gifts which imply some disadvantage to the community, the courts must find in the trust which is to be deemed 'charitable' some real advantages to the public which more than offset the disadvantages arising out of special privileges accorded charitable trusts." G. Bogert & G. Bogert, Law of Trusts and Trustees § 361, p. 3 (rev. 2d ed. 1977) (hereinafter Bogert).

For other statements of this principle, see, *e.g.*, 4 Scott § 348, at 2770; Restatement (Second) of Trusts § 368, Comment *b* (1959); E. Fisch, D. Freed, & E. Schachter, Charities and Charitable Foundations § 256 (1974).

[17]Cf. *Tank Truck Rentals, Inc. v. Commissioner*, 356 U.S. 30, 35 (1958), in which this Court referred to "the presumption against congressional intent to encourage violation of declared public policy" in upholding the Commissioner's disallowance of deductions claimed by a trucking company for fines it paid for violations of state maximum weight laws.

[18]The dissent acknowledges that "Congress intended ... to offer a tax benefit to organizations... providing a public benefit," *post*, at 614-615, but suggests that Congress itself fully defined what organizations provide a public benefit, through the list of eight categories of exempt organizations contained in § 170 and § 501(c)(3). Under that view, any nonprofit organization that falls within one of the specified categories is automatically entitled to the tax benefits, provided it does not engage in expressly prohibited lobbying or political activities. *Post*, at 617. The dissent thus would have us conclude, for example, that any nonprofit organization that does not engage in prohibited lobbying activities is entitled to tax exemption as an "educational" institution if it is organized for the " 'instruction or training of the individual for the purpose of improving or developing his capabilities,' " 26 CFR § 1.501(c)(3)-1(d)(3) (1982). See *post*, at 623. As Judge Leventhal noted in *Green v. Connally*, 330 F.Supp. 1150, 1160 (DC), summarily aff'd *sub nom. Coit v. Green*, 404 U.S. 997 (1971), Fagin's school for educating English boys in the art of picking pockets would be an "educational" institution under that definition. Similarly, a band of former military personnel might well set up a school for intensive training of subversives for guerrilla warfare and terrorism in other countries; in the abstract, that "school" would qualify as an "educational" institution. Surely Congress had no thought of affording such an unthinking, wooden meaning to § 170 and § 501(c)(3) as to provide tax benefits to "educational" organizations that do not serve a public, charitable purpose.

institution must fall within a category specified in that section and must demonstrably serve and be in harmony with the public interest.[19] The institution's purpose must not be so at odds with the common community conscience as to undermine any public benefit that might otherwise be conferred.

B

We are bound to approach these questions with full awareness that determinations of public benefit and public policy are sensitive matters with serious implications for the institutions affected; a declaration that a given institution is not "charitable" should be made only where there can be no doubt that the activity involved is contrary to a fundamental public policy. But there can no longer be any doubt that racial discrimination in education violates deeply and widely accepted views of elementary justice. Prior to 1954, public education in many places still was conducted under the pall of *Plessy v. Ferguson*, 163 U.S. 537 (1896); racial segregation in primary and secondary education prevailed in many parts of the country. See, *e.g.*, Segregation and the Fourteenth Amendment in the States (B. Reams & P. Wilson eds. 1975).[20] This Court's decision in *Brown v. Board of Education*, 347 U.S. 483 (1954), signalled an end to that era. Over the past quarter of a century, every pronouncement of this Court and myriad Acts of Congress and Executive Orders attest a firm national policy to prohibit racial segregation and discrimination in public education.

An unbroken line of cases following *Brown v. Board of Education* establishes beyond doubt this Court's view that racial discrimination in education violates a most fundamental national public policy, as well as rights of individuals.

> "The right of a student not to be segregated on racial grounds in schools... is indeed so fundamental and pervasive that it is embraced in the concept of due process of law." *Cooper v. Aaron*, 358 U.S. 1, 19 (1958).

In *Norwood v. Harrison*, 413 U.S. 455, 468-469 (1973), we dealt with a nonpublic institution:

---

[19]The Court's reading of § 501(c)(3) does not render meaningless Congress' action in specifying the eight categories of presumptively exempt organizations, as petitioners suggest. See Brief for Petitioner in No. 81-1, pp. 18-24. To be entitled to tax-exempt status under § 501(c)(3), an organization must first fall within one of the categories specified by Congress, and in addition must serve a valid charitable purpose.

[20]In 1894, when the first charitable exemption provision was enacted, racially segregated educational institutions would not have been regarded as against public policy. Yet contemporary standards must be considered in determining whether given activities provide a public benefit and are entitled to the charitable tax exemption. In *Walz v. Tax Comm'n*, 397 U.S. 664, 673 (1970), we observed:

"Qualification for tax exemption is not perpetual or immutable; some tax-exempt groups lose that status when their activities take them outside the classification and new entities can come into being and qualify for exemption."

Charitable trust law also makes clear that the definition of "charity" depends upon contemporary standards. See, *e.g.*, Restatement (Second) of Trusts § 374, Comment *a* (1959); Bogert § 369, at 65-67; 4 Scott § 368, at 2855-2856.

"[A] private school—even one that discriminates—fulfills an important educational function; *however, ... [that] legitimate educational function cannot be isolated from discriminatory practices... [D]iscriminatory treatment exerts a pervasive influence on the entire educational process.*" (Emphasis added.)

See also *Runyon v. McCrary*, 427 U.S. 160 (1976); *Griffin v. County School Board*, 377 U.S. 218 (1964).

Congress, in Titles IV and VI of the Civil Rights Act of 1964, Pub. L. 88-352, 78 Stat. 241, 42 U.S.C. §§ 2000c, 2000c-6, 2000d, clearly expressed its agreement that racial discrimination in education violates a fundamental public policy. Other sections of that Act, and numerous enactments since then, testify to the public policy against racial discrimination. See, *e.g.*, the Voting Rights Act of 1965, Pub. L. 89-110, 79 Stat. 437, 42 U.S.C. § 1973 *et seq.* (1976 ed. and Supp. V); Title VIII of the Civil Rights Act of 1968, Pub. L. 90-284, 82 Stat. 81, 42 U.S.C. § 3601 *et seq.* (1976 ed. and Supp. V); the Emergency School Aid Act of 1972, Pub. L. 92-318, 86 Stat. 354 (repealed effective Sept. 30, 1979; replaced by similar provisions in the Emergency School Aid Act of 1978, Pub. L. 95-561, 92 Stat. 2252, 20 U.S.C. §§ 3191-3207 (1976 ed., Supp. V)).

The Executive Branch has consistently placed its support behind eradication of racial discrimination. Several years before this Court's decision in *Brown v. Board of Education, supra*, President Truman issued Executive Orders prohibiting racial discrimination in federal employment decisions, Exec. Order No. 9980, 3 CFR 720 (1943-1948 Comp.), and in classifications for the Selective Service, Exec. Order No. 9988, 3 CFR 726, 729 (1943-1948 Comp.). In 1957, President Eisenhower employed military forces to ensure compliance with federal standards in school desegregation programs. Exec. Order No. 10730, 3 CFR 389 (1954-1958 Comp.). And in 1962, President Kennedy announced:

"[T]he granting of Federal assistance for ... housing and related facilities from which Americans are excluded because of their race, color, creed, or national origin is unfair, unjust, and inconsistent with the public policy of the United States as manifested in its Constitution and laws." Exec. Order No. 11063, 3 CFR 652 (1959-1963 Comp.).

These are but a few of numerous Executive Orders over the past three decades demonstrating the commitment of the Executive Branch to the fundamental policy of eliminating racial discrimination. See, *e.g.*, Exec. Order No. 11197, 3 CFR 278 (1964-1965 Comp.); Exec. Order No. 11478, 3 CFR 803 (1966-1970 Comp.); Exec. Order No. 11764, 3 CFR 849 (1971-1975 Comp.); Exec. Order No. 12250, 3 CFR 298 (1981).

Few social or political issues in our history have been more vigorously debated and more extensively ventilated than the issue of racial discrimination, particularly in education. Given the stress and anguish of the history of efforts to escape from the shackles of the "separate but equal" doctrine of *Plessy v. Ferguson*, 163 U.S. 537 (1896), it cannot be said that educational institutions that, for whatever reasons, practice racial discrimination, are institutions exercising "beneficial and stabilizing influences in community life," *Walz v. Tax Comm'n*, 397 U.S. 664, 673 (1970), or should be encouraged by having all taxpayers share in their support by way of special tax status.

There can thus be no question that the interpretation of § 170 and § 501(c)(3) announced by the IRS in 1970 was correct. That it may be seen as belated does not undermine its soundness. It would be wholly incompatible with the concepts underlying tax exemption to grant the benefit of tax-exempt status to racially discriminatory educational entities, which "exer[t] a pervasive influence on the entire educational process." *Norwood v. Harrison, supra,* at 469. Whatever may be the rationale for such private schools' policies, and however sincere the rationale may be, racial discrimination in education is contrary to public policy. Racially discriminatory educational institutions cannot be viewed as conferring a public benefit within the "charitable" concept discussed earlier, or within the congressional intent underlying § 170 and § 501(c)(3).[21]

C

Petitioners contend that, regardless of whether the IRS properly concluded that racially discriminatory private schools violate public policy, only Congress can alter the scope of § 170 and § 501(c)(3). Petitioners accordingly argue that the IRS overstepped its lawful bounds in issuing its 1970 and 1971 rulings.

Yet ever since the inception of the Tax Code, Congress has seen fit to vest in those administering the tax laws very broad authority to interpret those laws. In an area as complex as the tax system, the agency Congress vests with administrative responsibility must be able to exercise its authority to meet changing conditions and new problems. Indeed as early as 1918, Congress expressly authorized the Commissioner "to make all needful rules and regulations for the enforcement" of the tax laws. Revenue Act of 1918, ch. 18, § 1309, 40 Stat. 1143. The same provision, so essential to efficient and fair administration of the tax laws, has appeared in Tax Codes ever since, see 26 U.S.C. § 7805(a); and this Court has long recognized the primary authority of the IRS and its predecessors in construing the Internal Revenue Code, see, *e.g., Commissioner v. Portland Cement Co. of Utah,* 450 U.S. 156, 169 (1981); *United States v. Correll,* 389 U.S. 299, 306-307 (1967); *Boske v. Comingore,* 177 U.S. 459, 469-470 (1900).

Congress, the source of IRS authority, can modify IRS rulings it considers improper; and courts exercise review over IRS actions. In the first instance, however, the responsibility for construing the Code falls to the IRS. Since Congress cannot be expected to anticipate every conceivable problem that can arise or to carry out day-to-day oversight, it relies on the administrators and on the courts to implement the legislative will. Administrators, like judges, are under oath to do so.

In § 170 and § 501(c)(3), Congress has identified categories of traditionally exempt institutions and has specified certain additional requirements for tax exemption. Yet the need for continuing interpretation of those statutes is

---

[21]In view of our conclusion that racially discriminatory private schools violate fundamental public policy and cannot be deemed to confer a benefit on the public, we need not decide whether an organization providing a public benefit and otherwise meeting the requirements of § 501(c)(3) could nevertheless be denied tax-exempt status if certain of its activities violated a law or public policy.

unavoidable. For more than 60 years, the IRS and its predecessors have constantly been called upon to interpret these and comparable provisions, and in doing so have referred consistently to principles of charitable trust law. In Treas. Regs. 45, Art. 517(1) (1921), for example, the IRS's predecessor denied charitable exemptions on the basis of proscribed political activity before the Congress itself added such conduct as a disqualifying element. In other instances, the IRS has denied charitable exemptions to otherwise qualified entities because they served too limited a class of people and thus did not provide a truly "public" benefit under the common-law test. See, e.g., *Crellin v. Commissioner*, 46 B.T.A. 1152, 1155-1156 (1942); *James Sprunt Benevolent Trust v. Commissioner*, 20 B.T.A. 19, 24-25 (1930). See also Treas. Reg. § 1.501(c)(3)- 1(d)(1)(ii) (1959). Some years before the issuance of the rulings challenged in these cases, the IRS also ruled that contributions to community recreational facilities would not be deductible and that the facilities themselves would not be entitled to tax-exempt status, unless those facilities were open to all on a racially nondiscriminatory basis. See Rev. Rul. 67- 325, 1967-2 Cum. Bull. 113. These rulings reflect the Commissioner's continuing duty to interpret and apply the Internal Revenue Code. See also *Textile Mills Securities Corp. v. Commissioner*, 314 U.S. 326, 337-338 (1941).

Guided, of course, by the Code, the IRS has the responsibility, in the first instance, to determine whether a particular entity is "charitable" for purposes of § 170 and § 501(c)(3).[22] This in turn may necessitate later determinations of whether given activities so violate public policy that the entities involved cannot be deemed to provide a public benefit worthy of "charitable" status. We emphasize, however, that these sensitive determinations should be made only where there is no doubt that the organization's activities violate fundamental public policy.

On the record before us, there can be no doubt as to the national policy. In 1970, when the IRS first issued the ruling challenged here, the position of all three branches of the Federal Government was unmistakably clear. The correctness of the Commissioner's conclusion that a racially discriminatory private school "is not 'charitable' within the common law concepts reflected in...the Code," Rev. Rul. 71-447, 1971-2 Cum. Bull., at 231, is wholly consistent with what Congress, the Executive and the courts had repeatedly declared before 1970. Indeed, it would be anomalous for the Executive, Legislative, and Judicial Branches to reach conclusions that add up to a firm public policy on racial discrimination, and at the same time have the IRS blissfully ignore what all three branches of the Federal Government had declared.[23] Clearly an educational institution engaging in practices affirmatively at odds with this declared position of the whole Government

---

[22]In the present case, the IRS issued its rulings denying exemptions to racially discriminatory schools only after a three-judge District Court had issued a preliminary injunction. See *supra*, at 578-579.

[23]JUSTICE POWELL misreads the Court's opinion when he suggests that the Court implies that "the Internal Revenue Service is invested with authority to decide which public policies are sufficiently 'fundamental' to require denial of tax exemptions," *post*, at 611. The Court's opinion does not warrant that interpretation. JUSTICE POWELL concedes that "if any national policy is sufficiently fundamental to constitute such an overriding limitation on the availability of tax-exempt status under § 501(c)(3), it is the policy against racial discrimination in education." *Post*, at 607. Since that policy

cannot be seen as exercising a "beneficial and stabilizing influenc[e] in community life," *Walz v. Tax Comm'n*, 397 U.S., at 673, and is not "charitable," within the meaning of § 170 and § 501(c)(3). We therefore hold that the IRS did not exceed its authority when it announced its interpretation of § 170 and § 501(c)(3) in 1970 and 1971.[24]

D

The actions of Congress since 1970 leave no doubt that the IRS reached the correct conclusion in exercising its authority. It is, of course, not unknown for independent agencies or the Executive Branch to misconstrue the intent of a statute; Congress can and often does correct such misconceptions, if the courts have not done só. Yet for a dozen years Congress has been made aware—acutely aware—of the IRS rulings of 1970 and 1971. As we noted earlier, few issues have been the subject of more vigorous and widespread debate and discussion in and out of Congress than those related to racial segregation in education. Sincere adherents advocating contrary views have ventilated the subject for well over three decades. Failure of Congress to modify the IRS rulings of 1970 and 1971, of which Congress was, by its own studies and by public discourse, constantly reminded, and Congress' awareness of the denial of tax-exempt status for racially discriminatory schools when enacting other and related legislation make out an unusually strong case of legislative acquiescence in and ratification by implication of the 1970 and 1971 rulings.

Ordinarily, and quite appropriately, courts are slow to attribute significance to the failure of Congress to act on particular legislation. See, *e.g.*, *Aaron v. SEC*, 446 U.S. 680, 694, n. 11 (1980). We have observed that "unsuccessful attempts at legislation are not the best of guides to legislative intent," *Red Lion Broadcasting Co. v. FCC*, 395 U.S. 367, 382, n. 11 (1969). Here, however, we do not have an ordinary claim of legislative acquiescence. Only one month after the IRS announced its position in 1970, Congress held its first hearings on this precise issue. Equal Educational Opportunity: Hearings before the Senate Select Committee on Equal Educational Opportunity, 91st Cong., 2d Sess., 1991 (1970). Exhaustive hearings have been held on the issue at various times since then. These include hearings in February 1982, after we granted review in this case. Administration's Change in Federal Policy Regarding the Tax Status of Racially Discriminatory Private Schools: Hearing before the House Committee on Ways and Means, 97th Cong., 2d Sess. (1982).

Nonaction by Congress is not often a useful guide, but the nonaction here is significant. During the past 12 years there have been no fewer than 13 bills

---

is sufficiently clear to warrant JUSTICE POWELL's concession and for him to support our finding of longstanding congressional acquiescence, it should be apparent that his concerns about the Court's opinion are unfounded.

[24]Many of the *amici curiae*, including *amicus* William T. Coleman, Jr. (appointed by the Court), argue that denial of tax-exempt status to racially discriminatory schools is independently required by the equal protection component of the Fifth Amendment. In light of our resolution of this litigation, we do not reach that issue. See, *e.g.*, *United States v. Clark*, 445 U.S. 23, 27 (1980); *NLRB v. Catholic Bishop of Chicago*, 440 U.S. 490, 504 (1979).

introduced to overturn the IRS interpretation of § 501(c)(3).[25] Not one of these bills has emerged from any committee, although Congress has enacted numerous other amendments to § 501 during this same period, including an amendment to § 501(c)(3) itself. Tax Reform Act of 1976, Pub. L. 94-455, § 1313(a), 90 Stat. 1730. It is hardly conceivable that Congress—and in this setting, any Member of Congress—was not abundantly aware of what was going on. In view of its prolonged and acute awareness of so important an issue, Congress' failure to act on the bills proposed on this subject provides added support for concluding that Congress acquiesced in the IRS rulings of 1970 and 1971. See, *e.g., Merrill Lynch, Pierce, Fenner & Smith, Inc. v. Curran*, 456 U.S. 353, 379-382 (1982); *Haig v. Agee*, 453 U.S. 280, 300-301 (1981); *Herman & MacLean v. Huddleston*, 459 U.S. 375, 384-386 (1983); *United States v. Rutherford*, 442 U.S. 544, 554, n. 10 (1979).

The evidence of congressional approval of the policy embodied in Revenue Ruling 71-447 goes well beyond the failure of Congress to act on legislative proposals. Congress affirmatively manifested its acquiescence in the IRS policy when it enacted the present § 501(i) of the Code, Act of Oct. 20, 1976, Pub. L. 94-568, 90 Stat. 2697. That provision denies tax-exempt status to social clubs whose charters or policy statements provide for "discrimination against any person on the basis of race, color, or religion."[26] Both the House and Senate Committee Reports on that bill articulated the national policy against granting tax exemptions to racially discriminatory private clubs. S. Rep. No. 94-1318, p. 8 (1976); H.R. Rep. No. 94-1353, p. 8 (1976).

Even more significant is the fact that both Reports focus on this Court's affirmance of *Green v. Connally*, 330 F. Supp. 1150 (DC 1971), as having established that "discrimination on account of race is inconsistent with an *educational institution's* tax-exempt status." S. Rep. No. 94-1318, *supra*, at 7-8, and n. 5; H.R. Rep. No. 94-1353, *supra*, at 8, and n. 5 (emphasis added). These references in congressional Committee Reports on an enactment denying tax exemptions to racially discriminatory private social clubs cannot be read other than as indicating approval of the standards applied to racially discriminatory private schools by the IRS subsequent to 1970, and specifically of Revenue Ruling 71- 447.[27]

III

Petitioners contend that, even if the Commissioner's policy is valid as to nonreligious private schools, that policy cannot constitutionally be applied

---

[25][Omitted.]

[26]Prior to the introduction of this legislation, a three-judge District Court had held that segregated social clubs were entitled to tax exemptions. *McGlotten v. Connally*, 338 F. Supp. 448 (DC 1972). Section 501(i) was enacted primarily in response to that decision. See S. Rep. No. 94-1318, pp. 7-8 (1976); H.R. Rep. No. 94-1353, p. 8 (1976).

[27]Reliance is placed on scattered statements in floor debate by Congressmen critical of the IRS's adoption of Revenue Ruling 71-447. See, *e.g.*, Brief for Petitioner in No. 81- 1, pp. 27-28. Those views did not prevail. That several Congressmen, expressing their individual views, argued that the IRS had no authority to take the action in question, is hardly a balance for the overwhelming evidence of congressional awareness of and acquiescence in the IRS rulings of 1970 and 1971.* * *

to schools that engage in racial discrimination on the basis of sincerely held religious beliefs.[28] As to such schools, it is argued that the IRS construction of § 170 and § 501(c)(3) violates their free exercise rights under the Religion Clauses of the First Amendment. This contention presents claims not heretofore considered by this Court in precisely this context.

This Court has long held the Free Exercise Clause of the First Amendment to be an absolute prohibition against governmental regulation of religious beliefs, *Wisconsin v. Yoder*, 406 U.S. 205, 219 (1972); *Sherbert v. Verner*, 374 U.S. 398, 402 (1963); *Cantwell v. Connecticut*, 310 U.S. 296, 303 (1940). As interpreted by this Court, moreover, the Free Exercise Clause provides substantial protection for lawful conduct grounded in religious belief, see *Wisconsin v. Yoder*, *supra*, at 220; *Thomas v. Review Board of Indiana Employment Security Div.*, 450 U.S. 707 (1981); *Sherbert v. Verner*, *supra*, at 402-403. However, "[n]ot all burdens on religion are unconstitutional.... The state may justify a limitation on religious liberty by showing that it is essential to accomplish an overriding governmental interest." *United States v. Lee*, 455 U.S. 252, 257-258 (1982). See, *e.g.*, *McDaniel v. Paty*, 435 U.S. 618, 628, and n. 8 (1978); *Wisconsin v. Yoder*, *supra*, at 215; *Gillette v. United States*, 401 U.S. 437 (1971).

On occasion this Court has found certain governmental interests so compelling as to allow even regulations prohibiting religiously based conduct. In *Prince v. Massachusetts*, 321 U.S. 158 (1944), for example, the Court held that neutrally cast child labor laws prohibiting sale of printed materials on public streets could be applied to prohibit children from dispensing religious literature. The Court found no constitutional infirmity in "excluding [Jehovah's Witness children] from doing there what no other children may do." *Id.*, at 171. See also *Reynolds v. United States*, 98 U.S. 145 (1879); *United States v. Lee*, *supra*; *Gillette v. United States*, *supra*. Denial of tax benefits will inevitably have a substantial impact on the operation of private religious schools, but will not prevent those schools from observing their religious tenets.

The governmental interest at stake here is compelling. As discussed in Part II-B, *supra*, the Government has a fundamental, overriding interest in eradicating racial discrimination in education[29]—discrimination that prevailed, with official approval, for the first 165 years of this Nation's constitutional history. That governmental interest substantially outweighs whatever burden denial of tax benefits places on petitioners' exercise of their religious beliefs. The interests asserted by petitioners cannot be accommodated with that compelling governmental interest, see *United States v. Lee*, *supra*, at

---

[28]The District Court found, on the basis of a full evidentiary record, that the challenged practices of petitioner Bob Jones University were based on a genuine belief that the Bible forbids interracial dating and marriage. 468 F. Supp., at 894. We assume, as did the District Court, that the same is true with respect to petitioner Goldsboro Christian Schools. See 436 F. Supp., at 1317.

[29]We deal here only with religious *schools*—not with churches or other purely religious institutions; here, the governmental interest is in denying public support to racial discrimination in education. As noted earlier, racially discriminatory schools "exer[t] a pervasive influence on the entire educational process," outweighing any public benefit that they might otherwise provide, *Norwood v. Harrison*, 413 U.S. 455, 469 (1973). See generally Simon 495-496.

259-260; and no "less restrictive means," see *Thomas v. Review Board of Indiana Employment Security Div.*, *supra*, at 718, are available to achieve the governmental interest.[30]

IV

The remaining issue is whether the IRS properly applied its policy to these petitioners. Petitioner Goldsboro Christian Schools admits that it "maintain[s] racially discriminatory policies," Brief for Petitioner in No. 81-1, p. 10, but seeks to justify those policies on grounds we have fully discussed. The IRS properly denied tax-exempt status to Goldsboro Christian Schools.

Petitioner Bob Jones University, however, contends that it is not racially discriminatory. It emphasizes that it now allows all races to enroll, subject only to its restrictions on the conduct of all students, including its prohibitions of association between men and women of different races, and of interracial marriage.[31] Although a ban on intermarriage or interracial dating applies to all races, decisions of this Court firmly establish that discrimination on the basis of racial affiliation and association is a form of racial discrimination, see, *e.g.*, *Loving v. Virginia*, 388 U.S. 1 (1967); *McLaughlin v. Florida*, 379 U.S. 184 (1964); *Tillman v. Wheaton-Haven Recreation Assn.*, 410 U.S. 431 (1973). We therefore find that the IRS properly applied Revenue Ruling 71-447 to Bob Jones University.[32]

The judgments of the Court of Appeals are, accordingly,

Affirmed.

JUSTICE POWELL, concurring in part and concurring in the judgment.

I join the Court's judgment, along with Part III of its opinion holding that the denial of tax exemptions to petitioners does not violate the First Amendment. I write separately because I am troubled by the broader implications

---

[30]Bob Jones University also contends that denial of tax exemption violates the Establishment Clause by preferring religions whose tenets do not require racial discrimination over those which believe racial intermixing is forbidden. It is well settled that neither a state nor the Federal Government may pass laws which "prefer one religion over another," *Everson v. Board of Education*, 330 U.S. 1, 15 (1947), but "[i]t is equally true" that a regulation does not violate the Establishment Clause merely because it "happens to coincide or harmonize with the tenets of some or all religions." *McGowan v. Maryland*, 366 U.S. 420, 442 (1961). See *Harris v. McRae*, 448 U.S. 297, 319-320 (1980). The IRS policy at issue here is founded on a "neutral, secular basis," *Gillette v. United States*, 401 U.S. 437, 452 (1971), and does not violate the Establishment Clause. See generally U.S. Comm'n on Civil Rights, Discriminatory Religious Schools and Tax Exempt Status 10-17 (1982). In addition, as the Court of Appeals noted, "the uniform application of the rule to all religiously operated schools *avoids* the necessity for a potentially entangling inquiry into whether a racially restrictive practice is the result of sincere religious belief." 639 F. 2d 147, 155 (CA4 1980) (emphasis in original). Cf. *NLRB v. Catholic Bishop of Chicago*, 440 U.S. 490 (1979). But see generally Note, 90 Yale L. J. 350 (1980).

[31]This argument would in any event apply only to the final eight months of the five tax years at issue in this case. Prior to May 1975, Bob Jones University's admissions policy was racially discriminatory on its face, since the University excluded unmarried Negro students while admitting unmarried Caucasians.

[32]Bob Jones University also argues that the IRS policy should not apply to it because

of the Court's opinion with respect to the authority of the Internal Revenue Service (IRS) and its construction of §§ 170(c) and 501(c)(3) of the Internal Revenue Code.

* * *

Federal taxes are not imposed on organizations "operated exclusively for religious, charitable, scientific, testing for public safety, literary, or educational purposes...." 26 U.S.C. § 501(c)(3). The Code also permits a tax deduction for contributions made to these organizations. §170(c). It is clear that petitioners, organizations incorporated for educational purposes, fall within the language of the statute. It also is clear that the language itself does not mandate refusal of tax-exempt status to any private school that maintains a racially discriminatory admissions policy. Accordingly, there is force in JUSTICE REHNQUIST's argument that §§ 170(c) and 501(c)(3) should be construed as setting forth the only criteria Congress has established for qualification as a tax-exempt organization. See *post*, at 612-615 (REHNQUIST, J., dissenting). Indeed, were we writing prior to the history detailed in the Court's opinion, this could well be the construction I would adopt. But there has been a decade of acceptance that is persuasive in the circumstances of these cases, and I conclude that there are now sufficient reasons for accepting the IRS's construction of the Code as proscribing tax exemptions for schools that discriminate on the basis of race as a matter of policy.

[The remaining portion of Justice Powell's concurrence is omitted.]

JUSTICE REHNQUIST, dissenting.

The Court points out that there is a strong national policy in this country against racial discrimination. To the extent that the Court states that Congress in furtherance of this policy could deny tax-exempt status to educational institutions that promote racial discrimination, I readily agree. But, unlike the Court, I am convinced that Congress simply has failed to take this action and, as this Court has said over and over again, regardless of our view on the propriety of Congress' failure to legislate we are not constitutionally empowered to act for them.

In approaching this statutory construction question the Court quite adeptly avoids the statute it is construing. This I am sure is no accident, for there is nothing in the language of § 501(c)(3) that supports the result obtained by the Court. Section 501(c)(3) provides tax-exempt status for:

> "Corporations, and any community chest, fund, or foundation, organized and operated exclusively for religious, charitable, scientific, testing for public safety, literary, or educational purposes, or to foster national or international amateur sports competition (but only if no part of its

---

it is entitled to exemption under § 501(c)(3) as a "religious" organization, rather than as an "educational" institution. The record in this case leaves no doubt, however, that Bob Jones University is both an educational institution and a religious institution. As discussed previously, the IRS policy properly extends to all private schools, including religious schools. See n. 29, *supra*. The IRS policy thus was properly applied to Bob Jones University.

activities involve the provision of athletic facilities or equipment), or for the prevention of cruelty to children or animals, no part of the net earnings of which inures to the benefit of any private shareholder or individual, no substantial part of the activities of which is carrying on propaganda, or otherwise attempting, to influence legislation (except as otherwise provided in subsection (h)), and which does not participate in, or intervene in (including the publishing or distributing of statements), any political campaign on behalf of any candidate for public office." 26 U.S.C. § 501(c)(3).

With undeniable clarity, Congress has explicitly defined the requirements for § 501(c)(3) status. An entity must be (1) a corporation, or community chest, fund, or foundation, (2) organized for one of the eight enumerated purposes, (3) operated on a nonprofit basis, and (4) free from involvement in lobbying activities and political campaigns. Nowhere is there to be found some additional, undefined public policy requirement.

The Court first seeks refuge from the obvious reading of § 501(c)(3) by turning to § 170 of the Internal Revenue Code which provides a tax deduction for contributions made to § 501(c)(3) organizations. In setting forth the general rule, § 170 states:

"There shall be allowed as a deduction any charitable contribution (as defined in subsection (c)) payment of which is made within the taxable year. A charitable contribution shall be allowable as a deduction only if verified under regulations prescribed by the Secretary." 26 U.S.C. § 170(a)(1).

The Court seizes the words "charitable contribution" and with little discussion concludes that "[o]n its face, therefore, § 170 reveals that Congress' intention was to provide tax benefits to organizations serving charitable purposes," intimating that this implies some unspecified common-law charitable trust requirement. *Ante*, at 587.

The Court would have been well advised to look to subsection (c) where, as § 170(a)(1) indicates, Congress has defined a "charitable contribution":

"For purposes of this section, the term 'charitable contribution' means. a contribution or gift to or for the use of ... [a] corporation, trust, or community chest, fund, or foundation...organized and operated exclusively for religious, charitable, scientific, literary, or educational purposes, or to foster national or international amateur sports competition (but only if no part of its activities involve the provision of athletic facilities or equipment), or for the prevention of cruelty to children or animals;...no part of the net earnings of which inures to the benefit of any private shareholder or individual; and...which is not disqualified for tax exemption under section 501(c)(3) by reason of attempting to influence legislation, and which does not participate in, or intervene in (including the publishing or distribution of statements), any political campaign on behalf of any candidate for public office." 26 U.S.C. § 170(c).

Plainly, § 170(c) simply tracks the requirements set forth in § 501(c)(3). Since § 170 is no more than a mirror of § 501(c)(3) and, as the Court points out, §

170 followed § 501(c)(3) by more than two decades, *ante*, at 587, n. 10, it is at best of little usefulness in finding the meaning of § 501(c)(3).

Making a more fruitful inquiry, the Court next turns to the legislative history of § 501(c)(3) and finds that Congress intended in that statute to offer a tax benefit to organizations that Congress believed were providing a public benefit. I certainly agree. But then the Court leaps to the conclusion that this history is proof Congress intended that an organization seeking § 501(c)(3) status "must fall within a category specified in that section *and must demonstrably serve and be in harmony with the public interest.*" *Ante*, at 592 (emphasis added). To the contrary, I think that the legislative history of § 501(c)(3) unmistakably makes clear that *Congress has decided* what organizations are serving a public purpose and providing a public benefit within the meaning of § 501(c)(3) and has clearly set forth in § 501(c)(3) the characteristics of such organizations.·In fact, there are few examples which better illustrate Congress' effort to define and redefine the requirements of a legislative Act.

* * *

The Court suggests that unless its new requirement be added to § 501(c)(3), nonprofit organizations formed to teach pickpockets and terrorists would necessarily acquire tax exempt status. *Ante*, at 592, n. 18. Since the Court does not challenge the characterization of *petitioners* as "educational" institutions within the meaning of § 501(c)(3), and in fact states several times in the course of its opinion that petitioners *are* educational institutions, see, *e.g.*, *ante*, at 580, 583, 604, n. 29, 606, n. 32, it is difficult to see how this argument advances the Court's reasoning for disposing of petitioners' cases.

But simply because I reject the Court's heavyhanded creation of the requirement that an organization seeking § 501(c)(3) status must "serve and be in harmony with the public interest," *ante*, at 592, does not mean that I would deny to the IRS the usual authority to adopt regulations further explaining what Congress meant by the term "educational." The IRS has fully exercised that authority in Treas. Reg. § 1.501(c)(3)- 1(d)(3), 26 CFR § 1.501(c)(3)-1(d)(3) (1982), which provides:

"(3) *Educational defined*—(i) *In general.* The term 'educational', as used in section 501(c)(3), relates to

"(a) The instruction or training of the individual for the purpose of improving or developing his capabilities; or

"(b) The instruction of the public on subjects useful to the individual and beneficial to the community.

"An organization may be educational even though it advocates a particular position or viewpoint so long as it presents a sufficiently full and fair exposition of the pertinent facts as to permit an individual or the public to form an independent opinion or conclusion. On the other hand, an organization is not educational if its principal function is the mere presentation of unsupported opinion.

"(ii) *Examples of educational organizations.* The following are examples of organizations which, if they otherwise meet the requirements of this section, are educational:

"*Example (1).* An organization, such as a primary or secondary school, a college, or a professional or trade school, which has a regularly scheduled curriculum, a regular faculty, and a regularly enrolled body of students in attendance at a place where the educational activities are regularly carried on.

"*Example (2)*. An organization whose activities consist of presenting public discussion groups, forums, panels, lectures, or other similar programs. Such programs may be on radio or television.

"*Example (3)*. An organization which presents a course of instruction by means of correspondence or through the utilization of television or radio.

"*Example (4)*. Museums, zoos, planetariums, symphony orchestras, and other similar organizations."

I have little doubt that neither the "Fagin School for Pickpockets" nor a school training students for guerrilla warfare and terrorism in other countries would meet the definitions contained in the regulations.

Prior to 1970, when the charted course was abruptly changed, the IRS had continuously interpreted § 501(c)(3) and its predecessors in accordance with the view I have expressed above. This, of course, is of considerable significance in determining the intended meaning of the statute. *NLRB v. Boeing Co.*, 412 U.S. 67, 75 (1973); *Power Reactor Development Co. v. Electricians*, 367 U.S. 396, 408 (1961).

In 1970 the IRS was sued by parents of black public schoolchildren seeking to enjoin the IRS from according tax-exempt status under § 501(c)(3) to private schools in Mississippi that discriminated against blacks. The IRS answered, consistent with its longstanding position, by maintaining a lack of authority to deny the tax exemption if the schools met the specified requirements of § 501(c)(3). Then "[i]n the midst of this litigation," *Green v. Connally*, 330 F. Supp. 1150, 1156 (DC), summarily aff'd *sub nom. Coit v. Green*, 404 U.S. 997 (1971), and in the face of a preliminary injunction, the IRS changed its position and adopted the view of the plaintiffs.

Following the close of the litigation, the IRS published its new position in Revenue Ruling 71-447, stating that "a school asserting a right to the benefits provided for in section 501(c)(3) of the Code as being organized and operated exclusively for educational purposes must be a common law charity in order to be exempt under that section." Rev. Rul. 71-447, 1971-2 Cum. Bull. 230. The IRS then concluded that a school that promotes racial discrimination violates public policy and therefore cannot qualify as a common-law charity. The circumstances under which this change in interpretation was made suggest that it is entitled to very little deference. But even if the circumstances were different, the latter-day wisdom of the IRS has no basis in § 501(c)(3).

Perhaps recognizing the lack of support in the statute itself, or in its history, for the 1970 IRS change in interpretation, the Court finds that "[t]he actions of Congress since 1970 leave no doubt that the IRS reached the correct conclusion in exercising its authority," concluding that there is "an unusually strong case of legislative acquiescence in and ratification by implication of the 1970 and 1971 rulings." *Ante*, at 599. The Court relies first on several bills introduced to overturn the IRS interpretation of § 501(c)(3). *Ante*, at 600, and n. 25. But we have said before, and it is equally applicable here, that this type of congressional inaction is of virtually no weight in determining legislative intent. See *United States v. Wise*, 370 U.S. 405, 411 (1962); *Waterman S.S. Corp. v. United States*, 381 U.S. 252, 269 (1965).

These bills and related hearings indicate little more than that a vigorous debate has existed in Congress concerning the new IRS position.

The Court next asserts that "Congress affirmatively manifested its acquiescence in the IRS policy when it enacted the present § 501(i) of the Code," a provision that "denies tax-exempt status to social clubs whose charters or policy statements provide for" racial discrimination. *Ante*, at 601. Quite to the contrary, it seems to me that in § 501(i) Congress showed that when it wants to add a requirement prohibiting racial discrimination to one of the tax-benefit provisions, it is fully aware of how to do it. Cf. *Commissioner v. Tellier*, 383 U.S. 687, 693, n. 10 (1966).

*   *   *

This Court continuously has been hesitant to find ratification through inaction. See *United States v. Wise, supra*. This is especially true when such a finding "would result in a construction of the statute which not only is at odds with the language of the section in question and the pattern of the statute taken as a whole, but also is extremely far reaching in terms of the virtually untrammeled and unreviewable power it would vest in a regulatory agency." *SEC v. Sloan*, 436 U.S. 103, 121 (1978). Few cases would call for more caution in finding ratification by acquiscence than the present one. The new IRS interpretation is not only far less than a long-standing administrative policy, it is at odds with a position maintained by the IRS, and unquestioned by Congress, for several decades prior to 1970. The interpretation is unsupported by the statutory language, it is unsupported by legislative history, the interpretation has led to considerable controversy in and out of Congress, and the interpretation gives to the IRS a broad power which until now Congress had kept for itself. When in addition to these circumstances Congress has shown time and time again that it is ready to enact positive legislation to change the Tax Code when it desires, this Court has no business finding that Congress has adopted the new IRS position by failing to enact legislation to reverse it.

I have no disagreement with the Court's finding that there is a strong national policy in this country opposed to racial discrimination. I agree with the Court that Congress has the power to further this policy by denying § 501(c)(3) status to organizations that practice racial discrimination.[3] But as of yet Congress has failed to do so. Whatever the reasons for the failure, this Court should not legislate for Congress.[4]

Petitioners are each organized for the "instruction or training of the individual for the purpose of improving or developing his capabilities," 26 CFR § 1.501(c)(3)-1(d)(3) (1982), and thus are organized for "educational purposes" within the meaning of § 501(c)(3). Petitioners' nonprofit status is uncontested. There is no indication that either petitioner has been involved

---

[3]I agree with the Court that such a requirement would not infringe on petitioners' First Amendment rights.

[4]Because of its holding, the Court does not have to decide whether it would violate the equal protection component of the Fifth Amendment for Congress to grant § 501(c)(3) status to organizations that practice racial discrimination. *Ante*, at 599, n. 24. I would decide that it does not. The statute is facially neutral; absent a showing of a discriminatory purpose, no equal protection violation is established. *Washington v. Davis*, 426 U.S. 229, 241-244 (1976).

in lobbying activities or political campaigns. Therefore, it is my view that unless and until Congress affirmatively amends § 501(c)(3) to require more, the IRS is without authority to deny petitioners § 501(c)(3) status. For this reason, I would reverse the Court of Appeals.

Grove City College v. Bell

United States Supreme Court, 465 U.S. 555, 104 S.Ct. 1211 (1984).

Syllabus*

Section 901(a) of Title IX of the Education Amendments of 1972 prohibits sex
discrimination in "any education program or activity receiving Federal financial
assistance," and § 902 provides that a recipient's compliance with regulations
of a federal agency awarding assistance may be secured by termination of assistance "to the particular program, or part thereof, in which...noncompliance
has been...found." Under the statute a federally assisted program must be
identified before Title IX coverage is triggered. Petitioner Grove City College
(College), a private, coeducational, liberal arts college, accepts no direct federal
assistance, nor does it participate in the Regular Disbursement System (RDS)
of the Department of Education (Department), whereby amounts for federal
grants to students are advanced to the institution, which then itself selects eligible students and calculates and distributes the grants. However, the College
enrolls students who receive direct federal Basic Educational Opportunity Grants
(BEOG's) under the Department's Alternative Disbursement System (ADS).
The Department concluded that,-under applicable regulations, the College was
a "recipient" of "Federal financial assistance," and when the College refused
to execute an Assurance of Compliance with Title IX's nondiscrimination provisions, as required by the regulations, the Department initiated administrative
proceedings, which resulted in an order terminating assistance until the College
executed an Assurance of Compliance and satisfied the Department that it was
in compliance with the regulations. The College and four of its students then
filed suit in Federal District Court, which held that the students' BEOG's constituted "Federal financial assistance" to the College but that the Department
could not terminate the students' aid because of the College's refusal to execute
an Assurance of Compliance. The Court of Appeals reversed, holding that the
Department could terminate the students' BEOG's to force the College to
execute an Assurance of Compliance.

Held:
    1. Title IX coverage is triggered because some of the College's students re-
ceive BEOG's to pay for their education. In view of the structure of the Education Amendments of 1972, the clear statutory language, the legislative history
(including postenactment history) showing Congress' awareness that the student
assistant programs established by the Amendments significantly aided colleges
and universities, and the longstanding administrative construction of the phrase
"receiving Federal financial assistance" as including assistance to a student who
uses it at a particular institution, Title IX coverage is not foreclosed merely
because federal funds are granted to the students rather than to the College's
educational programs. Pp. 261-265.
    2. However, the receipt of BEOG's by some of the College's students does
not trigger institutionwide coverage under Title IX. In purpose and effect, BEOG's
represent financial assistance to the College's own financial aid program, and it
is that program that may properly be regulated under Title IX's nondiscrimination provision. Under the program-specific limitations of §§ 901 and 902, the
College's choice of participating in the ADS rather than the RDS mechanism
for administering the BEOG program neither expands nor contracts the breadth
of the "program or activity receiving Federal financial assistance." The fact that

---

*The syllabus constitutes no part of the opinion of the Court but has been prepared
by the Reporter of Decisions for the convenience of the reader.

federal funds eventually reach the College's general operating budget cannot subject it to institutionwide coverage. Pp. 266-268.

3. A refusal to execute a proper program-specific Assurance of Compliance warrants the Department's termination of federal assistance to the student financial aid program. The College's contention that termination must be preceded by a finding of actual discrimination is not supported by § 902's language. Pp. 268-269.

4. Requiring the College to comply with Title IX's prohibition of discrimination as a condition for its continued eligibility to participate in the BEOG program infringes no First Amendment rights of the College or its students. P. 269.

687 F.2d 684, affirmed.

WHITE, J., delivered the opinion of the Court, in which BURGER, C.J., and BLACKMUN, POWELL, REHNQUIST, and O'CONNOR, JJ., joined, and in all but Part III of which BRENNAN, MARSHALL, and STEVENS, JJ., joined. POWELL, J., filed a concurring opinion, in which BURGER, C.J., and O'CONNOR, J., joined, *post*, p. 269. STEVENS, J., filed an opinion concurring in part and concurring in the result, *post*, p. 271. BRENNAN, J., filed an opinion concurring in part and dissenting in part, in which MARSHALL, J., joined, *post*, p. 272.

JUSTICE WHITE delivered the opinion of the Court.

Section 901(a) of Title IX of the Education Amendments of 1972, Pub. L. 92-318, 86 Stat. 373, 20 U.S.C. § 1681(a), prohibits sex discrimination in "any education program or activity receiving Federal financial assistance,"[1] and § 902 directs agencies awarding most types of assistance to promulgate regulations to ensure that recipients adhere to that prohibition. Compliance with departmental regulations may be secured by termination of assistance "to the particular program, or part thereof, in which... noncompliance has been... found" or by "any other means authorized by law." § 902, 20 U.S.C. § 1682.[2]

---

[1]Section 901(a), 20 U.S.C. § 1681(a), provides in pertinent part:
"No person in the United States shall, on the basis of sex, be excluded from participation in, be denied the benefits of, or be subjected to discrimination under any education program or activity receiving Federal financial assistance...."
Nine statutory exemptions, none of which is relevant to the disposition of this case, follow. See §§ 901(a)(1)-(9), 20 U.S.C. §§ 1681(a)(1)-(9)

[2]Section 902, 20 U.S.C. § 1682, provides:
"Each Federal department and agency which is empowered to extend Federal financial assistance to any education program or activity, by way of grant, loan, or contract other than a contract of insurance or guaranty, is authorized and directed to effectuate the provisions of section [901] with respect to such program or activity by issuing rules, regulations, or orders of general applicability which shall be consistent with achievement of the objectives of the statute authorizing the financial assistance in connection with which the action is taken. No such rule, regulation, or order shall become effective unless and until approved by the President. Compliance with any requirement adopted pursuant to this section may be effected (1) by the termination of or refusal to grant or to continue assistance under such program or activity to any recipient as to whom there has been an express finding on the record, after opportunity for hearing, of a failure to comply with such requirement, but such

This case presents several questions concerning the scope and operation of these provisions and the regulations established by the Department of Education. We must decide, first, whether Title IX applies at all to Grove City College, which accepts no direct assistance but enrolls students who receive federal grants that must be used for educational purposes. If so, we must identify the "education program or activity" at Grove City that is "receiving Federal financial assistance" and determine whether federal assistance to that program may be terminated solely because the College violates the Department's regulations by refusing to execute an Assurance of Compliance with Title IX. Finally, we must consider whether the application of Title IX to Grove City infringes the First Amendment rights of the College or its students.

I

Petitioner Grove City College is a private, coeducational, liberal arts college that has sought to preserve its institutional autonomy by consistently refusing state and federal financial assistance. Grove City's desire to avoid federal oversight has led it to decline to participate, not only in direct institutional aid programs, but also in federal student assistance programs under which the College would be required to assess students' eligibility and to determine the amounts of loans, work-study funds, or grants they should receive.[3] Grove City has, however, enrolled a large number of students who receive Basic Educational Opportunity Grants (BEOG's), 20 U.S.C. § 1070a (1982 ed.), under the Department of Education's[4] Alternate Disbursement System (ADS).[5]

---

termination or refusal shall be limited to the particular political entity, or part thereof, in which such noncompliance has been so found, or (2) by any other means authorized by law: *Provided, however,* That no such action shall be taken until the department or agency concerned has advised the appropriate person or persons of the failure to comply with the requirement and has determined that compliance cannot be secured by voluntary means. In the case of any action terminating, or refusing to grant or continue, assistance because of failure to comply with a requirement imposed pursuant to this section, the head of the Federal department or agency shall file with the committees of the House and Senate having legislative jurisdiction over the program or activity involved a full written report of the circumstances and the grounds for such action. No such action shall become effective until thirty days have elapsed after the filing of such report" (emphasis in original).

[3]See, *e.g.*, 20 U.S.C. § 1071 *et seq.* (1982 ed.); 34 CFR pt. 674 (1983) (National Direct Student Loans); 42 U.S.C. § 2751 *et seq.* (1976 ed. and Supp. V); 34 CFR pt. 675 (1983) (College Work Study Program); 20 U.S.C. § 1070b (1982 ed.); 34 CFR pt. 676 (1983) (Supplemental Educational Opportunity Grants).

[4]The Department of Health, Education, and Welfare's functions with respect to BEOG's were transferred to the Department of Education by § 301(a)(3) of the Department of Education Organization Act, Pub. L. 96-88, 93 Stat. 678, 20 U.S.C. § 3441(a)(3) (1982 ed.). We will refer to both HEW and DOE as "the Department."

[5]The Secretary, in his discretion, has established two procedures for computing and disbursing BEOG's. Under the Regular Disbursement System (RDS), the Secretary estimates the amount that an institution will need for grants and advances that sum to the institution, which itself selects eligible students, calculates awards, and distributes the grants by either crediting students' accounts or issuing checks. 34 CFR §§ 690.71-690.85 (1983). Most institutions whose students receive BEOG's participate

The Department concluded that Grove City was a "recipient" of "Federal financial assistance" as those terms are defined in the regulations implementing Title IX, 34 CFR §§ 106.2(g)(1), (h) (1982),[6] and, in July 1977, it requested that the College execute the Assurance of Compliance required by 34 CFR § 106.4 (1983). If Grove City had signed the Assurance, it would have agreed to

> "[c]omply, to the extent applicable to it, with Title IX...and all applicable requirements imposed by or pursuant to the Department's regulation...to the end that...no person in the United States shall, on the basis of sex, be...subjected to discrimination under any education program or activity for which [it] receives or benefits from Federal financial assistance from the Department." App. to Pet. for Cert. A-126—A-127.[7]

When Grove City persisted in refusing to execute an Assurance, the Department initiated proceedings to declare the College and its students ineligible to receive BEOG's.[8] The Administrative Law Judge held that the federal financial assistance received by Grove City obligated it to execute an Assurance of Compliance and entered an order terminating assistance until Grove City "corrects its noncompliance with Title IX and satisfies the Department that it is in compliance" with the applicable regulations. App. to Pet. for Cert. A-97.

Grove City and four of its students then commenced this action in the District Court for the Western District of Pennsylvania, which concluded

---

in the RDS, but the ADS is an option made available by the Secretary to schools that wish to minimize their involvement in the administration of the BEOG program. Institutions participating in the program through the ADS must make appropriate certifications to the Secretary, but the Secretary calculates awards and makes disbursements directly to eligible students. 34 CFR §§ 690.91-690.96 (1983).

[6]The Title IX regulations were recodified in 1980, without substantive change, at 34 CFR pt. 106 in connection with the establishment of the Department of Education. 45 Fed. Reg. 30802, 30962-30963 (1980). All references herein are to the currently effective regulations.

"Federal financial assistance" is defined in 34 CFR § 106.2(g)(1) (1983) to include:

"A grant or loan of Federal financial assistance, including funds made available for:

.   .   .   .

"(ii) Scholarships, loans, grants, wages or other funds extended to any entity for payment to or on behalf of students admitted to that entity, or extended directly to such students for payment to that entity."

A "recipient" is defined in 34 CFR § 106.2(h) (1983) to include:

"[A]ny public or private agency, institution, or organization, or other entity, or any person, to whom Federal financial assistance is extended directly or through another recipient and which operates an education program or activity which receives or benefits from such assistance...."

See also 34 CFR §§ 106.11, 106.31(a) (1983).

[7]The Assurance of Compliance form currently in use differs somewhat from the version quoted in the text. See App. to Brief for Federal Respondents in *Hillsdale College v. Department of Education*, O.T. 1982, No. 82-1538, pp. 1a-2a. The substance, however, is the same in that it refers to "education programs and activities receiving Federal financial assistance."

[8]The Department also sought to terminate Guaranteed Student Loans (GSL's), 20 U.S.C. § 1071 (1982 ed.), received by Grove City's students.

that the students' BEOG's constituted "Federal financial assistance" to Grove City but held, on several grounds, that the Department could not terminate the students' aid because of the College's refusal to execute an Assurance of Compliance. *Grove City College v. Harris*, 500 F.Supp. 253 (1980).[9] The Court of Appeals reversed. 687 F.2d 684 (CA3 1982). It first examined the language and legislative history of Title IX and held that indirect, as well as direct, aid triggered coverage under § 901(a) and that institutions whose students financed their educations with BEOG's were recipients of federal financial assistance within the meaning of Title IX. Although it recognized that Title IX's provisions are program-specific, the court likened the assistance flowing to Grove City through its students to non-earmarked aid, and, with one judge dissenting, declared that "[w]here the federal government furnishes indirect or non-earmarked aid to an institution, it is apparent to us that the institution itself must be the 'program.'" 687 F.2d, at 700.[10] Finally, the Court of Appeals concluded that the Department could condition financial aid upon the execution of an Assurance of Compliance and that the Department had acted properly in terminating federal financial assistance to the students and Grove City despite the lack of evidence of actual discrimination.

We granted certiorari, 459 U.S. 1199 (1983), and we now affirm the Court of Appeals' judgment that the Department could terminate BEOG's received by Grove City's students to force the College to execute an Assurance of Compliance.

II

In defending its refusal to execute the Assurance of Compliance required by the Department's regulations, Grove City first contends that neither it

---

[9]The District Court held, first, that GSL's were "contract[s] of insurance or guaranty" that could not be terminated under § 902 of Title IX. The Department did not challenge this conclusion on appeal, and we express no view on this aspect of the District Court's reasoning. The court also concluded that Grove City could not be required to execute an Assurance of Compliance because Subpart E of the Title IX regulations, which prohibits discrimination in employment, was invalid. As the Court of Appeals recognized, we have since upheld the validity of Subpart E. *North Haven Board of Education v. Bell*, 456 U.S. 512 (1982). The District Court held, in the alternative, that § 902 permitted termination only upon an actual finding of sex discrimination and that Grove City's refusal to execute an Assurance could not justify a termination of assistance. Finally, the court reasoned that affected students were entitled to hearings before their aid could be discontinued.

[10]In reaching this conclusion, the Court of Appeals accepted the position argued by respondents. As respondents acknowledged in the oral argument before this Court, the Department's position has not been a model of clarity. Tr. of Oral Arg. 33-35. The Department initially took the position that the receipt of student financial aid would trigger institutionwide coverage under Title IX and construed its regulations to that effect. It pressed that position in the lower courts. In their brief in opposition to the petition for certiorari, respondents did not defend this aspect of the Court of Appeals' opinion, but argued instead that the question need not be resolved to decide this case. In their brief on the merits and in the oral argument, however, respondents conceded that the Court of Appeals erred in holding that Grove City itself constituted the "program or activity" subject to regulation under Title IX. The Department's regulations, it was represented, may be construed in a program-specific manner and hence are not inconsistent with the statute. This concession, of course, is not binding on us and does not foreclose our review of the judgment below.

nor any "education program or activity" of the College receives any federal financial assistance within the meaning of Title IX by virtue of the fact that some of its students receive BEOG's and use them to pay for their education. We disagree.

Grove City provides a well-rounded liberal arts education and a variety of educational programs and student services. The question is whether any of those programs or activities "receiv[es] Federal financial assistance" within the meaning of Title IX when students finance their education with BEOG's. The structure of the Education Amendments of 1972, in which Congress both created the BEOG program and imposed Title IX's nondiscrimination requirement, strongly suggests an affirmative conclusion. BEOG's were aptly characterized as a "centerpiece of the bill," 118 Cong. Rec. 20297 (1972) (Rep. Pucinski), and Title IX "relate[d] directly to [its] central purpose." 117 Cong. Rec. 30412 (1971) (Sen. Bayh). In view of this connection and Congress' express recognition of discrimination in the administration of student financial aid programs,[11] it would indeed be anomalous to discover that one of the primary components of Congress' comprehensive "package of federal aid," id., at 2007 (Sen. Pell), was not intended to trigger coverage under Title IX.

It is not surprising to find, therefore, that the language of § 901(a) contains no hint that Congress perceived a substantive difference between direct institutional assistance and aid received by a school through its students. The linchpin of Grove City's argument that none of its programs receives any federal assistance is a perceived distinction between direct and indirect aid, a distinction that finds no support in the text of § 901(a).[12] Nothing in § 901(a) suggests that Congress elevated form over substance by making the application of the nondiscrimination principle dependent on the manner in which a program or activity receives federal assistance. There is no basis in the statute for the view that only institutions that themselves apply for federal aid or receive checks directly from the Federal Government are subject to regulation. Cf. *Bob Jones University v. Johnson*, 396 F.Supp. 597, 601-604 (SC 1974), affirmance order, 529 F.2d 514 (CA4 1975). As the Court of Appeals observed, "by its all inclusive terminology [§ 901(a)] appears to encompass *all* forms of federal aid to education, direct or indirect." 687 F.2d, at 691 (emphasis in original). We have recognized the need to " 'accord [Title IX] a sweep as broad as its language,' " *North Haven Board of Edu-*

---

[11]See, e.g., Discrimination Against Women: Hearings on Section 805 of H.R. 16098 before the Special Subcommittee on Education of the House Committee on Education and Labor, 91st Cong., 2d Sess., 235 (1970) (Rep. May); id., at 433 (Rep. Mink); id., at 739 (Rep. Griffiths); 118 Cong. Rec. 3935-3940, 5803-5809 (1972) (Sen. Bayh).

[12]Grove City itself recognizes the problematic nature of the distinction it advances. Although its interpretation of § 901(a) logically would exclude from coverage under Title IX local school districts that receive federal funds through state educational agencies, see, e.g., 20 U.S.C. § 3801 et seq. (1982 ed.), Grove City wisely does not attempt to defend this result. In fact, the College concedes that "[b]ecause federal assistance is often passed through state agencies, this type of indirect assistance leads to Title IX jurisdiction *over the education program or activity* which ultimately receives the assistance." Brief for Petitioners 17, n. 17 (emphasis in original). Grove City has proposed no principled basis for treating differently federal assistance received through students and federal aid that is disbursed by a state agency.

cation v. Bell, 456 U.S. 512, 521 (1982) (quoting *United States v. Price*, 383 U.S. 787, 801 (1966)), and we are reluctant to read into § 901(a) a limitation not apparent on its face.

Our reluctance grows when we pause to consider the available evidence of Congress' intent. The economic effect of direct and indirect assistance often is indistinguishable, see *Mueller v. Allen*, 463 U.S. 388, 397, n. 6 (1983); *id.*, at 412 (MARSHALL, J., dissenting); *Committee for Public Education v. Nyquist*, 413 U.S. 756, 783 (1973); *Norwood v. Harrison*, 413 U.S. 455, 463-465 (1973), and the BEOG program was structured to ensure that it effectively supplements the College's own financial aid program.[13] Congress undoubtedly comprehended this reality in enacting the Education Amendments of 1972. The legislative history of the Amendments is replete with statements evincing Congress' awareness that the student assistance programs established by the Amendments would significantly aid colleges and universities.[14] In fact, one of the stated purposes of the student aid provisions was to "provid[e] assistance to institutions of higher education." Pub. L. 92-318, § 1001(c)(1), 86 Stat. 381, 20 U.S.C. § 1070(a)(5).

Congress' awareness of the purpose and effect of its student aid programs also is reflected in the sparse legislative history of Title IX itself. Title IX was patterned after Title VI of the Civil Rights Act of 1964, Pub. L. 88-352, 78 Stat. 252, 42 U.S.C. § 2000d *et seq.* (1976 ed. and Supp. V). *Cannon v. University of Chicago*, 441 U.S. 677, 684-685 (1979); 118 Cong. Rec. 5807 (1972) (Sen. Bayh). The drafters of Title VI envisioned that the receipt of student aid funds would trigger coverage,[15] and, since they approved identical language, we discern no reason to believe that the Congressmen who voted for Title IX intended a different result.

The few contemporaneous statements that attempted to give content to

---

[13]Grove City's students receive BEOG's to pay for the education they receive at the College. Their eligibility for assistance is conditioned upon continued enrollment at Grove City and on satisfactory progress in their studies. 20 U.S.C. §§ 1091(a)(1), (3) (1982 ed.). Their grants are based on the "cost of attendance" at Grove City, 20 U.S.C. § 1070a(a)(2)(B)(i) (1982 ed.), which includes the College's tuition and fees, room and board, and a limited amount for books, supplies, and miscellaneous expenses. 34 CFR § 690.51 (1983). The amount that students and their families can reasonably be expected to contribute is subtracted from the maximum BEOG to ensure that the assistance is used solely for educational expenses, 20 U.S.C. § 1070a(a)(2)(A)(i) (1982 ed.), and students are required to file affidavits stating that their awards will be "used solely for expenses related to attendance" at Grove City. 20 U.S.C. § 1091(a)(5) (1982 ed.); see 34 CFR §§ 690.79, 690.94(a)(2) (1983).

Grove City's attempt to analogize BEOG's to food stamps, Social Security benefits, welfare payments, and other forms of general-purpose governmental assistance to low-income families is unavailing. First, there is no evidence that Congress intended the receipt of federal money in this manner to trigger coverage under Title IX. Second, these general assistance programs, unlike student aid programs, were not designed to assist colleges and universities. Third, educational institutions have no control over, and indeed perhaps no knowledge of, whether they ultimately receive federal funds made available to individuals under general assistance programs, but they remain free to opt out of federal student assistance programs. Fourth, individuals' eligibility for general assistance is not tied to attendance at an educational institution.

[14][Omitted.]
[15][Omitted.]

the phrase "receiving Federal financial assistance," while admittedly somewhat ambiguous, are consistent with Senator Bayh's declaration that Title IX authorizes the termination of "all aid that comes through the Department of Health, Education, and Welfare." 117 Cong. Rec. 30408 (1971).[16] Such statements by individual legislators should not be given controlling effect, but, at least in instances where they are consistent with the plain language of Title IX, Senator Bayh's remarks are "an authoritative guide to the statute's construction." *North Haven Board of Education v. Bell*, 456 U.S. at 527. The contemporaneous legislative history, in short, provides no basis for believing that Title IX's broad language is somehow inconsistent with Congress' underlying intent. See also 20 U.S.C. § 1094(a)(3) (1982 ed.).

Persuasive evidence of Congress' intent concerning student financial aid may also be gleaned from its subsequent treatment of Title IX. We have twice recognized the probative value of Title IX's unique postenactment history, *North Haven Board of Education v. Bell, supra*, at 535; *Cannon v. University of Chicago, supra*, at 687, n. 7, 702-703, and we do so once again. The Department's sex discrimination regulations made clear that "[s]cholarships, loans, [and] grants...extended directly to...students for payment to" an institution constitute Federal financial assistance to that entity. 40 Fed. Reg. 24137 (1975); see n. 6, *supra*. Under the statutory "laying before" procedure of the General Education Provisions Act, Pub. L. 93-280, 88 Stat. 567, as amended, 20 U.S.C. § 1232(d)(1) (1982 ed.), Congress was afforded an opportunity to invalidate aspects of the regulations it deemed inconsistent with Title IX.[17] The regulations were clear, and Secretary Weinberger left no doubt concerning the Department's position that "the furnishing of student assistance to a student who uses it at a particular institution...[is] Federal aid which is covered by the statute."[18] Yet, neither

---

[16]See 117 Cong. Rec. 30158-30159 (1971) (Sen. McGovern); *id.*, at 39260 (Rep. Erlenborn); 118 Cong. Rec. 5814 (1972) (Sen. Bentsen). Grove City relies heavily on a colloquy between Senators Bayh and Dominick:

"Mr. DOMINICK. The Senator is talking about every program under HEW?

"Mr. BAYH. Let me suggest that I would imagine that any person who was sitting at the head of [HEW], administering this program, would be reasonable and would use only such leverage as was necessary against the institution.

"It is unquestionable, in my judgment, that this would not be directed at specific assistance that was being received by individual students, but would be directed at the institution, and the Secretary would be expected to use good judgment as to how much leverage to apply, and where it could be best applied." 117 Cong. Rec. 30408 (1971).

Grove City contends that Senator Bayh's statement demonstrates an intent to exclude student aid from coverage under Title IX. We believe that his answer is more plausibly interpreted as suggesting that, although the Secretary is empowered to terminate student aid, he probably would not need to do so where leverage could be exerted by terminating other assistance. The students, of course, always remain free to take their assistance elsewhere.

[17]The statutory "laying before" procedure and the actions taken by Congress pursuant to it were more completely summarized in *North Haven Board of Education v. Bell*, 456 U.S., at 531-534.

[18]Sex Discrimination Regulations: Hearings before the Subcommittee on Postsecondary. Education of the House Committee on Education and Labor, 94th Cong., 1st Sess., 482 (1975) (1975 Hearings). The Secretary added:

"Our view was that student assistance, assistance that the Government furnishes,

House passed a disapproval resolution. Congress' failure to disapprove the regulations is not dispositive, but, as we recognized in *North Haven Board of Education v. Bell, supra*, at 533-534, it strongly implies that the regulations accurately reflect congressional intent. Congress has never disavowed this implication and in fact has acted consistently with it on a number of occasions.[19]

With the benefit of clear statutory language, powerful evidence of Congress' intent, and a longstanding and coherent administrative construction of the phrase "receiving Federal financial assistance," we have little trouble concluding that Title IX coverage is not foreclosed because federal funds are granted to Grove City's students rather than directly to one of the College's educational programs. There remains the questions, however, of identifying the "education program or activity" of the College that can properly be characterized as "receiving" federal assistance through grants to some of the students attending the College.[20]

---

that goes directly or indirectly to an institution is Government aid within the meaning of Title IX. If it is not, there is an easy remedy. Simply tell us that it is not. We believe it is and base our assumption on that." *Id.*, at 484.

[19]Although "Congress has proceeded to amend § 901 when it has disagreed with HEW's interpretation of the statute," *North Haven Board of Education v. Bell, supra*, at 534, it has acquiesced in the Department's longstanding assessment of the types of federal aid that trigger coverage under Title IX. In considering the 1976 Education Amendments, for example, Congress rejected an amendment proposed by Senator McClure that would have defined federal financial assistance as "assistance received by the institution directly from the federal government." 122 Cong. Rec. 28144 (1976). Senator Pell objected that the amendment would remove from the scope of Title IX funds provided under the BEOG program and pointed out that, "[w]hile these dollars are paid to students they flow through and ultimately go to institutions of higher education ..." *Id.*, at 28145. Senator Bayh raised a similar objection, *id.*, at 28145-28146, and the amendment was rejected. *id.*, at 28147. See also *id.*, at 28013-28106 (treatment of Hatfield amendment).

It is also significant that in 1976 Congress enacted legislation clarifying the intent of the Privacy Act to ensure that institutions serving as payment agents for the BEOG program are not considered contractors maintaining a system of records to accomplish a function of the Secretary. Pub. L. 94-238, § 2(f), 90 Stat. 727, 20 U.S.C. § 1070a(c). This legislation responded to concerns expressed by educational institutions over "the additional and unnecessary administrative burdens which would be imposed upon them if [they] were deemed 'contractors.' " S. Rep. No. 94-954, p. 3 (1976). In sharp contrast, Congress has failed to respond to repeated requests by colleges in Grove City's position for legislation exempting them from coverage under Title IX.

The statutory authorization for BEOG's, moreover, has been renewed three times. Pub. L. 94-482, § 121(a), 90 Stat. 2091; Pub. L. 95-566, § 2, 92 Stat. 2402; Pub. L. 96-374, § 402(a), 94 Stat. 1401. Each time, Congress was well aware of the administrative interpretation under which such grants were believed to trigger coverage under Title IX. The history of these reenactments makes clear that Congress regards BEOG's and other forms of student aid as a critical source of support for educational institutions. See, *e.g.*, Reauthorization of the Higher Education Act and Related Measures: Hearings before the Subcommittee on Postsecondary Education of the House Committee on Education and Labor, 96th Cong., 1st Sess., pt. 3, p. 400 (1979) (Rep. Ford). In view of Congress' consistent failure to amend either Title IX or the BEOG statute in a way that would support Grove City's argument, we feel fully justified in concluding that "the legislative intent has been correctly discerned." *North Haven Board of Education v. Bell, supra*, at 535.

[20]JUSTICE STEVENS' assertion that we need not decide and have no jurisdiction to

III

An analysis of Title IX's language and legislative history led us to conclude in *North Haven Board of Education v. Bell*, 456 U.S., at 538, that "an agency's authority under Title IX both to promulgate regulations and to terminate funds is subject to the program-specific limitations of §§ 910 and 902." Although the legislative history contains isolated suggestions that entire institutions are subject to the nondiscrimination provision whenever one of their programs receives federal assistance, see 1975 Hearings 178 (Sen. Bayh), we cannot accept the Court of Appeals' conclusions that in the circumstances present here Grove City itself is a "program or activity" that may be regulated in its entirety. Nevertheless, we find no merit in Grove City's contention that a decision treating BEOG's as "Federal financial assistance" cannot be reconciled with Title IX's program-specific language since BEOG's are not tied to any specific "education program or activity."

If Grove City participated in the BEOG program through the RDS, we would have no doubt that the "education program or activity receiving Federal financial assistance" would not be the entire College; rather, it would be its student financial aid program.[21] RDS institutions receive federal funds directly, but can use them only to subsidize or expand their financial aid programs and to recruit students who might otherwise be unable to enroll. In short, the assistance is earmarked for the recipient's financial aid program. Only by ignoring Title IX's program-specific language could we conclude that funds received under the RDS, awarded to eligible students, and paid back to the school when tuition comes due represent federal aid to the entire institution.

---

decide this question is puzzling. Title IX coverage is triggered only when an "education program or activity" is receiving federal aid. Unless such a program can be and is identified, there is no basis for ordering the College to execute an Assurance of Compliance. The Court of Appeals understood as much and ruled that the entire College is the covered educational program. Until and unless that view of the statute is overturned, there will be outstanding an authoritative Court of Appeals' judgment that the certificate Grove City must execute relates to the entire College and that without such a certificate the Department would be entitled to terminate grants to Grove City students.

Grove City asks to be relieved of that judgment on the grounds that none of its educational programs is receiving any federal aid and that if any of its programs is receiving aid, it is only its administration of the BEOG program. Grove City is entitled to have these issues addressed, for otherwise it must deal with the undisturbed judgment of the Court of Appeals that the entire College is subject to federal oversight under Title IX. Even though the Secretary has changed his position and no longer agrees with the expansive construction accorded the statute by the Court of Appeals, it is still at odds with Grove City as to the extent of the covered program; and, in any event, its modified stance can hardly overturn or modify the judgment below or eliminate Grove City's legitimate and substantial interest in having its submissions adjudicated.

[21]There is no merit to Grove City's argument that the Department may regulate only the administration of the BEOG program. Just as employees who "work in an education program that receive[s] federal assistance," *North Haven Board of Education v. Bell*, 456 U.S., at 540, are protected under Title IX even if their salaries are "not funded by federal money," *ibid.*, so also are students who participate in the College's federally assisted financial aid program but who do not themselves receive federal funds protected against discrimination on the basis of sex.

We see no reason to reach a different conclusion merely because Grove City has elected to participate in the ADS. Although Grove City does not itself disburse students' awards, BEOG's clearly augment the resources that the College itself devotes to financial aid. As is true of the RDS, however, the fact that federal funds eventually reach the College's general operating budget cannot subject Grove City to institutionwide coverage. Grove City's choice of administrative mechanisms, we hold, neither expands nor contracts the breadth of the "program or activity"—the financial aid program—that receives federal assistance and that may be regulated under Title IX.

To the extent that the Court of Appeals' holding that BEOG's received by Grove City's students constitute aid to the entire institution rests on the possibility that federal funds received by one program or activity free up the College's own resources for use elsewhere, the Court of Appeals' reasoning is doubly flawed. First, there is no evidence that the federal aid received by Grove City's students results in the diversion of funds from the College's own financial aid program to other areas within the institution.[22] Second, and more important, the Court of Appeals' assumption that Title IX applies to programs receiving a larger share of a school's own limited resources as a result of federal assistance earmarked for use elsewhere within the institution is inconsistent with the program-specific nature of the statute. Most federal educational assistance has economic ripple effects throughout the aided institution, and it would be difficult, if not impossible, to determine which programs or activities derive such indirect benefits. Under the Court of Appeals' theory, an entire school would be subject to Title IX merely because one of its students received a small BEOG or because one of its departments received an earmarked federal grant. This result cannot be squared with Congress' intent.

The Court of Appeals' analogy between student financial aid received by an educational institution and non-earmarked direct grants provides a more plausible justification for its holding, but it too is faulty. Student financial aid programs, we believe, are *sui generis*. In neither purpose nor effect can BEOG's be fairly characterized as unrestricted grants that institutions may use for whatever purpose they desire. The BEOG program was designed, not merely to increase the total resources available to educational institutions, but to enable them to offer their services to students who had previously been unable to afford higher education. It is true, of course, that substantial portions of the BEOG's received by Grove City's students ultimately find their way into the College's general operating budget and are used to provide a variety of services to the students through whom the funds pass. However, we have found no persuasive evidence suggesting that Congress intended that the Department's regulatory authority follow federally aided students from classroom to classroom, building to building, or activity

---

[22]Until 1980, institutions whose students received BEOG's and other forms of assistance were required to provide assurance that they would
"continue to spend on [their] own scholarship and student-aid program[s], from sources other than funds received under [the federal programs], not less than the average expenditure per year made for that purpose during the most recent period of three fiscal years." 20 U.S.C. § 1088c.
This requirement was altered in the Education Amendments of 1980, Pub. L. 96-374, § 487(a), 94 Stat. 1451, 20 U.S.C. § 1094(a)(2) (1982 ed.), and no longer applies to schools whose students receive only BEOG's.

to activity. In addition, as Congress recognized in considering the Education Amendments of 1972, the economic effect of student aid is far different from the effect of non-earmarked grants to institutions themselves since the former, unlike the latter, increases both an institution's resources and its obligations. See Pub. L. 92-318, § 1001(a), 86 Stat. 375, 20 U.S.C. § 1070e, S. Rep. No. 92-346, p. 43 (1971); 118 Cong. Rec. 20331 (1972) (Rep. Badillo). In that sense, student financial aid more closely resembles many earmarked grants.

We conclude that the receipt of BEOG's by some of Grove City's students does not trigger institutionwide coverage under Title IX. In purpose and effect, BEOG's represent federal financial assistance to the College's own financial aid program, and it is that program that may properly be regulated under Title IX.

IV

Since Grove City operates an "education program or activity receiving Federal financial assistance," the Department may properly demand that the College execute an Assurance of Compliance with Title IX. 34 CFR § 106.4 (1983). Grove City contends, however, that the Assurance it was requested to sign was invalid, both on its face and as interpreted by the Department, in that it failed to comport with Title IX's program-specific character. Whatever merit that objection might have had at the time, it is not now a valid basis for refusing to execute an Assurance of Compliance.

The Assurance of Compliance regulation itself does not, on its face, impose institutionwide obligations. Recipients must provide assurance only that "each education program or activity operated by... [them] *and to which this part applies* will be operated by in compliance with this part." 34 CFR § 106.4 (1983) (emphasis added). The regulations apply, by their terms, "to every recipient and to *each education program or activity* operated by such recipient *which receives or benefits from Federal financial assistance.*" 34 CFR § 106.11 (1983) (emphasis added). These regulations, like those at issue in *North Haven Board of Education v. Bell*, 456 U.S. 512 (1982), "conform with the limitations Congress enacted in §§ 901 and 902." *Id.*, at 539. Nor does the Department now claim that its regulations reach beyond the College's student aid program. Furthermore, the Assurance of Compliance currently in use, like the one Grove City refused to execute, does not on its face purport to reach the entire College; it certifies compliance with respect to those "education programs and activities receiving Federal financial assistance." See n. 2, *supra*. Under this opinion, consistent with the program-specific requirements of Title IX, the covered education program is the College's financial aid program.

A refusal to execute a proper program-specific Assurance of Compliance warrants termination of federal assistance to the student financial aid program. The College's contention that termination must be preceded by a finding of actual discrimination finds no support in the language of § 902, which plainly authorizes that sanction to effect "[c]ompliance with any requirement adopted pursuant to this section." Regulations authorizing termination of assistance for refusal to execute an Assurance of Compliance with Title VI had been promulgated, 45 CFR § 80.4 (Supp., Jan. 1, 1965), and upheld, *Gardner v. Alabama*, 385 F.2d 804 (CA5 1967), cert. denied,

389 U.S. 1046 (1968), long before Title IX was enacted, and Congress no doubt anticipated that similar regulations would be developed to implement Title IX. 118 Cong. Rec. 5807 (1972) (Sen. Bayh). We conclude, therefore, that the Department may properly condition federal financial assistance on the recipient's assurance that it will conduct the aided program or activity in accordance with Title IX nd the applicable regulations.

V

Grove City's final challenge to the Court of Appeals' decision—that conditioning federal assistance on compliance with Title IX infringes First Amendment rights of the College and its students—warrants only brief consideration. Congress is free to attach reasonable and unambiguous conditions to federal financial assistance that educational institutions are not obligated to accept. *E.g.*, *Pennhurst State School and Hospital v. Halderman*, 451 U.S. 1, 17 (1981). Grove City may terminate its participation in the BEOG program and thus avoid the requirements of § 901(a). Students affected by the Department's action may either take their BEOG's elsewhere or attend Grove City without federal financial assistance. Requiring Grove City to comply with Title IX's prohibition of discrimination as a condition for its continued eligibility to participate in the BEOG program infringes no First Amendment rights of the College or its students.

Accordingly, the judgment of the Court of Appeals is

Affirmed.

JUSTICE POWELL, with whom THE CHIEF JUSTICE and JUSTICE O'CONNOR join, concurring.

As I agree that the holding in this case is dictated by the language and legislative history of Title IX, and the regulations of the Department of Education, I join the Court's decision. I do so reluctantly and write briefly to record my view that the case is an unedifying example of overzealousness on the part of the Federal Government.

Grove City College (Grove City) may be unique among colleges in our country; certainly there are few others like it. Founded more than a century ago in 1876, Grove City is an independent, coeducational liberal arts college. it describes itself as having "both a Christian world view and a freedom philosophy," perceiving these as "interrelated." App. A-22. At the time of this suit, it had about 2,200 students and tuition was surprisingly low for a private college.[1] Some 140 of the College's students were receiving Basic Educational Opportunity Grants (BEOG's),[2] and 342 had obtained Guaranteed Student Loans (GSL's).[3] The grants were made directly to the students through the Department of Education, and the student loans were guaranteed by the Federal Government. Apart from this indirect assistance,

---

[1]Yearly tuition for 1983 for fees, room, and board was $4,270. Brief for Petitioners 3, n. 2.
[2]*Grove City College v. Harris*, 500 F.Supp. 253, 259 (WD Pa.1980).
[3]*Ibid.*

Grove City has followed an unbending policy of refusing all forms of government assistance, whether federal, state or local. It was and is the policy of this small college to remain wholly independent of government assistance, recognizing—as this case well illustrates—that with acceptance of such assistance one surrenders a certain measure of the freedom that Americans always have cherished.

This case involves a regulation adopted by the Department to implement § 901(a) of Title IX (20 U.S.C. § 1681(a)). it is well to bear in mind what § 901(a) provides:

> "No person in the United States shall, on the basis of sex, be excluded from participation in, be denied the benefits of, or be subjected to discrimination under any education program or activity receiving federal financial assistance. . . ."

The sole purpose of the statute is to make unlawful *"discrimination"* by recipients of federal financial assistance on the "basis of sex." The undisputed fact is that Grove City does not discriminate—and so far as the record in this case shows—never has discriminated against anyone on account of sex, race, or national origin. This case has nothing whatever to do with discrimination past or present. The College therefore has complied to the letter with the sole purpose of § 901(-a).

As the Court describes, the case arises pursuant to a regulation adopted under Title IX that authorizes the Secretary to obtain from recipients of federal aid an "Assurance of Compliance" with Title IX and regulations issued thereunder. At the outset of this litigation, the Department insisted that by accepting students who received BEOG awards, Grove City's entire institution was subject to regulation under Title IX. The College, in view of its policies and principles of independence and its record of nondiscrimination, objected to executing this Assurance. One would have thought that the Department, confronted as it is with cases of national importance that involve actual discrimination, would have respected the independence and admirable record of this College. But common sense and good judgment failed to prevail. The Department chose to litigate, and instituted an administrative proceeding to compel Grove City to execute an agreement to operate all of its programs and activities in full compliance with all of the regulations promulgated under Title IX—despite the College's record as an institution that had operated to date in full accordance with the letter and spirit of Title IX. The Administrative Law Judge who heard the case on September 15, 1978, did not relish his task.

On the basis of the evidence, which included the formal published statement of Grove City's strong "nondiscrimination policy," he stated:

> "It should also be noted that there was *not the slightest hint of any failure to comply with Title IX* save the refusal to submit an executed assurance of compliance with Title IX. This refusal is obviously a matter of conscience and belief." App. to Pet. for Cert. A-94 (emphasis added.)[4]

The Administrative Law Judge further evidenced his reluctance by emphasizing that the regulations were "binding" upon him. *Id.*, at A-95. He concluded that the scholarship grants and student loans to Grove City constituted

These findings of the Administrative Law Judge have not been questioned.

indirect "federal financial assistance," and in view of the failure of Grove City to execute the Assurance, the regulation required that the grants and loans to its students must be "terminated." *Id.*, at A-96. The College and four of its students then instituted this suit in 1978 challenging the validity of the regulations and seeking a declaratory judgment.

The effect of the Department's termination of the student grants and loans would not have been limited to the College itself. Indeed, the most direct effect would have been upon the students themselves. Absent the availability of other scholarship funds, many of them would have had to abandon their college education or choose another school. It was to avoid these serious consequences, that this suit was instituted. The College prevailed in the District Court but lost in the Court of Appeals. Only after Grove City had brought its case before this Court, did the Department retreat to its present position that Title IX applies only to Grove City's financial aid office. On this narrow theory, the Department has prevailed, having taken this small independent college, which it acknowledges has engaged in no discrimination whatever, through six years of litigation with the full weight of the Federal Government opposing it. I cannot believe that the Department will rejoice in its "victory."

JUSTICE STEVENS, concurring in part and concurring in the result.

For two reasons, I am unable to join Part III of the Court's opinion. First, it is an advisory opinion unnecessary to today's decision, and second, the advice is predicated on speculation rather than evidence.

The controverted issue in this litigation is whether Grove City College may be required to execute the "Assurance of Compliance with Title IX" tendered to it by the Secretary in order to continue receiving the benefits of the federal financial assistance provided by the BEOG program. The Court of Appeals affirmed the District Court's decision that Grove City is a "recipient" of federal financial assistance, and reversed its decision that the Secretary could not terminate federal financial assistance because Grove City refused to execute the Assurance. The Court today holds (in Part II of its opinion) that Grove City is a recipient of federal financial assistance within the meaning of Title IX, and (in Part IV) that Grove City must execute the Assurance of Compliance in order to continue receiving that assistance. These holdings are fully sufficient to sustain the judgment the Court reviews, as the Court acknowledges by affirming that judgment.

In Part III of its opinion, the Court holds that Grove City is not required to refrain from discrimination on the basis of sex except in its financial aid program. In so stating, the Court decides an issue that is not in dispute. The Assurance of Compliance merely requires that it comply with Title IX "to the extent applicable to it." See *ante*, at 560. The Secretary, who is responsible for administering Title IX, construes the statute as applicable only to Grove City's financial aid program. All the Secretary seeks is a judgment that Title IX requires Grove City to promise not to discriminate in its financial aid program. The Court correctly holds that this program is subject to the requirements of Title IX, and that Grove City must promise not to discriminate in its operation of the program. But, there is no reason for the Court to hold that Grove City need not make a promise that the Secretary does not ask it to make, and that it in fact would not be making by signing the Assurance, in order to continue to receive federal financial assistance. It will be soon enough to decide the question discussed in Part III when and if the day comes that the Secretary asks Grove City to make some further promise in order to continue to receive federal financial assistance.

Moreover, the record in this case is far from adequate to decide the question raised in Part III. See *Consolidated Rail Corp. v. Darrone, post*, at 635-636. Assuming for the moment that participation in the BEOG program could not in itself make Title IX applicable to the entire institution, a factual inquiry is nevertheless necessary as to which of Grove City's programs and activities can be said to receive or benefit from federal financial assistance. This is the import of the applicable regulation, upheld by the Court today, *ante*, at 574-575, which states that Title IX applies "to every recipient and to each education program or activity operated by such recipient which receives or benefits from Federal financial assistance." 34 CFR § 106.11 (1983). The Court overlooks the fact that the regulation is in the disjunctive; Title IX coverage does not always depend on the actual receipt of federal financial assistance by a given program or activity. The record does not tell us how important the BEOG program is to Grove City, in either absolute or relative terms; nor does it tell us anything about how the benefits of the program are allocated within the institution. The Court decides that a small scholarship for just one student should not subject the entire school to coverage. *Ante*, at 572-573. But why should this case be judged on the basis of that hypothetical example instead of a different one? What if the record showed—and I do not suggest that it does—that all of the BEOG money was reserved for, or merely happened to be used by, talented athletes and that their tuition payments were sufficient to support an entire athletic program that would otherwise be abandoned? Would such a hypothetical program be covered by Title IX?* And if this athletic program discriminated on the basis of sex, could it plausibly be contended that Congress intended that BEOG money could be used to enable such a program to survive? Until we know something about the character of the particular program, it is inappropriate to give advice about an issue that is not before us.

Accordingly, while I subscribe to the reasoning in Parts I, II, IV and V of the Court's opinion, I am unable to join Part III.

JUSTICE BRENNAN, with whom JUSTICE MARSHALL joins, concurring in part and dissenting in part.

The Court today concludes that Grove City College is "receiving Federal financial assistance" within the meaning of Title IX of the Education Amend-

---

*Indeed, if we are to speculate about hypothetical cases, why not consider a school comparable to the private institutions discussed in *Blum v. Yaretsky*, 457 U.S. 991 (1982), in which over 90% of the patients received funds from public sources? See *id.*, at 1011. It is at least theoretically possible that an educational institution might be financed entirely by tuition, and that virtually all of the students at an institution could receive a federal subsidy. Again, I do not suggest that Grove City College is such an institution, but I do suggest that it is improper for the Court to decide a legal issue on the basis of hypothetical examples that are selected to support a particular result.

ments of 1972, 20 U.S.C. § 1681(a), because a number of its students receive federal education grants. As the Court persuasively demonstrates in Part II of its opinion, that conclusion is dictated by "the need to accord [Title IX] a sweep as broad as its language," *ante*, at 564; by reference to the analogous statutory language and legislative history of Title VI of the Civil Rights Act of 1964, *ante*, at 566; by reliance on the unique postenactment history of Title IX, *ante*, at 567-568; and by recognition of the strong congressional intent that there is no "substantive difference between direct institutional assistance and aid received by a school through its students," *ante*, at 564, 565-566, 569-570, and nn. 12-14, 19. For these same reasons, however, I cannot join Part III of the Court's opinion, in which the Court interprets the language in Title IX that limits application of the statute to "any education program or activity" receiving federal moneys. By conveniently ignoring these controlling indicia of congressional intent, the Court also ignores the primary purpose for which Congress enacted Title IX. The result—allowing Title IX coverage for the College's financial aid program but rejecting institutionwide coverage even though federal moneys benefit the entire College—may be superficially pleasing to those who are uncomfortable with federal intrusion into private educational institutions, but it has no relationship to the statutory scheme enacted by Congress.

[The remaining portion of Justice Brennan's opinion is omitted.]

INDEX

ACCIDENTS
Generally, 76-88
Athletic injuries
See Athletics
Charitable immunity, 76
Abolished, 77
Deaths, 76
Dram shop/social host liability, 81, 82
Duty of care, 77
Negligence, 77
Private camps, 83
Wrongful death, 83

ACHIEVEMENT TESTS
Home instruction, 21, 26
Licensing, criteria for, 22

ACCREDITATION
Generally, 6-8
Accrediting Associations, 6

ACTIVITY ASSOCIATIONS
See Athletics

ADMISSIONS
Generally, 8-12
Age discrimination, 10
Age Discrimination Act, 167
Civil Rights Act of 1964, 136
Handicap discrimination, 11, 157
Racial policies, 8-10
Reconstruction Civil Rights Statutes,
189
Rehabilitation Act of 1973, 157
Sex discrimination, 10
Title VI, 136
Title IX, 145

AFFIRMATIVE ACTION
PROGRAMS
See Federal Statutory Requirements

AGE DISCRIMINATION
See Discrimination, Age

AMERICAN ASSOCIATION OF
UNIVERSITY PROFESSORS
Generally, 40-47

ATHLETICS
Activity Associations, 33-35
Coaches
Equal Pay Act, 36
Duty of Care, 36
Discrimination
Race, 37
Sex, 37
Eligibility of players, 33-35

Eligibility of schools, 35
Injuries
Generally, 84-86
Spectators, 86
Title IX, 145
Transfer eligibility rules, 33-35

ATTENDANCE
Generally, 20-26

BONA FIDE OCCUPATIONAL
QUALIFICATION
See Discrimination, Title VII

BREACH OF CONTRACT
Employment
Generally, 40-50
Benefits, 43
Investigations, hearings and
procedural disputes, 49
Letters of intent, 48-49
Retirement plans, 50
Tenure denials, 45-48
Fundraising
Bingo games, 37
To educate
Generally, 12-18
Dismissals, 15, 16
Educational malpractice, 16
Implied privacy rights, 18
School closing, 13
Tuition refunds, 14, 15

BUCKLEY AMENDMENT
Application of, 17
Statutory and regulatory text, 169-189

BUILDINGS
Construction and maintenance pro-
grams, 112
Disposal of Federal property, 114
Fire regulations
See Licensing
Zoning, 113

BUS TRANSPORTATION
See State Aid

CIVIL RIGHTS ACTS
Age Discrimination in Employment
Act, 165
Age Discrimination Act, 167
Civil Rights Act of 1964, 136
Employment, 53, 73
Equal Pay Act, 144
Handicapped children, 128
Racial discrimination, application to,
8, 9, 10, 128, 136

CIVIL RIGHTS ACTS (cont'd)
Reconstruction Civil Rights Statutes,
189
Rehabilitation Act of 1973, 157
Title VI, 136
Title XI, 145

COLLECTIVE BARGAINING
Generally, 69-73
Managerial employees, 72

COMPULSORY ATTENDANCE
Generally, 20-27
Amish exception, 21, 24
Home instruction
Generally, 21, 26
Achievement testing, 26
Minimum standards, 21
Teacher certification, 21, 23, 24

COOPERATIVE EFFORTS, PUBLIC
AND PRIVATE SCHOOLS
See State Aid

CORPORAL PUNISHMENT
Licensing regulations, 3

DEFAMATION
See Employment Practices

DISCRIMINATION
Age discrimination, 165-169
Involving students, 10-11, 167
Involving teachers, 58, 165
Employment
Generally, 51-60
Age, 58, 165
Handicap, 58, 157
In benefits, 63
Investigation of charges, 60
Racial, 51, 136
Rehabilitation Act of 1973, 157
Religious, 57
Retaliatory discharge, 59
Sex, 54, 60
Title VII and statutory text, 139
Handicap, 11-12, 157
Racial
Student admissions, 8, 9, 10, 136
Title VI, 136
Sexual, 8, 145, 152

DISMISSAL FROM SCHOOL
Generally, 15-16

DUE PROCESS
Accreditation, 7

Dismissals from school, 15
Employment disputes, 44

EDUCATIONAL MALPRACTICE
See Breach of Contract

EMPLOYMENT PRACTICES
Generally, 40-73
Age discrimination, 58, 165
Benefits, 43, 63, 64
Breach of contract, 40
Collective bargaining
First amendment limitations, 69
National Labor Relations Board,
69-73
Defamation, 62
Discrimination, benefits, 63
Discrimination, investigation of, 60
Equal Employment Opportunity
Commission, 139
Handicapped teachers, 58
Income tax, 64
Letters of intent, 48
Managerial employees, 72
Racial discrimination, 51, 52, 53
Religious discrimination, 57
Retaliatory discharge, 59
Sex discrimination, 54-57
State action, 73
Tenure denial, 45, 61
Unemployment taxation, 65
Unlawful employment practices, 141-
144
Wrongful termination, 40-50

EQUAL EMPLOYMENT
OPPORTUNITY COMMISSION
See Employment

ESTABLISHMENT CLAUSE
See First Amendment

FEDERAL AID
Grants and loans, 111

FEDERAL STATUTORY
REQUIREMENTS
Affirmative action programs, 136, 139
Age discrimination, 165-169
Age Discrimination in Employment
Act, 165
Application and compliance, 136
Buckley Amendment, 169-189
Civil Rights Act of 1964
Title VI: Racial discrimination, 136
Title VII: Employment discrimina-
tion, 136, 138, 139
Equal Pay Act, 63, 144

FEDERAL STATUTORY
  REQUIREMENTS (cont'd)
  Reconstruction Civil Rights Statutes,
  189
    Section 1981, 189
    Section 1983, 189
  Rehabilitation Act of 1973, 157-165
  Title IX, 136, 145-157

FINANCIAL AID
  See Scholarships

FIRST AMENDMENT
  Generally, 3-6
  Establishment clause, 19, 41, 67,
    70-71, 99
  Free exercise clause, 70
  Freedom of Speech, 4
  Limits on collective bargaining, 69
  Racial policies, 9
  State Aid to religion, 90

FUNDING
  Federal, 10

FUNDRAISING
  Generally, 37-38

GRANTS   .
  See Scholarships

HANDICAP DISCRIMINATION
  See Discrimination, handicap

HANDICAPPED STUDENTS
  Generally, 120
  Civil rights, 128
  Committee on the handicapped, 126-
    127
  Contract disputes, 131
  Education for All Handicapped Child-
    ren Act (EAHCA)
    Generally, 120
    Status quo provision, 125
  Facilities and programs, 130
  Handicapped Children's Protection
    Act, 128
  Individualized education program,
    121, 123, 125
  Placement of students, 122, 127
  Private school eligibility to educate,
    128
  Rehabilitation Act of 1973, 157
  Related services, 120
  States' duty to educate, 120
  Tuition reimbursement, 121

HOME INSTRUCTION
  Generally, 26-27
  Achievement testing, 26
  Monitoring of, 26-27

INSURANCE
  Liability, 87-88

INTERVIEWING
  See Recruiting on Campus

LEASING OF FACILITIES
  Generally, 19-20

"LEMON" TEST
  Generally, 90-111

LICENSING
  Generally, 3-6
  Fire regulations, 5
  Literature distribution, 5
  Scope of investigations, 4
  Special use permits, 5

NATIONAL HONOR SOCIETY
  See Student Organizations

NATIONAL LABOR RELATIONS
  BOARD
  See Employment, Collective
    Bargaining

PARENTAL OBLIGATIONS
  To educate, 17

PRIVACY RIGHTS OF PARENTS
  AND STUDENTS
  Generally, 173-189

RACIAL DISCRIMINATION
  See Discrimination, Racial

RECRUITING ON CAMPUS
  Interviewing, 31

REHABILITATION ACT
  Admissions, 11
  Athletics, discrimination, 37
  Statutory and regulatory text, 157

RELEASE TIME
  See State Aid

SCHOLARSHIPS
  Generally, 27-30
  Financial Aid, 27
  Grants, 27

SEXUAL DISCRIMINATION
See Discrimination, Sexual

STATE ACTION
Athletic associations, 34
Employment, 73

STATE AID
Generally, 90-118
Bus transportation, 92
Classroom equipment, 106
Cooperative efforts, public and private
schools
Instruction on public school
property, 100
Leasing of public or private school
facilities, 102
Public school personnel on parochial
school grounds, 98
Release time programs, 95
Diagnostic and therapeutic services,
107
First Amendment, 90
Instructional services, 103
"Lemon" test, 90-111

STUDENT AID
Incidental expenses, 109
Tax deductions and credits, 110
Tax refunds, 111
Textbook loans, 90
Tuition assistance, 107, 108, 109

STUDENT AID
See State Aid

STUDENT ORGANIZATIONS
Fraternities, 30
Gay rights groups, 31
National Honor Society, 32

STUDENT RIGHTS
Buckley Amendment, right to privacy,
17, 169
Implied right to privacy, 18

TAXATION
Effect of racial policies upon, 114, 115
Federal income tax, 64, 114
Local property taxation, 116-117
Exemptions, 117
Tax credits and deductions, 110
Tax refunds, 111
Unemployment taxes, 65

TEACHER CERTIFICATION
Compelling state interest, 3
Not enforced, 3

TENURE
Generally, 40
Denials, 45, 61
Employment practices, 44

TRESPASSING
Nonstudents, 12

TUITION REFUNDS
Generally, 14-15

UNEMPLOYMENT TAXATION
Generally, 65-69

ZONING
See Buildings

Use the attached order cards to order your own or extra copies of **PRIVATE SCHOOL LAW IN AMERICA.**

Faculty lounge? Orientation workshops? School library? Your own office? Board members?

Order extra copies of **PRIVATE SCHOOL LAW IN AMERICA** now. The attached cards may be removed from the book for your order.

Please send me_____copies of **PRIVATE SCHOOL LAW IN AMERICA** at $45.00 per copy.

Name_____

Title_____

Address_____

City_____ State_____ Zip_____

Telephone Number_____

Purchase Order Number, if needed _____

Send order and check payable to: DATA RESEARCH, INC., P.O. Box 490, Rosemount, MN 55068

Please send me_____ copies of **PRIVATE SCHOOL LAW IN AMERICA** at $45.00 per copy.

Name_____

Title_____

Address_____

City_____State_____Zip_____

Telephone Number_____

Purchase Order Number, if needed _____

Send order and check payable to: DATA RESEARCH, INC., P.O. Box 490, Rosemount, MN 55068